AMERICAN EARTH

BY CARLETON BEALS

THE STORY OF THE PEOPLES

American Earth

America South

Fire on the Andes

The Crime of Cuba

Mexican Maze

CONTEMPORARY CHRONICLES

The Coming Struggle for Latin America

Rome or Death: The Story of Fascism

Mexico: An Interpretation

PERSONAL EXPERIENCE

Glass Houses: Ten Years of Free-Lancing

Banana Gold

Brimstone and Chili

BIOGRAPHY

The Story of Huey P. Long

Porfirio Díaz: Dictator of Mexico

NOVELS

The Stones Awake

Black River

Destroying Victor

CARLETON BEALS

AMERICAN EARTH

The Biography of a Nation

J. B. LIPPINCOTT COMPANY
PHILADELPHIA   NEW YORK   TORONTO

PRINTED IN THE UNITED STATES OF AMERICA

CONTENTS

PART ONE

I	POPPIES IN CALIFORNIA	9
II	MOTHER AMERICA	26
III	WAR FOR LAND	37
IV	THE AMERICAN DILEMMA	65
V	LAND FOR THE FEW	96
VI	THE WESTWARD URGE	121
VII	THE RELIGIOUS URGE	136
VIII	MORMONS	161
IX	SETTLING UP THE COUNTRY	177
X	OLD MAN RIVER	198
XI	WHITE MEN CAN TAKE IT	219
XII	REVOLT	238

PART TWO

XIII	WARS IN WYOMING	259
XIV	THE END OF THE TRAIL	280
XV	DON'T MONKEY WITH THE BUZZ-SAW	293
XVI	THE GREAT FLOOD	307
XVII	FUR EMPIRE	318

6   *CONTENTS*

XVIII	Black Alabama	334
XIX	Red Clay	358
XX	Georgia: The Swan Song of Utopia	378
XXI	Migs: Shantytown on Wheels	393
XXII	Lost Empire	409
XXIII	Beyond the Last Frontier	431
	Bibliography	471
	Index	477

PART ONE

CHAPTER I

POPPIES IN CALIFORNIA

Every spring, when I was a boy in California, carpets of golden poppies covered fields that stretched unbroken for miles, north from Altadena to the blue Sierra Madre.

Along the roads south to Los Angeles, poppies and lupins bordered grainfields, vineyards and orchards of oranges, lemons, apricots, peaches and gnarled olive trees. Smiling cultivated fields opened to placid skies.

Today the many miles of orchards from Los Angeles to Pasadena have become mostly city blocks of brick and steel, in places interspersed with the ugly black ribs of oil derricks. Other avenues, gracefully curving over low hills, fling an easy embrace around wealthy homes, rich chalets and high-walled estates. Farther north, where once were only poppies, are now bungalows and concrete highways and gas stations and a smell of dust and carbon-monoxide fumes.

Over that carpet of gold, I once strode like a young god, happy and free. No lasting cares wrinkled my countenance. Gophers peered at me with their grandfather faces; cottontails darted along the little gullies; garden snakes matched their color with poppies. Crimson flowers painted the face of white rocks. The air was scented with yucca and sage. From the underbrush whined bevies of quail, and on hot afternoons grasshoppers shrilled in a hushed world that lifted toward the sky in layers of green citrus, sepia fields and majestic purple mountains.

But the golden carpet has been rolled up by the years. Today there are concrete roads and motorcycle cops, stop-signs; and from the hills,

9

now carved with skyline boulevards, one gazes down upon endless miles of city blocks, vanishing in a haze of factory smoke and dust. Progress has rolled up the golden carpet of youth.

Where neat, sleek Hollywood now rises, were boulders, cactus and sagebrush; and there, out under live oaks and cottonwood trees, we used to enjoy family picnics. Now, all the hills over which I used to wander, hills that sloped clear to the sea, are slashed up everywhere with more roads and with the homes of movie stars and new Croesuses of wealth—the Beverly Hills area, screaming Veblen's observations of leisure-class ostentation and waste—much of it a veritable school-girl's dream of brass-button flunkydom. Tucked near there is the new campus of the southern branch of the State University—culture, Greek letter societies and football have not been neglected.

Across those hills, one finally comes to Santa Monica. There my folks used to rent a little two room summer cottage, crudely decorated with faded, blue-striped wallpaper, and on the beach there as a boy I used to swim. The waves of the breasted sea, those fretted shapes, that silver sheen, aroused some of my first poetic notions.

The little cottages are gone now, and glittering Coney Island amusements have multiplied.

But the coast and the sea are still beautiful. This afternoon of my return is very sunny and clear; I can just make out the little pencil line on the sea that is Catalina Island. Over there as a small boy I went camping, wandered freely up hill and down dale, and swam naked in the goat lakes and swam naked in the sea. But now there is merely more Coney Island, and the rest of it is enclosed by a great wealthy estate.

Behind Pasadena and Riverside, up the great tawny sagebrush *barrancas,* and the nearby timbered mountain slopes, a few years ago one could run into a snarling wildcat or really get lost and die—the papers told of cases. The virgin heart of nature still pulsed free and untamed.

Now in many of those canyons of old-time mystery are merely more concrete roads; here and there noisy tin-can summer camps; and in some ravines stand palatial residences, duly blessed with Crane's streamlined fixtures.

Progress has rolled up the golden carpet of youth; progress has laid its neat commonplace lacquer over all the mysteries of yesterday.

Not all of these handsome and less handsome palaces are owned by Californians. This garden spot of white house and red tiles, all this jumble and hash of the thousand architectural motifs of the world, tell the tale of how balmy climate, the odorous fruits, the prodigal vegetation, the massed flowers, have attracted the *nouveaux riches* of all the country.

It occurs to me now, in an idle moment not tinged with the slightest regret, that had I stayed home and saved my nickels and bought city blocks, today the brass-button footman in blue, swinging open the stately gate before which I stand musing, would be bowing obsequiously to me as I roll in, slightly obese, in my latest model Cadillac.

Or just as easily I might have overloaded with 1929 stocks or have juggled bank funds and have put a pistol to my head and spattered my brain against a Ming Dynasty vase. Or more probably, I might be shoving great hunks of scrap iron into a raw red furnace—as I did for a while during arduous years of getting an education—and be living now down among the narrow cobbled streets of the endless blocks of squalid tenements; and those tenements—Frick Hollow, where the Mexicans fester and die, and Bunker Hill, where disease and crime breed—are as vicious as any in the country.

As it is, I am just a wanderer over the face of the earth, unencumbered by any excess baggage, unworried about the stock market, merely observing the ways of men and society, and now observing happily, and often sadly, this varied world of my America, this explosive world of miracles, of progress, of speed—where men find concrete pavements better, or at least more necessary, than poppies.

This is no elegy, no lament for the dead, no sighing for the good old days. The poppies are gone—though not from memory or my hopes—and this new latter-day world, despite its occasional rawness, its ostentation, its greater swank, its more violent contrasts between wealth and misery, is a world where other beauties unknown when I was a boy catch me in a giant grip of silent wonder.

Wealth can often buy beauty it does not know how to create; and in the midst of hectic growth, of realty grabbing, and hurried greed for power and luxury, more than in many an American community, folk here have taken into account something more than mere material expediency. Los Angeles is even a bit quixotic and mad, and other-worldly, a place of star-gazers as well as real-estate sharks—and for that it should be given due credit. One need but call the roster of the McNamara dynamiters, Harrison Gray Otis, Aimee McPherson, Upton Sinclair and the Epic plan, Hollywood, Mexican exiles, the Magón brothers, the Mount Wilson Observatory, Gaylord Wilshire of Socialist and gold-mine fame, Marion Davies, the Brotherhood of the White Temple, Townsend and pensions, to sense some of the curious contours. Here, along with smug Native Son pride, are found the bizarre, the ambitious, the untamed, the unusual—that which seeks to burst through all contours and become boundless; that which refuses to be content merely with commonsense things. The frontier note of religious extravagance still bursts over these hills like the fire-spray of a many-colored rocket.

The throbbing city that now stretches across this vast plain from sea to mountains—sprawling out, despite its magnificent new planned civic center—in the accidental way that it grew without regard for logic, merely utility and speed—has obeyed some great human rhythm, some tremendous cycle of power, some law of development that challenges the future and seems to imply that human energy and ambition, human hopes and dreams, are limitless. However haphazard, discordant and blaring, however raucous with crudities is this new metropolis, it is reckless with power and ambition. Though it be pimpled with bad taste, with honky-tonk ice-cream and hot-dog parlors, with Arabian Nights movie palaces and ushers bringing the gold braid of the *Prisoner of Zenda* royalty to five-and-ten girls, even so, within the womb of this fantastic growth is some peculiar pattern and beauty both American and typical of the locale.

If compared to the free world of those golden fields of poppies, this newer city now seems to me a relatively tawdry and closed-in place, actually that one great circling horizon of youth has been exchanged for a thousand new horizons, many of them not at all visible to the naked eye. For those who like horizons, life has put on layer after layer of complexity.

Those earlier days of my childhood, in my father's library of glass doors on rollers, was a book entitled *That's the Talk for American Freemen*. The swagger of that independent title—probably Populist propaganda—made a permanent impress upon my life. I was too young to read the book; I don't know to this day what its subject matter was. But ever since, I have always associated the word "America" with the word "freemen," with the idea of freedom of expression and ample opportunity, above all else a land where men could always talk boldly of what lay close to their souls and their desires, and without fear or favor.

All these early ideas—not even consciously expressed to myself—were intimately interwoven with that simple world of wide coastal plain, of mountains, untamed and open, where the free spirit could roam. That free world of Nature symbolized a society also, where men could roam freely—in search of ideas, of truth, of spiritual enrichment.

America was truly a land of opportunity. If its full promise of life were to remain unabridged, it must always remain a land of opportunity for all men, an opportunity ever growing more meaningful so that the resources of each and every individual could always be used to the maximum to benefit both himself and his neighbors. That was the widening circle that I early saw. Its axis matched that of the long golden meadows, the bold blue peaks of the Sierra Madre, the circle of the sea, crashing along the beaches from San Pedro, north and south. That circle stretched far beyond to the towers of great cities I had never seen but knew that someday I would know.

Even in those earlier days, California had already become the Mecca of the wealthy seeking a paradise in which to retire. Along the upper hills of Pasadena, overlooking the Arroyo Seco, stretched famous Orange Grove Avenue where were being built palace after palace, each arrogantly striving to surpass the other. One enormous mansion—the grounds of which, surrounded by a fifteen foot iron fence, covered a whole city block—was said to have doorknobs and fixtures of solid gold. We boys used to make pilgrimages there and peer awestruck through the gates.

But there was not the slightest envy in our gaping wonder. America had yielded up this richness to these folk generously, and beyond the palaces still stretched the golden fields and more and more wealth to be garnered. Even if a man had few of this world's goods, there were innumerable things to which he could turn his hand; the gates of opportunity seemed wide. Wherever one went, the land beyond would be endlessly smiling and golden.

There was the mansion of Mr. Thum, or Mr. Foote or some such name, the inventor of sticky flypaper, who had retired to California, a millionaire. Just daub a little syrup on a piece of paper and you became richer than Alexander or Cleopatra! Who could not imitate him? The matter of wealth, those days, struck me as such a simple thing, I never bothered my head about it. Though we were lower middle-class folk, it never occurred to me to express my ambition in terms of dollars and cents. Even in those childhood days I thought merely of writing, of pouring out songs worthy to match the land and the mountains and the sea all about me.

As for pocket money, any enterprising boy could make that. I mowed lawns and hoed weeds. I got up before dawn, rain or shine, to deliver newspapers. I even came to believe that calamities, if they were majestic enough, were quite desirable things, for when the San Francisco earthquake wiped out a great city (without putting even a stitch in the side to halt the swift stride of California's Progress), I learned that all evils bring some good to somebody. My "extras" went up to a dollar a copy. What I did not then know was that the rebuilding of the hill-perched city would provide still easier pickings for others—the lushest graft ever plucked in this plunder-built America.

I remember no envy because others were more fortunate than myself. If anyone ever snubbed me because I was not well off or did not come from a Grand Avenue family, I was never conscious of it. The feeling of complete equality was in the air. One took it for granted in that free and easy world of the gold-rush state that all men were men, to be taken as such, regardless of their origins, their status, or the size of their bankroll. At a certain stage, the booster spirit is genuinely democratic—except toward hoboes and critics. Why snub your neighbor if in a year or so he might likely be sitting on the plush of luxury?

In actuality—as I recalled many years later—there was much discontent. I have vague memories of a serious strike of Japanese, Filipinos and Mexicans. The Mexicans were to keep on coming into the country, once wholly theirs, in ever greater numbers until they made up nearly a fourth of Los Angeles' population. Not merely the rich were called to the western paradise. On the roads those early days—as these later days—one saw many blanket-stiffs, hoboes, men out of work. Scarcely a day went by without such knocking at the door for hand-outs. But for all that ilk we then had great contempt. They were idlers unwilling to seize their opportunities. It was quite right for the sheriff to pick them up, thrust them in jail, run them out of town.

But Mexicans and Japs and Filipinos and hoboes now, these later years, take on a social meaning I never suspected. They were the footloose slaves who built the West as the Blacks built the South. Their starvation still makes possible the most profitable and scientific agriculture in the world.

My eyes were still on the fields of poppies when they fled while I was pointing their place. But philosophically I now quite accept at least the beauty of Bobby Burns' lines on the subject. If the flowering fields have gone, and concrete has been poured over their graves, there are other joys to take their place. Progress is progress. America must become puissant and wise—as I dreamed of it as a boy. It must become great and joyous and free—like the Prometheus of Shelley—only more so: physically as well as spiritually free.

Has it done so? Is it doing so?

During the years in which the perfume of lupins and sagebrush and pennyroyal has given way to the scent of many other flowers never known before, now cultivated in precisely kept private gardens, scents that now mingle with the puffing fumes of gasoline, has America kept the promise of those boyhood expectations? Is it the America I thought it to be? That I expected it to become?

Today, as I motor through Southern California, I find that many of the places where as a youngster I camped out among desolate sand

and cactus, are now irrigated. The desert has been made to bloom as it never bloomed in former days—all those once barren stretches over toward Old Baldy, the snow-clad flanks of which, with tireless youthful eagerness, knapsack on my back, I used to climb. The way to it those earlier days led through bone-dry canyons, torrents during brief, violent cloud-bursts. Then only a few orchards and gardens bloomed wearily, laden with dust. Today, aloft on that summit one can see on every hand the fruits and grains and the grass of man's handiwork, luxuriating on lands that once knew only the rattlesnake and the lizard. The orchards that elsewhere went down like lost-cause soldiers before the march of cement and brick have been replaced a hundred-fold elsewhere. Does not all this represent a better life?

Thirty years ago, San Bernardino and Riverside were scraggly little towns, mostly of old cracked adobe, full of dust and flies. Today I motor through the broad palm-lined avenues of Riverside, a city now sweet with pungency of oranges and lemons. Even in a car, the redolence sweeps into my nostrils and fills me with a long-forgotten zest. The gray concrete street lights have been fashioned with singularly appropriate taste to look like old mission bells. Everything is neat, bustling. Air-cooled restaurants serve food more sophisticated than any I ate as a boy, food not equaled for many a long weary stretch through the whole Middle West. Riverside, today, is the playground of the wealthy sojourner.

Into the restaurants saunter folk that would have been "queer" in my boyhood days; women wearing scanty sunsuits that would have been considered immoral; women with closely bobbed hair and flaunting the bizarre jackets of Bohemia. Today they cause not the lift of an eyebrow, not a second glance—unless their good looks merit it. Here, certainly, is a remarkable emancipation from former narrow provincialism. Or has Greenwich Village merely become cliché, its old rebellion against the *mores* of Puritanism now merely a Main Street commonplace?

In any case, the new atmosphere of freedom is welcome, and I can now perceive that though poppy-beds stretched so wide, many a strait-laced concept of human conduct was stunting the artistic

and cultural growth of America—barriers derived from Old World
thought, from the tight-lipped coon-skined Calvinist, the hard-
mouthed dissenter. Many a noble idea was held in by the false dykes
of a grimmer world of early conquest; by grimly moral pioneers,
muscular and hard, uncultured, mostly narrow or ignorant. Many
such dykes now have given way to release the human spirit; to open
up different horizons that stretch further than any golden acres.

But all too soon for me—now on my return—the neat tastefulness
of these Southern California cities takes on a surface touristy touch,
glittering and thin; everything soon becomes like a painted poster,
like a cardboard doll set. Too new, too hastily improvised, they do
not weld with their traditions like any French town. All traditions
here are merely grist in the mill of the booster spirit to be ground
out deftly into seasoned hamburgers of pat showmanship. Thus the
old Riverside mission has become a swank hotel; the time-worn vaults
and corridors have been turned into a curio shop that attempts to
retain historical accuracies but merely makes old reverences and
beauties a side show for penny postcards, tiny miniature crates of
oranges and owls carved out of redwood.

As I drove into Riverside from the desert one balmy March twilight—after thirty years' absence—it seemed all over again the promised land, so dazzlingly beautiful I ached to settle down there for good.
But by the following morning, its charm became so obviously stressed,
so tinsel-covered, so forcedly artificial that with equal pleasure I fled
from it. The old dusty scraggly Riverside with its unkempt arroyos,
its adobe, its loafer Mexicans, its bucolic insouciance seems realer to
me still than this more perfected smooth-piston creation. I do not find
women with plucked eyebrows distasteful; in fact they often excite
my concupiscence. But society, somehow, should not pluck its eyebrows into such a perfect line as does Riverside.

I pushed on to the great annual "National Orange Fair" in San
Bernardino. In a mammoth hall towered mountains of the fairest
fruit in the history of the human race. I felt proud of that. I could
even endure seeing God's handiwork, so improved by man, here
converted into caricatures of Donald Duck, Mickey Mouse and Minnie, Pluto, the Three Little Pigs, the Big Bad Wolf. There were

manikins of Joan Crawford and Marlene Dietrich lolling in lawn chairs among garden paths laid out with lemons and grapefruit, and pretty-boy Clark Gable in neat white flannels and open-throat shirt under a fake orange tree glistening with too large golden globes. And most brave attempt of all—a store-window, glass-eyed dummy of Will Rogers, dressed up in a neck-bunched hand-me-down, a stuffed stiff figure turning round and round, like a department store ad, but in a Chinese pagoda made of oranges. Just why Will Rogers should be grinning under a Chinese pagoda I haven't the slightest idea, though surely he, most of all, would have hugely enjoyed seeing himself there—it would have excited his love and tolerant humor for this callow, over-serious, still provincial America.

That great annual orange fair of San Bernardino showed such gorgeous taste, and yet such hybrid mixtures, that at bottom it was garish, a bit crude, lacking in pure form and subtlety, devoid of finesse, largely boosterism run amuck. And yet I loved every bit of it.

Its boasting placards, its brave figures of production, of profits and wages revealed such blatant unblushing faith. I fully expected a check-suit, cigar-tilted, Pullman-car smut-story to pop out from a gold-tinsel heaven. Here was the old go-getter spirit I had always known, the eternal optimism, all the raw edges of a folk still a bit uncomfortable in expressing good taste, not yet conscious of art forms, yet so hungry for beauty; hungry for beauty, and yet their very self-assurance defeats beauty. But in spite of all I reveled in that blatant faith, I could not feel too censorious.

I reveled also in the side show; the African glass-trading dwarf in the inevitable moth-eaten leopard skin, the sword swallower, the man who pulled a woman on a car with his eyelids, the hermaphrodite, the three-legged man, and the other monstrosities—so horrible, so crude. They held for me the pathos of a dying, naïve phase of America, an era of yokel wonder as remote from the world of Matthew Arnold or Emerson or Schiller as the huts of an Australian bushwhacker; something out of another generation of the days of the pink *Police Gazette* and the gay 'nineties; a holdover that soon must steal away into the chance crossroad corners of our lives, something that once was lusty and brightly depraved but is now precious as a memory rather than a reality—its reality quite too incongruous along-side of attempted streamlining of mass-production of oranges.

I opened the editorial page of the local paper:

"The two great assets of San Bernardino are the National Orange Fair and our mountains. We must promote both, with all our energies. . . . To do this, we must solve our parking problem."

The ensuing account of the parking problem was sprinkled with all the phraseology of a lyric prospectus, not entirely grammatical, but Californian to the core.

Oh, beloved boosters with undimmed optimism and eye on the main chance, what you write is as glorious—almost—as the booster blurbs of a golden shore that John Law once used to lure the folk of the French cafés to their death in the Mississippi swamps, that Columbus wrote for the virtuous Queen of Spain about the shiny cities of the New World!

California is full of fair-haired queens, stature a bit above the country's average, Junoesque in type. It is a beauty that strikes me—as I wander over these forty-eight states—as almost too superlative, too fresh and perfect. It, too, almost falls over into the meretricious. The fruit, so perfected in color and size, with such concern for visual appeal and marketability, has lost just a bit of its once half-wild pungency and its virile resistance; the tang has turned to juice and sugar. Something similar has happened to the women, so lush in the eye, but so monotonously streamlined with neat marcelled hair, so sugar-water in their senseless patter about moviedom, all their technical blatting about late-model auto cars.

What is this little flaw in perfection, this universal harboring of smugness, this unblushing optimism, this world of constant "juicit" up? Is it that I no longer quite wish for the perfect? Is there perhaps some mote in my own eye, some blemish in my soul, some twisted vision of things?

It seems almost unfair—as I walk out of that great cornucopia of golden glory which is the National Orange Fair of California—to recall that despite all this brave showing, all this "sunkist" boosterism, half the crop that particular season was ruined by a freeze! That every year the pursuit of perfection, of a standardized product and the maintenance of top prices, cause the dumping of tons of low-grade oranges, this in a nation where millions of people cannot afford oranges and are deprived of good health because of lack of essential vitamins. It seems unfair to recall tales out of school of striking workers in the groves, of tree trunks splattered with human blood by armed Vigilantes.

None of the statistics in the National Orange Fair, glowing with accounts of "richest in Vitamin C and A"; of fruit, "tree-ripened in all-year sunshine—irrigated by clear mountain snow-waters," fruit, "highest in healthfulness," none of this blah-blah told of the wage-levels, the facts of ownership, the nasty political lobbies at Sacramento and Washington, the arrogant and unnecessary state border inspections. It seems unfair to remind this unblushing provincialism that an orange fair without the participation of Florida, Texas, New Mexico, Louisiana and Arizona has no proper claim to label itself "national."

Many such things were not mentioned on the exultant bronze plaques beneath the exhibits. But after all the fruit *is* so perfect; if not always in taste, at least in size, uniformity, color and visual appeal!

And those lovely California girls—it seems particularly unfair to recall a secret medical bulletin detailing the number of abortions among California sorority girls that tells, not of romance nor sophisticated and subtle sin, with the pensive accents of Baudelaire, but just mess-'em-up, hip-flask lust.

Was I so much under the spell of the boosters during boyhood days when I used to work all night helping to decorate our High School float for the New Year's Tournament of Roses—the super-booster show of boosterdom which has become a folklore and a joy and a revel of splendor—that I failed to notice some harsher things?

Now I do recall that during those earlier days occurred the free speech fight in San Diego, in which men, taking the American Constitution as seriously as do the economic royalists of today, thought they had a right to utter their bizarre opinions—until good solid citizens, bankers, storekeepers and boosters taught them differently. Those early believers in free speech were whacked out of town by cactus clubs in the preferred style of the Yaqui Indians. The too naïve upholders of our naïve Bill of Rights were beaten up, or tarred and feathered, or castrated or killed. Folk like them still are.

Mayor Hague of Jersey City, who among others has inherited those righteous wings of false patriotism to waft his crass stupidity, is a pink ribbon cherub compared to the tough but panicky boosters of California. In fact Jersey City thuggery and suppression is still today such a commonplace in California that it rarely excites much comment.

On the borders of the state today arrogant police officers have tried to hold out of the Western Paradise the swarms of broken folk— except during the rush harvest season when starvation labor is needed —all the "rubber tramps," rolling in from the disaster of the mid-west dust bowl. And Los Angeles, as other cities of the state, has long had one of the most corrupt gangster-police set-ups to be found anywhere. There in that city the police long terrorized citizens who were political foes by threats of death, imprisonment, or with faked obscene pictures—just as crude as all that! Police of California cities or plantation Vigilantes have dynamited labor headquarters and lynched harvest-hands. Bravely they throw bricks through the windows of liberal-minded persons of the various communities, with death threats attached to them. There are times when bloody murder stalks under the red sun of California, though mostly it skulks in cowardice in the dark of the scented nights that spill such riches so inequitably distributed.

One pokes through the tinsel showmanship in the state and finds corruption everywhere. One walks over the fake marble floors of newly, hurriedly built palaces, and everywhere one suddenly falls from the sunkist seedless heights into a Cloaca Maxima.

And yet it would be wrong to over-exaggerate such evils. Despite the gangsters, the intolerance, the haste, the general lack of historical perspective, the futility of periodic reform, there is ever a gesture of great free deeds that have shaped all efforts to a grandiose pattern, a constant faith in the future. Los Angeles represents a typical American credo more pronounced still than in most parts of our broad land where it is withering so fast.

In few places of our great nation have wealth and power of late accumulated faster than in California. Nowhere does man seem quite so puissant. But has human justice kept pace with the new flaunt of abundance?

I think of Tom Mooney falsely jailed for twenty-two years. I think of Ford and Suhr. I think of Anita Whitney, jailed for fourteen years for addressing a public meeting. I think of the ignorance and viciousness of politicians in high places, scarcely equaled in any state in the Union. How did the conscience of California become so dulled, so complacent, in all its sun and surface prosperity? Time, perhaps, turns the tide everywhere. In the last elections Governor Merriam was finally turned out of office. Mooney has been freed.

But are these latter-day people of my long-adopted state happy?

Another little cloud of doubt casts a shadow upon the pleasing show of magnificence that so quickly greets the eye. What is the reason for all the restless new sects, the constant seeking of otherworldly salvation, amid such a living utopia of opulence? Why all the odd food cranks in a state that provides healthy food in abundance and with a marvelous climate in which health should create the best of appetites? Why Epic plans and munificent old age plans? And what is the reason for bloodshed and lawless Vigilantes?

Across the Golden Gate and San Francisco Bay—once the haunt of Jack London and Joaquin Miller and Filibuster Walker—have been flung two magnificent new flying spans. And under those spans, on an artificial island lifted up from the mud flats, is one of the most magnificent and modern expressions of California boosterism, the San Francisco Fair, built with energy, enthusiasm, hope, a fairyland replete with bigger and better and more showy boosterism, a super-Barnum-and-Bailey display.

But also those bridges fling their spans out from one of the most politically corrupt cities in America, a city repeatedly rocked by graft exposures, scandals which persistently emerge into the light every decade or so.

The city was hailed for its bravery in quickly rebuilding itself after the earthquake—or "the fire" as the boosters call it there—but that rebuilding was also an achievement in graft and filth that left a trail of slime on the doorsteps of nearly all prominent politicians from the prominent nabobs on Nob Hill to the lesser breed by the Ferry Building and the fish wharves. Abe Ruef went to jail, taking the rap for the bigger boys and joking boisterously about the stylishness of prison stripes—then everybody felt virtuous for a while, although the same practices, as everyone knew, were continued a bit more discreetly by the same bellwethers.

Federal Agent John B. Densmore only a few years ago found "cases framed . . . fabricated evidence . . . blackmail, intimidation." One case involved the bribing of a Supreme Court judge for $410,000. But nothing was done about these mostly suppressed findings. People gasped, and graft went on, and Mooney stayed in jail.

In March, 1937, once more the police department and other civic agencies were rocked with disclosures of graft, abetting of crime, prostitution and racketeering. Some of the same famed underworld figures and back-scenes bosses were found to be, though previously exposed, still at work. Once more, except for punishing a few petty scapegoats, the matter was mostly quashed. Perfume was cast on the ruffled smelly waters by mayor and bishop.

The golden soil of California has grown some strange fruits that do not always meet the eye.

Is this also the story everywhere else in America? Has democracy grown dry-rot?

And in the very shadows of those Golden Gate spans, bloody battles go on along the mud-caked waterfront. Labor and capital coiled into violent hates. Criminal yeggs and strike-breakers are sent into action much as the Medicis might have used a private army.

Here indeed is the end of one frontier and the beginning of class frontiers. Here is the end of a long trail. It is a blood-drenched trail.

Yesterday it was the blood of Indians. The hunter and trapper cheated the red man with gewgaws and fire-water to get the furs of animals that gave him food and happiness; the missionaries stole his soul and his happy hunting grounds of hereafter; and the settlers and cattlemen stole his lands.

And the railroads, lawyers, judges, timber men and speculators stole the land in turn. In California, Stanford and his gang grabbed millions of acres and piously founded a university which—though now a great and noble institution—must still blush for shame every time its name is mentioned.

Today the blood is that of our own kind—and unless industrial warfare can be ended with justice, perhaps all America will have a bitter price to pay.

What then is the full story, the complete picture, the true picture, of this America of mine? This America of my boyhood? and this America of manhood?

Have the horizons held? Are the new horizons better? Or are the horizons closing in on us? Is the American dream of opportunity in America narrowing? What doors have been closed—and why?

In a few decades a great, powerful nation has been born, great towers have been flung against the sky, and wings of flying boats have been flung still higher; and proudly we can say that, whatever the methods used, a people has grown mighty, that America has given a better way of life, so far as material things go, to a larger number and proportion of people than any empire in the history of mankind.

But we have also cast a large share of our population down into misery and treadmill tasks. Today we have millions of unemployed amid wealth. We are fast depleting our soil. Most of our rural population, once prosperous, then poor, now is in pauperdom. What is the answer to that—we who are so rich, so powerful, so wise?

Certainly we can say, now that we have spanned a continent, that the need to take hold of our resources with such wasteful speed no longer prevails. A great industrial and social plant has been built; we merely don't know how to keep it going properly. The wild continent has been tamed; a great community has been founded. Now the laws of that community's growth and progress must necessarily change, along with the relation of man to his tools of production and the soil that gives him food and wealth. The days of our careless economic youth are behind us.

In any case, this America has become a mysterious and complicated land, the meaning of which no single person may dare to presume to measure with too much self-assurance.

My concern in this book is with the rich earth of America and man's relation to the earth where he lives and labors in pain and joy and hope.

Not to me will all the answers be vouchsafed—nor to the next man. But perhaps it is appropriate to begin the quest for this knowledge out in my boyhood poppy fields of California on the last, vanishing free land of America.

CHAPTER II

MOTHER AMERICA

What greater love for the American earth and its fruits and life therefrom was ever expressed than by Arapooish, Chief of the Crows, speaking of the Big and Little Horn River country?

"The Crow country. The Great Spirit put it exactly in the right place; while you are in it, you fare well; whenever you get out of it, whichever way you travel, you fare worse.

"If you go to the south, you have to wander over great barren plains; the water is warm and bad, and you meet fever and ague.

"To the north it is cold; the winters are long and bitter; with no grass, you cannot keep horses there, but must travel with dogs. What is a country without horses?

"On the Columbia they are poor and dirty, paddle about in canoes and fish. Their teeth are worn out; they are always taking fishbones out of their mouths. Fish is poor food.

"To the east they dwell in villages; they live well, but they drink the muddy water of the Missouri—that is bad. A Crow's dog would not drink such water.

"About the folks of the Missouri is a fine country; good water; good grass; plenty of buffalo. In summer it is almost as good as the Crow country; but in winter it is cold; the grass is gone; and there is no salt weed for the horses.

"The Crow country is in exactly the right place. It has snowy mountains and sunny plains; all kinds of climates and good things for every season. When the summer heats scorch the prairies, you can draw up under the mountains, where the air is sweet and cool, the

26

grass fresh, and the bright streams come bubbling out of the snow
banks. There you can hunt the elk, the deer, and the antelope when
their skins are fit for dressing; there you will find plenty of white
bears and mountain sheep.

"In the autumn when your horses are fat and strong from the
mountain pastures, you can go down on the plains and hunt the buffalo or trap beaver on the streams. And when winter comes on you
can take shelter in the woody bottoms along the rivers; there you
will find buffalo meat for yourselves, and cottonwood bark for your
horses; or you may winter in the Wind River valley where there
is salt weed in abundance.

"The Crow country is exactly in the right place. Everything good
is found there. There is no country like the Crow country."

This was the sort of patriotism that Walt Whitman knew. This
was the expression of a deep patriotism that makes our latter-day flag
oratory, the blat-blat of our Daughters of the Revolution, our Frank
Hagues and our Legionaires seem shallow as the beating of brass
cymbals.

One can understand better why the Crows and other native folk
fought so long, so desperately, so bravely, against insuperable odds
to hold on to the soil that nourished not only their bodies but such a
deep and abiding love.

The official historian of Natrona County, Wyoming, Alfred J.
Mokler, remarks: "Volumes have been written about the wonderful
resources of Central Wyoming, but all that has been said and all that
has been written could be boiled down into the few words of praise
of Chief Arapooish nearly a hundred years ago."

In the early days our forefathers did not lack wonder, even
though their creed so soon became spoliation. They marveled, though
rarely did they, or could they, love the new earth deeply.

If the Spanish Conquistadores gaped in awe at the gold and the
palaces and the gorgeous feather robes of the native people to the
south, the northern settlers marveled more often at the amplitude
and lavishness of this new land, its teeming water, its fertility; the
great falls of Niagara, of which "no words can express the conster-
nation of travellers"; the mighty rivers and forests; the Indian

mounds, "fashioned with as much military skill, as if designed by Vauban himself"; the coiled rattlesnakes, the epic battles of alligators in southern bayous and everglades, the wild horses that ran ahead of the most daring explorers and tossed their manes on the very crags of the Rockies; the cloudbursts, the floods, the terrible flail of hail.

The new climate was a constant amazement to them, as it is today to alien travelers in our midst. The great sweep of wind, the high drifts of snow, the alternating glare of sun, the over-dramatic thrust of spring, the extravagant burning fires of autumn, have had their effect in shaping the life and thought of Americans, even though we are usually quite unaware of the source of much of our spirit of rest- lessness and have so little tenderness, respect or affection for the beau- ties unrolled before us.

The autumn colors were "part of the tumult;" in no other land such autumns: "a great burial fire," tongues of flame going up to the sky, "the garnet of black and red oaks, the leaping maples and the flickering aspens, and out of the midst of it all one exulting spire of light where a cottonwood shakes primal yellow at the virginal blue of the American sky. The thickets filled with the cymbal colors of the sumach—orange and scarlet and stain of wine; the leaning dwarf forest of the hawthorns begins to drop its shower of little poems—ruby color overcast with purple bloom." [1]

If much of our original natural riches has vanished, the climate is still with us, still keeps its dramatic tempo, its power to astonish folk. In a recent number of *Harper's Magazine* Mary Borden writes:

"I returned to America in December. . . . I looked out of the car window and shuddered, for the wind was screaming down from the north, there was not a blade or leaf of green to be seen, and the land was hard and gray as slate. I thought, 'It is dead.' I felt the world of winter in America to be an unnatural, frightening world. And I remembered that at that moment there were roses growing out of doors in England. . . .

"In America . . . the climate is too militant, too exciting. It is America's one great danger" (if this were only true!); and Miss

[1] Donald Culross Peattie, *A Prairie Grove.*

Borden goes on to say with a faint hint of truth, though with rather childish sociological reasoning: "It has produced more skyscrapers, more religious maniacs, more psychoanalysts, more nervous wrecks, more drunkards, gamblers, gunmen and yellow journalism than any country in the world. Its keynote is extravagance. It is ultra-stimulating; it impels men to work, to undermine mountains, irrigate deserts, build cities in the sky, and fill the silent places of the earth with noise. . . .

"It . . . makes every American feel in a hurry. Get rich quick, get up quick, jump abroad quick, and divorce me quicker, live quick, get old quick. If only it would rain for six months in America without stopping. . . .

". . . the climate of the United States is dangerous. . . . Life burns in America with too bright a flame to burn long. . . ."

It would be nice to solve all our problems with a little rain and soggy drizzle, as of course perishing England has done so well: Mary Borden's passage is not cited here for its common sense, but as an example of the extravagant surprise which for so long has been the keynote of descriptions of the natural world of America, an amazement never stronger than in our first colonists.

In the mixed grammar of the early chronicler Daniel Denton, there is almost Freudian excitation and unconscious symbolism that in spots has almost the true aboriginal touch, when in 1670 he described the fruits of Long Island:

"Mulberries, persimmons, grapes great and small, huckleberries, cranberries, plums of several sorts, raspberries and strawberries, of which last is in such abundance in June, that the fields and woods are dyed red: which the country people perceiving, instantly arm themselves with bottles of wine, cream, and sugar, and instead of a coat of mail, everyone takes a female upon his horse behind him, and so, rushing violently into the fields, never leave till they have disrobed them of their red colours, and turned them into the old habit."

About this time Thomas Ashe was marveling at the *chur, chur, chur* of Carolina hummingbirds, their needle-like bills, their deep green plumage, "shadowed with murrey, not unmuch like the colour of some dove's necks." He marveled at the fireflies, "enlightening" the state "with their golden spangles," and the strong musk smell of the alligators and the eatable flesh of the young ones.

Down in the Carolinas, says another commentator, the little-mouth bass were "thick as leaves." The woods teemed with chincapins, wild grapes, huckleberries and big blackberries.

Soon after Maryland was founded, George Alsop was sending back word to the old country of the furs of "multitudes" of beavers, otters, muskrats, wildcats, elk, buffalo and "divers others." Herds of deer, he said slyly, were "as numerous as cuckolds can be in London, only their horns are not so well drest and tipt with silver."

Best of all, thought the newcomers, was that native food "weachin" —maiïs or maize—domesticated from a wild plant and improved by the Indians through untold centuries of residence. Well-described by John Winthrop, Jr., to the Royal Society, it was "of various colors, as red, white, yellow, blue, olive, greenish, black, speckled, striped, etc.," with ears "defended from the cold and storms by strong, thick husks; the stalk grows six or eight feet high. . . . It is jointed like a cane, is full of sweet juice like the sugar-cane, and a syrup as sweet as sugar may be made out of it. . . . At every joint there are long leaves or flags, and at the top a branch of flowers like rye blossoms."

Down South, James Adair was telling of the abundant crops of the Indians: "Corn is their chief produce, and main dependence." There were "three sorts." The "yellow and flinty" kind they called "hominy-corn." The largest, "of very white and soft grain," was termed "bread-corn." In July, "when chestnuts and corn are green and full-grown, they half boil the former, and take off the rind; and having sliced the milky, swelled long rows of the latter, the women pound it in a large wooden mortar, which . . . wide at the mouth . . . gradually narrows to the bottom; then they knead both together, wrap them up in green corn-blades, . . . about an inch thick, and boil them well, as they do every kind of seethed food. This sort of bread is very tempting to the taste, and reckoned most delicious to their strong palates."

Over in Jersey, Mahlon Stacy was exulting over fruit trees that destroyed themselves of their own weight; peaches, strawberries, cranberries, huckleberries; the plenitude of venison and turkey; how the Indians brought in seven or eight plump ducks a day; how by merely agitating a stream with birch boughs, he and his cousins stirred up thousands of herring and in half an hour filled a three bushel sack—"a brave, plenteous country."

The early Dutch and Swedish settlers in Delaware told similar tales; meadows covered with great flocks of cranes that rose up in clouds, fish so swarming they could be taken with the hand, the water crowded like drifting snow with ducks and wild geese that fell in scores with each shot.

John Smith and his men, cruising up the Potomac, found such an abundance of fish, "lying so thick with their heads above the water," they tried to catch them with frying pans; and found no difficulty, standing in shallow water, in "nailing" the fishes to the bottom with their swords, "and thus we tooke more in one houre than we could eate in a day."

Later Father Andrew White, missionary and chronicler, wrote of this same Potomac, "the sweetest and greatest river I have ever seene, so that the Thames is but a little finger of it," and he told of "the soyle" round about where one could not "set down a foote, but tread on strawberries, raspires, fallen mulberrie vines, acchorns, walnutts, saxafras," and of the "infinite" swarms of birds.

And in these later days of turkey at forty cents a pound, we can recall perhaps wistfully enough the early years when John Brickell, a North Carolina doctor, was wont to shoot any number of wild turkeys weighing from forty to sixty pounds, as one writer has put it, "gobblers as heavy as a child of five." Flocks of five hundred or more flew by. Teals were told of, so well fed they burst when they fell on hard ground.

The Indians brought in fat bucks every day in return for a few pipes of tobacco or a measure or two of powder.

The Governor of Virginia with "His Gentlemen" on the Rappahannock River forks saw "the largest timber, the finest and deepest mould and the best grass" he "ever did see. . . . We killed three bears this day." He told of plentiful killing of deer and turkeys, of graving the trees in the name of King George, the First, of England;

and though the Governor's health was drunk in "Virginia red wine and white wine, Irish usquebaugh, brandy, shrub, two sorts of rum, champagne, canary, cherry, punch, water [sic], cider, etc.," there is no reason, even so, if we are to judge from other corroborating accounts of the countryside, that the chronicler and his friends exaggerated what they saw.

As hunters, explorers and settlers pushed on West, new astonishment at the wonders of the land are revealed. And into the rough-hewn souls of the earlier adventurers inevitably crept the wine of poetry. From school-day memories I recall merely that Daniel Boone was a practical trapper, woodsman, and dare-devil Indian fighter. No teacher imparted to me the hope, the ambition, the hidden dream of such characters, which ever flared up like a flaming beacon when they stood on the edge of great beckoning landscapes. Boone speaks simply and strongly:

"One day I undertook a tour through the country, when the diversity and beauties of nature I met with in this charming season [May], expelled every gloomy thought. . . . I had gained the highest summit of a commanding ridge, and looking around with astonishing delight, beheld the ample plains and beauteous tracts below. On one hand I surveyed the famous Ohio, rolling in silent dignity and marking the western boundary with inconceivable grandeur. At a vast distance, I beheld the mountains lift their venerable brows and penetrate the clouds. . . .

"In March, 1771, I returned to my family, being determined to bring them, as soon as possible, at the risk of my life and fortune, to reside in Kentucky, which I esteemed a second paradise."

F. A. Michaux, considerably later, is astonished at plane trees—at Marietta, Ohio, the first capital of the old Northwest Territory—which measured forty-seven feet in circumference at a distance of four feet above the ground, and whose girth was undiminished to a height of fifteen or twenty feet.

The great Audubon tells us of the passenger pigeons in the Green River country of Kentucky, such dense flocks that they covered the sun with the close network of their wings.

Farmers drove hundreds of hogs hundreds of miles to fatten on them at the roosts. The dung at such roosts lay several inches deep, "like a bed of snow." Many trees two feet in diameter were broken off not far from the ground and branches everywhere were torn off by the weight of the pigeons, "as if the forest had been swept by a tornado."

When the pigeons finally appeared, the sun was lost to view, and the noise they made, "though yet distant," reminded Audubon "of a hard gale at sea, passing through the rigging of a close-reefed vessel, and as they passed created a surprising current of air."

Arriving by thousands, they alighted everywhere, until solid masses, "as large as hogsheads," were formed on the branches all around.

Perches gave way under the weight with a crash, destroying hundreds of birds. "It was a scene of uproar and confusion. I found it quite useless to speak, or even to shout to those persons . . . nearest . . . me. Even the reports of the guns were seldom herd. . . . It was past midnight before I perceived a decrease in the number of those that arrived. The uproar continued the whole night."

When the pigeons took off at dawn next day, wolves howled, and the foxes, lynxes, cougars, bears, raccoons, opossums and pole-cats were seen sneaking off, jowls probably red with the feast; and eagles, hawks and vultures in crowds fearlessly took over their places to gorge.

The early settlers in Pennsylvania also told of the pigeons that filled the air with the humming of their wings. The place where they roosted, called Moyamensing, became the name of part of Philadelphia.

Samuel Griswold Goodrich saw such flocks as late as 1806, flying over Fairfield County, Connecticut, in a stream all day, "from rising to the setting sun."

Hamlin Garland, too, remembered the pigeons: "Countless myriads . . . when they settled to earth, they covered acres of meadow like some prodigious cataract from the sky . . . rose . . . like the rumbling of thunder."

Father Pierre Jean De Smet exclaimed about the mighty herds of buffalo, "majestic elk," and "clouds" of antelopes, and big sporting herds of ashata; the black-tailed roebuck scarcely touching its feet to the earth; the abundance of grizzly bears, wolves, panthers, badgers and wildcats. Prairie hens and the mountain-cock started up from the heather; lakes and rivers were covered with swans, geese and ducks; the beaver, the otter, the muskrat and fishes were in "peaceable possession of their solitary waters."

Donald Culross Peattie in his *Prairie Grove* vividly recreates the buffalo days—when many millions of the monarch bison—half a ton hefty, six feet high and sometimes nine feet in length—pounded the prairies from the eastern forest to the Rockies, from Canada down to Texas through the salt-licks of Kentucky and the watering holes of the great plains, and made the buffalo "traces" that in time became the Kentucky road, the Vincennes road, and are today concrete highways. They ground the grass "with many million molars" and covered the land—where today the prairie states spend millions every year buying fertilizers—"with the returned fertility of their great flaps."

"The buffalo means abundance, warmth, excitement. . . . They put the manhood into man, they gave his way of life; they were what he could win by bravery. His art and his song, his prayers and his dances, exulted in the perilous opportunity that thundered on him in a golden pillar of dust."

The buffalo served the earlier settlers as it had the Indian. Many a snowed-in colonist on the plains survived the weeks and months of thirty-degree-below weather only by burning up the accumulated hills of buffalo bones and dung. The meat was cured, the fat and grease run for winter months. The hides made sleeping bags, leggings, moccasins, and provided a very spongy sole leather. The hair growing on the head and neck of the animal was long and shaggy but so soft it spun into a thread "not unlike mohair, which might be wove into a sort of camlet." "Some people," wrote William Byrd two centuries ago, "have stockings knit of it, that would have served an Israelite during his forty years' march through the wilderness."

Great was the buffalo feast when, after the hunt, the slaughtered animals lay mountainous on the prairie. "Around the feasting circle passed the tenderloin and fat, offered first to the old," then to visitor tribesmen, finally to the chiefs and great warriors, "until bellies were gorged."

One of the early ostentations of the American leisure class became eating or, better said, gorging in almost Indian fashion—an inherited devotion to the abundance of the land. This is reflected in a very simple dinner given by Secretary Woodbury in Washington in which there were thirty meat dishes. The simplest, most simple dinner, described by Margaret Bayard Smith, was bouilli at the foot of the table and boiled fish at the head, then canvas-backs followed by pheasant; as side dishes, a small ham, a small turkey, partridges, mutton chops, sweetbreads, a macaroni pie and oyster pie, together with stewed celery, spinach, salsify, cauliflower. For dessert, ice-cream, fruit, jellies, custards, blanc mange, cakes, sweet-meats and sugar-plums, etc., etc.

The lyric note of Dan Boone carries on across the continent, on through the Rockies and Yellowstone to the Northwest, on to California where "the owls woo-whoo-ed and the rattlesnakes rattled and waved their tails in greeting."

Many an excited immigrant saw not merely beautiful land and rivers, majestic mountains and sweeping sky, but lofty visions, as did the marveling chap who beheld around the conical peak of Pilot Mountain "shapes like men, with wings, flying the clear blue sky." Others, seeing the big footprints in the snow of beforehand travelers, sent back reports that the region was inhabited by a race of giants. Everything was so marvelous and new that everything could be believed. Scientific observation was mostly a waste of time.

Frémont on one of the first expeditions, though a fairly prosaic man, able to survive on a prairie dog diet, waxed poetical about those snow-dazzling heights, which if not the Alps, have "their own character of grandeur and magnificence," which he prophesied would find "pens and pencils to do them justice."

And in a later day, John Muir was to continue the spirit of wonderment in the Far West, but by then science was mingling more and more with poetry. He tells in his prolix journals of the totem poles on Wrangel Island, records the dimensions of cedar rafters in Indian houses, the glacial origin and majesty of the Yosemite; but most repeatedly he speaks in awe and delight of the *pinus monticola*, his beloved sequoias, "the most venerable-looking of all the Sierra giants, standing erect and true, in poise so perfect they seem to make no effort,—their strength so perfect it is invisible."

Before that Robert Rogers, walking the shores of mighty Lake Superior, marveled at the tall grass, at the "fish, fowl and beasts of every size and kind . . . in the greatest abundance . . . a rich and valuable country, should it ever be inhabited by a civilized people."

In 1833 Cleng Peerson, walking, walking, walking alone across a continent into the buffalo grass, over the broad acres lush with wild pea vines, dense with thick forests, finally sensing that paradise was at last at hand, dug his knife into the prairie and beneath the matted grass roots found fine black soil—and thereby he led the first Norwegian colony into the upper Mississippi basin.

By 1855 at Bishop Hill they plowed two mile furrows for their cornfields and never hit a boulder.

And soon in the Dakotas the Norsemen were singing, to the squawking fiddle at their round dances: [1]

"In America they give land for nothing, . . .
And the grain just pops out of the ground. . . .

The grain threshes itself in the granary
While I stretch out at ease in my bunk. . . .

You just ought to see the potatoes!
You can distill a quart of whiskey out of each one.

The salmon leap like mad in the rivers
And hop into the kettles and cry out for a cover.

And little roast pigs rush about the streets,
Politely inquiring if you wish for ham.

And the hens lay eggs big as a gourd,
And the cocks strike the hour like an eight-day clock. . . .

Oh, I'd much rather live in America
Than drag the chain of slavery over yon in Norway."

[1] Quoted by Walter Havighurst, *Upper Mississippi*.

CHAPTER III

WAR FOR LAND

Hunters, trappers, traders, missionaries, settlers, tamed a continent. They tamed a continent by fighting two great contenders: the people who already possessed it and Nature herself. They tamed both with brawn, hardship, love of freedom (for themselves), greed, astuteness. Their weapons were the civilization and techniques of England and Western Europe and their faith in an imaginary Protestant God.

All told, the Indians also had some excellent techniques for living, for procuring food and clothing, for fighting enemies of their own kind. Their pursuits gave them enjoyment, art, time for worship.

Thomas Jefferson was convinced that the Indian societies enjoyed "in their general mass an infinitely greater degree of happiness than those who live under the European governments."

But the natives did not have the wheel and had not yet discovered iron; and such things, putting them at an unexpected disadvantage, helped spell their doom. The White man also had rum and other strong drinks, and these, too, spelled the Indian's doom. Rum went side by side with the Christian religion—though the two were not often on speaking terms—in breaking down native resistance. A hundred missionary and other accounts prove this. Rum, according to one missionary to the Mohawks, caused "the Indians to waste away. . . . Indeed the Christians selling the Indians so much rum as they do is sufficient bar against their embracing Christianity." But even when Christianity won out over rum, religion itself likewise broke down native morale.

And so, if the Indians' techniques were sufficient for the good life according to their own lights, if their culture and thought and art fed their spirit, such things were not sufficient to combat the White settlers.

The Indians, like the Whites, had many contradictory traits. They were hospitable, generous, and highly courteous, with a dignified etiquette in dealing with outsiders. They were also warlike, and when on the war-path, cruel. Their cruelties, though, mostly followed a religious pattern. If they scalped their enemies, that was to keep them out of the happy hunting grounds of the hereafter. It had much the same significance as a priest who refuses to give unction to a dying enemy.

In any case, the Indians had no copyright on cruelty, even in its worst forms; and the conquerors, though they had better tools, had no exclusive copyright on morality or beauty. The Indians, in fact, had religions and literatures and art that in many ways, so far as kinship with the American earth is concerned, have never been surpassed by their White despoilers.

For, whatever the technical limitations of their culture, the Indian people, with thousands of years of adjustment to their environment, as compared to our own very short span, had achieved a thorough-going regard for the common welfare, a great honesty and disdain of all petty evasion, and a dislike of hypocrisy that often filled them with utter contempt for the White man, who so often cloaked cunning and greed in religion. There was many a noble note in Indian character.

Mary Jennison, long a prisoner of the Indians, gives us a Seneca lament for one of their lost warriors that seems more heart-felt than any oration said over the tomb of a modern Unknown Soldier.

"Oh, our brother! Alas! He is dead—he is gone; he will never return! Friendless he died on the field of the slain, where his bones are yet lying unburied! . . . No tears dropped around him; oh, no! No tears of his sisters were there! He fell in his prime, when his arm was most needed to keep us from danger. . . . The deer he could take on the chase! The panther shrunk back at the sight of his strength! His enemies fell at his feet! He was brave and courageous in war! as the fawn he was harmless; his friendship was ardent; his temper was gentle; his pity was great! Oh! Our friend, our companion is gone! . . .

"Though he fell on the field of the slain, with glory he fell, and his spirit went up to the land of his fathers in war! Then why do we mourn? With transports of joy they received him, and fed him, and clothed him, and welcomed him there! Oh, friends, he is happy; then dry up your tears!"

And so they took and adopted a woman, a White woman, of those who were their enemies, to take his place in their hearts.

Imagine an American in 1917 taking in and protecting a German woman to replace one of our fallen soldiers on the Argonne battlefront. Such civilized charity would seem ridiculous to us.

But the lowly Indians, whom we dispossessed from a continent, chanted, "Dickewamis has come: then let us receive her with joy! She is handsome and pleasant! Oh, she is our sister, and gladly we welcome her here. In the place of our brother she stands in our tribe. With care we will guard her from trouble; and may she be happy till her spirit shall leave us."

After about four years, Mary Jennison became so accustomed to Indian ways she no longer had any "anxiety" to leave them, "was warmly attached in consideration of the favors, affection and friendship" with which they had "uniformly" treated her, from the day of adoption.

James Smith was captured and adopted into the Caughnewago nation. "My son, you are now flesh of our flesh, and bone of our bone. . . . My son, you now have nothing to fear—we are now under the same obligations to love, support, and defend you that we are to love and defend one another."

Smith remarks: "I did not believe this fine speech, but since, . . . I have found that there was much sincerity in said speech; for, from that day, I never knew them to make any distinction between me and themselves in any respect whatever until I left them. If they had plenty of clothing, I had plenty; if we were scarce, we all shared our fate."

Thus many of the captives the Indians took were treated no worse than they treated themselves, sometimes better. John Gyles, taken

prisoner one winter, told how the Indians gave him rags to bind up
his frozen feet and showed him how to cure himself with fir-balsam;
and when he got better, they thoughtfully fixed up a special snow-
shoe for him to travel on.

Captain John Smith addressed the British Queen herself to tell
what great courtesy he was tendered by Chief Powhatan, his son
Nantiquaus and the lovely Pocahontas. He told how the weak and
miserable thirty-eight settlers in Jamestown would surely have perished "had not the savage fed us."

Mrs. Rowlandson, taken prisoner by the Iroquois, writes with hate
of her captors. But the picture of cruelty (of which little intentionally
fell her way) and kindness (of which she was the constant recipient)
that she paints is none too flattering to the lady herself. One captive,
who complained too much, was finally stripped naked and knocked on
the head. But many an Indian captive was dealt with just as cruelly
or worse by the Whites; and other captives of this particular tribe of
Indians, and among them Mrs. Rowlandson, were admirably treated,
often with sensitive consideration.

When she wept, fearing they intended to kill her, they told her
gently they wouldn't hurt her, and one of them came and gave her
several spoonfuls of meal to comfort her, and another a half a pint
of peas. When she sewed for them, she was honestly paid in money
or in kind. She carried a piece of bear meat around in her pocket
till it stank, afraid to cook it, lest the hungry captors would take it
from her; but when she finally did, she was given ground nuts to
eat with it. She, the more civilized person, herself snatched away
a piece of meat the Indians had given to a captive English child,
"and savory it was" to her taste. She comforted herself from Job 6:7:
"The things that my soul refuseth to touch, are as my sorrowful
meat."

On another occasion a warrior, returning with bloody bullet-torn
clothes, frightened her, but "the Lord suffered not this wretch do
me any hurt, yea, instead of that . . . five or six times did he and
his squaw refresh my feeble carcase. . . . They would always give
me something, and yet they were strangers that I never saw before."

And when Mrs. Rowlandson was finally ransomed, the tribe,

on her departure, gave her bread and tobacco and a hood and scarf —all prized possessions.

She concludes, building up to terror and letting us down with a little *shsh:*

"I have been in the midst of those roaring lions, and savage bears, that feared neither God nor man, nor the devil, by night and day, alone and in company; sleeping all sorts together, and yet not one of them ever offered the least abuse of unchastity to me, in word or action."

Could a young Negro woman say the same of the Whites in the South even today?

The Indians tried to punish those of their members who committed depredations without the consent of the group against White folk. But the Caucasian settlers never held their members especially accountable for evil deeds against the Indians, though during later treaty periods some futile attempts were made in this direction and several centuries later one White man was actually sentenced to be hanged for murdering an Indian. In New York and Massachusetts in very early days, a drunken Indian was subject to fine or imprisonment or worse, but no punishment was meted out to the Whites who got him drunk.

The Indians often tried to be generous and helpful toward the alien invaders. Benjamin Trumbull, in his *Complete History of Connecticut* (1818), states that at the Englishmen's first settlement, the natives "performed many acts of kindness," instructing them "in the manner of planting and dressing Indian corn. They carried them upon their backs, through rivers and water . . . served them instead of boats and bridges. They gave them much useful information about the country, and when the English or their children were lost in the woods, and were in danger of perishing with hunger or cold, they conducted them to their wigwams, fed them, and restored them to their families and parents."

There is real nobility in the later word of Pied Riche, chief of the Potawatomi, to the leaders of the migrating Mormons. Previously the Potawatomi had been woefully treated, forced to leave their homes. The Mormons had also been persecuted and, though the

Mormons were of the White people from which he had suffered so
much, Pied Riche was above narrow race prejudices.

"The Pottawatamie came, sad and tired, into this unhealthy Missouri bottom not many years back," driven out of his "beautiful
country beyond the Mississippi which had abundant game, timber
and clear water everywhere. Now you are driven away the same
way from your lodges and lands . . . and the graves of your
people. So we have both suffered. We must help one another and
the Great Spirit will help us both." And so he allowed the Mormons
to live where they pleased, cut all the wood they needed, make new
homes. Neither people need "always suffer." We may both live "to
see all right yet. However, if we do not our children will."

Later the Indians, as usual, were to repent of their open-handed-
ness. Irritations arose. The Mormons proved to be no angels.

In upper New York, the arrogant warlike Mohawks generously
gave hospitality to miserable half-starved Palatine peasant refugees,
carried them over the winter, gave them land. Their kindness was
their undoing. They were little by little overwhelmed, and in 1782
the last Indian rode forever out of the valley.

Our textbooks tell repeatedly of the trials and tribulations of the
early transcontinental travelers at the hands of the Indians, but
they never tell of the wrongs to the Indians committed by rough
and ignorant White men, the wiping out of whole Indian settlements—men, women and children. Stories and movies of massacres
by Indians are dramatic; so is the reverse, but even-handed truth
would anger the box office. Rarely is it revealed that the pioneers
who crossed the continent (often without having gotten proper permission and in violation of established treaty rights, recognized by
the United States government itself), often received fine hospitality
and merciful aid from the Red man. Far more often than accounts
of attacks by Indians, the records tell of friendly fraternizing and
Indian helpfulness.

The Journal of Stanislaus Lasselle, who went overland to California from Indiana in '49, tells how, day after day, friendly Indians
came into camp. They played and danced, let the immigrants gaze
upon their intimate religious festivals. They came to show the trav-

elers where to get water and game, how to find the right trail, helped them pack up on leaving. They brought gifts. Only when the expedition approached its destination did some of the Indians, near civilized towns, try to steal a few things. In contrast Lasselle's record is replete with stories of quarrels, gambling, drunkenness and thievery among the Whites themselves. Fights were common.

In 1820, Jedidiah Morse, commissioned by the President of the United States to investigate Indian affairs, reported to Congress that there was no reason to look down on the Indians "as an inferior race." He objected bitterly to the way people profited by Indian ignorance and weakness by taking their property "for a small part of its real value," and for oppressing them in other ways. He condemned the heartless removal of settled agricultural Indians "far away from their present homes . . . into a wilderness, among strangers, possibly hostile," thus forcing them back into the hunting stage to which they were not at all accustomed and which was "incompatible with civilization" and could not at all be "reconciled with the professed . . . objects of the Government in civilizing them."

He describes some of the eastern Indians, the hospitable Choctaws, who to assist travelers had set up inns excelling in cleanliness and comfort many of those among Whites, of the equally hospitable and progressive Chickasaws, and others. Of the Cherokees he states that their "courage, fidelity, hospitality and cleanliness" stood high. They were "generally of a fine figure, as to their persons, polite in their manners, and fond of learning and improvement in the arts." He praises their civil government, their jurisprudence and the skill and judgment of their political institutions.

After these and other accounts by the few men who really lived among the Indians, studied their ways, attempted to understand them sympathetically, and in nearly all cases found boundless hospitality, we can sympathize better with Cannasateego, the Onondaga Chief, who remarked feelingly to Conrad Weisser:

"If a White man in traveling through our country enters one of our cabins, we treat him as I do you. We dry him if he is wet; we warm him if he is cold; and give him meat and drink that he may allay his hunger and thirst, and we spread soft furs for him to rest and sleep on. We demand nothing in return. But if I go into a White house and ask for victuals and drink, they say, 'Where is your money?' and if I have none, they say, 'Get out, you Indian dog.' "

Almost from the first the Indians had a foreboding of their fate. As Nathaniel Hawthorne put it: "The forest track trodden by the hobnailed shoes of these sturdy Englishmen has now a distinctness it never could have acquired from the light tread of a hundred times as many moccasins . . . and the Indians, coming from their distant wigwams to view the White man's settlement, marvel at the deep track which he makes, and perhaps are saddened by a flitting presentiment that the heavy tread will find its way over all the land."

Soon enough the Indians everywhere began to doubt the good intentions of the Whites. The Mohawk Sachems, visiting Queen Anne in London in 1710, in representation of the one group of Indians continuously loyal to the English, reveal their perplexity over being merely the pawns of imperial policy. It was a Mohawk who told Missionary Andrews: "You Christians were so wicked to crucify your God and now He is angry with you and therefore to pacify Him you endeavor to persuade us to serve Him, but why should we? We never heard of Him until Christians came here; He is not angry with us."

The Indians were not long in taking the true measure of a good part of the invaders and exactly what they wanted and their unethical ruthlessness in getting it. As the Abenakis of St. François early said to the delegate of the Governor of Massachusetts, whom they addressed as "Brother":

"It is in vain that you charge us with bad hearts; it is always you, our brothers, who have attacked us; you have a sweet tongue, but a heart of gall. . . . We like nothing better than . . . peace. . . . We wish to keep possession of the lands on which we live. . . . As soon as you cease to encroach upon those lands we shall be at peace." It sounds almost like President Roosevelt talking about "aggressor nations."

In 1811, Red Jacket of the Senecas said to a missionary: "They told us they had fled from their country for fear of wicked men. . . . They asked for a small seat. We took pity on them, granted their request; and they sat down amongst us. We gave them corn and meat; they gave us poison in return."

More came, and called the Indians brothers and were given a large seat. "They wanted more land; they wanted our country. Our eyes were opened. . . . Wars took place. . . . Many of our people were destroyed. They also brought strong liquor among us. It was strong and powerful and has slain thousands. . . . Now . . . we have scarcely a place left to spread our blankets. You have got our country, but are not satisfied; you want to force your religion upon us. . . ."

Soon enough the Indians realized that the friendship they had at first mistakenly tendered could never survive—only war. More and more the natives had to "hang up the kettle and take up the hatchet."

If the Indians when at war were ferocious, or when organized warfare degenerated in times of simulated peace into brutal reprisals on both sides, the Indians were thereby conforming to the best military traditions of all peoples. In such traits there was not much to choose between the two contenders. The White settlers, when they descended on the native villages, also killed Indian women and children ruthlessly, frequently submitting them to frightful tortures.

The fact was, it was the White man who was ever persistently encroaching, however much at moments the tables might be reversed. Commercial greed and land greed were paramount, and constant factors impelled the Caucasians to try to get the best of the Indians in every possible way. From the very first the Indian was mostly an object to be tricked, beaten or destroyed without compunction.

Peter Kalm in his *Voyage to North America* indicates that it was often customary to try to get the Indians drunk in order to cheat them, and this was even more true in the later days of licensed traders, whose account-books still reveal how universally shameless they were in robbing the natives.

When Captains Amadas and Barlow appeared in Pamilco Sound in 1584, the native king's brother, accompanied by forty or fifty men, came out in boats, "very handsome and goodly people, and in their behavior as mannerly and civil as any of Europe. . . . The king made all signs of joy and welcome, striking on his head and his breast, and afterwards on ours, to show we were all one, smiling and making show the best he could of all love and familiarity."

This did not prevent the Englishmen from fleecing the natives; exchanging a tin dish for twenty skins worth twenty crowns and a copper kettle for fifty skins worth fifty crowns.

Whenever Martin Pring and his men, who happened along in 1603, tired of the "savages," who graciously sought to entertain them with convivial music and dancing, the civilized visitors would set their mastiffs on them.

Sargent, long ago in his *Introductory Memoir to the Journal of Braddock's Expedition,* described the aggressive Scotch-Irish settlers, a sweet people who gouged out the eyes of adversaries with thumb and forefinger.

"They hated the Indian while they despised him, and it does not seem, in their dealing with this race, as though there were any sentiments of honor or magnanimity in their bosoms that could hold way against the furious tide of passionate blind resentment." The physician, the Reverend Joseph Doddridge who treated the settlers' ailments, tells us that the cruelty and brutality of the Scotch-Irish warfare were almost beyond belief. Both sides scalped each other; both sides killed prisoners.

Often the Indians paid high for their generosity to captives. One night, Hannah Dustin, Mary Neff and Samuel Lennerson sneaked up on their captors, bashed their heads in with tomahawks, then cut off the scalps of "ten of the wretches," for at that time the General Assembly of Massachusetts was paying five pounds each for Indian scalps. It did not take the American settlers long to imitate all the Indian cruelties without relinquishing any of their own.

Scalp bounty raids, even upon peaceful Indians, were common. Caleb Lyman tells of a raid in the Connecticut Valley. His party came back with six scalps (for which they received thirty-one pounds reward), much plunder, guns, skins, canoes, etc., and concluded that they "should be rich enough."

Connecticut had a complicated schedule of awards for scalps, depending on who did the gory deed and how, and whether the Indian scalped was man, woman or child.

Dunbar's war broke out over a very common incident. White frontiersmen, in cold blood, murdered all the family and relatives of the Iroquois Chief, Logan, whose sense of honor, dignity, fairness, loyalty and unwavering kindness had won for him the respect, even the admiration, of many prominent Whites. One April day nine Indians, including women and babies, all of Logan's family, left their village at Yellow Creek on the upper Ohio and made a friendly visit to the trading camp of a settler named Greathouse. There the grown-up natives were made drunk, and when they had become helpless, Greathouse and two companions slaughtered the whole lot, women, babies and all. This was nothing compared to the good Reverend J. M. Chivington, who as colonel of the 2nd Colorado Cavalry, in November, 1864, perpetrated the Sun Creek Massacre, cold-bloodedly butchering an encampment of 300 Indians, men, women, children, babes in arms. General Nelson A. Miles characterized it as "the foulest and most unjustifiable crime in the annals of America." The Black Hole of Calcutta was mild in comparison, and though it precipitated three decades of bloody reprisal and trouble, it is omitted from our school textbooks.

We like to tell of Indian or Spanish cruelties in Latin America, but our own forefathers could often give both the native and the hidalgos lessons in such things.

If among the New World settlers themselves inevitably contradictions between deed and creed multiplied constantly, there was rarely any such doubt, only a common welding of utility and faith, in the driving out of the Indian. It was a long story of over two centuries of war when peace occasionally broke out, of hypocritical peace pacts with the natives, of treaties made and torn into scraps, of increasingly treacherous reprisals; misunderstanding and mutual resentments, brutality and theft and murder. It was the inevitable clash of two cultures in which all moral scruples, except in the mouths of politicians, went by the boards.

The settlers, so as not to be late to church, figuratively, wiped their tomahawks, with which they so soon learned to scalp, with the leaves of the Bible and the Sermon on the Mount. As someone has said: "Calvinists in coonskins, once started, were devils, and they shot with the logic of John Knox." The White man's religion definitely aided the prolonged conquest.

Though the Indian's gods stood staunchly by him, they also led him to futile slaughter; and with defeat, gradually his old assurance in his long-cherished beliefs faded away; the old religions cracked apart, and as the native race was even more dependent on religion than the White, the crack soon yawned through his whole culture and broke up the cement of his community life, paralyzing his productive as well as his defensive powers. The rupture of his older faith was part of the process by which he was subdued. Breaking down his older faith facilitated conquest, hastened his defeat. The preacher and the missionary, as in all conquests, were powerful instruments for the annihilation of the Red man.

The Indians themselves had a tolerance about religious matters unknown to the Puritan. In the early years of first settlement, if Mrs. Rowlandson wrote of her Iroquois captors with such consuming rancor, it was because they were heathen, not because they treated her illy. God was always in her mouth, but not in her soul. The Indians displayed no such bigotry. In fact she tells how, after the Indians had victoriously attacked a settlement and had come back whooping with triumph, one of the warriors gave her a Bible he had stolen, carefully brought home in a basket for her, to try to comfort her. The Puritans tried to destroy the religion of the natives wherever they could, but the Indians respected hers and let her read her Bible.

Indian religious and race tolerance, the very moral values they had, opened the gates through which the settlers charged pell-mell. Captain Bonneville reported of the Nez Percés: "Simply to call these people religious would convey but a faint idea of the deep hue of piety and devotion which pervades their whole conduct. Their honesty is immaculate. . . . They are more like a nation of saints than a horde of savages."

That could not be said a few years later. When their group faith cracked, their character definitely changed; and they became the bravest, most remarkable and implacable foes the Whites ever faced.

An observer, who had lived long among the Sioux at Prairie du Chien, wrote in the *Indiana Centinel*, May 29, 1819 (quoted by Dunbar), that though the so-called pagans had no knowledge of the Bible, but worshiped a Great Spirit that would someday call them to his side, nevertheless they lived by a golden rule and were the most "innocent, benevolent and moral part of the human race" he had ever seen. "The moral perfection of these Indians and their creed are . . . as good as the Articles of the multiformed churches of Christendom."

Their high morality, however, merely led the Sioux to become easier victims of the Christian White traders, caused them to lose lands and to be driven west—their customs destroyed, their social fabric broken, their lives uprooted—to become the worst of the so-called "bad men" of the plains, among those most bitterly denounced for their banditry, violence and assassinations of White people.

If a few religious groups, especially the Quakers and the Moravians, were often kind, even helpful to the Indians in more intelligent ways, their work was frustrated by others. The Christianized Indian settlement, founded by the Moravians in Ohio, was brutally wiped out by other settlers. But even if now and then we find the good ministers of the Gospel busily trying to convert the "savages," and bring them to the light of Christ, this was really quite as destructive of the natives as White raids and scalp bounties. In the next breath the same Christian pastors called out the dogs of war in brimstone and chile sermons; then no invective was too harsh.

Pious Increase Mather wrote delightedly of how King Philip, who had shown great kindness to many White prisoners, had his head cut off and carried to Plymouth, his hands to Boston, and his four quarters "hanged up as a monument of revenging Justice," and concluded, "So let all thine enemies perish, O Lord!"

The righteous Cotton Mather frequently poured out invectives on the "tawney serpents" and from the fullness of his Christian heart, incited the colonists to violent action. Reverend Solomon Stoddard of Northampton—with the sedentary viciousness that often is characteristic of a few well-protected members of the cloth in time of war—urged the use of dogs "to hunt the Indians as they do beasts" and in 1706 Massachusetts officially went in for dog-breeding for this purpose.

But between battles, some settlers often sought to convert the natives to Christianity. In the northern colonies, John Eliot was the outstanding "apostle" in this effort, and his work was supported as early as 1649 by the English "Society for the Propagation of the Gospel in New England," a work taken over in 1787 by the more patriotic "Society for Propagating the Gospel Among the Indians and Others in North America"—the oldest incorporated missionary body in the United States.

But it cannot be said that the new doctrines were any improvement on the beautiful nature-rites of the natives. Sir William Johnson, surveying the matter with jaundiced Established Church eyes, tells of the work of the dissenting Presbyterian missionaries: They caused the Christian Indian to imbibe "an air of the most enthusiastical cant," and were "in short intermixed with the greatest distortion of features and zealous belchings of the spirit." The singing of psalms among them by the "bigoted Puritans" merely caused the Indians to "neglect their hunting and most worldly affairs," and become "very worthless members of society."

Mary Jennison, wife of an Indian, wrote: "The use of ardent spirits among the Indians, and the attempts which have been made to civilize and Christianize them by the white people, have constantly made them worse and worse; increased their vices, and robbed them of many of their virtues; and will ultimately produce their extermination."

Thus evangelization became—along with the rifle and the ax, and soon enough the Indian's own tomahawk—a weapon that disintegrated native society. The field reports of the missionary body just mentioned show the missionary plunging into unexplored wilderness, Bible in one hand, life in the other—the former more valued than the latter. But in this courageous self-sacrificing role, unconsciously he served the conquest of the continent; he and his fellows were shock-troops in exposed places, and their self-righteous fervor blazed trails and drove wedges into the native culture, causing moral and spiritual cracks which were soon to widen enough so that not only

Gabriel could trumpet through, but an army of settlers and the United States cavalry could drive in to complete the Christian process.

If bullets and land-theft were in large part the newcomer's answer to the New World hospitality, Christianity (as all phases of the culture of the invaders) inevitably became one of the major weapons of subjugation, either to fortify the spirit of the settlers with the loftiest stated motives or to weaken and disrupt the cultural, psychological and moral integrity of the defenders. Christianity definitely helped the newcomers to achieve security and power. Religion, in its dual role, served as motivating force and an instrument for wiping out the native race.

In all this process, White atrocities mostly were conveniently forgotten. Indian atrocities were magnified and have grown large over the years. There is little charity or justice in the views people hold of their opponents in war—neither then nor today. We need but recall the tall yarns we gulped down about the Germans during our last war.

Our tendency to blacken the Indian's character was accentuated by the fact that we were the interlopers, stealing the Indian's lands, destroying his wealth, curtailing his means of livelihood, violating treaty after treaty—and when one is the aggressor it becomes all the more necessary, in order to justify one's civilizing aims, to smear over the reputation of your adversary, to emphasize your own superior ways, and justify your own actions in high moral terms, when in reality what you want is land and power and wealth—be it an advance along the Alleghenies or upon Addis Ababa.

Nothing is more curious than the pseudo-legal haggling over the titles of vast stretches of wilderness, arguments resulting from the confusing overlapping of regions obtained by pacts with the Indians, who often gave where they had no jurisdiction or without being aware, beyond the petty gifts lavished upon them, of what was occurring. There was similar pettifogging legal conflict resulting from various Royal charters and grants, often for the same areas, though everybody concerned knew perfectly well that the only real title lay in seizure, occupation, the fighting off of the rival settlers with guns—

as in the massacre of Connecticut folk over the Wyoming Valley in Pennsylvania.

Even more amusing is to follow the solemnity with which even our contemporary historians discuss the pros and cons of such paper claims.

Such legal niceties at such a time merely represented one more effort at the general rationalization of theft, the outwitting of the Indians, the taking from him whatever the White settler wanted or needed. Such legality was really conscience salve.

In the long battle were interludes when the pioneers paused to consolidate their gains. Then peace with the natives became advantageous, and we could reassume a lofty attitude, talk bleedingly of our love and benevolence for the Red man, our desire to protect and "civilize him."

From the battle of Fallen Timbers in 1794 until approximately 1840, with the exception of several wars, such as that of Black Hawk in 1832, relative peace prevailed. We were somewhat stalled until roads and canals could be built; and on their side the Indians, realizing the futility of armed conflict, sought to organize their societies in better fashion and to secure what rights they could by treaty. The federal government found it temporarily convenient to recognize the complete sovereignty of various "Republics," "Nations," "Confederations," "Kings" and "Councils." White men were excluded entirely for a time from some areas; they could cross others only by special permit or treaty arrangements; in many places they were restricted to recognize trails from which they might not diverge.

But the *putsch* of the Whites was too determined. The Americans knew these treaties were subterfuges; they never really accepted them; they felt that the country was theirs to go where they wanted; and despite the legal restraints, they did so whenever they felt they could and wanted to. And the federal government did little or nothing to make its own citizens respect its laws and its solemn obligations with the Indians. Treaties were violated constantly. They were then amended; more and more land ceded or arbitrarily taken. There were a hundred Munich accords in the expansion of the United States, a hundred Czechoslovakias.

As early as 1821 President Monroe, salving his conscience by talking solemnly of America's duty to educate the Indians, declared that "their sovereignty over vast territories should cease." Inevitably from 1830 on, tension grew greater. In 1837 the Indian Lands Bill dispossessed the "Five Civilized Tribes" of the South, the Choctaws, Cherokees, Seminoles, Creeks and Chickasaws, some sixty thousand people. They were herded west to Indian Territory—"a greedy and cruel business."

As usual in other cases high officials patted themselves on the back for the kindly way the Indians were dispossessed, talked of their noble civilizing motives. The only motive at all was land greed. The best witnesses of kindliness were the Choctaws themselves. Thomas W. Owen, in his *History of Alabama*, gives the picture: "On the banks of the Bodaka Creek, there are two or three high hills, and all the Choctaws rendezvoused on these hills, just before their emigration. Here they remained for three days, lifting their voices in wailing lamentations, performing their religious rites, and here from the summits of the hills, they took their last look over the beautiful country which they were to see no more."

Among two of the counties carved out from Choctaw land are Sumter, Alabama, and Kemper, Mississippi, today two of the most debased, illiterate lynch centers of the United States, with rough roads impassable in winter, where only $2.41 a year (Sumter) is spent on each Negro child for education, and Negro teachers receive $171 per year. Arthur E. Raper, in his *Tragedy of Lynching*, describes Sumter County as a place of "Sorry schools, poorly paid and poorly trained teachers, indifferent parents, uninspired children and dogmatic landlords," with "no public library, hospital or Red Cross organization, and no public health officer or social worker in the county." Kemper County, nicknamed "Bloody Kemper," is even lower in the scale. It is doubtful whether the mass of the population of either county is as well off, as cultured, as clean, as decent, as the ousted Choctaws. Such is one triumph of civilization!

And so from 1840 on the old ways of war between Indians and Whites were resumed.

And so through war, the defrauding of the Indians, the seizure of their land, went on from Colonial times down until late in the nineteenth century. During the more peaceful treaty interlude, our people, little enamored of that peace, became alarmed at the obvious success with which, in many instances, the Indians were advancing in settled agriculture, political solidarity, education and rejuvenated cultural integrity. The remaining Indians were steadfastly refusing to sell more land and were visibly acquiring a civic pride and social state comparable to that of the Whites, in some instances superior to that of White Americans in the same areas today a century later.

It would be too much to claim that the Indians were not restless, that they did not have malcontents and trouble makers, but it was the American settlers who crowded across Indian boundaries, did trick trading, appropriated land, perpetrated violences, caused most trouble. The Americans wanted land, furs, profits from rum selling; the Indians mostly wanted merely to be left alone.

We need merely look at the way in which the Potawatomi Indians of the Wabash, in a space of two years, lost their lands to the federal government, paid out $130,974.60 in cash and still owed $22,761.04 —all very legal. The Whites usually never rested in such cases until they had the land the federal government had paid for and the money paid out besides. Whenever the government bought land from the Indians, a crowd of White crooks, speculators and adventurers swarmed about. In a mob scramble they intimidated the Indians, whose morale was already gone from having lost their homes, to snatch their money away. A whole concerted system of looting both the federal government and the Indians was built up. Enormous fake claims would be created. The government would buy out and dispossess the Indians with the proviso that all such claims be paid at once. The Indians would be moved away at governmental expense, and the same buzzards, or others like them, would usually get their cash and their homes too. Some Indians fought, though they knew it to be hopeless, rather than permit themselves to be so easily despoiled by the United States government and trick speculators, traders and land-grabbers.

"In Alabama, Georgia and elsewhere," says one authority, "the Southern plantation gentlemen, by the liberal use of whiskey, defrauded the Indians of their official reservations and used pressure at Washington to get the holders removed elsewhere at government expense."

In Georgia, though the poorer Uplanders hated the rich Lowland planters, they were all one with the latter in desiring the expulsion of the Cherokees from the large northern area of the state. The poor folk saw, in the probable land lottery, a chance to grab good farms. The planters of the coast had depleted their soil, through tobacco-growing, and were beginning to emigrate, seeking new lands.

The Cherokees, however, had become the most prosperous civilized, and peaceful of all the Indians. Rapidly, they had matched the White neighbor in agriculture. In 1825—Sequoyah, an enlightened Cherokee chieftain, having invented an alphabet—a printing press was set up in New Echota, the capital. A newspaper, the *Cherokee Phoenix*, was printed and a written constitution drawn up. Many pamphlets and books were published, schools were founded. Population was increasing. The group was so prosperous it even owned 1,277 Negro slaves. All told the Cherokees were probably superior in physical stamina, moral habits, civilized manners, and had a better per capita income than the majority of Whites who now occupy that same region a century later. The Indians did not want to move when the Georgians kept demanding it and told the President: "The Cherokees are not foreigners, but the original inhabitants of America, and they now stand on the soil of their own territory."

But in due time out they went—given only a month by army decree to abandon their homes and fields.

A chance traveler from Maine down South gives us a vivid account (*New York Observer*, 1839) of General Scott's harsh methods of dispossessing them.[1]

On a Tuesday evening this traveler fell in with the large group be-

[1] Quoted by Henry Beston, *American Memory*, pp. 303-4.

ing deported: about "two thousand Indians with horses and mules in proportion. The forward part of the train was found just pitching their tents for the night, and notwithstanding some thirty or forty wagons were already stationed, we found the road literally filled with the procession for about three miles in length. The sick and feeble were carried in wagons—about as comfortable for traveling as a New England ox cart with a covering over it—a great many ride on horseback and multitudes go on foot." And he adds: "Even aged females, apparently nearly ready to drop into the grave, were traveling with heavy burdens attached to the back—on the sometimes frozen ground, and sometimes muddy streets, with no covering for the feet except what nature had given them. . . . We learned from the inhabitants on the road where the Indians passed, that they buried fourteen or fifteen at every stopping place. . . ."

The Indians carried in their countenances "everything but the appearance of happiness." Many had "a downcast dejected look, bordering upon the appearance of despair; others a wild frantic appearance as if about to burst the chains of nature and pounce like a tiger upon their enemies." Even so, he claimed, "most of them seemed intelligent and refined." Some were "wealthy" and traveled "in style," one lady road in "a hack" with her husband, "apparently with as much refinement and equipage as any of the mothers of New England; and she was a mother too and her youngest child about three years old was sick in her arms. . . .

"When I passed the last detachment of those suffering exiles and thought that my native countrymen had thus expelled them from . . . their much loved homes, and that too in this inclement season of the year in all their suffering, I turned from the sight with feelings which language cannot describe and wept like childhood then."

He reported that several missionaries were accompanying the Indians to their destination. One missionary, the Baptist Evans Jones, wrote: "The Cherokees are nearly all prisoners. They have been dragged from their houses and encamped at the forts and military posts. . . . Multitudes were allowed no time to take anything with them except the clothes they had on. Well-furnished houses were left prey to plunderers, who, like hungry wolves, followed in the train of the captors. . . . Females . . . habituated to comforts and comparative affluence are driven on foot before the bayonets of brutal men, their feelings . . . mortified by vulgar and profane vociferations. . . . The property of many has been sold before their eyes for almost nothing—the sellers and buyers in many cases, have combined to cheat the poor Indians . . . stripped of the whole at one blow."

The Commissioner of Indian Affairs, like most politicians, had only honeyed words for the crime: he spoke of it as "a striking example of the liberality of the government in all its branches . . . refreshing to well-constituted minds. . . ." The 18,000 Indian "friends" had been "quietly and gently transported to the west bank of the Mississippi."

The Secretary of War was equally hypocritical, quite unctuous about the "generous and enlightened policy . . . ably and judicially carried into effect. . . . Humanity no less than good policy directed this course toward the children of the forest." Page Uriah Heep! The Cherokees, of course, were not "children of the forest" any longer.

The House Committee on Indian Affairs, which investigated and brought in a report in 1842 (our customary conscience salve, a Congressional investigation), exposed elaborate fraud throughout the whole affair. Both the federal government and the Indians were mulcted by agents of the federal government in cahoots with private contractors.

In October, 1877, a group of Nez Percé Indians—of the tribe called by Bonneville "a nation of saints"—surrendered at Bear Pan Mountain, Montana. The Secretary of the Interior reported in 1882 that they had been "forced into war and, contending with an army far outnumbering them, had made a fight almost without parallel in the annals of history, extending over a district of more than 1,300 miles, and then, though entrenched on the rocks where they could not have been dislodged without great loss of life in the army, as well as to themselves, surrendered as Joseph [their leader] says, because he didn't want any more lives sacrificed."

They were faithfully promised on surrender that they would be put on the Nez Percé reservation in Idaho. Instead of that the government took between 430 and 450 of them off to Leavenworth. Within eight months only 410 were left alive, and these were dumped into the Indian Territory where they continued to dwindle. But there they were made to adopt "citizen's clothing" and were converted to Presbyterianism—all told two notable victories for civilization and Christianity. Even after subduing them and tricking them, thus breaking a solemn pledge, we insisted on pulling down their morale further by trying to regiment them to American habits. Even after Indians became the protected wards of the nation, we continued to harass them with narrow religious importunities; we continued to destroy them.

"In no other manner and by no other means," piously reports the Commissioner of Indian Affairs in 1882, "can our Indian population be so speedily and permanently reclaimed from barbarism, idolatry and savage life, as by educational and missionary operations of the Christian people of our country," and he ignorantly adds: "If we expect to stop sun dances, snake worship and other debasing forms of superstition and idolatry, we must teach them the better way."

The federal agent on the Moquis Pueblo post was even more vehement in displaying prejudice and complete ignorance of anthropology and sociology. Under the head of "Morals" he states: "I have never yet attended any of their dances, and cannot speak from personal knowledge; but . . . the great evils in the way of their ultimate civilization lie in these dances. The dark superstitions and unhallowed rule of heathenism, as gross as that of India or Central Africa, still infects them with its insidious poison, which unless replaced by Christian civilization, must sap their very life-blood." One of the first steps to civilization, he never missed an opportunity to impress upon them, was "to cover their nakedness even with only the cheapest material. . . . I have also talked to them . . . to induce them to cut their hair like Americans, and I am happy to say that in a few instances I have succeeded." He also persuaded them to quit painting themselves, a "foolish and disgusting practice."

Looking at the 1938 bathing beauty cheese-cake pictures, the plucked eyebrows, the painted lips and eyes, we are impressed with the fact that the Indians were merely too advanced for their day. By the time we got them quite subdued to prudery, we went Indian on them.

The decay of a noble race continued. Up in Caster, Wyoming, presently famous Chief Red Cloud is arrested for shooting game out of season—a final humiliation, a final warning that he must be "civilized" or die. Soon they serve for artists' models. Out on a trading post, George Catlin paints Chief Stu-Mick-o-Sucks (Buffalo's Black Fat) of the Blackfeet. Remington will catch the vanishing pathos and will splash over-sweet sentimentality about them.

Pretty soon we find the Indians in war-paint and feathers, with their queer tom-toms, dancing in western towns for pennies—the brave and magnificent festival turned into a circus side show. Down in Yuma, soon they will be photographed by enraptured eastern tourists. Soon we find dummies in front of cigar-stores, and an Indian on a penny, and an Indian and a buffalo on a nickel coin—a gracious gesture toward the fallen.

They are mostly a memory, now, though with certain poetic justice their more notable sons will be recorded in the *Dictionary of American Biography*. In that monumental work, including the names of 15,000 notable Americans, there is just one native of Wyoming—Spotted Tail; but one native of Arizona—Gerónimo; two natives of Idaho—Kamaiakan and Sacagawea, the latter a woman; South Dakota contributed only three names, three Sioux Indians—Gall, John Grass and Sitting Bull.

The story of our attitude toward the Indian is a part of our history and our psychology, a measure of our group mentality, and in general a reminder to us of the lack of logic, the opportunism, and the disregard for facts that feature most group-thinking. The hate-versus-romance literature, against or for the Indian, has waxed and waned from time to time and place to place according to the intensity or danger of the struggle. The early curiosity about the picturesque forest dweller that occasionally tinctured our very first chronicles, soon gave way to hymns of hate as in the writings of William Bradford, or the sermons of the Cottons and Mathers. Such hate literature moved West with the frontier, and even now is encountered in more recently settled points, viz., the harsh onslaught by Alfred James Mokler, official historian of Natrona County, Wyoming, in his *Transition of the West*. But back East, by the eighteenth century, the virile Indians had been mostly driven over the Alleghenies; and in more settled seaboard country, the race was represented by fragmentary settlements or individuals lounging about towns. Indians there had sunk to indifferent lethargy. If their frequent drunkenness and thievery made them a bit feared, mostly they became objects of contempt, though their condition was due to the White man.

After a time many easterners never saw an Indian their life long. Then the native was gradually romanticized, became the noble Red man, the type that at times invades the sentimental fiction of Cooper. In a still later day of mere reminiscence, Helen Hunt Jackson will write her completely sentimental but beautiful *Ramona*, to cause people to weep over past injustices. People are always ready to weep over *past* injustices or those committed by other nations.

Some few Americans began to rediscover the Indian as a man—as such he is portrayed by Catlin and Schoolcraft; and others belatedly perceived the beauty of his arts and crafts. In our own century, indifference has mostly ruled, coupled with a frequent revival of the old mode of considering him as picturesque and unusual; occasionally he is the butt of tolerant, fairly uncomprehending jokes. Now and then he is the victim of "Indian laments," cloying poetry, or the object of escape literature, literary stereotypes, of which the Pulitzer Prize winner *Laughing Boy* is the most competent.

In time Greenwich Village discovered him, and the artists of Taos. They began to discover his mysterious soul, his kinship with the secrets of the world's *élan*.

But a few anthropologists have brought him into better focus with scientific understanding; and as our relations with Latin America grow more significant, he is likely to resume even contemporary importance as part of an Indian-mestizo culture extending from Alaska to Patagonia, embracing over 50,000,000 people, which means that he is still imbedded deep in the life of the Americas, past, present and future; and that his culture, his art, his attitude toward life, may yet exercise a remarkable influence, even on us.

Before 1920, the native population in the United States had been reduced to about a quarter of a million. Today the American land nearly all belongs to the Whites, or better said a few of the Whites. The plow has gashed the buffalo plains—but perhaps had we listened a little more closely to what the Great Spirit said about that process, we might have avoided some of our later ills.

War it was between the races, of one sort or another, war for nearly three centuries, war and White man's education and White man's religion, all indistinguishably part of that war, all poison for the Indian—a war in which the aborigines were pushed back and back, stubbornly contesting the relentless advance, growing every year more bitter, more desperate, crueler, more ruthless. The Whites, victory assured, had less and less need for brutality. Gradually our cruelty became an incident, not so much a national trait.

It was iron, among other things, that carried the day, and not merely in muskets and shot, which the Indians promptly learned to use, but the iron of the rails that soon enough spanned the continent, and the iron of the steam boilers in boats that chugged over rivers and lakes; the Thorpe and Sprague stage-coaches, stuck on trucks, chained together and jerked over rails; the Boulton and Watt engines and boilers stuck in dumpy boats—both trains and boats to become in time as streamlined as the Indian's original birch-bark canoe.

Early in the nineteenth century, the Indians lined the banks of the Ohio to stare unbelievingly at Nicholas Roosevelt's spark-throwing *New Orleans;* and in 1818, they gathered on the shores of Lake Erie to watch a strange new craft being pulled—so they were told— by sturgeons. Trustingly, even before the vessel appeared, they grunted their awe at the power of the Whites that made even the fishes obey them. Soon they perceived the joke played on their credulity—fire-machinery drove the new *Walk-in-the-Water*—and they turned away sadly. "We are children," they said.

Those vessels and the railway engines roaring across what a few years before were buffalo trails, were more powerful than Custer and his men in subduing an ancient people and an old way of life.

We find amusing now, proof of our superiority, the account of "Porcupine," a Plains Indian, who in savage defiance faced a Union

Pacific train. Right after a fight in which the soldiers of Ash Creek defeated the Sioux and Cheyennes, Porcupine tells of his first glimpse of a train, "puffing out smoke and steam"; and as it came on, they said to each other that "it looked like a White man's pipe when he was smoking."

After it passed by, the Indians went down to see what kind of a trace it made.

As they sat talking over their troubles, they said: "Now the White people have taken all we had and have made us poor and we ought to do something. In these big wagons that go on this metal road, there must be things that are valuable—perhaps clothing. If we could throw these wagons off the iron they run on and break them open, we should find out what was in them and could take whatever might be useful to us."

So they tied a big stick to the rails—and captured a hand-car, and killed two men. But soon a real train loomed. "We saw a small light close to the horizon, and someone said: 'The morning star is rising.' 'No,' said another, 'that is one of those things that we have seen.' "

They sent men along the track to find out what the lights were, to yell and shoot that they might frighten it.

When they discovered that it was the same sort of White man's wagons running on rails, they fired at it, and one tried to throw a rope over the engine, but their horses were frightened and ran away. "When they fired, the train made a loud noise—puffing—and threw up sparks into the air, going faster and faster, until it reached the break, and the locomotive jumped into the air and the cars all came down together."

There is something ludicrous, yet sublimely pathetic, in this spectacle of an Indian trying to lasso a locomotive. But perhaps it tells the story of defeat better than any moral pros and cons.

The mechanical equipment of Europe, modified by American inventiveness, carried the day, and—despite hardships, the occasional bloodiness and in general the long persistence of the struggle—the outcome was soon so visible, and the conquest could be carried on with such victorious ease whenever the Whites decided on a new frontier thrust, that America was given an arrogant self-confidence and boastful optimism little warranted had we been obliged to face a more equal foe.

This chapter is no effort to sing a sentimental elegy over the Redskin. The past can bury its own dead. This is not a lament for those who perished or a race that has gone from our shores, though it still bulks large in the rest of the continent. My interest is in Americans of today and tomorrow. In fact the whole matter of conquering, defrauding, ejecting the Indians then and recently is cluttered up with entirely too much wild-eyed moral invective one way or the other.

In the process itself, of course, morals and legality had really little or nothing to do with the whole thing except as slogans, hypocritical justification of coercion. The relative worth of the character of the Indians and Americans had little to do with it, except that frequent Indian generosity permitted easier conquest, not true the other way around. Ruthless, cunning and greedy men took advantage of a situation.

What was really involved was the conflict of two cultures, widely different; two ways of life, of which the victorious one did not have all the superior qualities. The most powerful, clever and brutal won. An inevitable historical process forced these unpleasant exhibitions. The Indian was facing not merely a handful of settlers, but the whole population thrust of Europe, and the whole might of its evolved warlike machinery. Against that he had no chance.

If I have endeavored to see the Indian point of view, to set up a more tolerant understanding of him, this is not because of outraged sentiments on my part, not because of any romantic feeling, but because it is necessary in order for us to understand what conquering him has done to us as a people and a nation. The conquest did something to us in terms of character, in forming our individual and group habits; it helped determine the shape and direction of our institutions, and in good part the relation of Americans to the American earth.

The long, very crude, historical process resulted in our material gains being so great that they have largely obscured for us the moral cost of our ruthless enterprise. That process of fraud, corruption, trickery, violence, spread like a sickness through all the American body politic; and those methods, plus violence, are often methods used still in settling political, social, racial and international problems—"mobs and ruffianism and tarring and feathering," of which "one reads all too often," suggests Henry Beston, are the outcome.

The constant eloquent speeches of our politicians (for more than a century) regarding their noble aims toward the Indians, obviously —this was patent to even the most stupid—were never born out by our deeds and policies toward the Indians. Has not this perhaps led us into demanding no proper accounting from public servants so long as they feed us righteous pap, mention civilization, God, the home, but don't go realistic on us? Our most successful politicians are those who talk noble language in hazy generalities and permit skulduggery under their noses. They may be rightly termed following the beloved "American way."

Perfect training for later financial plundering, not of Red men, but of fellow Whites by more cunning Whites, the whole ethic of later corporation growth and monopoly—here in the Indian struggle is to be observed the whole American psychology of getting something for nothing, or at most for a little trickery.

In this way, also by war, force, murder and conquest, were created those sacred property rights which our sacred Supreme Court and our Constitution are supposed to defend and do defend. The theft of Indian lands promoted and always condoned the subsequent thefts of lands and resources from the national domain: the timber and coal steals, the cattle-king steals, the railroad grabs, Teapot Dome—all these abuses and more are but a few of the latter-day links in the same long chain. Such things in the past give us the clue to the agricultural evils that have overtaken us. The record of the Great Conquest helps give us part of an explanation of the ruin of so much of the American earth, the destruction of the equivalent of a whole empire of soil, and the present maladjustment of our rural population to the land; part of the reason for our low standard of living in rural areas, our dispossessed farmers, our distressed serf-like croppers, our pauper migrants; it is part of the explanation of why, as a people, we have a far less satisfactory relation to the soil than the Indian had before us.

CHAPTER IV

THE AMERICAN DILEMMA

The aboriginal Americans achieved a religious relationship to the mystery and richness and beauty of the American earth. Their few surviving legends, almost literally translated immediately after the conquest, reveal a curious symbolism, interwoven with subtle word magic, which leads one to the brink of some unique, mysterious knowledge of the universe and of Nature not granted to all other peoples—a deep-delving earth-wrought poetry almost suggesting sense apparatuses missing or at least atrophied in other races, a deep sex-soil vitality that D. H. Lawrence, at too late a date, strove so desperately and fearfully to penetrate.

The aboriginal festivals were nearly all earth festivals: the song and dance of fertility, of the first-born, of field and stream. Their magic was rain-making magic.

Those fiestas—even though described during the border years mostly by unfriendly and quite uncomprehending eyes—remind us that the continent lost something very valuable in song, rhythm and beauty when the native races vanished: the dances to the music of pounded deerskin, stretched over earthen porridge-pots, and of shaken gourds; the bright feathers, the animal and God masks, the bells on ankles and knees, the hawk-bells on dusky necks, the weaving steps and the chanted legends of passing greatness.

This and more was a heritage of the plains of America that melted away far too quickly: a loss of soil-knowledge, life-wisdom and beauty, all integrated with earth and sky, for which it will take many centuries still for us Americans to find comparable substitutes. With

65

more patience, did history work that way, we might have comprehended some of those beauties and absorbed part of them to our own enrichment.

Implicit even in the more brutal native rites—as those of the Aztecs in Mexico—were mighty tides, the majestic cycle of day and night, the passing of the seasons, the great epochal sweep of the fifty-two years. Their wars were the "flowering wars," that blood might "flower" on the altar: symbolical enactment of fertility, fruition, continuity, the vital flow of the cosmos.

Such rites were to increase their control over the forces of Nature. To reinforce their own kinship with Nature, the Mayas sought the secrets of the influential magic stars and thereby created the magnificent temples of Chichen Itza and Uxmal and worked out to scientific accuracy the movements of the most prominent of the heavenly bodies, enabling them to create a calendar, which they carved in stone, more accurate than that which we use today in the United States of buy-a-book-a-week.

For the American Indian, the land of America, the earth of America, was his mother—and so was pictured in many a legend and holy rite. One did not attempt to conquer one's mother, as did the White invader. One rather went gratefully to her embrace. The Indian lived within the coils of Nature—a trait that still characterizes the race—from Alaska to Patagonia.

They lived within the interstices of nature, were a portion of Nature themselves, felt the continuity of themselves with their soil, their forests, their world. Through the common veins of themselves and Mother Nature pulsed the blood from one heart, nourishing them. They sought far more to shape their lives to Nature rather than shape Nature to their will. Their trails threaded the forests with as little disturbance as possible. Their feet, moccasined, went soft and fleet. They shared in the Great Purpose and did not attempt to remold it. They were fluid, within the flux of day and night and of the seasons, with the germination and ripening and harvesting of the crops. Their whole existence was instinct with Oneness.

They did not seek to conquer but to placate Nature. Hence they did not seek individual wealth, but collective well-being. Their tools and techniques for this were limited enough, but adequate most of the time for their desires. They did not seek to live so much by tools and techniques as by religion. Every act was holy, and in this deep sense they were far more religious, as well as more spiritually sensitive to Nature, than the hard-ribbed, dogma-ruled Puritans who invaded their realm.

Their rites to persuade Nature to endow them with the good life, in turn produced a creative art that only now, too late again, we are beginning somewhat to appreciate. It also included a large body of nature-lore, medicine, war technique, soil and human fertility wisdom. Many a White plantation owner, despairing of the limited resources of the best English doctors and their phobias of leeching and bleeding, turned to the Indians for help and sometimes found quick relief by using their herbs and roots and potions, some of which in time became part of the kit of every frontier housewife. When I was a boy sassafras tea was a requisite blood-cleaner every spring, and when we went camping in the wilds, our beverage was steeped pennyroyal leaves, plucked fresh and pungent from the mountain side. The greatest of early American painters, Benjamin West, learned the secret of preparing colors, it is claimed, from the Cherokee Indians.

But today we call the Indian's great reliance upon religion mostly a gross superstition, though the number of superstitious folk among us is by no means small: quack curers, quack ministers, quack fortune-tellers, fake magic, race-track diviners, card-prognosticators still flourish among us, but without providing us with any integrated group knowledge or philosophy. Some of them are college professors and publish books that go into the best-seller lists and are even applauded editorially. Some are religious leaders who refuse the findings of science for curing disease. Some are politicians who use word-magic, shouting out our numerous tribal tabus. Some are "gold money" economists. Some talk of the business cycle as though it were the Virgin of Lourdes. But not for love of Nature or of Beauty or man's happiness do they do these things.

In other ways, too, we also are ignorant and superstitious: We have merely moved the wonder of magic further away from our daily tasks, though uncomprehendingly, in marrying off our daughters, in burying our dead, in the rites of our churches; we still follow slavishly, through habit, a thousand and one customs derived from the dim past of pagan magic.

Our artists no longer paint pictures directly to placate, to inveigle the Great Spirit into good humor. And yet, unless an artist is commercialized, he paints in a creative spirit, with an ideal of beauty, sometimes with a social purpose. To the extent that such artists are not personally acquisitive or ambitious, they are painting in an Indian way, which was closer to the pure creative urge than is our present-day mercantilism.

Beauty was part of the creative relationship the Indian had with land—like that of an artist graduated far beyond mere copy-book realism. Such a relationship few rural Americans have ever had with the American soil. They have it less today than they did a century ago. Commercialized mass-production agriculture breeds no such attitude.

Perhaps the early settlers came closer to a healthy relationship with the American earth than did most later cultivators, forced into becoming merchants rather than providers; for although quite a number of the colonies were founded as ventures in commercialism, by companies seeking profits, many of the early settlers, since they came to seek religious freedom, had no deep acquisitive motivation. They came to found new homes, to take root, to live happily.

But the native Indian culture already had roots. It had grown out of the soil. Their forebears had come to this brave New World apparently more than twenty thousand years before. Their ancestors were probably here when mastodons crunched cottonwood trees and made traces for later buffaloes; before Niagara Falls existed; when Lakes Erie and Ontario drained through the Wabash and the Ohio into the Mississippi River.

The Indian way of life was interlaced with the continent, with its soil, its vegetation, its wind and rain and snow, its animal life. Their mode of living was well correlated with the vital phenomena all about them. Even those natives who had little settled agrarian economy, who lived mostly in the hunting stage, had deep communion with bounteous Nature; and when the Midwest pioneers plowed up the plains partly to the sorrow of modern drouth-ridden descendants, the early Red folk knew that the newcomers were compounding evil. When the settlers broke the sod of the plains in this reckless fashion, they plowed up not merely the Indian's livelihood, but also his gods and his faith. The two divine parents of the Sioux folk were Wakan-Takka, the Great Mystery, and Makka, their Earth-Mother—nothing was more evil than this White tampering with the divine gifts of grass and buffalo. The new iron plows violated sacred beliefs. The Indian's soul was shaken by those murderous weapons gashing the generous breast of Makka, and he sang sad laments and prayers to win his own pardon from the Great Mystery and the Great Mother, certain that someday the great curse would fall. There is something prophetic, pathetic and majestic in this clash of an ancient way with the new.

In Alabama we have the legend of the great chief Tush-ka-lusa. Over the dead body of his son, accidentally killed by one of De Soto's men, Tush-ka-lusa drew himself up to his seven-foot height and called down on the White invaders the vengeance of the Great Spirit; and Alabamans still tell how the Black Warrior River (named after the giant Redskin) to this day constantly claims victims. Something of that same old magic, almost of disaster, still broods over the state these later days. As Carl Carmer puts it: "Hill-billies and niggers, poor whites, and planters, cajuns and Lintheads are sometimes aware of the intangible net that encompasses them." Out of that deeper knowledge of the American soil-heritage—from that world now so immersed in poverty and ignorance—may come, one of these days when the crude drive of our nation for material power slackens, a new creative urge, something akin to the early Redskins' wonder and praise—but truly our own, not his. Until now we have been too busy using our new world to live with it comfortably.

If the Indian coiled within Nature, if its sap was the sap of his deeds and his philosophy, the Englishman slashed straight across Nature. He nullified its direct force or bent it more directly to his will. The ax and rifle belong on his coat of arms. The Indian conceived geometric abstractions, symbols of power over Nature. The

White man brought the reality of such abstractions, and no shape more practical than the wheel that rolled, yet went straight to its goal. That very imposition of our force and ability, while in keeping with our earlier religious methods, our intolerance, was so in contrast with the meaning of our religious dogmas, that it has created in America psychological contradictions which are still the despair of all foreign observers.

The English newcomers sought bluntly, without much finesse or tolerance, to impose an alien religion and an alien technique upon the New World, and if out of that came greatness, they nevertheless blindly destroyed much of worth, lost many things of value, set up many antagonisms between their own rigid concepts and the actualities of the land where they found themselves. Had they been less intolerant in their ideas, they might have reaped more knowledge; they and their descendants might have come to know their new world sooner and better.

The French pioneer was of different texture, far more imaginative and far more adaptable. He threaded the forest, fraternized amicably with the Indian we thought so terrible and ferocious, and turned half native to please him, for the most part getting along famously. From the human angle the French have always been the world's best colonizers.

As Duquesne told the Iroquois (quoted by Turner), not without a touch of self-interested hypocrisy: "Go see the forts that our King has established, and you will see that you can hunt under their very walls. They have been placed for your advantage. . . . The English, on the contrary, are no sooner in possession of a place than the game is driven away. The forest falls before them as they advance, and the soil is laid bare so that you can scarce find the wherewithal to erect a shelter for the night."

Like the Spaniard to the South, the Frenchman might likely have built a new hybrid race, a new culture, more truly American in blood and tradition and to that extent in many ways more beautiful; but the English settler swept all before him, hard in his self-assurance, his creeds, his certainty that he knew and understood all earthly and supernatural wisdom and the best way to achieve things.

Our forefathers came in the dual role of conquerors and settlers. Unlike the Spaniards to the South, they did not enslave the natives and make them labor to produce a quick civilization of wealth, luxury and culture; the American settlers killed them off. The Latin folk exploited man; our forefathers exploited Nature. They drove back and exterminated the native people, then exploited the land fertilized by the bones of those slain. There can be little debate as to which was the more civilized and Christian process, whatever the final results.

Only in our South did the importation of Negro slaves introduce an almost entirely feudal system, based on race-oppression, somewhat similar to that of Hispanic America, a system which was largely to persist down to our own day. If all the colonies were founded mostly in the twilight of the medieval ecclesiastical age, so that the settlers brought many social myths already losing their validity, nevertheless they were all greatly imbued with the new mercantile spirit and except in the South, hard work, common danger, a free continent, all broke down feudal traditions still further, promoted more equalitarian traditions and paved the way rapidly for individualistic capitalism. The new colonists soon put a bit on Nature, more and more drove Nature to their will by their own efforts, and inevitably, sooner or later, they felt the equality of all *White* men in the struggle against the Indian and the forests: they became eventually, except in the South, more democratic in spirit, increasingly so as they spread over the vast plains. At a time when so many disciplines were lacking, they gave us the most potent of all disciplines, that of hard work, the most democratic force of all. This enslaving of Nature rather than man for a time gave us a juster, more democratic society—for ourselves if not for Indians or Negroes. By thus ruthlessly sweeping aside other peoples, we were not obliged to create caste differences; our forefathers affirmed their own man to man equality.

But this engendered a great feeling of race superiority. Our overt disregard of the native human element, plus the hardness of our will, created for us one of our first and deepest dilemmas as a people: an inability to understand foreign nations and above all those of different race. As for the New World south of the Rio Grande, we mostly still peer through opaque spectacles of self-satisfied superiority and a thousand needless prejudices; and our diplomacy there has nearly always depended more on our overwhelming wealth and power and financial desire than on justice or comprehension.

The American folk took hold of the new land very greedily, with immediate practical-mindedness, though otherwise not over-intelligently. The natural abundance of the continent for quite some centuries concealed the many evils of their gross carelessness and poured into their laps as reward for buoyant optimism and industriousness the jewels of her opulence. Nature, so wild and abundant, once tamed, ran with them to golden pastures, provided the new kinetics of rapid development. Nature, with such titanic masters, became a lavish provider of wealth—like a woman forced to bear too many children.

But if the American earth was forced to yield to the practical and greedy onrush of the folk from the Old World, it was not obliged to accept their ideas and their dogmas. Not even yet have all the American plains accepted all the imposed European philosophy of the colonists, and never will.

This has created another dilemma. The newcomers clung desperately to European ideas. Though reluctantly enough they were forced to discard many Old World methods in order to survive, they were much more doubtful about discarding Old World thinking. The concentrating of energies on almost wholly practical and material success, caused the newcomers to shrink (just as we mostly do today) from facing the full meaning of their conquest.

In this manner, they were at once stretched to the breaking point between their inherited ideas and customs and the practical needs of their new environment—the problem of trying to remain English, or Dutch or Scotch and yet become American. The bitter struggles in the Dutch Reformed Church vividly attest to this conflict.

Transplanted communities in an alien setting usually become more rigid in their beliefs than previously, because of an attempt to withstand the strain of new outside forces which tend to break down dogmatic opinions, habits and old customs—a phenomenon of the emigrant everywhere. Thus today, Americans, long resident, say in a country like Mexico, fiercely resist all invasion of their cultural habits and attitudes, hence become more reactionary than at home; they become more Main Street than Main Street. Their ideas and beliefs freeze into the pattern they had when they left the United States many years before. In the meantime Main Street itself has been evolving. But the emigree has cast his mind in the steel of the changeless.

Thus many of our early colonists answered the problems of their new environment, for the time being at least, by trying to circumscribe their new unknown world both physically and spiritually. They tried to create definite land boundaries, and most of them tried to create mental and spiritual boundaries by means of dogmatic tyrannies.

The first colonists—English—had been an insular people. Their insularity had been even more narrowed by their minority rebellion against the powers-that-were in England. They already represented hard little islands of dogma. Transplanted to the New World, though suddenly exposed to the stresses of a great continent and confronted with a consciousness of great space they had never before known, even so they could not at once meet its challenge by ceasing to be insular or dogmatic. Though most of the old compressive forces of England were suddenly gone, except from their minds, though old laws did not so hedge them about, though economic opportunities beckoned, the colonists could not immediately change shape, were slow to expand and breathe free air. They had been tempered to steel, were neither fluid nor gas. They sought rather to live as though all the compressive forces still operated on them. They held their social shape as rigidly as they could. The more they were challenged, the more sternly, desperately, did they try to hold to their preconceived notions.

Although they faced land empire, they at first tried to convert their domain into a little island. In 1690 the Massachusetts General Court named a committee to determine the frontier and line it with settled garrisons, each with exactly forty guards. Connecticut followed almost identical methods. Settlers in frontier towns were forbidden to leave under pain of property-confiscation or imprisonment. The colonists wanted a political island with boundaries as fixed as though carved out forever by encircling waters. The colonists, ruled by overseas ideas, sought to erect a Chinese Wall—artificially narrow boundaries such as had existed in Old Europe.

And so, the early settlers did not, like the Spaniards to the South, at once run down dale and up. It took the methodical, organizing English settlers much longer than the Spaniards to know and explore their New World. The great early explorers of the mainland were Frenchmen and Spaniards.

The English settlers tried to hold to their old spiritual boundaries even more rigidly than they did physical boundaries. The harsher aspects of Colonial rule affirm for us the bitterness of creeds held by people unwilling as yet to face the realities of the new environment and the times—a second Chinese Wall. Rebels though they had been in England, now in the new America they promptly suffered from the warped psychological characteristics that affect all violently transplanted people; most soon became rigid conservatives, loath to accept any further doctrinal changes. Fear of the new *mores* thrust upon them and lack of security merely caused a quicker hardening of their intellectual fibers, a panicky adherence to homeland habits and ideas, however ill-suited, however lacking in utility in their new habitat. This psychological resistance was at once reflected in their political rule.

Though the American faiths were already abysmally democratic compared to the Catholic Church or Calvin's Geneva hierarchy, John Cotton, fearful now in turn of dissenters, jealous of his own power, thundered: "Democracy, I do not conceive that God did ever ordain as a fit government for either Church or commonwealth."

The intolerant Colonial régimes—where on the Sabbath even "the obstreperous hen deposited her egg and cackled not"—were efforts in part to stay the onrush of religious and political evolution.

Three centuries of repeated evasion resulted. Instead of rebelling or forcing necessary social change in established communities, men simply went West and escaped. The history of America, despite its notable achievements in new settlement and growth, in mechanical greatness, was until lately basically a history of evasion, mental and—to the extent that many people emigrated—also physical. Such evasions are practiced by all peoples at all times, but more crowded populations are forced to choose new practical, if not always equitable, systems much sooner. The early Americans, though, could escape many such decisions almost indefinitely, and the nation thus grew to greatness doomed to a prolonged adolescence that has not yet vanished. To this day many of our people confuse the reason for our greatness with our failure to think realistically about it; they elevate ignorance of our social institutions to a creed of success; analysis becomes the enemy of the state.

All this partly explains that queer way we Americans have—though it is also a universal trait—of seeking non-related idealisms to explain our actions. As Americans—for all our talk of the "American way," for all our parading of sacred American institutions, for all our harping upon democracy—in good part we still utilize symbols of speech, ideas, thought-habits, derived from the medieval mists and slums and dogmas of Europe. Ironically enough when you hear a super-patriot shouting for 100 per cent Americanism, if you examine his creed closely enough, you find that frequently it is really a cry to preserve the very European fetishes we should be rid of, an ignorant refusal to come to terms with the American earth and a hatred of those who would do so.

Eventually the breath of a great continent, with its drafty, violent sweep down from the Arctic to the tropics, and from the hot southern Gulf and deserts northward, was to rush through the carefully guarded halls of the early colonists, their neat little societies with their neatly patterned ideas, and wrench the walls of older securities apart. Creeds, ideas, set modes of thought, crumbled before the tidal wave of imperial forces, the heavy tide-rip of western emigration, of new jostling peoples, parties and religions. A constant humming tension replaced much of the former narrow set mental routine. "Granite faith" in the soul's righteousness soon was "cracking and weathering." Travel, new occupations, the rise of industry, caused doubts and new doctrines to blow over them and wear down their intolerance—though Tennessee and other southern states with their anti-evolution laws reveal still how little the gulf between dogma and the American earth has been bridged in many of the corners of our fair land.

For in spite of the ample dimensions of America and forced adjustment, all that earlier insularity, all that ingrowing individualism, has shaped many of the ways, much of the thinking of Americans to this day, and still stands as a barrier to our proper realization of the meaning and proper organization and direction of American life. The alien creeds our fathers brought to American shores still create difficulties between thought and reality. The transition from European to American culture is not yet completed.

The up-sap out of the soil of America has not yet completely taken hold of our lives, does not yet fully shape our deeds and institutions and ways. That may take centuries yet.

This book is in part the story of the manner in which our fathers and subsequent generations sloughed off older habits and prejudices, their struggle to become Americans, as did the Indian, in his own way long before them; the story of the mutual adjustment and adaptation of an alien people—we Americans—to the strange soil of this New World.

The colonists could not at once make proper contact with the new land, and it was the savage, who—at the very moment when the colonists expected to be destroyed by him—suddenly relented and "brought such plenty of their fruits and provision that no man wanted."

But of course it was "God, the patron of all good endeavors," who "changed the hearts of the savages."

And so the colonists' first concern was with the God of their fathers and next their stomachs—even though mentally they were unable successfully to correlate the two necessities. Thomas Studly, writing of the first awful July at Jamestown, told how "all received the Communion: the day following, the savages voluntarily desired peace," and thereupon the newcomers proceeded to survive on "half a pint of wheat and as much barley, boiled with water, for a man a day," until they could find native substitutes, which from May to September consisted of sturgeon and sea crabs. The Pilgrims, one good day in 1623, were reduced to a few kernels of parched corn per person—and even that meant full dependence on the New World where they found themselves and not on England whence they had come.

From the very first, therefore, the settlers at least had to put down the necessary physical roots to survive; so that even if the New World sap did not immediately nourish their brains or souls, it did nourish their stomachs, altered the very metabolism of their bodies. They ate wild turkeys, and corn and cranberries and pumpkins and new kinds of fish. The very chemistry of their bodies had to change and has been changing ever since. Even the odor of their sweat glands changed. Ere long Americans of English descent no longer smelled like Englishmen across the water.

So from the very first, Americans had to make *practical* use of the resources at hand. The early Dutch settlers long had to live in crude huts and holes. Nicholaes Van Wassenaer, who visited the colony in 1626, found folk living in houses made "of the bark of trees." Even as late as the end of the Nineteenth Century Timothy Dwight noted that log houses were still built "in the same manner as the weekwans."

Gourd shells became dippers. Oak logs became salt mortars and crooked saplings provided sled runners. The newcomers learned to use and manufacture native moccasins, snowshoes and canoes. They used the Indian tripod for suspending pots and cooking over wood fires. Out of native woods they had to fashion, by laborious whittling, their own utensils, buckets, firkins, spoons, trays, candle-rods, toys, even though the objects and their shapes remained mostly European. In fact "whittling" in time became such a national characteristic that early in the Nineteenth Century, Europeans were wont to caricature the "idle, fidgety and frivolous" qualities of Americans by sketches of home-spun, hang-mouth whittlers.

Many immigrants had to change their occupations. In New York and Pennsylvania, the Palatine vintners had to turn farmers and often grew corn. The first cargo sent back by Plymouth Pilgrims was of beaver and lumber.

"The main staple," wrote Captain John Smith, "to be extracted from the present to produce the rest, is fish . . . however, it may seem a mean and base commodity . . . and never could the Spaniard with all his mines of gold and silver pay his debts, his friends, and army so truly as the Hollanders still have done by this contemptible trade of fish."

"Is it not a pretty sport," he wrote back to England, "to pull up two pence, six pence, to twelve pence" as fast as you can toss out the line.

Soon enough the prosperity of much of the South came to depend upon a most typical New World product—tobacco.

Though George Alsop, one of the first comers, was something of a poet who could rave about the beauties and abundance of the new colonies, his keen, practical eye—and how deathly practical were all these early folk even in the midst of all their poetry and religious nonsense—rested still more determinedly on the details of tobacco husbandry, which provided the wealth of the colony, and brought "twenty sail and up-wards," merchant-men landed with wares—"silks, hollands, serges, broad-cloths and other necessary goods"—to be traded for the black leaf, a commerce carried on at "fair and legal rates," with "fair and honest decorum," an ethic, however, reserved for Christian gentlemen, but not to be kept when dealing with mere natives.

It was a beautiful sight in a place like Port Tobacco, to watch the gangs of singing Negroes, hauling and heaving the packs into the many ships "that lay like a flock of birds on the smooth tidal river." But tobacco, we must ruefully note, was cultivated by men trying desperately to keep the culture and airs of English gentlemen, and holding their noses and their brains as much aloof from New World crudeness as possible, priding themselves rather on being *"au fait"* as to the literary, dramatic and personal gossip of London.

This capable handling of *materials* by our forefathers—while often at the same time they rejected the meaning, the causes, the beauty of the things with which they worked and forgot to ask most of the time where they were going—has helped create, though in deeds we have become so indistinguishably American, further evasiveness and a superficiality that still dominates much of American thought.

And yet, soon enough, insidious cultural changes, enforced by realities of American life, intruded. American heresies soon enough appeared in the diamond diaper work of the Dutch masons; and often, the builders, with sadness, abandoned the accustomed roof pantiles of the old country for thatch, planking or wooden shingles; and in the south and central regions of New Netherlands, they built a new kind of house altogether. Their eight-cornered-mill churches gradually gave way to square buildings.

Quaker architecture, writes Wertenbaker, "in its new environment, immediately felt the influence of local conditions—building material, climate, labor costs, isolation. . . . America gripped the English houses and slowly but irresistibly remoulded them into American houses."

Painters, but little encouraged in the crude new colonies, were perhaps thereby partly benefited in that they came closer to the actual American scene by being obliged to travel about, semi-vagabonds, painting portraits, sign boards, stage-coaches and fire-engines.

But if the New World was whittled to the dimensions of the colonists' physical needs, the chronicles of the first few years often show little real love for the new environment that the newcomers were forced reluctantly to accept and utilize—and love is the real test of adoption as of adaptation. Everything was astonishing, but quite too strange, even terrifying, to be easily embraced.

William Bradford called it "hideous and desolate wilderness, full of wild beasts and wild men!"

"Our fathers were Englishmen," he wrote, "ready to perish in this wilderness, but they cried unto the Lord, and he heard their voice, and looked on their adversity (etc.) . . . he hath delivered them from the hand of the oppressor. . . ."

For all good things the settlers were ever grateful to God, but rarely to the strange soil that gave them its fruits or the Indian who often aided them.

As New World things were often entirely too astounding for the newcomers, naturally they then fell back upon that great "common-law" base of religion—superstition. That is frequent enough everywhere in every age, but it had special psychological reinforcement those early days of settlement. All the pagan sub-strata of Christianity rose muddily in the minds of the first settlers to help them explain (falsely) the odd phenomena about them, the reality with which physically they so capably grappled, but which mentally they rejected.

The lambs were frightened by wolves? Then as John Winthrop tells us solemnly, most of them brought forth were "of Monsieur Reynard's complexion and colour."

When ships were wrecked, it was "a correction from God."

The northern lights—in bright "blood red arch from horizon to zenith, and light enough to read out of doors," immediately made them think of the day of final judgment, which might come, in accordance with the best pagan fairy-tales, "at midnight or at cock-crowing."

Increase Mather and Cotton Mather were constantly observing the most frightful things going on. For Increase Mather—and he was an intellectual and moral leader—"small pocks" was "an arrow shot by God into the town." The keeper of the Swan Inn was a drunkard. His daughter therefore got the pox because of "God's displeasure." Why God didn't take it out on the innkeeper himself, Mather doesn't elucidate.

The Devil was busy those days, and the colonists at times descended to grosser and less justifiable superstitions than the so-called savages about them. This Christianized paganism and superstition— if common enough in Europe also—in the New World was often also the blind reflex of great fear: fear of the unaccustomed, fear of insecurity, fear of the vastness of the wild-swept continent. They met mysterious or fancied dangers with their own brand of supernatural logic.

Cotton Mather constantly tells us of inexplicable events; or rather, events explicable only by inventing a phantom world of evil spirits and ogres. A girl with odd fits was "*diabolical*," a symptom of the "*Sadducism*" of that "debauched age." And yet this was the curious man, so contradictory and pathological, who as early as 1721 was to introduce anti-smallpox inoculation in the face of opposition from the one graduate doctor in the colony.

In June, 1682, he relates, the wife of Antonio Hortado, dwelling near Salmon Falls, heard a voice calling, "What do you here?" and about an hour after, she received a blow on her eye "that almost spoiled her," and several days later, a great stone was thrown along the house, but no one could find the stone. A frying pan in the chimney "rang so loud, that the people at a hundred rods distance heard it"; and Mary and her husband saw in the river the head of a man, and three feet away, with no body to join them, the tail of a cat. Later a stone from an invisible hand caused a swelling on her head; she was "bitten on both her arms black and blue and her breast scratched; the impression of the teeth, which were like a man's teeth, being seen by many."

We would not, at this late date, suggest that Mary had been up to things not becoming a lady of that Puritan community, or that the loneliness of her cabin got on her nerves, that she was suffering from well-known symptoms of hysteria; but the fact that the leader of the community could then and constantly rehash such mysterious superstitions seriously and base his political and ecclesiastical power on them and witchcraft hangings is indicative of the jitters which had overtaken the handful of folk in the New World. Perhaps Cotton Mather was like a modern southern demagogue, or a Hitler, beating up strange brutal stories to fan hatred, though evidently he was able to believe implicitly all the terror he helped create and used so ruthlessly and cunningly. Certainly the witch who turned out to be "Roman Catholik" was not helped thereby; and in various tests of bewitched folk, it was shown beyond doubt that the Quakers and other "heretics" were exercising vicious powers in league with Satan over the afflicted persons.

Down South settlers became infected with Negro superstition. The Guinea Negroes, large of stature and black as black, were especially considered to be in league with the Evil One, and magic charms, rabbits' feet and other mummery were often resorted to by the Whites as well. Many White folk were careful not to point their fingers at certain old negresses, considered to be witches. Perhaps, also, the hysteria in New York in 1841 that caused the legal lynching, by burning thirteen Negroes at the stake, the hanging of eighteen more, and the deportation of seventy, obeyed similar psychological and political causes.

The exaggerated preoccupation with law became another symptom of the newcomers' confusion. Since settlement and development were forging ahead so rapidly, and forcing such hurly-burly changes in every phase of life, perplexed folk, bitter against change, hating to relinquish bigotry and intolerance, turned for security to the stable rules of old. They quibbled over the legal niceties of Indian grants, though war, murder and occupation were more than nine-tenths of the law. They saw all in flux, and sought to cling, not merely to old religious dogmas, but to the familiar outlines of English law transplanted.

We have a parallel in the present when a crisis forces a rapid readjustment to new conditions, of those folk who turn with exaggerated hysteria to the sacredness of an unchangeable Supreme Court, forgetting that Supreme Courts and laws were originally made by men; that the court even now is composed of fallible old men, made more fallible by age.

In Colonial days, too, the legal standards dragged behind while the facts of life were changing in such apparently dizzy fashion. For no laws could keep pace with the rapid changes the colonists themselves were bringing about. Their intense faith in law was a mighty urge for stability, a fear of change, a desire for order and frozen habits, at a time when pioneering, war, experiment, were the true masters. To this day the folk of the Atlantic seaboard are far more prone to dash into a law court about petty things. "We Down Easterners," wrote John Neal, a Maine Quaker, in 1869, "are a litigious people, and lawyers are always to be had." As I write, a Connecticut townsman not far from me, is suing one of his best friends, because, on leaving the latter's house, he tripped (without seriously injuring himself) on a loose board.

As the frontier moved away from the first settlements, men's habits and even their ideas, in spite of themselves, became more fluid; they accepted their environment more, became more self-reliant, and lost many fears.

The trappers and foresters who went out alone and became part Indian learned best to know and love the American earth. If they stopped to pray instead of crawling through the brush they got scalped. They influenced the next settlers who came with ax and hoe and cleared the ground. Such men came sooner to grips with the new soil.

Hence the West naturally became most "American," more and more removed from Europe and tradition. There on the recurring frontier zones, men were stripped down to the primitive and partly forgot old useless dogmas.

Frederick Jackson Turner ably described the process. The frontier receives the immigrant, "a European in dress, industries, tools, modes of travel, and thought. It takes him from the railroad car and puts him in the birch canoe. It strips off the garments of civilization and arrays him in the hunting shirt and the moccasin. . . . Before long he has gone to planting Indian corn and plowing with a sharp stick; he shouts the war cry and takes the scalp in orthodox Indian fashion. . . . He follows Indian trails."

Such men could not help but adopt many useful Indian ways—dress, foods, medicines, the smoking, chewing and snuffing of tobacco. Presently we find even a President's wife, Mrs. Madison, using snuff, but of course in *her* hands the snuff-box seemed "only a gracious implement with which to charm." Mrs. Andrew Jackson was very fond of her corncob pipe.

Joseph Doddridge gives us a vivid picture of the dress of the Allegheny frontier that tells us more than volumes of the ready adaptability of the man on the border: The universally worn hunting shirt—generally of linsey, sometimes of coarse linens, a few dressed deerskins, the last "cold and uncomfortable in wet weather" —was a "kind of loose frock, reaching half way down the thighs, with large sleeves, open before, and so wide as to lap over a foot or more when belted." The large cape was often "handsomely fringed" with raveled pieces of cloth "of a different color from that of the hunting shirt. . . . The bosom of the dress served as a wallet to hold a chunk of bread, cakes, jerk, tow for wiping the barrel of the rifle." The belt, always tied behind, in cold weather served to hold "the mittens and sometimes the bullet-bag."

On the right was supended the tomahawk, on the left the "scalping knife in its leathern sheath." In the later years of the Indian wars, young men "became more enamored of the Indian dress throughout." Drawers were laid aside and "the leggins made longer, so as to reach the upper part of the thigh," where they were attached by strings to the belt. The Indian breech clout, "a piece of linen or cloth nearly a yard long, and eight or nine inches broad . . . ornamented with some coarse kind of embroidery work," passed under the belt, with end flaps before and behind, leaving the upper part of the thighs and part of the hips naked.

"The young warrior instead of being abashed by this nudity was proud of his Indian-like dress," but in places of public worship, their appearance "did not add much to the devotion of the young ladies."

The picture repeated itself as the frontier moved westward. Henry Harmon Spaulding tells how the free trapper of the Rockies felt most complimented when mistaken by the tenderfoot for an Indian brave. Often he was accompanied by an elegantly outfitted native wife. His own hair, "suffered to attain full length, is carefully combed out, and suffered to fall carelessly over his shoulders, or plaited and tied up with otter or white weasel skin. A hunting shirt of buskin, with heavy phylacteries and circles of porcupine quills, falls to his knees, below which, leggings of the same, closely fitted to his calves, and beautifully ornamented with fine beads and heavy fringes, reaches to a pair of moccasins curiously wrought with scarlet beads and porcupine quills. His blanket is girt about him with a red sash of otter skin, in which is bestowed his pipe, knife and tobacco pouch, the latter wrought with beads. His gun is lavishly decorated with brass tacks, vermilion, and eagle's feathers. His horse . . . is often caparisoned in the most dashing and fantastic style."

As the frontier emerged into a settled, organized system the westerner emerged to become a product that at least in part was American, and increasingly so with each new area of conquest. New laws evolved, new state constitutions, new outlooks, new ideas. We can laugh a bit now, but there was talk at the time of not admitting Oklahoma, later Arizona, to the Union because of too radical constitutions.

But though the pattern of habits slowly changed, intellectual evasion often continued. Men escaped into the wilderness rather than face settled problems. American thinking was thus dulled by this constant fleeing from temporary homelands to grasp at new material utopias further west. It is a deep urge within us still. I recognize it in my own insistent journeys to far parts, my long concern with the problems of Latin America rather than with those at home. I was the son of frontier folk and Populist revolters who landed up in California, then dreamed of going to Australia.

This rejuvenation, via the primitive, this augmenting Americanization, was a periodical phenomenon of American life almost to the end of the Nineteenth Century. Up until then, a portion of America was being constantly re-born in new forms, a repeated swift cycle of primitive conditions up through to the most advanced of the time. This has provided American life with a curious fluidity and also inconsistency, a variety of political and social conditions and outlooks that gradually since have been going down before the regimenting force of machine-production.

The reiterated process of primitive settlement promoted individual self-reliance, trained men in military methods and aggression, and created an abiding but unfortunate contempt—that is today almost a national trait—for races imagined to be inferior.

The general frontier process, if so necessary to create a real America, had its disadvantages. The unrelenting struggle with the Indians and with Nature brutalized the early American, thinned out his inherited culture, reduced him temporarily to a primitive level. By the early part of the Eighteenth Century, social habits and intellect in the New World colonies had reached their lowest ebb. A hiatus lay between two eras, while American forces slowly organized themselves. Had it not been for certain factors, the descent might have been still lower, and our re-emergence from a semi-savage state much longer delayed, though perhaps the results might eventually have proved sounder.

Factors that modified and held back the Americanization of Americans via the primitive, but which still more confused our mental attitudes, were varied.

The steadfastness of creeds was one factor. Not by creating an integrated life with interlocking religion and material interests, but by dualism, by splitting reality and thought, did the American avoid the reality of his new world.

Intellectually he often lived in a dead world; practically, materially, he lived in a live, vital world. The more encased in the past, the more useless, dead and hence unchangeable became his religious concepts, the more doggedly did he often cling to them—all his mental capacities went merely into the practical, the making of new gadgets for new ends.

Among few settlers was this schizophrenia so marked as among the Pennsylvania Quakers. Their doctrine of Quietism, which subdued the intellectual processes to mystic adoration, was originally an escape, not merely from Roman Catholic ritual, but from the realities of their world in Europe.

In the New World, where the Quakers sought a real haven for Quietism, the doctrines they so sternly retained and the reality they faced were constantly thrown into ludicrous contrast. Anarchists that they were, the Quakers were opposed to war, official oaths, politics and organized government. But when they went to Pennsylvania to be free of such things, they were at once constituted into a governing body responsible for the economic and political management of the country. To help their members in the frontier, they had to hold "meetings for sufferings"; when they made friendly peace treaties with the Indians, the compact was an oath, whatever the Quakers succeeded in calling it.

The Quakers were pacifists, but not all the Indians were peaceful, and when the good Friends attempted to conduct their colony without war or force they failed, and finally on occasion had to take musket in hand, as when the Paxton boys moved in on Philadelphia, but they clung to their beliefs little changed. The Indian war whoop often resounded on their frontiers, and the Quakers long resisted taking proper defense, especially as those endangered were Presbyterians, Episcopalians, and other despised sects. But finally in order not to lose control of the colony they did take decisive warlike measures, but in such hypocritical ways as to provide incessant amusement to later observers. They voted money "for the relief of the distressed Indians" of the Six Nations, although they knew the "relief" was to be used for bullets and war equipment. They supported the expedition against Louisburg, voting money to purchase "bread, beef, pork, flower, wheat or other grain," the last named being grains of gunpowder. When the angry Scotch-Irish brought the mutilated bodies of a family, murdered by the Indians, to Philadelphia and displayed them in the streets and before the State House, the Quakers found means to vote over $1,000,000 for forts and armed expeditions.

"Oh, how sweet," remarked William Penn from his forest retreat, "is the quiet of these parts, freed from the troubles and perplexities of woeful Europe." It sounds very like the present false rejoicing of our modern isolationists. But it was a vain sigh he emitted. Not only was he tied up with constant Old World law suits, and so had Europe on his neck until the end of his days, but the difficulties of settlement threw most of his ideas into the junk heap of purely mental stubbornness.

In contrast to the Puritan, who was an apostle of politics, force and intolerance, the Quaker, though the lamb of gentleness never before seen, managed, whatever his beliefs, by force, politics, and intolerance, to protect his rights and his territory far better than many a more frankly Machiavelian colony. Nerve-racking problems of conscience were induced in the broad-hatted members of the sect, but these did not prevent them from hanging on to power by hook or crook, nor did they halt their economic advance because of conflicting theories on tracts on simple living. In fact so well did they take to politics that William Penn had to chide them various times not to be so "governmentish." Thus in practice they managed to ignore almost all their doctrines, while clinging to them tightly. This divergence between doctrine and need had the effect, actually, of often making the Quakers tougher, more cunning, and more relentless in their pursuit of practical matters.

The Quakers produced some of the most prominent men of America, who became outstanding by remaining Quakers and violating all the fundamental doctrines of Quakerism. Perhaps it was largely because the Episcopalians took over the cultural life of the colony that such talents found a chance to expand in the face of the general hatred of knowledge on the part of the Quaker sect. But the Quakers who did participate in the Episcopalian flowering did not relinquish the contradictions of soul and deed. Though the Quakers were pacifists, they produced two leading generals; they frowned on science, but gave us John Bartram, the famous botanist, contemporary of Linnaeus, and Thomas Godfrey, the inventor of the quadrant. The Quakers also despised poetry and the arts, yet gave us two of our outstanding bards, including Whittier, and also John Dickson, famous for his *Farmer's Letters;* also two of our early painters, Benjamin West, who had to go to England to find scope, and Robert Feke.

The Quakers decried ostentation, yet even in the early Colonial period many became wealthy, and, though they built mansions with severe exteriors, furnished them luxuriously. In the face of strictures against immoderate eating, the Quaker *nouveaux riches* provided more costly banquets than almost anywhere, piling the board high with showy extravagance. Nor does Herbert Hoover's success in life rest upon strict adherence to his Quaker precepts. To point out the contrast between men's deeds and their creeds, their hypocrisies, has been an amusing pastime in all ages; but the two horns of dilemma were never further apart than in the case of the Quakers.

Thereby the Quakers, like the other sects, added their moiety to the lack of realism that is one of the outstanding characteristics to this day of much American thinking. Our forefathers had extensive philosophies, dogmas and popular sayings regarding the laws of Nature, the laws of God; but not by obeying such imaginary truths but by fighting and subduing nature by energy and mechanical intelligence was the continent brought under the yoke. Though Americans never have forgotten the old sayings, nor should they, our forefathers soon learned to separate their Calvinistic and other creeds from practical things. Their thoughts often lived in a vacuum unrelated to the workaday world. They divide the world into more or less exclusive spheres, a projection of the division in their own minds and souls: the division between inherited culture and the realities of a world never part of that original culture.

But they were shaken, and at times this has had startling results in the field of religion; for emotions, suddenly released from old restraints, sweeping up like a bursting geyser with no mental controls derived from the immediate social environment, produced some of the most pathological religious aberrations in the history of mankind.

Another factor besides rigidly held dogma, which delayed or modified the Americanization of America, was a continuous emigration from England and elsewhere that renewed the blood of the descendants of the first colonists. Later comers brought with them the continuous fresh challenge of English and continental culture to check our more savage ways. This retarding process—though mass immigration was so necessary in order to build up America rapidly—has operated throughout our history, still operates. We know only too well of the psychology and the activities of hyphenated Americans, the Nazi-Americans, the Fascist-Americans, the Russo-Communist Americans, the English-Empire Americans; we know of their divided loyalties, their psychological struggles to adopt American ways but to deny the change in their own minds. All our early settlers were hyphenated Americans. Though our own loyalties and emotions are no longer so divided, our thinking in many ways still obeys the compulsives derived long ago from distant shores. It is affected constantly by that process of evading the meaning of the things right before our eyes, which despite such mental blindness, we often handle so capably from purely short-range or mechanical view.

This separation from the more integrated European world from which people came to the schizophrenic world of America, meant that thought patterns were no longer grooved by deeds into reliable service, and that thought patterns rarely directed deeds. This meant a rigidity of doctrines, a loss of universality, and a concentration on the practical in turn robbed of its philosophical significance.

We catch this from Charles G. Leland's *Hans Breitmann's Ballads*: America abounded with Germans who, though having received in their youth a "classical education," later passed through such varied adventures, they often presented the most startling paradoxes of thought and personal appearance.

"I have seen . . . a porter, who could speak Latin fluently . . . a beer shop kept by a man . . . [once] distinguished in the Frankfort Parliament . . . a graduate of the University of Munich in a Negro-minstrel troupe."

There was at all times among Americans an eclectic selection from the lore of the past whenever deeds needed false rationalization. Our forefathers were held under the "tyranny of words," though mostly unaware of it, long before Stuart Chase came along—only they had less need to be perturbed about it, hence weren't.

Each new wave of European immigration repeated this process, thereby creating a queer unreality and belatedness to all American thinking.

A third restraint on "Americanization" operated. As more settlers came and productive life expanded, a certain amount of wealth and corresponding leisure were accumulated in more established centers. Trading increased rapidly on the eastern seaboard, bringing riches, and also setting up another intellectual barrier by creating a class-isolated group able to cherish European rather than American culture. Leisure was granted to a few enterprising souls or their immediate descendants.

People did thereby become more preoccupied with appearances, physical and mental, less concerned about their intangible souls. "Why," complains Julia Cowles of Farmington, Connecticut, in 1794, "should the rich spend a fortune upon dress and other equipage, why not share with the poor?" Entertainment, in which as a rule the elders sullenly refused to participate, became more frequent, playing pawns, hunting the whistle, threading the needle, etc. Styles appeared. We hear of "pompedore" shoes and gloves, of coats and bonnets costing £45, no less, of "lokets" and jewelry galore. Anna Green Winslow (1772) tells proudly how she was dressed in her "yellow coat, black bib and apron, black feathers . . ." and adorned with her "past comb" and all her "past garnet marquesett & jet pins," together with her "silver plume . . . loket, rings, black collar . . . black mitts & 2 or 3 yards of blue ribbin (black and blue is high taste), striped tucker and ruffels . . . & silk shoes."

Amid carved chairs and showy curtains, men and women over-proud of their faked aristocratic origin and lavishly robed in ruffles, silver buckles, gold-embroidered waistcoats, and rich brocade dressing gowns—the folk pictured in the Boston canvases of John Singleton Copley—found knowledge, even art and music of interest; they kept

older cultural values alive. It was all somewhat artificial, though out
of it was to come, in part, the later flowering of New England. "The
Boston style" even in very early times was a phrase used elsewhere
"to denote a florid, pompous manner of writing." Would-be Europeans, grown rich in a real America, unconsciously were trying hard
not to accept it.

In the South, the plantations grew wealthy, and the slave system
early permitted considerable leisure for a few. Though one wonders
whether the consequences have not been more grievous than the gain,
this for a time also conserved more civilized manners, which merely
meant, so far as possible, European leisure-class manners. In those
more southern climes, the slaves, as more and more came in, provided
a cushion which for centuries softened the conflict of the newcomer
with a strange land, the strange new earth.

But even so, as William Howard Russell of the *London Times*
noted at the outbreak of the Civil War: although those "tall, thin-
faced Carolinians" boasted eternally of their dubious aristocracy,
nevertheless they were "great materialists." Slavery perhaps had
"aggravated the tendency to look at all the world through parapets
of cotton bales and rice bags." They were "not less prostrate before
the 'almighty dollar' than the Northerners."

In 1861, Rhett told Russell: "We are an agricultural people, pursuing our own destiny, breeding up men and women with some other
purpose than to make them vulgar, fanatical and cheating Yankees—
hypocritical, if as women they pretend to real virtue; and lying, if
as men they pretend to be honest. We have gentlemen and gentle-
women in your sense of it. We have a system which enables us to
reap the fruits of the earth by a race which we save from barbarism,
in returning them to their real place in the world as laborers, whilst
we are enabled to cultivate the arts, the graces and accomplishments
of life, to develop science, to apply ourselves to the duties of government, and to understand the affairs of the country."

Leisurely owners, living in fine mansions behind box-wood hedges
and crêpe myrtles, were thus able to continue to toy with their relatively useless European lore, culture and customs, less undisturbed
by reality. But science got little boost; their understanding of the

affairs of the country, except for that first galaxy of brilliant Virginia minds at the time of independence—and even they had the limited slant of the ruling plantation class—has ever been mostly lamentable; and creative originality soon languished.

From that day to this, the bulk of southern Whites have lived, more than have those anywhere else in the nation, in an unreal dream world, a world of fantasy—not of the creative imagination, but of a fantasy created by others in a long dim past, an embalmed fantasy, without vigor or renewal. As late as 1931 the editor of the *Charleston News and Courier*, William Watts Ball, wrote a book, which, despite its surface humor, demanded in bitter denunciation of demagogy in his state that it be delivered back politically to the very plantation aristocrats who ruined and despoiled it—a screed against "the deadly and foreign poison of democracy." This is seventeenth century Bourbonism with a vengeance.

The real vitality in the South, the real soil wisdom (I am not talking of enforced technical misuse of the soil), the real creative force of song and poetry, mostly has been Negro vitality. But that too was aborted, at least distorted, by slavery and later oppression.

Nowhere else on our American continent has the earth, our American soil, been more grievously wounded and destroyed and betrayed than below the Mason and Dixon line.

But thus it was that in early days our first important leaders came chiefly from the mercantile aristocracy of New England and plantation aristocracy of Virginia. Neither represented the true genius of America, the latter less than the former. They were rather the vehicles, as Wertenbaker would put it, of the "transit and survival of European ideas"; by means of a preliminary stabilization, they did, in a sense—we should not, however critical, rob them of their true stature and their notable accomplishments—help save America, which was to lie mostly beyond the Alleghenies, for its true genius and its truer fruition, whatever that may prove eventually to be.

Incidentally they built America on two conflicting economic systems, feudal and mercantile. In the very foundation of our nation can be seen the great crack upon which it rested, which was to widen until the whole superstructure fell apart—the Civil War.

But however valuable those leisure-class holders of civilized traditions and dead art slowly withering in the newer breaths of the New World, much of the real American was to be born elsewhere. The founding fathers built a state and wrote a constitution based on a hundred and fifty years of vivid European political polemics; but, despite their wisdom, the true but anonymous founders of America were even then creating economic, legal and political forms never known to the world, let alone to the Founding Fathers—forms more definably American.

Thus the early years of America were a race between the process of settlers becoming American and yet not becoming too ignorant and primitive. This constantly created a problem of unstable balance within Colonial institutions, later between the more Europeanized eastern seaboard and the hardier if more benighted, yet more soil-rooted culture of the hinterland.

The newcomers put their wills unitedly to producing workable gadgets, but they divided their brains, high-walled between faith and mechanics. Intellectual equipment, resting on the Bible (in some instances more extensively on Fox's *Book of Martyrs,* John Bunyan, and *Bowels Opened; or, A Dictionary of the Union betwixt Christ and the Church*), the sole literary meat of many settlers, may have been very admirable, but it also helped draw a mental screen in front of the world before them.

This has accentuated two psychological characteristics over the years: a constant mental evasion of all theory and universal principles except those inherited, and hard-eyed realism toward material things. We have a singular inability to achieve objective thought, or any thought, apart from the immediately practical, apart from self-interest, personal desire and personal efforts. As a result our ideas have usually been demeaned to excuses. They have been whittled down to selfishness. Curiously enough, though self-interest so strongly determines our intellectual process, our rationalizations (when they are not merely echoes of long-standing inherited prejudices and stock group symbols), we have ever displayed as a group and a nation very lavish material generosity toward all stricken peoples. But intellectual and spiritual generosity (I am not referring to tolerance, of which we now have our fair share) are not especially characteristic of the American's thinking. The self-interested basis of the American's thinking leads him to become part of a sort of camorra against all thinking that is not based on self-interest. Thus the average American instinctively listens to and puts faith in the arguments of the man who has a selfish ax to grind rather than those of the man who comes forward free of any personal stake. The latter is considered an impractical visionary. Thought has thus been broken on the wheel of efficiency and mechanical aims. Or we have merely avoided thought by founding ever new crazier sects to escape either complete pragmatism or the consequences of our activities; or we have quite subordinated our explanations to our immediate purpose.

As long as Nature, as long as the material thing, so easily obeyed our people, naturally they had no need of deep thought or of clear philosophy. Hence our people became the greatest "pragmatists" since the days of the Roman Empire. William James, among others, developed precisely a pragmatic philosophy to fit more comfortably the intellectual need, both of frontiersman and our later business man; John Dewey has done likewise for our hazy, sentimental liberals. But it has been an unnecessary rationalization. Most Americans long have clung to time-honored fetishes and quaint religious motives and have been sufficiently served by them, all the thoughtless maxims of yesteryear. Those sacred fetishes have never disturbed our go-getter energy and achievement or our Horatio Alger faith.

This has created in the American—though this also is a universal characteristic of man—a queer duality, singularly pronounced, that leads other nations to brand us as the world's worst hypocrites. We kept our eye on the ball, in as simple, direct, honest manner as a cat, but out of the store of our inherited notions about God and Nature often we draw grandiose, idealistic and noble but untruthful explanations for what we do. Usually these have had little real relation to our accomplishment. But in our haste to conquer a continent and to affirm our national power, we have had little time and little need to challenge our thoughtless slogans or to explain our acts or even to chart our course.

But thereby lies part of the explanation why our power to handle the material Frankenstein we have created has broken down; thereby we have rifled the soil without thought of the morrow; thereby, though we are still crop-rich, we now face the growth of a pauper peasantry instead of a nation of free men.

CHAPTER V

LAND FOR THE FEW

Far down South in 1718, near the mouth of the Mississippi, behind a hastily constructed levee, Jean Baptiste Le Moigne Bienville founded New Orleans, and forthwith there came to settle there, besides many an honest French citizen, shiploads of unemployed from the Paris slums, gamblers, criminals, smugglers, deserters, adventurers. The jails were emptied. To wive came shiploads of young prostitutes and women from houses of correction, herded through the streets and on to ships in sixes, chains about their middles. Orphanages and reform schools were stripped of girls: *"les filles cassette,"* so-called because of the little basket of effects given each by the Crown—"the king's dowery." Out of the mire of France and Louisiana grew the lily-snob families of today.

This general stampede to the New World was largely promoted by John Law, whose great financial extravagances provided one of the major scandals of the ages—the Mississippi bubble, which, with its barrels of fiat money, well-nigh ruined France financially for a generation.

Law and his followers, who hired the best writers and artists of the day to turn out mass propaganda, pictured Louisiana as a paradise —*"un nouveau Pais de cocagne"*—a land of milk and honey, of gold and silver, filled with docile Indians eager to become slaves. Mobile, which sounded unstable, was changed to Immobile; Massacre Island was renamed Dauphin Island. The previous truthful reports of Bienville, with their savor of fresh forest verdure; their keen, if poetic, observations measured deftly into the dignified prose of official exactitude, gave way now to the booster extravagances, commercialized distortions, all the doctored-up slap-stick of go-getterism. A great publicity campaign!

According to Law, New Orleans (but a huddle of palmetto huts in the marsh beside a yellow stream) had become a great city, a place of tropical luxury and golden towers, vying with Arabian Nights dream cities, a land of palm trees and vineyards and blue moonlight by calm seas. The booster stories ran like wildfire through the Paris cafés. In the New World all Frenchmen, however humble, lived like kings, surrounded with beautiful, seductive bronze women, waited on by naked Nubian slaves. One publicity placard of the cafés showed an Indian giving a white man nuggets of gold in exchange for a small knife.

Gullible people from all classes scrambled to emigrate. They begged, borrowed, or stole, or sold their homes, their ultimate possessions:

> *Les femmes vendent jusqu'à leurs bijoux*
> *Pour mettre à ce nouveau Perou.*

The country had to be settled quickly if Law and France itself were not to collapse. When volunteers failed, so much per head was offered, and the streets were scoured at night of their human refuse. "It was dog-catchers' work; and dog-catchers performed it." The horrors perpetrated on human beings became in time the theme of satirists and of painters—the notable canvas of Watteau—and of famous writers, the notable *Manon Lescaut* of Michelet. As is the case when any great and extravagant steal is on, those who ridiculed it at the time or told the truth were hushed up, bribed, ridiculed or persecuted.

And so, shipload after shipload of colonists were dumped on Dauphin Island, only to find there no food, no shelter. They wandered about starving, heart-broken, chewed up by mosquitoes, blistered by the sun. Men went insane. Men, women and children died and rotted unburied on the beaches—mingled heaps of putrefying Black slaves and White folk.

But a few survived, made their way up the Mississippi through the swamps and the bayous, founded homes, plantations, and shortly some even prospered. An empire was founded, an empire even from the first in good part owned by rich concessionaires.

To the Hudson and the Delaware Rivers, much earlier, came the Dutch. Hendrik Hudson anchored the *Half Moon* three times on the way up the river where in a few years would stretch great baronial estates. Indian canoes "brought great store of very good oysters aboard, which we bought for trifles." And in the Delaware: "Six hours of tacking and sailors' oaths and ten lines of Juet's handwriting in a log-book, were enough," writes Sidney George Fisher, "to give the Dutch an empire of thousands of square miles." It included a large part of Pennsylvania.

Dutch settlers stuck up a tin painted with the arms of Holland. An Indian took it down to make a tobacco-pipe. For this insult to a great nation, he was killed. The Dutchmen were themselves wiped out. But during fifty years they planted wide estates under patroons, expanded their claims everywhere.

Then came the Swedes, for seventeen years. Printz, the Governor, was a jovial *bon vivant*, weighing four hundred pounds. He lived high, extended his domain, built a mansion, an estate, a "pleasure house," and a yacht.

The Dutch came back for nine years. Then the region went into the hands of the Duke of York. Finally, in 1682, William Penn came over, having been granted as well, all of Pennsylvania, to set himself up as one of the largest landholders in the whole world.

William Penn and his family thereafter fought for their landed rights with all the tight Bourbon greed that characterized the spirit of land-feudalism everywhere. Charter in hand, the Penns made treaties to their own distinct advantage with the Indians, and in 1736 bought from them for a song a permanent option on all the territory in Pennsylvania. The land was never free to settlers, who had to pay for it or become tenants. Though some squatters, and even several whole squatter settlements, made good their right of possession, this was never with the willing consent of the Penn family, which sometimes years after, as with certain settlements of Scotch-Irish, made them pay up on the land they had long occupied. In the case of Wyoming Valley, pitched battles were fought, massacres were perpetrated as a result of the speculative efforts of New England land companies, and if the Penns and the Quakers did not prevail, it was not for lack of shedding enough blood.

Pennsylvania, though the most tolerant of the colonies in religious matters, was far from being the ideal utopia ecstatically painted by Voltaire, though it may well have seemed such compared to France. Rule down to the Revolution rested on a rotten borough system by which an autocratic Quaker clique of rich planters and merchants retained nearly all political control. Voting was restricted to those with $250 "lawful money" or owning at least fifty acres of land. In the farming districts one person in ten, and in Philadelphia only one in fifty, had the right to vote. In addition, new non-Quaker counties were long denied all political rights, and even when they were eventually given legal status, they were allowed fewer seats in the General Assembly. Lancaster, York, Cumberland, Berks and Northampton were admitted with a total of only ten seats, as compared with the twenty-four from the Quaker counties, Chester, Bucks and Philadelphia. In 1775, the Quaker minority held twenty-eight out of thirty-six seats.

From the first, free settlers were not the ruling forces in the colonies. Many of the colonies were promoted by chartered companies, seeking private profit. Numerous colonists were desirable merely to augment commercial gains. Those companies had a free hand, were granted practically sovereign powers, and enjoyed enormous special privileges.

In New England, the most powerful concern was the Plymouth Company. When it was dissolved, the directors divvied up the land among themselves, and for the most part held their great estates and their powerful control against all comers. The New England Company was free from all financial obligations to the Crown for twenty-one years, and was relieved from taxes forever. Thus much of New England was held in large estates, run on a semi-feudal basis. The large individual holders assumed all of the rights accorded to the earlier companies, and together they so controlled the legislative processes as to retain and enforce all their privileges.

Only in a few instances were such property rights abrogated. After many suits and conflicts, the Lords of Trade, on the recommendation of Governor Bellomont of Massachusetts and New York, declared Colonel Samuel Allen's title to all of New Hampshire (which he had bought from a former director of the Plymouth Company) defective. But litigation by Allen and his heirs raged for sixty years, blocking settlement and development. John Usher, who had bought all of Maine from Sir Fernandino Gorges—grandson of the original owner, close to Queen Elizabeth—finally had to relinquish his title, for compensation, to the Massachusetts Company.

Such cases were exceptional. Most big owners kept firm grip on their properties and on political power. The recipients of large plantations were merely men of influence, new settlers not being able even to go to such plantation settlements without the consent of the majority of the magistrates of General Court. Absentee proprietors long continued to retain dominant economic interest in even freeholder Puritan towns. Salisbury, in the Merrimac Valley, was planted on lands granted to a dozen proprietors, mostly prominent in the political councils of the colony, only two of whom actually lived in the place. Dunstable, Lancaster, Mendon, Dedham, Deerfield, Woodstock, Leicester, and in fact most places, never saw the real owners of the land.

Absentee holders were mostly immune from taxes; the actual poorer settlers had to foot almost the entire bill of governmental costs. In Deerfield—runs an old complaint—"the very best principle & best for soil; the best for situation," that lying in the very center of the town, was nearly half owned by "eight or nine proprietors," who "never came or were likely to come to the settlement." They did not pay taxes; nor did they improve their land, or if in rare instances did so, they put in very undesirable tenants. In many places, those who were landless or became landless lost all their rights in the use of the commons. Property qualifications limited the voting right.

Churches, too, often got superlative grants, some of which still survive. I have recently been living on a small Connecticut bay across from such an extensive wooded and valuable *mort main* property. Such properties also paid no taxes.

Between 1715 and 1762, the General Court opened remaining lands to reckless speculation and monopoly. In the latter year whole townships in the Berkshires were sold out supposedly to the highest bidders—in short were grabbed without regard for social or colonizing needs. Around 1760, Governor Wentworth of New Hampshire job-lotted the land of 130 townships in what is now Vermont to specu-lators.

In New Netherlands, the patroon—a man who could plant a colony of fifty souls—was permitted to own sixteen miles of waterfront along a navigable river, or eight miles along a navigable river and as far into the interior as he could settle. Actually some holdings were much larger.

One director of the Dutch West India Company, Kiliaen Van Rensselaer, a name still encountered on the boards of high banking and business companies, bought from the Indians for a small quantity of duffels, axes, knives and wampum, a tract on the west bank of the Hudson twenty-four by twenty-eight miles, comprising over 700,000 acres and covering two counties and a goodly part of two others.

Such titles were perpetual and included a monopoly of all re-sources except furs and pelts, though the proprietor usually found means to monopolize this trade also.

When Governor Fletcher took over the colony for the English government—which assumed sovereignty in 1664—he rapidly ex-tended the existing feudal system, giving out enormous tracts for personal bribes or to friends. Captain John R. N. Evans of M. S. Richmond paid Fletcher, it is said, a beggarly £100 bribe and got a huge estate, thirty by forty miles, on the west bank of the Hudson— some of the richest, most picturesque land in the colony.

Nicholas Bayard, go-between for Fletcher and the pirates—who on the high seas and at the mouth of the Hudson, paid for immunity—

grabbed off an estate of equal size.[1] Chief Justice William Smith, hand in glove with Fletcher, got an equally large estate in Nassau, Long Island, for £10. One 160,000 acre estate was granted to the loan merchant and army-purveyor, the "soldier's belly-pincher," Robert Livingston, ten miles of it abutting on the river below Albany and covering seven modern townships clear to the Connecticut border, an estate which by ignoble means he expanded greatly during the rest of his lifetime.

These were but a few of numerous similar grants. By 1732, two and one-half million acres were tied up in manorial estates, blocking frontier expansion. By 1764, the governor reported that three grants alone contained over a million acres each, and that such grants, mostly unimproved, occupied a "great part of the province." Even today they would represent in area the equivalent of a fourth of the improved farmland of the state.

These newer English estates, granted after the Dutch departed, followed the English manor system, which had evolved out of Teutonic tendencies and Roman traditions, superimposed on a communal system; they were not, therefore, any authentic American evolution, were no indigenous product of the rolling hills of eastern New York or the meadows of the Hudson Valley or the wooded eminences of Bear Mountain and Lake Mohonk. In America that system was merely an artificial imitation, a transplanted product that would take time to be modified to the American needs. As in England, the feudal practices with copyholders and serfs or slaves to cultivate them were followed. Most owners paid only a symbolic rental: such as four-

---

[1] The mouth of the Hudson was infested with pirates who preyed on all legitimate commerce, but who, like modern bootleggers, often enjoyed, through graft, complete immunity for their depredations. At one time there were nine pirate ships in New York harbor at one time. "Captain William Trew was the honored guest of the royal Governor, and rode at his side in his 'coach and six,' a resplendent rascal . . . dressed . . . colorfully right down to the knitted girdle from which hung a dagger, its hilt blazing with jewels." The pirate Coates loaded the governor with gifts.

Today pirates still visit governor and mayor, but they have different names and usually wear silk hats.

pounds, payable yearly—"on the day of the Annunciation of the Blessed Virgin Mary" or "twenty bushels of good peas."

"With the great landed estates came tenantry, wage slavery and chattel slavery, the one condition the natural generator of the others," remarks Gustavus Meyers; and he quotes Savine's *Lives of the Loyalists* that it was tolerably accurate "to say that the political institutions of New York formed a feudal aristocracy. The soil was owned by a few. The masses were retainers or tenants, as in the monarchies of Europe." Meyers goes on to state: "The feudal lord was also the dominant manufacturer and trader. He forced his tenants to sign covenants that they should trade in nothing else but at his store; that they should grind their flour at his mill, and buy bread at his bakery, lumber at his saw mills and liquor at his brewery. Thus he was not only able to squeeze the last penny from them by exorbitant prices, but to keep them everlastingly in debt to him."

There was little room for the petty merchant, and as in the previous Middle Ages in Europe, the burghers could only operate in the new cities, which were small; and during the first century or so, landed proprietors reached out to control them also. The landlords everywhere monopolized much of the hunting, fur-trading, fishing, whaling, liquor and rum-running business, slave-traffic, and on occasion had secret arrangements with pirates to share the spoils of seizing or robbing British and other commerce.

The governor, in 1769, protested to London that, through monopoly of political power, the proprietors were "not only freed from quitrents but . . . from every other public tax on their lands" which "other land-holders . . . pay."

Even if the lord of the manor sold or subdivided any part of the estate, the new freeholders owed him complete political allegiance. The privately administered justice, the leet courts of the patroons, all the vexatious dues of the feudal privileged class, were in direct opposition to the later American spirit of independence and self-reliance.

Paul Wilstach wrote in *Hudson River Landings*: "Class distinction was marked during the eighteenth century; a few aristocrats . . . on an aloof pinnacle," and then "a gaping hiatus." Those aristocrats, "in the rarified atmosphere of the heights, were the families of the lords of the manors, of the greater business men and bankers. The professional classes developed slowly. Far below these aristocrats, in the absence of a well-developed middle class, were the small tradesmen, artificers and artisans, and farmers of whom the lesser portion owned small acreages and the larger portion rented from the lords of the manors and other landlords. This was a comparatively small group of indentured white servants, some of them convicts, some of them kidnaped and sold into servitude, and some of them redemptioners who worked their way to freedom. But there were far fewer of these on the Hudson than on the Chesapeake."

In Maryland Lord Baltimore ruled with regal powers and proprietary right over the entire province. There, within five years of the arrival of the first colonists, were planted great manor houses on hillocks of sheltering locust or oak groves, overlooking the river, with twelve to fifteen mile vistas. The owners of these estates had the privilege of "trial by peers, freedom from ignominious death, summons by special writ to every assembly, right to keep stray cattle, and right to escheat to tenements." All these special privileges created a closed world of class power, completely un-American as we use the word in our schoolbooks.

Thomas Cornwallis owned three manors totaling 8,000 acres. The first governor, Leonard Calvert, also owned three enormous manors. Margaret Brent, apparently his mistress, and her family, received 9,610 acres across on the Virginia shore. Thomas Gerrard, Gent., was awarded the St. Clements Manor of 11,400 acres and the adjacent Brasford Manor.

More than a decade before the Pilgrims landed, the people of Jamestown had planted themselves, and a year before the *Mayflower* hove-to off Cape Cod, twenty-two Virginia burgesses from the plantations, and some hundreds of colonists, met in the primitive church to set up a government, supposedly free and democratic, but from the start dominated by the wealthier landowners.

Virginia was in fact owned by the London Company, which had

an absolute monopoly on all land and resources, and carved it up into big plantations ruling over bond-servants and Guinea slaves, the first boat-load of the latter arriving in 1619. Many of the brave settlers who came to Virginia on the wind-buffeted *Sahra Constant* were not stepping into a free world; they wore certain shackles before they ever set out.

The company was dissolved in 1620, but the planters continued to control the life of the colony and to issue the legislation they desired. Even after Independence, a man had to have at least 100 acres to be able to vote.

The custom prevailed of making grants of 1,000 acres to the right people; but speculative planters, influential with the governor, secured grants of many thousands of acres. The Lord Fairfax Estate, surveyed by the youthful George Washington, which lay partly in the northern Shenandoah, covered six million acres. The Beverley Manor, near Staunton, was a grant of 118,000 acres. The Fontleroy Estate was also of vast proportions.

The first Lee by 1663 had accumulated 20,000 acres on both sides of the river; William Fitzhugh bequeathed nearly 50,000 acres on the Potomac, besides other holdings in Virginia and Maryland. He owned land on nearly every creek for sixty miles and, on the Occoquan alone, 21,000 acres. Mr. Nicholas Hayward of London, who never even saw America, received a grant of 30,000 acres. Robert Carter accumulated over 63,000 acres. The Jesuits also got big grants.

George Washington was himself a land speculator who did not hesitate—though he publicly denounced such practices—to buy soldiers' scrip cheap. Among other places, he owned acreages in Virginia, Maryland, Pennsylvania, New York, Kentucky, and the city of Washington.

His Mount Vernon estate, welded from five adjacent farms, though it contained only 8,000 acres, in organization was typical of the Colonial feudal system. The estate was divided into four plantations, besides the manor house (that grew between 1759 and 1787 to a mansion, resembling many a later nineteenth century town-hall) and outbuildings, all comprising a separate unit, and was manned with serfs and slaves. The manor alone required a superintendent, overseer and his wife, five male house-servants, four women house-servants, four laborers, six stablemen, a dozen skilled male workers and seven skilled women workers, three old people and twenty-six children. The manor house arrangements had ordered space, with convenient service and maximum personal privacy.

A grist mill demanded the attention of one miller and three coopers. The largest of the four plantations required an overseer and his wife, ten male laborers, seventeen female laborers, and twenty-three children.

In North Carolina, Lord Granville owned the whole northern half of the state and exacted quitrents.

In 1655 Charles granted to seven noblemen a charter for the land between Luke Island on the Virginia seas to the Matthews River, the borders of Florida and west clear to the South Seas; and in 1669, eighty-year-old William Sayles led an expedition that settled "Charles Town." The fundamental constitution of "South Carolina" provided for an elaborate aristocracy, to "avoid erecting a numerous democracy"—a set-up devised by no less a person than John Locke, thus giving the colony a curious Platonic touch.

The new province was grandiosely divided into eight signories, eight baronies and four precincts. Titles were spewed out like iris-colored soap-bubbles. The oldest proprietor was Palatine; there were admirals, chancellors, chamberlains, constables, chief justices, high stewards and treasury offices to be distributed to the "true and absolute lords proprietors." The proprietors were to be "landgraves," receiving 48,000 acres, and "casiques" receiving 24,000 acres. The latter title curiously returned an Aztec word to the New World, for so the high political feudal bosses of Moctezuma's empire were originally named. At first these big estates were cultivated with indented servants, later slaves. The owners—the "nigger-rich" folk, the fox hunters—dominated the colony long after it became a state. By the 1790 constitution, the Low country with a fourth of the population, was allowed twenty of the thirty-two senators and seventy of the one hundred and twenty-four members of the Assembly; and the 1808 constitutional revision, if it extended representation more generously to Up country districts, nevertheless restricted suffrage on the basis of White population and the amount of taxes paid. Plurality voting by property owners further weighted the scale.

This pseudo-aristocracy that so dominated, boasted of lineage from cavaliers, though only one family originally had remote connections with English nobility; a few came from the gentry, and the Huguenots had been mostly artisans and tradesfolk. But by 1835 the state had the wealthiest planter in America, Wade Hampton, with estates —one worth a million and a half dollars—there and in Mississippi; and it was Hampton who in 1868 led the "Red-Shirt Regulators" to smash Reconstruction rule and put the lower classes and the Negroes back down in their places. Except for interludes, ignorance and terrorism have governed the state from that day to this. The great aristocratic commonwealth is today the most illiterate state in the Union.

Oglethorpe, the founder of Georgia, thought in terms of Utopia. He wished to provide a refuge for people suffering from oppression, a place of honest labor, without envy, harshness or riotous living. The attempt was made to restrict all individual holdings to inalienable fifty acre plots. No grants larger than five hundred acres (and this only provided the recipient actually settled ten colonists) were permitted.

But plantation agriculture was required on the warm coast country first settled. Negro slaves completed the process of destroying human equality through toil. The original Oglethorpe ideal began to break down in the Eighteenth Century. Much of the land—despite various revolts—was increasingly gathered into large holdings. By 1750 the democratic system had largely vanished, never to return unless the ill-balanced Reconstruction period or the various strident demagogic upsurges can be so characterized.

State rule, right up to the Civil War, remained mostly in the hands of the richer Low country planters. The Georgia delegation at the 1789 national constitutional convention represented such planters; and their spokesman, Abraham Baldwin, though contented with the proposed arrangement for the Senate (to be constituted of members elected by state legislatures), demanded that the House of Representatives be based on ownership of property. Whatever the ostensible issues—usually that of state rights—in the politics of subsequent generations, the voting, down to the Civil War, split sharply along regional and economic lines. The Up country folk were poor and ignorant among the pine woods. The wire grass and wild oats furnished sustenance for ill-kept cattle. Few wagon roads existed. Clothing was homespun. Political power, concentrated on the coast in the hands of relatively rich landowners, prevented the spread of population and public improvements. For many years, for instance, Georgia politics were run by George Michael Troup (whose father had probably been a Tory), a distinct aristocrat, a states' rights man, a member of the plantation class. He ruled by majorities from the slaveholding counties.

Ironically, today, in the once ideal colony of Oglethorpe, human misery, poverty and ignorance is equaled in few corners of the globe. An average southern Mexican or Guatemala highland Indian is a marvel of moral integrity, prosperity and enlightenment compared to the average poor tenant farmer of Georgia.

The large New World feudal estates, and even smaller farms, constantly clamored for labor. One of the principal defects in our husbandry, Timothy Dwight noted even at a much later date, was "a deficiency in the quantity of labor." Earlier the emergency was partly met by buying White servants in England (later, on the Continent also) to be resold in Massachusetts, New York, Pennsylvania, Maryland, Virginia and South Carolina—a traffic almost as vile as the slave trade itself. Many a wealthy American family was founded on such traffic.

This traffic was also promoted by the Golden Books of the Queen Anne, propaganda by which the British Government sought to fill up the colonies with people from across the Channel. British agents were sent all over the Palatinate to round up emigrants.

This traffic was drummed up by shipping agents, and seekers of indented servants, called "new landers" or "soul-sellers." Big rewards were reaped by the recruiting agents, and they knew how to share their profits in the right quarters. Preachers, for a free passage, or for a split in the profits, often helped such agents hook the people. Many an English judge who thus trafficked in human flesh for the American colonies did not become the poorer thereby.

Low folk in the London slums, and especially along the waterfront, were bamboozled with drink into signing papers of indenture; others were shanghaied. Poor people were arbitrarily arrested for any one of the multitude of petty offenses that cluttered the statute books of the day, and were then transported to the New World as criminals to be White slaves.

The system had its drawbacks. Robert Beverley of Virginia remarked that malefactors, "condemned to transportation," were readily bought by "the greedy planter," but that it was to be feared they would be injurious to the New Country which had already suffered "many murders and robberies."

Mittleberger tells of how people from the Palatinate were brought over packed in the holds like herring. "The filth and stench of the vessels no pen could describe, while the diverse diseases, sea-sickness in every form, headaches, biliousness, constipation, dysentery, scarlet fever, scrofula, cancers, etc., caused by the miserable salt food and the vile drinking water, are truly deplorable, not to speak of the deaths which occur on every side." Lice could literally be taken in quantities from the bodies of the passengers. Some passengers became so desperate, they ran amuck and killed those about them. During the voyage, body after body was "committed to a watery grave." Women who gave birth to children often tossed them overboard. One woman, having trouble giving birth, was "shoved through an opening in the ship . . . into the water, because it was not convenient to attend her." Food was served three times a week, so filthy the very sight of it was "loathsome," and drinking water was "black, thick, and full of worms."

Mr. Bamfylde Moore Carew, an indented servant who escaped, tells how, after the vessel he was on cast anchor in Miles's River, the captain had a gun fired to bring the planters. He ordered all men prisoners to be close-shaved, the women to have their best headdresses on; and all, "near a hundred," brought up on deck, where "a large bowl of punch was made." After mail and news, the planters' first inquiry was "if the captain had brought them a good store of joiners, carpenters, blacksmiths, weavers and tailors." One Griffy, "a tailor, who had lived at Chumleigh, in the county of Devon, and was obliged to take a voyage to Maryland, for making too free with his neighbor's sheep," was called forward. He was purchased by Parson Nichols and Mr. Tolles, after they decided he was "sound wind and limb."

The poor tailor "cried and bellowed like a bellwether, cursing his wife who had betrayed him. . . . Wherefore all these wailings, say our hero, have we not a fine glorious country before us? pointing to the shore. . . . The beauty of the prospect, the fragrancy of the fields and gardens, the brightness of the sky, and serenity of the air, affects the ravished senses; the country being a large plain, and the hills in it so easy of ascent, and of such moderate height, that they seem rather an artificial ornament to it, than one of the accidents of nature."

When all the best tradesmen had been disposed of, a planter asked Mr. Carew "what trade he was of: Mr. Carew, to satisfy him of his usefulness, told him he was a rat-catcher, a mendicant, and a dog-merchant. 'What the devil trades are those?' replied the planter in astonishment, 'for I have never before heard of them.' Upon which the Captain, thinking he should lose the sale of him, takes the planter a little aside, and tells him, he did but jest, being a man of humour, for that he was a great scholar, and was only sent over on account of having disobliged some gentlemen . . . that he would make an excellent schoolmaster." He offered to sell him for seven years.

None of these inducements prevailed, so the next day the Captain asked Carew to go on shore with him to see the country, "but indeed with a view of getting a purchase for him among the planters." They went to a tavern where three planters showed up. The bowl of punch went round "merrily." In the midst of their mirth, Mr. Carew, "who had given no consent to the bargain they were making for him, thought it no breach of honor or good manners to take an opportunity of slipping away, without taking any leave of them; and taking with him about a pint of brandy, and some biscuit cakes, which by good luck, he chanced to lay his hands on, he immediately betook himself to the woods as the only place of security for him."

Laborers, men and women, for transportation, often bound themselves for four to seven years for keep, a total remuneration of £3, and several suits. Still, there are nearly two million farm hands today in the United States working only for keep.

If in a few places those indented were promised land at the expiration of their term of bondage—in South Carolina a hundred acres—such generosity was rare. The land so given was often promptly taken away by declaring them to be squatters—or by other ruses—especially in New York from where many fled into Jersey and Pennsylvania.

Many women were also sent over, some to work, some for sexual purposes, some to wive. Gustavus Meyers tells how, when a cry went up for females, London sent over 60 young women, who were auctioned off at from a hundred to one hundred and sixty pounds of tobacco each. Beverley remarks that the Virginia planters, instead of demanding dowries, were so hard up for women "it was a common thing for them to buy a deserving wife, that carried good testimonials of her character, at the price of one hundred pounds, and make themselves believe they had a bargain."

Children, too, especially orphans, were indented. Ten-year-olds were bound for nine years or more. In that time, they could not contract matrimony and had to be at the master's services day and night. They were supposed to be taught their letters and a trade, and at the expiration of the period, to receive two good suits. Young girls, as described so vividly in Van Wyck Mason's novel, *Three Harbours*, had no redress against the toil, the floggings or sexual abuses inflicted by their masters.

In New York the immigrants were turned over to grafting Governor Hunter, who quartered them on Governors Island. The able-bodied were sent up the Hudson to work on Livingston Manor and the estates of friends. Perfidy, fraud and extortion featured this activity. The immigrants had to remain in helpless slavery from three to four or more years, unless, getting into communication with the Indians, they could escape.

In New York, after those freed or escaped had settled in some place and were about to bring in their crops, the governor would descend on them anew to tell them they had no valid title to their lands and to demand payment so exorbitant they would have to become bonded servants again or scatter elsewhere, losing all.

In most places paupers were subject to being sold into slavery. Thomas Low Nichols noted that this occurred in New Hampshire far into the nineteenth century, long after Independence. Speaking of personal knowledge of his own town of Orford, he says: "Every year at town-meeting, the paupers of the town were sold at auction. . . . The pauper was a slave, sold for a year at a time, but sold yearly as long as he lived."

But bad as were conditions, they were not as bad as in the old country. On feudal estates the democratic touch prevailed to a degree it never had in Europe. The days, twice a year, when the tenants came to pay their rent, in cash or in kind, became, as in New York, gala occasions on which the landlord entertained with a barbecue and "plentiful draughts" of "Sopus ale." It was a relatively cheap *beau geste* to keep folk contented. The freeholders under the political domination of the estates, even the tenants, were not always badly off, and certainly in few places any worse off than most of the same group today nearly three centuries later. Slaves were often handsomely treated. Lyman Beecher says that in North Guilford—which may have been more genial about such things than the South—"slavery was very lenient." He tells us of Moses, "quite the man of business," who sent his master's son to college, paid the bills, managed the farm, rang the church bell, and was factotum. "He lived a slave because he was a king." In America many indented servants worked their way to liberty easier than was ever done in the old country. Many eventually became freeholders. Many with little more than the clothes on their backs, a gun and an ax, trudged into the wilderness to settle. The tenant who presumed to evade these landlord monopolies became a criminal and was so punished.

Even so it was hard to control these semi-slaves on the open frontier. Many escaped to other colonies and squatted on new lands, preferring the danger of death from Indian arrows, storms, snows, and hardship rather than the cruelties on the estates and manors. By 1726,

100,000 squatters had moved into Pennsylvania; between 1732 and 1740, 400,000 acres were taken without grants. The great Livingston Manor, the largest estate in New York, at one time was left with only five hands. It was pretty good evidence that the mass of colonists were not keen about remaining in subservience to the feudal lords. Probably most of the baronial landlords of the Washington type treated their serfs, slaves and tenants with sufficient largess for the times, which is not saying too much. Their rule was firm. There were even stories told of overseers being locked in dungeons and Negroes being whipped to death. George Turberville of Hickory Hill used to chain his coachman to the seat. Most of the owners had a fondness for Negro wenches.

But they were all semi-aristocrat gentlemen, signing "Gent." after their names, a recognized title that had legal safeguards and privileges, so that it is little wonder that even today a southerner cannot say five sentences without using the word with pious and self-incriminating inflection, although the title as such, together with its later snob inflections, has now largely no practical application, except in our 95th Article of War and the minds of the American officer caste.

The owner of Mount Vernon enjoyed the full pre-eminence of his class in society: the best luxury of the times; a range of apparel now considered flamboyant; a fine array of wigs; much fox-hunting in blue coats, white cassimere waistcoat, black breeches and boots. He had full access to the best findings of knowledge, all the latest gadgets, among them quite a number of false teeth, most remarkable those days, that flopped up and down when he ate or talked. He had the best physicians of the day at his beck and call, which merely meant that he was killed off before his time. His library was strong on books of husbandry, such as *Parterres, Groves, Wilderness, Labyrinths, Avenues, Parks, etc. After a more Grand and Rural Manner than has been done Before.* In accordance with this volume he kept up a great expanse of turf, *"the parterre en grande"* (page Veblen!), and a deer park without deer. He bumped over the countryside in the big carriage, or "chariot," with high-perched coachman, a lumbering equipage which required four to six horses straining at the traces to get it through muddy highways.

Many of the feudal Colonial lords, in their powdered wigs, knee-breeches and silver buckles, silk, gold, lace and ruffles, comported themselves with real pomp, often licentiousness, knowing no restraint except their own individual and usually arrogant wills. Colonel Smith used only the finest silks, wore only embroidered belts worth $550, used a Turkish scimitar, and had twelve Negro slaves as personal attendants. A powdered wig and a cocked hat, apparel none too well anchored in place, were also useful in promoting a careful starchy, stiff-necked carriage, so essential to appear highborn and important, and in fact made the leaders of society "look like the born lords of creation."

Laws, in some cases, prevented inferiors from imitating their dress or using articles of luxury.

Often the feudal baron, like the good feudal lords they were, had their distinct flags and insignias; many estates were fortified and protected by armed soldiery; often the indented colonists had to take an oath of fealty and allegiance.

They controlled the political and religious life of the colonies even after the proprietorships and company controls broke down. In Virginia this control was very enduring. In New York larger land grants provided the owner the privilege of "patronage of all and every church," and the sending of a representative to the General Assembly. Landed proprietors automatically became legislators—a hereditary right.

In 1764 Lieutenant Governor Cadwallader Colden protested to the Lords of Trade in London that the landed proprietors in conjunction with wealthy New York merchants, both utilizing "deluded" common farmers, had set themselves up as the law-making class.

In other colonies also they so controlled property and the voting apparatus. The right to vote was everywhere so hedged about with property and other restrictions that they were bound to be elected. They naturally voted to free themselves not only of all quitrents but of every other tax on their lands.

Gradually the merchants of New Amsterdam and Fort Orange, superseded the "sham lords" of the patroon grants, and formed the backbone of the colony. The merchants of Boston very early overshadowed the farming class and everywhere many of the plantation owners, who with their highly commercial crops were engaged in trade, were thoroughly imbued with the mercantile spirit. They were far from being feudal aristocrats in the European sense.

But for our story, they are important as great planters ruling over the lives of others, for they were the instruments for an initial betrayal of the American earth and of the people in relation to the soil—a betrayal still strongly mirrored in the present.

The plantation system, with its unfree labor and plentiful land, began those habits in American agriculture that depleted the soil, which disregarded conservation or replacement of fertility. Absenteeism aggravated the evil. If a few planters concerned themselves with sound husbandry, and we find very early records in Virginia of associations formed for that purpose, most merely lived off the cream. William Smith, writing about 1750, noted of New York that "Gentlemen of estates rarely reside in the country, and hence few or no experiments have yet been made in agriculture . . . little recourse to art for manuring and improving their lands." In many places the plantation emphasized the single cash crop. Careless methods became the rule, because land and labor were cheaper than machinery or improvements, an attitude which has ruined a vast area of America, much of it forever, and much of it for a thousand years or more.

However much in so many places large landholding overshadowed the economic and political system, it would be a grave distortion of the Colonial picture to give only the land-monopoly and feudal side of it. If in much of New York, Virginia, Maryland, the Carolinas, later in Georgia, and in other large regions, there were only the well-to-do landlords, contrasted with the indented servants, Negro slaves and very poor White, by no means all rural inhabitants—especially in New England, New Jersey and Pennsylvania or the uplands of the southern states—belonged to the two extremes of life.

Many settlers, if their mode of life was humble and restricted, were intrinsically free men, who would (or their sons would) build themselves into independent prosperity. Many communities came with a common fund to buy land. Many individuals had enough sav-

ings to make a good start. The buying up of the shares of the Massachusetts Bay Company by the immigrants themselves, and their
transference to the colony, indicates the prompt determination of
many of the New Englanders to gain complete economic and political
autonomy.

Numerous pictures of New England and of the Quakers in Pennsylvania give us the feeling of solid, pleasant communities, based on
kindliness and democratic tolerance and the satisfaction of material
and spiritual needs. "The terms democrat and aristocrat had not got
into use," said one writer, speaking of his boyhood in New England
just before the arrival of the Nineteenth Century. "These distinctions
and the feelings now implied by them had indeed no existence in the
hearts of the people. . . . The feuds between Ups and Downs, which
have since disturbed the whole fabric of society, had not yet begun."

Toward the time of the Revolution, we read more and more accounts of comfortable middle-class living, especially as to food. "Nuts,
raisins, cakes, wine, punch, hot & cold; all in great plenty," and similar descriptions thread through the tales of social and family gatherings. Every girl was supposed to have a pillowcase full of stockings
of her own knitting before she was married after due "chimney-
corner courtship." Geese feather beds and enormous woodpiles became indexes of prosperity and naïve social status. Men got gloriously
drunk on rum, and the ladies on "Hopkins' Elixir." And no morning
prayer was complete without its Tansey bitters. This tippling was for
many part of a lusty, industrious and ever-expanding life.

More and more there was a fervent desire to impart education to
all, even when heating was so poor that the ink froze on the pen.
The "attachment to education" in New England, wrote Timothy
Dwight, "is universal." In settlements where the inhabitants were
still roughing it in log huts, one would see neat schoolhouses erected.

Of the more middle-class farming communities which gradually
grew up after several centuries, Samuel Griswold Goodrich has given
a good picture of Ridgefield—a place of 1,200 people, comprising
two-hundred families—as he remembered it in his boyhood, in 1790,
shortly after the Revolution: Society was exclusively English, the
manners and customs modified by the "influence of existing circum-

stances." To our modern amusement, he adds, "I remember but one Irishman, one Negro, and one Indian in the town. . . . We had a professed beggar, called Jagger, and one settled pauper, Mrs. Yabacomb, who . . . was my standard type for the witch of Endor. . . ."

"All could read and write, but in point of fact, beyond the *Almanac* and Watts' *Psalms and Hymns,* their literary acquirements had little scope . . ." though there were then four newspapers in the state, and in Ridgefield "a public library of some two hundred volumes."

Nearly all the Ridgefielders were farmers. "Even the persons not professionally devoted to agriculture, had each his farm or at least his garden and home lot, with his pigs, poultry, and cattle. . . ."

His father carried on a well-stocked farm of forty acres "besides preaching two sermons a week, and attending to other parochial duties—visiting the sick, attending funerals, solemnizing marriages, etc. . . ."

There is also much of the good life of contentment, industry and honest conscience in the memoirs of Dr. Lyman Beecher of North Guilford, Connecticut, an account written on the very eve of the Revolution:

"Our living was very good. Rye bread, fresh butter, buckwheat cakes and pie for breakfast. . . . Anne and I helped aunt milk. Then they made cheese and spun until dinner. We dined on salt pork, vegetables, and pies; corned beef also; and always on Sunday, a boiled Indian pudding. We made a stock of pies at Thanksgiving, froze them for winter's use, and they lasted till March. . . .

"In the evening we visited, chatted, ate apples, drunk cider and told stories. On Sunday nights the boys went a courting."

Thomas Low Nichols, who had a trenchant pen for any and all abuses, wrote of Orford, New Hampshire, in the early Nineteenth Century in a way that showed the rapid progress of democracy in that earlier land-monopolized state. "There were no landlords in this country, almost every man owned the land he cultivated," and the "proprietor of hundreds of acres worked harder than any man he could hire." Employers and employees "associated on terms of perfect equality." He paints attractive pictures of the laborious and contented, often gay life, the tinkling sleigh rides over the moonlit frozen landscape, the suppers and dances, of the lucky chap who in husking bees came on a red ear of corn which entitled him to kiss the girl next to him.

Such accounts as these, though they also tell of dawn-to-dark industriousness, of never-ending husbandry and toil, hint that many of the European interlopers on this continent had gradually come to pretty decent terms and understanding with their environment.

However, the dominant large plantation system in many places weighed heavily enough, and echoes of discontent were constant.

In petition after petition from the frontier towns of Massachusetts, folk protested against absentee proprietors and their own unfair burden of taxes, the forced labor of building forts and patrolling the region for the benefit of others. In 1681 the people of Mendon reported they could not build a Lord's house "unless others who are proprietors as well as ourselves (the price of whose land is much raysed by our carrying on public work and will be nothing worth if we are forced to quit the place) doo beare an equal share in Town charges."

Jonathan Edwards declared in 1751 that in Northampton, for half a century, politics was divided between "our great proprietors of land" and those "concerned about land and other matters." Class conflicts against the large proprietors over the ownership and disposal of common lands were frequent in Massachusetts towns throughout the Eighteenth Century.

In many of the colonies discontent flared into open armed rebellion as that of Bacon in Virginia, when Charles II, after his restoration, granted large tracts of land belonging to the colony to favorites. The dispossessed and the small farmers, denied the vote, seeing themselves submerged by the Church-State combination of wealthy planters, took arms in hand. Later, the revolt of small farmers, immigrants and freed indented servants, against Governor Alexander Spotswood, obeyed similar causes.

In 1734 and subsequently, disorder racked Georgia—even under the mild proprietary rule set up by philanthropist Oglethorpe—as people saw their equitable system falling to pieces by the grabbing landholders.

North Carolina was long turbulent, right down to the Revolution, with agrarian disorder, directed against Lord Granville and other proprietors. The poorer farmers, crowded on scrubby lands, resented the broad fertile tobacco acres cultivated by swarms of Blacks. The "piney wood" folks, who put "Christian character and kindness before rank and position," hated the delicate women of the plantation coast, reared in luxury, steeped in ignorance and affectations, and the men, who if well-educated in England, were often so effeminate-looking, more pucker-lipped than their women. The people of the coast did not talk openly in economic terms; their economics mostly took the twice-removed form of disliking folk knowing nothing of rice, indigo or the Episcopalian prayer book; their text was "you can't raise a gentleman above tidewater." Some poor freeholders, getting neither political rights nor economic justice, went off west to be really free men, founders of empire; but not all could thus solve their problems and merely had to eke out a bare existence, to become "poor white trash" (in the Low country "poor buckra")—and a blight on the nation.

In South Carolina, as William Watts Ball points out, from the very first "proprietors and colonists were far apart. Proprietors were investors. They wanted dividends. Colonists were pioneers. They wanted loans." This authentic difference was finally to bring about the 1719 revolution under Colonel James Moore, which established home rule, not however for the real settlers who backed the movement, but for the local plantation class. Then the relative division between rich profit-makers and pioneers wanting credit and also good land became that between Low country planters and the Up country "wool-hats."

Much of the agrarian unrest in the Carolinas, from even before Independence on, often found its expression in banditry. Upcountrymen, many of them disgruntled soldiers of the Indian wars, rustled cattle and robbed. Bands of "Regulators" used lynch law tactics to keep them in order—and, as usually happens, became a greater menace to orderly folk than the original marauders. Ill-feeling and violence marred the relations of the two classes right down to the Civil War, when regional patriotism brought temporary unity.

The Leisler revolt in New York at the end of the Seventeenth Century, though it involved controversies within the Dutch Reformed Church, also struck a blow, if only temporary, at vested interests of the planters. Wealthy owners were flung into jail; plantations were confiscated. But Leisler was soon enough executed.

In Western Pennsylvania in 1754, the frontier "Paxton boys" demanded by their actions—though they based their rebellion on Quaker failure to protect them from Indians—the right to share in political priviliges along with the older part of the colony, and behind this was the idea also of redressing agrarian and taxation wrongs. For Pennsylvania, the Revolution was largely a dual revolt: against England, and also of the interior against the Quaker and Episcopalian land aristocracy and commercial dominance of the coast.

Every colony had its local issues, differing from those elsewhere, but these and other revolts were outbursts of popular discontent, largely against the oppressive form in which land was held, against discriminatory taxation, and lack of political rights. These evils were a contributing cause of the American Revolution, and of westward migration. Many crossed the Alleghenies, risking danger, suffering hardships, to seek the land and the opportunity they could not obtain on the seaboard.

CHAPTER VI

THE WESTWARD URGE

The settlement of America is pictured in the schoolbooks as an experiment in freedom. But America was founded, in good part, upon class lines, on principles of economic and political injustice, often tyranny and religious bigotry. Tolerance was not a strong point with the early comers.

The so-called democratic liberties of the United States have all been won by hard struggle. The westward movement was part and parcel of that struggle.

We do not need to turn to the hob-nailed ridicule in Butler's *Hudibras* or the Cavalier jibes of Macaulay to remind us of the intolerable solemnity and ignorance that featured many sides of ecclesiastical rule in Colonial times. Self-righteous Massachusetts was for years a tight little theocratic tyranny, long ruled by terror, based on dogmatism and superstition. The witchcraft trials were an expression, not merely of ignorance, superstition, and fear of a new environment, but of terrorism as definite in its implications of power-politics as the Inquisition or the O.G.P.U. For a considerable time only church members could vote, and in places Congregationalist pastors were paid by public tax until into the Nineteenth Century. Massachusetts was long as definitely a totalitarian régime as Germany or Russia is today.

When in 1656 two Quakeresses, Ann Austin and Mary Fisher, arrived in the colony, they were at once arrested, threatened with trial for witchcraft, finally deported to Barbados. Other Quakers were whipped out by cat-o'-nine-tails, had their tongues bored, or were murdered. Quakers were hung in Boston in 1659 and 1660. Baptist Obadiah Holmes, visiting Lynn, was given thirty strokes on the bare back with a three-corded whip. Too compassionate bystanders were arrested, fined, threatened with whipping. Religion had become a bully. At Dover, three Quakeresses were tied, stripped to the waist, to the end of a cart in bitter winter cold and forced to trudge "half-leg deep" through the snow. At each town they were whipped on their bare backs. The sadism of religious bigotry, perverted sexual suppression, and narrow-mindedness could go no further. Such things remind us of Chesterton's description of the place as "a madhouse where religious maniacs had broken loose and locked up their keepers."

New York under Governor Peter Stuyvesant had its own period of persecution. Quakers were imprisoned; the hosts of Quakers were banished or otherwise punished. Robert Hempstead was whipped on his bare back with a thick pitch rope till he keeled over. He was left on the ground, the sun beating down on his bruised, swollen body until nightfall.

Maryland in 1649, school children are brightly told, passed America's first law of religious tolerance permitting another sect, besides the state church, to function; but school children are not taught that that law punished seditious speeches and acts by unlimited imprisonment, slitting the nose, boring of the tongue, cutting off one or both ears, whipping, branding with a hot iron on hand or forehead, amputation of the right hand or being nailed by the ears in pillory. Hitler is almost a gentleman compared to our good ancestors.

Obviously many of the folk who soon enough moved on west were people who found Colonial society little to their liking.[1] They

[1] Of course no single-track theory explains westward migration. Soil depletion often forced even the wealthy to go west. The cattle and dairy industry caused well-to-do New Englanders to search constantly for new wide grass meadows. Conservative elements, disgusted with the breakdown of religious structures or the adaptation of new liberal laws, went off in a huff to the West in large groups to attempt once more to create and maintain a rigid closed-in system. And wonder, love of adventure, hope, excitement, swept over communities in recurrent waves of contagious enthusiasm to break the moorings of even the most contented, successful and sober-minded. Here I am merely examining certain persistent economic factors of major importance.

sensed its hypocrisies or felt its harshness; often were hedged about economically, deprived of a voice in affairs of state, unwilling to bend the knee to severe religious laws, or appalled by the superstitions and the intolerance. They were social rebels, who instead of rebelling (having no need to rebel because of the spaciousness of the continent) moved to new lands.

Many of the original settlers—though there were also adventurers, criminals, paupers, folk seeking their fortunes—had come to American shores in the same way, to escape evil situations. Rebels in the Old World, they preferred to escape to a freer haven to become colonizers on an unknown shore, rather than face the music at home.

But soon after their escape, they hardened the shell of their beliefs still more. And so we have this repeated phenomenon in American life of people emigrating to escape intolerance, emigrating from a too rigid social scheme, emigrating from land monopoly and abridged economic opportunity, and settling down in new places, then elevating their own rebellious creed to the same intolerant dominance. The westward urge is a consistent repetition of this pattern. Folk escaped from hard little islands of political and economic and spiritual dogma, only to build new little islands equally intolerant. New schism was the inevitable result. It is all like the biological life-cycle of the jellyfish, in which polyps affixed to rocks are converted into mobile medusae, and medusae into polyps, an alteration of generations.

Just as the English and other governments looked contemptuously down upon the malcontents who fled to the New World, so, in very human fashion, the new rulers of the arbitrary seaboard colonies, despite their own history, similarly looked down on many of those who went as shiftless, shameless troublemakers—a good riddance.

Timothy Dwight, President of Yale College (a stuffy Eighteenth Century reactionary, unreflectively faithful to the myths of his institutions and his class in society), in his four volumes of *Travels in New England and New York* (New Haven, 1821-24), harshly describes the type:

Those "first inclined to emigrate," he says, "are usually such, as have met with difficulties at home!" These pioneers were unable to "live in regular society . . . too idle; too talkative; too passionate;

too prodigal; and too shiftless; to acquire either property or character." They were "impatient of the restraints of law, religion and morality," grumbled about taxes, "by which Rulers, Ministers and school-masters are supported"; they complained "incessantly, as well as bitterly, of the extortions of mechanics, farmers, merchants, and physicians," to whom they were always indebted.

At the same time they were usually possessed "in their own view, of uncommon wisdom," understood "medical science, politics, and religion" better than those "who studied such things all their lives"; although they managed their own concerns "worse than other men," they felt perfectly satisfied that they could manage those of the nation "far better than the agents, to whom they are committed by the public."

Of course, "the public," during early days, consisted only of those who had property and university presidents. Others could not vote. And as late as the eighteen-twenties, the wage of common laborers in Boston was only twenty-five cents a day. Governor Bellomont of Massachusetts and New York advised the Lords of Trade in 1700 that the reason colonists were leaving for Pennsylvania and New Jersey was that people were "cramped . . . for want of land," and would be fools "to become a base tenant."

Dwight (with punctuation that these later days would flunk a freshman) continues: "After displaying their own talents, and worth; after censuring the weakness, and wickedness of their superiors; after exposing the injustice of the community in neglecting to invest persons of such merit with public offices; in many an eloquent harangue uttered by many a kitchen fire, in every blacksmith's shop, and in every corner of the streets; and find all their efforts in vain; they become at length discouraged; and under the pressure of poverty, the fear of gaol, and consciousness of public contempt, leave their native places, and betake themselves to the wilderness. . . . We have many troubles even now; but we should have many more, if this body of foresters had remained at home."

We have heard this same chant from the smug prosperous in all ages, and in our own times, and quite as frequently from our college presidents. But a vast continent was not seized and settled merely by misfits, radicals and quarrelsome folk; it was filled up by people seeking opportunities denied them by the class for which the good Yale president was unconsciously the dutiful spokesman.

Hamlin Garland, born of those western settlers, saw far more truly "that these plowmen, these wives and daughters had been pushed out into these lonely ugly shacks by the force of landlordism behind. These plodding Swedes and Danes, these thrifty Germans, these hairy Russians had all fled from the feudalism of their native lands and were here because they had no share in the soil from which they had sprung, and because in the settled communities of the eastern states, the speculative demand for land had hindered them from acquiring even a leasing right to the surface of the earth."

The discontented ones saw reason enough to emigrate. They were often better educated than the small pseudo-aristocratic circle that excluded them. They resented the pompous "powder-heads"—the upstage users of powdered wigs—who often could not spell their names or "do the rule of three." In old records such remarks as, "It was the remains of feudalism in Virginia that my father came more and more to dislike, and that finally determined him to move to a newer country."

Whole counties in the East were practically depopulated. People squeezed in upon poor lands by big landlords, simply pulled up stakes and left and whole towns followed along. People burned down their cabins and store buildings in order to salvage the nails with which to build anew far in the wilderness.

Dwight tells how these foresters, going into the wilderness, cut down the trees, girdled others, furnished themselves with an "ill-built log house, and a worse barn," and reduced the forest to fields. "The forests furnish browse; feed a few cattle; and with these, and the penurious products of their labour, eked out by hunting and fishing, they keep their families alive."

Even as Dwight meagerly describes the process it does not sound like the life of an easy-going idler. But for him the foresters were merely shiftless no-accounts. When a less energetic but perhaps more frugal and systematic settler would come along with a little money, but unwilling to tackle the hardships of the wilderness, Dwight notes, the forester would sell out, because he hated "sober industry and prudent economy, by which his bush pasture might be changed into a farm, and himself raised to thrift and independence." Receiving "more money than he ever before had had in his life"—Dwight fails to note, precisely because of his efforts—the forester pushed on to repeat the process.

Benjamin Rush of Pennsylvania was little less eulogistic: "The first settler in the woods is generally a man who has outlived his credit or fortune in the cultivated parts of the state. His time for migrating is the month of April."

The log cabin he built was small, usually windowless, the floors of earth, the roof of split logs. Corn was sowed "with but little cultivation," and yielded "in the month of October following from forty to fifty bushels by the acre."

In 1936, the average national yield, despite all our present-day science and efficiency, was only 16.5 bushels per acre. In Colonial times, yields of even sixty bushels were not uncommon, and out in Tennessee and Kentucky, the yield came up to eighty, even ninety bushels. The settlers would have been foolish indeed to have worked especially hard—they had no market for surplus production; and until they could accumulate live-stock, pigs particularly, excess crops merely depleted the soil and rotted in the fields and the granaries. The nation would someday need the fertility they so frequently did waste.

The settler's family, continues Rush, was "fed during the summer by a small quantity of grain which he carried with him, and by fish and game. . . . He endures a great deal of distress from hunger, cold, and a variety of accidental causes, but he seldom complains or sinks under them. As he lives in the neighborhood of Indians, he soon acquires a strong tincture of their manners. . . . He eats, drinks and sleeps in dirt and rags. . . .

"In proportion as population increases around him, he becomes uneasy and dissatisfied." He has to confine his cattle, put up fences. The wild game disappears. "Above all he revolts against the operation of laws. He cannot bear to surrender up a single natural right for all the benefits of governments—and therefore he abandons his little settlement, and seeks a retreat in the woods, where he again submits to all the toils . . . mentioned."

But even self-satisfied Dwight is obliged to admit that "a considerable number of even these people [the foresters] become sober, industrious citizens, merely by the acquisition of property," and he concludes with smug assurance: "The love of property to a certain degree seems indispensable to the existence of sound morals," a generalization that reflects the authentic triteness of the great American middle class and its cramped respectability and lends itself to many somber reflections.

Dwight's lack of understanding of social and psychological forces is monumental. Nor did he glimpse, from his staid polished security, that majestic call of the continent that made America what it is today. His limited understanding, his love of precise neatness, do not compare favorably in the light of today with the fierce passion of liberty which pushed out the frontier—love of personal liberty, the poetry of far, free places, the manly fortitude of matching the individual will with untamed Nature—all that genius of untrammeled freedom and contempt for the petty routine of organized life based on injustices; in all, a dream which spelled progress and greatness. The loss of it by any people or any nation soon enough brings about decay and eventual meanness of life.

Dwight's words are far more censorious for the courageous clearers of the forest than those who followed on their heels, "allured by the prospect of gain [which] is presented in every new country to the sagacious, from the purchase and sale of lands." The latter, not the American settler, not those who risked their lives and whose labor built America, but the speculators, those who are eventually to steal the better part of the continent, aroused Dwight's admiration.

But the frontiersman and the forester, however savage they became, were the men who made the great westward movement possible. They were the shock troopers, endowed with both realism and vision, the men who risked death—for parsons and college presidents. They have received some scant post-mortem reward. Today Daniel Boone is a school-child hero, but Timothy Dwight is known only to historical researchers.

Dwight, whatever his stodgy smugness, was an able observer, and —quite inconsistent with his thesis of shiftlessness—tells vividly of the bold, difficult process of taming the frontier.

The settler "after he has completed his shelter . . . begins to clear a spot of ground: i.e. to remove the forest, by which it is covered. This is done in two ways; *girdling* and *felling* the *trees*. . . . The latter has now become the almost universal practice; and wherever it can be adopted, is undoubtedly to be preferred. The trees are cut down, either in the autumn, or as early as it can be done in the spring; that they may become so dry as to be easily burnt up in the ensuing summer. After they have lain a sufficient time, he sets fire to them, lying as they fell. If he is successful, the greater part of them are consumed in the conflagration. The remainder he cuts with his axe into pieces of convenient length; rolls them into piles; and sets fire to them again. In this manner they are all consumed; and the soil is left light, dry and covered with ashes. These, so far as he can, he collects and conveys to a manufactory of potashes if there be any in the neighborhood; if not, he leaves them to enrich the soil. In many instances the ashes, thus gathered, will defray the expense of clearing the land. . . .

"After the field is burned over . . . *a drag*, with very stout iron teeth resembling in its form the capital letter A . . . is drawn over the surface a sufficient number of times to make it mellow, and afterwards to cover the seed. A plough . . . would soon be broken into pieces by the roots of trees. . . .

"His next labour is to procure a barn: generally large, well framed, covered, and roofed. Compared with his house it is a palace."

In many ways the pioneer and huntsman, though they were in more danger from Indians, lived a freer life than later more sedate settlers who followed behind and who, after a lifetime of toil, found themselves in old age, broken and with no great accumulation of property.

There was something pathetic, yet magnificent about all those escapists who sought freedom on the fringe. They toiled and suffered for that individual freedom as have few men. They also gave America in the end a freedom it did not have when it was founded. We have, for instance, the astounding but fairly typical record of Seth Hubbel, who in February, 1789, with an ox-cart team, one horse and cow, went from Norwalk, Connecticut, to Wolcott, Vermont, to start a farm, his family consisting of his wife and five children, all girls, the eldest nine or ten years old.[1]

A hundred miles before reaching Wolcott, one of his oxen failed, but Hubbel kept him yoked till about ten each day, then took the animal's place in the yoke, and thus managed to get within fourteen miles of his goal. The sick ox could go no further, and he left it with Thomas W. McConnel in Johnson. As the latter had no hay or grain, in near by Cambridge, Seth "interceded" with a man for a little hay, which he carried "a bundle at a time, five miles, for about ten days," through the snowdrifts, to keep the animal alive.

From McConnel's, Hubbel struggled on six miles farther to "Esq. McDaniels" at Hyde Park, where the road ended. By then it was the 20th of March, the snow was four feet deep; there was no hay for his animals and no way for them to browse.

But guided only by marked trees, he set out with his wife and the two oldest children on snowshoes to cover the eight miles to Wolcott, where an "Esq. Taylor," his wife and two small children were the only settlers. To the east and west the nearest inhabitants were eighteen to twenty miles away, but no road existed. To the north stretched only virgin wilderness clear to Canada.

He had reached the end of his journey, but had "not a mouthful of meat or kernel of grain" for his family, nor "a cent of money left to buy with." But he got some moose-meat from an Indian and had the good luck to catch "a saple," which he had to pack home five miles. He then carried the skin fifty miles to exchange it for a bushel of wheat which he carried home on his back. "We had then lived three weeks without bread."

He brought the three youngest children from Hyde Park eight miles away on his back, one at a time, and in the same way he gradually lugged his possessions to his new home.

Until the first crop could be put in and harvested, he had to make

[1] Quoted in *We Were New England*.

sixty mile trips into New Hampshire for the scant rations he had for his family.

He had expected to get fifty acres to farm, apparently on shares, but instead, he had to sell the yoke of oxen and his horse to get land. He kept only the cow, which died the next winter.

The second fall he bought another cow, but in June it was killed. It left a heifer calf that in the following fall was accidentally choked to death. He then bargained for two cows "to double in four years." But before that time was up; one of his own died in calving, one was killed in fighting, another was found dead in the yard. A neighbor's oxen hooked and killed a two-year-old bull. So he was left destitute and still had to pay for the lost cattle.

"But there was a door opened." He heard that a Haverhill merchant was buying snakeroot and sicili. With the help of the two oldest girls, he dug and dried "a horse-load," and carried it on his back. But this was "like most hearsay reports of fine markets, always a little way ahead, for he [the merchant] knew nothing about this strange article, and would not even venture to make an offer; but after a long conference, I importuned with another merchant to give me a three-year-old heifer for my roots, on certain conditions too tedious to mention. I drove her home, and with joy she was welcomed to my habitation."

When Hubbel came to Wolcott, his tools consisted of merely an ax and an old hoe, but he cleared about two acres. Then, being short of provisions, he had to work out most of the time till harvest "with scarce a sufficiency to support nature." When too faint, for want of food, to labor, he used to take fish from the river, broil it on the coals and eat it without bread or salt—"and then to my work again. . . ."

The first season he couldn't get a single potato to plant, but he secured eight quarts of seed corn for "two and half yards of whitened linen, yard wide"—an extortion, he calls it—and this he "had to go twenty miles for." Frost ruined his crop, so he got nothing at all the first year, not even his seed back.

Being out of bread-corn to alleviate the family's distress, he had to go off with his sickle to Lake Champlain for the harvest, some forty miles. But the grain there was not ripe yet, so he went on to Grand Isle, trading two lances in a case for boat passage. But on Grand Isle also it was too early. However, after pleading his case, he was allowed to stay on. He worked until he had received as pay a bushel and a half of wheat, a bit green at that.

A boat bound for Mansfield's mills on the Lemoille River took him and his grain along free. He had it ground, but it was so green and damp, it merely mashed. He then traded his sickle to get the meal carried to Cambridge borough, where he had it ground a second time. "It was still far from good meal." From the Borough he was fortunate enough to get the loan of a horse to get home on.

As he had been gone a fortnight, and his wife was frantic (he had had to leave his family without bread or meal), he "was welcomed home with tears." His wife baked a cake, and his children "again tasted bread."

Shortly after, he had the good fortune to buy on trust from a man in Cambridge twelve bushels of corn and one of wheat, and by digging on shares he also got twelve or thirteen bushels of potatoes. Friends helped him to get the produce part way, but even so he had to make twenty-six trips, sixteen miles a round trip, carrying the corn, wheat and potatoes home on his back.

He tells vividly of his problem of getting the grain home the first stage of the journey:

"Soon after I set out from home, sometimes in the month of March, it began to rain, and was rainy day and night. The Lemoille was raised—the ice become rotten and dangerous crossing—many of the small streams were broken up. The man of whom I purchased the grain was so good as to take his team and carry it to the mill. The owner of the mill asked me how I expected to get my meal home. I answered . . . that I knew not. The feeling man then offered me his oxen and sled to carry it to the Park, and I thankfully accepted his kind offer. He then turned to the miller, and directed him to grind my grist toll free. While at the mill a man requested me to bring a half hogshead tub on my sled up to Johnson. By permission of the owner of the oxen, he put the tub on the sled. . . . When I came to Brewster's branch, a wild stream, I found it broken up, run rapid and deep. . . . To go across with my bags on the sled would ruin my meal; I soon thought of the tub; this held about half of my bags, the other half I left on the shore, and proceeded into the branch and crossed with safety. Though I was wet nearly to my middle, I unloaded the tub and returned into the branch, holding the tub on the sled, but the stream was so rapid, the tub being empty, that in spite of my exertions, I was washed off."

He was carried down stream, holding on to the tub, more than twenty yards before he could make shore. The oxen, when they got across the stream, turned towards home, but happily stopped till he came up with the tub.

"I then . . . succeeded in getting the whole across the branch, and traveled about three miles and put up for the night. Wet as I was, and at that season of the year, it is easy to conceive my uncomfortable situation, for the thaw was over, and it was chilly and cold. In the morning I proceeded for home—came to the river; not being sensible how weak the ice was, I attempted to cross, but . . . when half across . . . I perceived the ice settling under my oxen. I jumped on to the tongue of my sled, and hastened to the oxen's heads and pulled out the pin that held the yoke. By this time the oxen were sunk to their knees in the water. I then sprang to the sled, and drawed it back to the shore. . . . By this time, they [the oxen] had broken a considerable path in the ice, and were struggling to get out. I could do nothing but stand and see them swim around—sometimes they would be nearly out of sight, nothing scarcely but their horns to be seen—they would then rise and struggle to extricate themselves from their perilous situation. I called for help in vain; and to fly for assistance would have been imprudent and fatal. . . . At length the oxen swam up to where I stood and laid their heads on the ice at my feet. Immediately I took the yoke from off their necks; they lay still till the act was performed, and then returned to swimming as before. By this time they had made an opening in the ice as much as two rods across. One of them finally swam to the down stream side, and in an instant, as if lifted out of the water, he was on his side on the ice and got up and walked off; the other swam to the same place and was out in the same way. . . . I then thought, and the impression is still on my mind, that they were helped out by supernatural means. . . . That a heavy ox six and half feet in girth, can of his own natural strength heave himself out of the water on his side on the ice, is too extraordinary to reconcile to a natural cause:— that in the course of Divine Providence events do take place out of the common course of nature, that our strongest reasoning can't comprehend, it is impious to deny."

He was fortunate enough to catch enough "saple" to pay for the grain, but soon was "destitute of meat." He had to have recourse to wild meat and had the good luck to purchase a moose from a hunter. Also he got the meat of two more, by bringing them in on shares. The latter two were uncommonly large, weighing seven hundred pounds each and requiring many trips, for he had to bring in the meat, the largest bones and the heads, on his back, packing them five or six miles over rough land, too cut up by ridges and hollows, too interspersed with underbrush and "windfalls," to utilize a handsled.

"My practice was to carry my loads in a bag, to tie the ends of the bag so nigh that I could but comfortably get my head through, so that the weight of the load would rest on my shoulders." Thaw made the task more severe; the coarse snow would hardly hold his snowshoes. Without any warning he would suddenly break through and slide under a log or into the bush in the snow, his load about his neck. Repeatedly he had "to struggle in this situation for some time to extricate" himself.

All winter he had to gather firewood; in fact "my snowshoes were constantly hung to my feet."

He continues: "Being destitute of team for four or five years, and without farming tools, I had to labor under great embarrassments; my grain I hoed in the first three years. After I raised a sufficiency for my family, I had to carry it twelve miles to mill on my back, for the first three years; this I had constantly to do once a week. My common load was one bushel, and generally carried it eight miles before I stopped to rest. My family necessities once obliged me to carry a moose-hide thirty miles on my back and sell it for a bushel of corn and bring that home in the same way."

Oftentimes he had to get out anyway and tramp down the snow for miles merely to be sure he and his family would not be marooned. The first snow after he came in, the year he settled there, was fully two feet deep. As it was vital to keep communications open with Hyde Park, he and Esq. Taylor started before sunrise. They sank deep into the light snow; by noon it gave still more; their snowshoes being buried at every step. "We had to use nearly our whole strength to extricate the loaded shoe from its hold. It seemed that our hip joints would be drawn from their sockets. We were soon worried— could go but a few steps without stopping; our fatigue and toil became almost insupportable—were obliged often to sit down and rest, and were several times on the point of giving up the pursuit and stop for the night, but this must have been fatal, as we had no axe to cut wood for a fire; our blood was heated, and we must have chilled."

They finally reached a deserted cabin, so tired they couldn't have gone "twenty rods further." The next day he returned home with a bushel of meal.

Once, having planned a trip, he woke up in the night, and the moon was shining so brightly he thought it was nearly day, so set out. Soon he could scarcely see, and as the route had pitfalls made by oxen, frequently fell. In his thin clothing, to keep warm he "had to exert the utmost strength to keep from freezing." He ran and jumped and fell some more. In all he ran nearly eight miles and reached Hyde Park just as the cocks were crowing day. He found the bottoms of his moccasins and socks cut through, his feet bare, but not frozen.

Once, setting traps for beaver, he and Taylor got caught in a snowstorm which wet them to the skin, so they had to keep on their feet all night. To get back, they followed streams through the alder bushes, their clothes frozen to their bodies. Hubbel's coat, when he managed to get it off, stood straight up on the floor. To save the traps they had to make another trip out and got—one solitary muskrat.

In 1806 an epidemic put five of his family in bed at the same time. His wife—who had borne her share of misfortunes "with becoming fortitude"—and a daughter died; another daughter was bedridden six months. Debts piled up, causing him to lose his farm—"my little all." But he adds, "Though I have been doomed by hard fortune, I have been blessed with numerous offspring; have had by my two wives, seventeen children, thirteen of them daughters; have had forty-seven grandchildren, and six great grandchildren, making my posterity seventy souls." He took little credit himself, instead ends his harrowing recital by "rendering" his "feeble thanks and praise" to his "benign Benefactor, who supplies the wants of the needy, and relieves the distressed."

Probably, even had stalwart Seth Hubbel known of the sneers of Timothy Dwight in his soft berth at the Yale University Chancellery, he wouldn't have given a damn. Seth was of the brave builders of the continent. Dwight, whatever his contributions, was mostly unctuous toward those who were to take the "little all" of the Hubbels.

CHAPTER VII

THE RELIGIOUS URGE

One of the impelling forces of westward migration was religion. The relation of man to the soil in America is interwoven with his religious creeds—not in the Indian sense of close communion—but because the American stepped out of a medieval era in which religion and ownership of the soil were closely interrelated. The new religious forms, both in Europe and America, were involved in the attempt to work out a new and freer utilization of the land.

The causes which drove men across the Atlantic and later out of the settled coast lands of the eastern seaboard, must in part be sought in the break-up of the traditional feudal religious pattern and culture of Europe itself and also in the still more accelerated break-up in America.

The weapons used in Europe against feudalism and Catholicism (which formed an integral part of feudalism) were (1) democracy, for that wrested political control from the monasteries, ecclesiastical authorities and the feudal estates and flung it into the city where the masses could be controlled by demagogic means; (2) land distribution, for that was a thrust at the economic control of both the feudal lords and the Church; (3) religious reform, for that broke down the reverence for the feudal Church and feudal power.

The break-up of authoritarian Catholicism obeyed mighty new economic forces, the rise of new social classes to power. As William Blake put it without finesse in *The World Is Mine:* "Protestantism was only parvenu capitalism too rapacious to divide with another master, the Church." The struggle demanded the stripping of the

Catholic Church of its economic prowess and political hegemony. The Church had been opposed to the amassing of wealth by the masses or the merchants, but it had fostered accumulation by the feudal landed aristocracy. The Church, one of the main instruments of that aristocracy to maintain its privileged position, was itself a mighty feudal property owner. The revolt of the mercantile class inevitably had to destroy, to the extent that it could, the religious and moral formulae by which the older class ruled. Also, the individual, discarding the Church's age-old strictures against the garnering of wealth, sought to justify his new obstreperous search for prosperity by approaching God on more intimate personal terms. And so, the religious battle, the false front of the economic battle—most men were quite unaware of the larger economic compulsives—raged bitterly.

Men—murdering each other in the name of God, flung about like so many atoms into the narrow sealed test-tubes of bitter sects—were merely trying to find a creed that fitted with the new facts of productive life. This new earnest searching for absolute religious truth—which of course does not exist—contributed unwittingly to the major economic battle. Few of the Crusaders probably thought beyond the holy impulses that led them across Europe to the Near East. Few even admitted their own personal love for adventure and hopes for personal gain; even less did they realize that they were thrusting at the Mohammedan forces, not merely because of religion, but because the old trade routes had been closed. In the name of religion, they were unconsciously fighting the new battle of the rising mercantile classes.

The various sects that broke away from Holy Rome and went overseas were also obeying and furthering this same mercantile urge—often they themselves openly combined religion and profit, and never once saw the connection.

The revolt against Catholicism took on various guises: (1) Opposition to the *forms* of Catholicism, an attempt to modify ritual, and thereby break down the moral monopoly of the Church. (2) Opposition to the political power of the Church, through the creation of democratic congregations. (3) Rebellion against the economic power of the Church by the formation of communal Church groups or individualistic embryo capitalist groups.

Two tendencies, diametrically opposite, though sometimes illogically intermingled, resulted from the revolt against the forms of the Church: (a) an attempt to rationalize religion in terms of the individual; (b) an attempt to recover the vital mysticism of the Church.

Also, certain of the early sects had a definite national race basis, behind which, of course, was the same thrust of the new trading class. In England long-smoldering hatred of the aristocratic Norman conquerors produced the Lollard movement, and probably also helped bring into existence the Church of England. The Normans were the feudal barons, the aristocrats; Catholicism, their religion. It was a conquest religion. This same belated nationalistic destruction of feudal Catholicism is occurring in Russia, Germany, Mexico and Spain in our own day.

The racial nationalism in the earlier English revolt represented a deep antipathy to the outsider, which in the New World may quite possibly have contributed a bit to the rigid resistance to mingling with the Indian.

Eventually the official English Church came to represent merely a new authoritarianism set up by a successful mercantile State which had largely, but not entirely, rid itself of feudal political domination —in short was a compromise institution resulting from the penetration of the feudal ranks by wealthy merchants become snobs, and the turning of members of the old aristocracy to the newer, lucrative, if despised, allurements of trade. It had its faint parallel in our own South after the carpet-bag era, in the gradual political fusion of the old slaveholding aristocracy with new industrialists and finance-politicians, except that Ku Klux Klanism (the political counterpart of the Inquisition or the witchcraft trials in earlier epochs, or the O.G.P.U. terror trials in a modern epoch) had merely to ally itself with one or another of the already dominant Protestant sects.

In the thirteen colonies Episcopalianism, breeding a mentality more loyal to the British Crown, was made up predominantly of the wealthier landholding and shipping class. It helped perpetuate English cultural practices. Plays were produced in "Charles Town,"

South Carolina, as early as 1703, decades before such a worldly delusion was allowed in Quaker Philadelphia or in Puritan Boston, which still periodically makes itself ridiculous by its suppression of the stage.

But the new British ruling groups were not able by means of a new established Church to stay the full tide of revolt that had surged up against Catholicism and old forms. In England and later America, religious revolt went on to extremes that menaced even the new aristocrat-industrialist order. An initial revolution is often overwhelmed by subsequent higher waves. *"The Great Awakening"* was already in the offing—inevitable. The new religious diaspora was at hand. The search for spiritual reality, and with it a lot of new freedom, could not be stopped.

Wycliffe, the first great Reformation leader, could rid himself of only one little dogma: transubstantiation. John Huss, the next great leader, at first merely attacked fraudulent miracles. Even a hundred years after Huss, Luther, in his ninety-five propositions (though, of course, he did see clearly that old property rights were entangled with Catholicism), merely chided at the excessive sale of indulgences. But brick by brick the edifice of Catholic ritual, and along with it feudal privilege, was pulled down. The dyke broken, religious change came in a tossing flood.

Practically all the sects rejected many Catholic forms, confession, sacraments and Church hierarchy; the Quakers completely rejected baptism.

Many inner Presbyterian struggles swirled about the pivotal question of democratic organization. Calvin's Geneva theocratic state broke down in Scotland. There, as early as 1560, a General Assembly of ministers and laymen struck down the hierachy, put their bishops, abbots and priests on an equal footing.

In outside political affairs, the Presbyterians stood for the democratic rights of the middle and lower classes against aristocracy and Crown. John Melville, who railed against "the bloody knife of absolute authority," dared pluck James VI by the sleeve and call him "God's silly vassal." Of course, like the Communists of today, the radical Presbyterians were not so much interested in democracy, as in the power of their own sectarian organization. But they made a pattern for future political democracy.

In America, too, questions of democratic control and liberal interpretation of doctrines exercised the minds of Calvin's disciples for a century or more, causing constant strife, often open schisms.

Similarly the Quakers, Baptists, Mennonites, were all opposed to a hireling ministry: the Church should be composed of equals all equal in the sight of God, all with an equal voice in the management of Church affairs. The Baptists, Friends, later the Methodists and Progressive Dunkers, permitted women to preach. The Baptists even extend this right to inspired children. The Familistic and Antinomian sects lacked nearly all organization, were almost formless. These sects, also the Seekers, Ranters, Pietists, Separatists, Enthusiasts, Soul Sleepers, Levelers, Adamites, Traskites, Anabaptists, and numerous others, all revolved around new subtle changes in the forms of faith, new democracy, new systems of property control.

Perhaps the most outstanding and successful form of communalistic organization, in reality a species of theocratic capitalism, was the Moravian Church; later those of the Mormons and Tunkers. The American continent is still dotted with the remnants of such communal farming societies of various sects. Among other things, they represented, in the beginning, an attempt to organize non-serf, new mercantile, new middle class elements along economic lines for survival. Unconsciously they borrowed much from the then-known feudal pattern. It was an immediate economic democratizing of the feudal pattern, of the Church monastic pattern, a new society within the shell of the old, and having its own peculiar shell.

Among the Moravians, though personal property was not surrendered, the Church owned all the land, and received into its treasury the result of the combined labor of the community. To each member were given the necessities of life, schooling, protection in sickness and old age. Bachelors lived in a common house, single women in another, widows in a third. Mates were chosen by lot (among them some of my ancestors). At the Bethlehem settlement some thirty trades were carried on for the benefit of the Church and its members, and the community became one of the advanced manufacturing centers during the later Colonial period. The similarity of the pattern to the Catholic monastic orders is apparent.

The Harmonists, or Rappites, north of Pittsburgh, who later settled Harmonie on the Wabash in Indiana, where the angel Gabriel left his footprint in a rock, destroyed all records of private property. All personal wealth was transferred to the common treasury; even the gravestones, symbols of earthly vanity, were forbidden. But if these experiments represented revolt against Catholicism, in their feudal collective features they had not fully caught up with the individualistic and private-property spirit of the new age. This was taking "primitive" Christianity entirely too seriously.

The group that stood most four-square with the future individualistic, private property tradition of America was that of the Puritans and Pilgrims. Long ago Max Weber, in his *Die Protestantische Ethik und der Geist des Kapitalismus,* pointed out that the capitalist spirit developed in Massachusetts and elsewhere in part because sheltered by Protestant religion, a claim disputed by Clive Day of Yale who has argued, on a basis of a too narrow range of documents and still narrower range of thinking, that the early Puritan spirit was more socialistic (really remnants of a democratized feudalism everywhere visible), and that the ministers of the Gospel did not clearly announce the new order. It is precisely the proper function of ministers of religion to disregard the source of their own economic support and evade the economic problem. New trends involve curious contradictions, but the dominant trend in Massachusetts was decidedly "capitalistic." The psychology and purpose of the Puritans, though many feudal patterns were retained, was never, except in isolated localities, toward collectivism, but rather toward individualism, private property, and the acquiring of personal wealth. "Business before friends" soon became a commonly heard New England expression—almost a regional motto.

Samuel Willard, at the close of the Seventeenth Century, elaborately justified private property by all law, human and divine: put such doctrines back a century or so, and one perceives how revolutionary they are with reference to feudalism. The fact that Willard utilized the argument of social benefit, the good of the group, to rationalize his doctrines, does not imply socialistic doctrine at all. Read the classic professorial American economists (not the Veblens) down through and beyond the last century and note how heavily they lean on God, in every other phrase, to justify ruthlessness, theft, and the damning of the new labor movement.

The Puritans, though denouncing covetousness, emphasized thrift and honesty, all those qualities that lead to prosperity. "Let Your Business Engross the most of your Time," wrote Cotton Mather. "It is a vice to refuse riches," says Baxter's *Christian Dictionary*, "for this is refusing the means and opportunities of doing good." This tunes in with the whole later Sunday school teaching and philanthropy of a Rockefeller. Most of our very rich men have been very pious—and the psychological explanation of their compartmental mind-processes is a very simple one. It is almost identical with that of the early Puritan, and with the subsequent careful separation in the American of spiritual and mental concepts from practical activity, except as false rationalizations and remote control.

When David L. Dodge, with four other "professors of religion," set up a cotton factory near Norwich, the Bozrah Manufacturing Company, they considered it their duty to "look to God for his guidance" and "blessing in our undertaking" and to maintain "a moral and religious establishment"—all the children who toiled in it were obliged to attend Sabbath school regularly.

Judge Samuel Sewall—a good Puritan—spending his Christmas in the "awful but pleasing diversion" of arranging the coffins in the family vault, to me symbolizes the banker in the steel vault of a later day. One senses the combination of piety and title-deeds.

Nowhere was the spirit of commercial gain more intimately linked with religion than in the settling of New Haven by merchants and tradesmen led by the Eaton brothers, one wealthy, the other a minister, and by Reverend John Davenport. The shareholders of the emigration wanted a place where they could enforce the worship of God in their own way and establish an impressive trading metropolis. The religious dictatorship helped guarantee commercial monopoly. Called by Wertenbaker "a Bible State, ruled by a narrow clique working in close affiliation with the clergy," quite as aptly it could be described as a Business State in which only Church members were free burgesses.

And Reverend Timothy Dwight of Yale, at the close of the Colonial period, with his aphorisms on the evils of idleness and prodigality, his praise for the settled industrious type, his hatred of restless independence, his staunch defense of government and laws favoring the well-to-do, his love of all the conventional aspects of the society of the day, shows all the mentality of contemporary capitalist folklore as interpreted by the upper middle class.

Part of the break-up of the set feudal mind was achieved by Renaissance thought and art, a general freeing of the mind and the individual will. This was part of movement which made possible the emergence of the new capitalist order, and one important Puritan characteristic was that they brought with them a broader culture than most of the dissenting sects; they had less hatred of culture. As V. F. Calverton trenchantly points out in his *Passing of the Gods*, most of the other sects represented not only a revolt against aristocracy but against the culture of which aristocracy had a monopoly; they became, in part, an ignorant revolt against all culture.

The planting of English North America, as one commentator has stated, may have begun "as a venture of the Elizabethan mind," but in many parts it was also in part an antagonism to the new freedom of the Elizabethan mind. Shakespeare's *Antony and Cleopatra* was in part "escape" literature and the colonization was an "escape" process, but though the great drama was probably written in 1607, the "hot and sickly" summer of the founding of Jamestown, it was over a century before plays were tolerated in Virginia or anywhere else in the colonies, except "Charles Town." But save for extremists among them, the Puritans, of all the rebel sects (though not so much so as the Episcopalians), were far less afraid of learning, schools or the arts.

More than any other sect, the Puritans, in the Scot rather than the English tradition, wished to rationalize religion, reduce it to logic; they were moved by ideas rather than emotions. Stubborn ideas, too divorced from human sympathy, led to their exaggerated theocratic tyranny. The Puritans warped all they touched, but that is characteristic of radical sects, which, for a few truths sternly held, reject universality. If they plunged into the morass of hysteria and witch-hunting in the end, their very love of ideas helped bring them back to common sense.

In the breakdown of traditional law and rules that the Reformation made inevitable, many of the sects wished to discard all law and find salvation purely in individual beatitude, but not in reason. As a result, they promptly struck away from most of the new knowledge brought by the Renaissance; most of them turned away from the new dazzling light of thought and learning in the hopes of finding a truer light in the dark mists of mysticism.

The mysticism of the Catholic Church had been neatly patterned into hierarchy and subordinated to a workable system of fees; but the Quakers, for instance, believed that the inner light, given by the Founder of Christianity, could be cultivated by silence and meditation—a sort of pseudo-Orientalism. This process, derived in part from Descartes and from the Spanish Catholic priest Molinos, whose movement was eventually put down in blood by the Inquisition, was known as Quietism and was common to a number of sects. It tended to make all sacraments quite unnecessary. The individual found God by a sort of self-hypnotism.

One should seek God by meditation until all soul doubts were subdued one by one. The individual then passed on into contemplation, in which the soul, no longer struggling, freed from reason or reflection from which doubts sprang, could rest at ease in the embrace of God, a return to the first principles of consciousness. Naturally such meditation, continually practiced, meant the decay of reason; it weakened the intellect; religion became an opiate dream.

Since doubts were thus dispelled by annihilating thinking, the corollary was a hatred of knowledge. For personal salvation, knowledge of anything except God was not required. A premium was put upon ignorance. Many sects, hating all learning, became apostolic in behalf of semi-illiteracy. The Quakers long fought higher education, in some locales still do. In the Colonial period this gradually weakened Quaker leadership and their influence, not only in their own colony but elsewhere, and after Independence reduced them to an inferior role in national affairs. But this dislike of knowledge had considerable importance, as we shall observe, in the settling up of the land.

The difference between Quakers and Puritans is no better illustrated than by an amusing anecdote of Elizabeth, New Jersey, founded by New England settlers. The Puritans ruled Elizabeth arbitrarily, but when under the Carteret grant, new state laws of religious tolerance permitted Quakers to intrude into the Puritan domain, the latter had no defense except argument. Debates were staged, but when the reasoning went against the Quakers, they "set to humming, singing, reeling their heads and bodies," and would threaten the Congregationalist minister that his "destruction was nigh at hand." They remind one—except that the Quakers were rarely violent—of the Communist method of breaking up a Socialist or Trotsky meeting. Strangely enough the Quaker Church grew more rapidly. Obviously it is easier to hum, sing and reel than patiently to argue or to try to think.

Unlike the Puritans, the Quakers disliked not only higher learning but nearly all forms of human entertainment, most of which had been linked up with leisure-class aristocracy.

"How many plays did Jesus Christ and his apostles recreate themselves at? What poems, romances, comedies, and the like did the apostles and saints make or use to pass away their time withal?" sternly demanded William Penn, during his youthful imprisonment in the Tower.

"Plays, parks, balls, treats, romances, musics, love sonnets," he averred on one occasion, would not sit well "with the righteous judgment of God." Gambling, dueling, profanity, drunkenness, playing with dice, cards, lotteries, etc., were punished by the Pennsylvania Quaker lawmakers with severe fines and imprisonment.

They tolerated no music (an "insidious, sensuous, frivolous" menace), novels, dancing ("leaps of hell"), elaborate dress, or titles.

"How many pieces of riband and what feathers, lace bands, and the like did Adam and Eve wear in Paradise or out of it?" demanded William Penn of his flock, though he did not go on to tell them what Adam and Eve did wear or to recommend his followers to copy the innocent pair. Nor did Abel, Enoch, Noah or Abraham, he went on to inform them, use embroideries or silks. Nor did Eve, Sarah, Suzannah, or the Virgin Mary "use powder, patch, paint, wear false locks of strange colors, rich points, trimmings, laced gowns, embroidered petticoats."

All this became helpful doctrine for frontiersmen, substituted piety for vanities which could easily have made frontier wives discontented.

Dislike of learning and pleasure was also characteristic of the German Tunkers or Dunkards, the Mennonites, and Lutherans. More than half of them were illiterate to begin with, and anything beyond reading and writing was considered sinful. The Tunkers openly boasted there were no educated men among them and often destroyed all books not religious. Throughout the history of Pennsylvania those sects have stood as enemies of good schools, many going to jail rather than pay school taxes. Such fanaticism found echo even in high official quarters in the colonies. Governor Berkeley of Virginia once said:

"I thank God there are no free schools or printing . . . for learning has brought disobedience and heresy and sects into the world and printing has divulged [them] and libels against the best government. God keep us from both."

William Smith in the Eighteenth Century observed that the people of New York neglected reading, "indeed all the arts for the improvement of the mind." Schools were of "the lowest order," the teachers semi-ignorant "through a long and shameful neglect of all the arts and science."

And so, the Dissenters' "religiosity shaped the early outlook of the nation," remarks Calverton, and "has continued ever since to function as a spiritual incubus in hampering and suppressing the creative spirit of the American people in the field of art and letters." But it helped settle up the country. The mind and spirit checked on the higher levels turned naturally to the American love of gadgets and more gadgets.

The schismatic tendencies of Europe continued in the New World, influenced in new ways, of course, by the facts of American environment, by contact with the American soil. Here, as in Europe, under the guise of religion and fine-spun theories of personal redemption, were carried on bitter economic and political battles. Religious oppression and sectarian differences also caused that constant shearing-off process which caused vast numbers to emigrate westward.

Early near-schisms in Quakerism, though they pivoted upon the question of Atonement and other doctrinal matters, were in part a reflection of recurring difficulties of Colonial rule and the tensions and resultant personal irritations thus set up. Among other things, schisms and competition (the Quakers were hard-pressed in Philadelphia by the Episcopalians and elsewhere on the frontier by the German sects and the Scotch-Irish Presbyterians) eventually destroyed Quaker political power. The sons of William Penn themselves turned Episcopalian and gradually swung much of the commonwealth away from Quakerism. Philadelphia to this day is divided between two "societies," Quaker and Episcopalian. Even in its respectable and affluent period, Quakerism, which, for instance, forced its members to free their slaves, was never so adequate an assurance for maintaining private wealth, or promoting scientific research, as was official Episcopalianism, more closely tied up with continental British rule.

It is significant that the more extreme the new faith, the more poverty-stricken and ignorant the holders. Even to this day economic disillusionment results in the founding of new extravagant sects. Studies among the southern tenant farmers show that periodically, usually about every fifteen or twenty years, a completely new sect is started, always by the poorest members of the community.

From home meetings and outdoor gatherings the sect progresses to the point of building a church. Slowly it becomes respectable, absorbs the better classes, whereupon once more the poverty-stricken, with their poor clothes and untutored manners, find themselves ill at ease in the house of worship and are ripe for a new religious experiment. It is merely an escapism from their intolerable economic situation for which they see no remedy. In the early days, such new sects, faced with poverty and persecution, emigrated west.

Several things happened to the colonist in the New World. The tendency ever present in the sects which gained control of Colonial governments, to prevent the inevitable disintegration induced by a new environment, was to try to stamp their dogmas ruthlessly on everybody. An iron shoe was slipped on the rapid foot of change. Vested interests never like change.

But if a new environment drives some folk to rigidity of belief, it drives others to throw all tradition aside recklessly. Many of the colonists, indented or otherwise oppressed, found emotional compensation by adhering to new heretical sects. As this struck at the ecclesiastical and economic stability of the earlier settlements, such dissidents were maltreated, accused of witchcraft, jailed, persecuted or deported. Some, like the visionary Huguenot Dutartres, who saw visions, became non-social in every sense of the word; non-taxpayers, non-resisters, and pacifists—though willing to fight the whole state militia when coerced—were assassinated or sent to the gallows.

Many to escape such treatment preferred to move west. Thus Roger Williams embracing Antinomianism, the idea of continuous revelation, had to go into the Connecticut wilderness to escape the ecclesiastical tyranny of Massachusetts. The story of Anne Hutchinson is an epic of such emigration.

In spite of religious tyranny, new sects wormed into the established commonwealths and in some cases we even find the conservative faction itself giving up the struggle and in a bitter mood moving west to found a new Zion where no breath of heresy might enter the tight confines of settlement, of brain or of soul. This explains much of the Puritan migration to New Jersey. The disillusion is reflected in John Davenport of New Haven, who finally saw "the cause of Christ" there "miserably lost." A large part of the population—the people of nearby Branford almost en masse—emigrated to Newark to recreate their lost religious monopoly, the freedom they so denied to others and wished still to deny them.

And so, in spite of all, the already well-defined, well-established sects had to face constant controversy between those seeking to conserve dependence upon European tradition and those awake to new American needs.

In nearly all the faiths constant conflict between reality and creed, between American needs and European tradition, inevitably brought exasperating controversies over beliefs, controversies that in turn were an escape from troublesome realities, and which led to schisms, to new migrations. The inner struggles of the Dutch Reformed Church, Congregationalists versus Unitarians; Quakers versus Keithites and Hicksites and Wilburites; the see-saw of Lutherans and Moravians are but a few samples. The Dutch Reformed Church, clinging to the rules of the Amsterdam Classis, yet torn with the demands of the Americanists, was shaken by repeated controversies in which religion, language and the land question form an intricate web of dissension.

An amusing incident is reported from the New Jersey Congregationalists. In 1773 Colonel Josiah Ogden, a leading member of the rigid Congregational community of Newark, dared to gather in his wheat, in danger of rotting from the rains, on a Sabbath, and thereby precipitated a prolonged feud of great animosity that lasted down until the Revolutionary War. It was one more case of sensible, practical American needs thrusting themselves commandingly within the iron walls of religious dogma and forcing religious adaptation.

Thus, rapid evolution of new brands of faith, besides mirroring the struggles for political and economic power in the colonies, represented partial adaptation to the American scene. The splintering-off process of religion occurred ever more frequently. The "hurly-burly of religious polemics" was speeded up. New sects developed with amazing rapidity; old sects divided and re-divided. These controversies and the new sects themselves stimulated the westward movement, which in turn forced the creation of still more numerous sects.

In the Old World, to become a member of a new sect usually meant persecution and continuous struggle. Definite boundaries were set to anarchy of opinion. In the New World, with a whole continent to hold dissenters, such outside restraints were largely removed, and all the inner energy of religious sentiment promptly exploded like corn popped over the fire. The frontier itself, a great releaser of the individual spirit, caused the casting off of nearly all community bonds. The explosive force of religion had even fewer restraints than in the little seaboard colonies. The spirit of the foresters sought to match the exuberance of the continent. They succeeded. The result was a wilder growth of spiritual vegetation than the world has ever known, quite as dazzling as the strange new botanical species encountered on the route of the westward march.

Even as early as 1742 among the Pennsylvania Germans, new sects were mushrooming everywhere. Vagabonds and frauds circulated, extorting money at the communion table. "A disorganized rabble," the settlers were a prey to every new eccentric the mystic German mind could invent. Muhlenberg, who came over to salvage the Lutheran Church, wrote:

"At the present time old and young self-appointed pastors, offended keepers of inns and groceries, silversmiths and beerhouse fiddlers, dancing masters, entire companies of recently arrived Nethinim (I Chron. ix: 2), and the insane rabble of Sichem (Sirach i, 28) gather together, throw dust in the air, and raise, with their cursing and blaspheming such a confusion that the town-clerk himself might be perplexed (Acts xix: 23-40)."

The sap of the continent had not yet begun to flow upward strongly through our institutions, and new religions were a symptom of perplexity and wonder and fear among an uprooted people. Old dogmas and customs seemed incapable of meeting the challenge of this New World. All the newcomers could do was to clutch out desperately for some new, more bizarre faith. The struggle within the various sects between American needs and established creeds and unworkable European ideas is to be noted in all the sects.

Such new sects keyed in with frontier individualistic characteristics, made it more feasible for frontiersmen to leave communities and be cheerful in the wilderness. Catholics, members of a feudally organized community sect, however magnificent their explorers and conquistadores, have never made good individualistic frontier dwellers. The Spanish expeditions into the wilderness nearly always went in groups and rarely were they undertaken without an accompanying priest. But the individualistic northern frontiersman naturally embraced the sects requiring the most extreme individual relationships with God. Social instincts were largely restricted to a sort of animal gregariousness and periodic religious orgies after long periods of isolation. This is what made the camp-meeting, tried out first in Kentucky in 1800, one of the best instruments of Methodist conversion.

The great camp-meeting of 1801 in Logan County, Kentucky, was attended by 15,000 people—"like a great army, covering hundreds of acres"—a mad mob of revivalists, turned into insane jerking, wailing, shrieking dervishes.

But the frontiersman, however much he might enjoy at intervals such group reunions, was individualistic. He was happy in this physical and spiritual isolation, and so he invented many new sects himself which laid still more stress on divine revelation to the individual soul. It was often impossible to support a regular preacher. The settlers had to depend upon appointed lay readers, and these, untrained in the niceties of traditional dogma, opened the doors to unbridled, if naïve and often foolish, speculation and discussion.

This did not necessarily mean new knowledge. Men argue most violently over things they know nothing about; the bitterness over religious doctrines and forms represented an escape from the harsh frontier facts. Rather was it emphasizing the factor, already mentioned, of antagonism to knowledge and the arts. The westward movement emphasized hatred of non-sectarian culture; it helped produce new sects, and these in turn reinforced the distrust of learning. Even had the immigrants been receptive, the frontier did not, for the moment, provide them with any means to acquire civilization or formal knowledge. They therefore made a pride of their ignorance, a fetish of illiteracy, a cocksureness in proportion to mental inadequacy.

After all, sagacity, courage, perseverance, and all the brute and animal characteristics of man, were far more important than learning. It did not require book-learning or art in the strict sense to girdle trees, clear the wilderness, fight Indians, plant crops. A premium was put upon anti-intellectualism, an ever greater emphasis upon all practical and bold deeds, an exaggerated individualism.

In regions where doctors were scarce—and most of those available knew little except "bleeding" and killed more folk than they cured— it became a further mainstay to believe in religions which denounced scientific medicine and placed the onus for all cures directly on God and faith in God. This has always been a belief comforting to the poor and oppressed. Such sects appeared long before in Europe, and man's fear of sickness and death, from the earliest times of primitive religions, has caused him to believe in miraculous cures. If this was and is a strong Catholic belief—as Lourdes so testifies—it is a much more emphasized peculiarity of many of the individualistic sects. It has been re-emphasized down to our own day, first by frontier needs, then after the closing of the frontier, by the growing economic and cultural degeneracy and terrible poverty of the greater part of our rural population. Thus we find that in 1907 in Hot Springs, Arkansas, was organized the Assemblies of God with divine healing as one of its principal tenets. Such reliance upon faith rather than knowledge animates many of the poor farmers and tenants, driven out from the Midwest dust-bowl, the Oklahoma "Migs," who in their desperation, lack of schooling and general ignorance, have been reaped like chaff into the folds of the Pentecostal healing sects. Other such cults bear an even more recent date.[1]

Inevitably the frontiersman—since his polygamous instincts, cut off by isolation on the frontier, could not be satisfied clandestinely as in urban centers, and as he did not often solve his sexual problem as did the Spanish conqueror by cohabiting promiscuously with the native women—was obliged by unrelieved monogamy or abstinence to sublimate his unsatisfied sexual desires. His religious aberrations were and are, in part, the symptom of sex-starved race.

[1] Among such at the present time, believing in divine healing, and rejecting scientific treatment in part or entirety are:

SECT	WHERE STRONGEST
The Church of God	Ohio, Indiana, Illinois, Michigan, Missouri, Kentucky, Pennsylvania, Oklahoma.
Church of God in Christ	Texas, Mississippi, Arkansas, Oklahoma, Louisiana, Illinois, Missouri, Tennessee.
Church of the Nazarene	Texas, Oklahoma, California, Indiana, Kansas, Arkansas.
Congregational Holiness	Georgia, South Carolina, Alabama.
Divine Science	Missouri, Washington.
Apostolic Faith Mission	Oregon, Missouri, Minnesota, Washington.
Missionary Church Association	Ohio, Indiana, Kansas, Michigan, California.
Pillar of Fire	New Jersey, Pennsylvania, Colorado.
Free Church of Christ in God	Colorado, Texas, Kansas, Oklahoma.

[Continued on page 153.]

Some sects carried abstinence to fanatic lengths, and the resultant unhealthful mental and physical reflexes induced hysteria that could find outlet only in bizarre ritual, the shaking, fit-like frenzies, the wailing and chanting orgies. Sexual abstinence was tied in also with queer apocalyptic theories of the end of the Universe. Thus the Rappites, for the ten years of their residence in Harmonie, convinced the millennium was near at hand, left not a single record of marriage or birth. Moravian religious ecstasy had at its roots something very debauched and sexual. The music of many of the more excitable sects —for music, too, joined the march of revolt—was often very orgiastic, with a scarcely veiled sexual content. This is very true of the Pentecostal liturgy.

Other sects were driven by the same sort of aberration to the opposite extreme. The Mormons swung over to polygamy; the Oneida Perfectionists, communalistic in all things, pooled all husbands and wives and all sex enjoyment. Warped sexual psychology twisted even sex conduct into rigid dogma. It was also part of the manifestation of the perplexity of the newcomer over the strange American earth where he found himself.

Likewise, in part because of the same sex motive and hatred of learning, the frontiersman turned to the most equalitarian and emotional sects. When these did not satisfy his desire for emotional orgy, he invented still more extravagant ones. In general, Quietism did not

SECT	WHERE STRONGEST
Holiness Church	California, Kentucky, Tennessee.
Latter Day Saints	Utah, Idaho, Arizona, California, Wyoming, Texas, Nevada, Montana.
Liberal Catholic Mennonites	California, Michigan, Minnesota, Pennsylvania, Indiana, Ohio, Nebraska.
Reformed Methodist	New York, Pennsylvania.
Original Church of God	Alabama, Tennessee, North Carolina, Maine, Missouri, Arkansas.
Pentecostal Assemblies	Ohio, Indiana, Illinois, Kentucky, Pennsylvania, California, Kansas, Michigan, Texas.
Pentecostal Holiness	North Carolina, South Carolina, Oklahoma, Virginia, Georgia, West Virginia, Florida, California.
Pilgrim Holiness	Indiana, Ohio, North Carolina, Pennsylvania, Michigan, Kentucky, Kansas, Colorado, Virginia.

prevail in America; even the Quakers found it a strain. But a more appealing type of worship also sought—by a different road—to defeat the mental process and get nearer to a mystical adoration of Jesus and God that should be devoid of all intellectual reefs. If one could smother one's doubts by Quietism, by brooding on doubts until the mind wearied and thus enter into a sort of vague trance where the mind no longer functioned, this could also be achieved by action and noise and slobbering madness. The latter style of worship was far more attuned to the active, aggressive life of the frontier. By shouting, shaking, whooping, screeching, the brain was atrophied, and a state of exhaustion and auto-hypnotism induced which was a counterpart to Quaker so-called spirituality.

Allen Tate, in his *The Migration*, a vivid piece published in the *Yale Review*, describes "the jerks" through the eyes of Rhodam Elwin: "I looked upon the jerking exercise with astonishment. Many fell down under the burden of sin, as men slain in battle, and lay for hours in nearly breathless and motionless state, sometimes for a moment reviving with symptoms of life, giving deep groans or piercing shrieks; and thus did they obtain deliverance from evil. Two or three of my particular acquaintance were struck down, and I patiently sat by one whom I knew to be a careless sinner, critically observing the contortions as they seized him. At one moment being still as death, he would begin to jerk in one arm, gradually and at regular intervals, till the motion spread over his entire body which heaved violently in all directions as if he were trying to tear himself apart. A grove of saplings had been cut down breast-high, and at each post a zealous Christian took his station, so that when the time came he would have something to jerk by. At these posts pretty girls and sober matrons waited, and it was wonderful to see my sister Emily Maxey jerk and kick so powerfully that the earth under her feet looked like a hitching-place for horses in fly time."

Many of these orgiastic sects were, in part, also derivative from places where Negro influences were absorbed. Few writers have ever admitted this, but the greater orgiastic abandon, the deep physical lascivity, the more erectile flesh of the Black man from the hot lands, pervaded and tinged religious life in the South, and contributed to the development of similar trends among new White sects everywhere.

We shall not attempt to find how the perpetuation of the very ancient foot-washing rite by the Mennonites, Moravians, and Tunkers with the frontier and its imposed poverty dove-tailed. It is a rite that has spread to many sects and still inspires new ones. It would, however, be easy, if one wished to be facetious, to indicate the utility of such hocus-pocus and its relationship to the subconscious repugnance to the sweaty toil in the fields and its aromatic consequences. The spirit of humbleness it symbolized was also valuable to the poorer elements of the frontier, especially in a secondary period when isolation reinforced the early emergence of class distinctions. It made folk more content to remain just "poor white trash." Also, by cleansing the most perceptibly unclean portion of the anatomy, the believers not only felt a sense of ease and relaxation, but their simple minds could easily rationalize on up to even the cleansing of the soul. In this rite, too, as in many, are involved definite Freudian and sexual connotations—even though in most cases the washing is done by members of the same sex—which need not be entered into here.

All in all the refined subtleties of Calvin were quite too much for the Westerners; they demanded a religion free of all necessity to think. Close-minded dogmatism made the frontiersman well-nigh impervious to all outside attacks. Since his faith was not of the mind —however much that had been implied in the original Reformation— he could and did, when forced by critics to utilize some slight mental effort, express his resentment by rising up and smiting his tormentor. Enmeshed in this emotional self-sufficiency, the frontiersman was thus fortified in his prowess as an individual. He was able to be contemptuous of the culture of the East, self-reliant in ignorance, not only self-reliant but unashamed. Not all the shafts of reason, learning or science could penetrate the charmed circle he had drawn about himself. The frontiersman became the divine possessor of a wisdom that no mundane minds, schoolmen, critics or professors could take away from him.

The Baptists and Methodists, for instance, putting their entire stress upon the individual and his right to salvation, ignored not merely class differences, but all theological differentiations. Redemption and salvation were emotional, not intellectual experiences, and not even dependent upon an established clergy. Thus any man could become a great preacher, not with theological training, but through religious inspiration. Lay preachers, thus inspired, swarmed over the plains. They were men with an intense emotional intimacy with God, who ranted and shouted hypnotizing phrases, thus providing an outlet for pent-up emotions otherwise denied expression on the culturally barren frontier.

Peter Cartwright described the frontier preacher vividly: "A Methodist preacher in those days when he felt that God had called him to preach, instead of hunting up a college or a Biblical institute, hunted up a hardy pony, or a horse, and some travelling apparatus, and with his library always at hand, namely the Bible, Hymn Book, and Discipline, he started, and with a text that never wore out or grew stale, he cried, 'Behold the Lamb of God, that taketh away the sin of the world!' In this way he went through storms of wind, hail, snow, and rain; climbed hills and mountains, traversed valleys, plunged through swamps, swam swollen streams, lay out at night, wet, weary and hungry, held his horse by the bridle all night, or tied him to a limb, slept with saddle blanket for a bed, his saddle or saddle-bags for his pillow, and his old big coat or blanket, if he had any, for covering."

Many of the ministers showed marvelous adaptability to frontier conditions. Mari Sandoz tells of the sky-pilot in Nebraska, who organized a church in a tent, using a pile of wagon tongues and empty whiskey kegs for a pulpit, and who afterwards joined the boys in the saloon to celebrate the inauguration.

Under the guise of religion, it is only fair to state, considerable knowledge was painlessly imparted. Walter Havighurst tells how the wandering ministers were the first schoolteachers, too, especially among "foreign" elements. Ministers taught the Swedes, the Norwegians, the various aliens their first vague notions of American history and democracy.

"Swimming rivers, sleeping under stars, driving through snowstorms so dense they could barely see their horses or trudging through spring mud, tending the sick, comforting the discouraged, patiently leading drunken Norse or Irish section hands back to the camps," the ministers, however narrow their creeds, were often "selfless, vigorous and pious men," through whom the frontiersmen and their wives gained assurance, outside contacts and a degree of garbled information.

Thus the explosive force of the original Reformation revolt against Catholicism continued in the Americas, like a series of internal telescoped rockets successively exploding in the ever-darkening sky of mysticism to startle God at the pyrotechnics of his own handiwork. Frontier conditions, by the release of nearly all outside barriers, merely made the sacred fireworks more fantastic. The excessive stressing of the individual—by the frontier and by the tenets of these creeds —made for, if not intellectual divergences, religious divergences.

It was all somewhat puzzling to the natives whom the Whites sought to convert. As Red Jacket of the Senecas said to a missionary: "If there is but one religion, why do you White people differ so much about it? Why not all agree, as you can all read the book? We do not understand these things."

This continuous schism is the process of all unseasoned radicalism —before it channelized into respectable institutions. The rebellious sect inevitably feels that it possesses all truth, all wisdom, all justice and all right. But if one minority sect believes this passionately enough, then inevitably a still smaller group within the rebellious group is still more wise and right. In the end, of course, you have the one man who is right: the outcome is dictatorship. Individualism has then quite completed the cycle. The only reason we did not have more ecclesiastical despotism in the New World, a continuation of the Massachusetts sort of thing, was because there were so many sects, so many creeds, and the frontier was wide enough to hold them all.[1]

---

[1] At present we have a counterpart of this religious schismatism in the revolt of economic sects against Capitalism. The Socialists begot Anarchists, Socialist Laborites, Social Democrats, Christian Socialists, Syndicalists, One-Big Unionists, Communists, Trotskyites, Lovestoneites and a dozen heresies, and provoked Fascism into life. Each schism has meant that a still smaller faction (unaware of its greed for power) has arrived at the true light. As might be expected, this could only end (even had Russia

After Kentucky and Tennessee filled up with piny-woods Methodists from the Virginia and Carolina uplands, they were followed by "tobacco-makers" from the plains, with Negro slaves, who were mostly Baptists. The earlier comers became restless, often emigrated further. Thus the various sects did not immediately seriously impinge. If they did, they moved on.

Thus none became strong enough to impose its will except for a short time in a small area. Inevitably the result was a reluctant tolerance which has done much to shape American liberties, however much in many localities such tolerance is still lacking even to this day.

Thus, as significant as the peculiar character of the religious sects, is their vast number. Even in the East, where for a time close-fisted ecclesiastical régimes tried to hold the separatist tendencies in check, an incredible number of new sects arose or were flung back upon them from the evolving frontier.

Of course, some of the eastern colonies were fairly tolerant even from the first, especially those where varied national groups made their home. New York, except for the harsh rule of Stuyvesant, was mostly fairly open even in early days, promising New Englanders and others "liberty of conscience according to the custom and manner of Holland."

As early as 1687 Governor Dongan reported that "New York has a first Chaplain belonging to the Fort of the Church of England; secondly, a Dutch Calvinist; thirdly, a French Calvinist; fourthly, a Dutch Lutheran." There were not many Episcopalians or Roman "Catholicks," but an "abundance" of Quaker preachers, men and women; Singing Quakers; Ranting Quakers; Sabbatarians; Anti-Sabbatarians; some Anabaptists, some Independents; some Jews; "of all sort of opinions there are some." Rhode Island welcomed other sects, and a number of Quakers even came to be governors.

The Quaker creed insisted upon religious freedom for all. Out-

been less inclined in that direction) in one-man dictatorship, the single possessor of the true light. Stalinism represents the recurrent and probably inevitable history of all violent rebel movements.

side sects were never persecuted, though the Quakers denied the members of other denominations equal political privileges, and by retaining control of the State Assembly right down to the Revolution—through gerrymandering and property qualifications for voting—the good Friends did enforce their own stringent blue laws and ideas of personal conduct.

The whole process of multiplication of sects is well revealed by present-day statistics. In 1916 there were still 202 religious denominations active in the United States, 35 with memberships of over 100,000.

Indiana—as one might expect—leads the patch-work parade with 107 denominations; New York has 92 (1926); Michigan, 87; Iowa, 85. Pennsylvania, which because of the principle of tolerance of the Quakers, served as a refuge wherever sects got into trouble elsewhere, still has 79 denominations. California has 79. Kansas, 77. Many of the California sects were brought in by immigration, but the splitting-up process and the invention of new sects has been more active there than in many places, perhaps partly because of the more recent exposure of immigrants to new environment.

Religious schism, product of the original anti-Roman Catholic revolt, accelerated in the New World to a great extent by unpleasant economic conditions in the East, and by the strange demands of new environment, conflicting ideas, the constant jostling of the melting pot, was then further accelerated by frontier conditions. Thus all this splintering up of sects was both a cause of western migration and likewise an outgrowth from it. Such sects represented readaptation on one hand, but on the other, a stubborn resistance to the realities of the new soil-world of America. They were a phenomenon of an attempt to cling to European concepts in a world where those concepts no longer had validity. Each new schism represented a breakdown of that effort, a new alignment of the spirit with the world about and at the same time an obstinate refusal to quite come to terms on any sensible basis except that of physical and material conquest. Mental and spiritual evasion and physical and material realism (in the direct primitive sense) continue to feature American development, American life and to hamper American thinking.

But religious schism was a major factor in keeping the western movement ever fluid and bringing about the rapid seizure and utilization of the American earth.

CHAPTER VIII

MORMONS

In 1811 the Astor overland expedition passed through or near the famous Wyoming South Pass, which marks the continental divide. Major Thomas Fitzpatrick and his party definitely traveled through this cleft in the Rockies in 1824. Twelve years later, Doctor Marcus Whitman and bride and Reverend H. H. Spalding and wife followed the same route; and there in the pass at the headwaters between two oceans, on July 4th, Doctor Whitman, the Holy Bible in his left hand, the American flag in his right (evidently a worthy predecessor of those who know the movie cameras are grinding), fell on his knees and in the name of God and America took possession of the land of the West as the home of American women and the Church of Christ. A monument there bears the names of the two women—the first White females ever to cross the continent.

These pioneers blazed the way for more than 300,000 people, who from 1840 to 1870 struggled through this gap in their long trek to claim a new land and build an empire. Untold thousands left their bones to the Indians, the snows, the rattlesnakes, to the grinning god of hunger.

Not the least of these emigrants were the Mormons, who came west to Utah in successive waves.

In the third decade of the nineteenth century, one of the most successful mumbo-jumbo artists of the Unknown, Joseph Smith of Vermont, pulled out of the silk hat of the Infinite Mystery divine revelations printed on golden plates. In the year 1820, when Smith was only fourteen, Trinity had communicated with him in person.

In the hills near his father's home, two glorious personages appeared in "a vision of great light," told him to join no existing church and laid upon him the solemn duty of prophesying to the people. This was very plausible in a period when everybody, if pious enough, was able to receive direct revelation; and between 1823 and 1827 numerous revelations were made to Joseph concerning the coming of Christ and other remarkable matters. To him was told the location of the auriferous plates of the sacred records of the ancient inhabitants of America. He was to visit the place each year until worthy to receive them.

September 22, 1827, the *Book of Mormons,* consisting of thin gold plates, about eight inches by seven, held together by three golden rings like a modern school notebook, and printed in "Reformed Egyptian," was put into his hands.

Part of the contents of this six-inch-thick metallic volume was sealed. But Joseph Smith also received two magic stones, called Urim and Thummin, set in silver bows like a pair of spectacles, so that whoever looked through them could read the sealed portion. Joseph was thus in possession of the power of revealing the unknown sections of the contents whenever any parts of it should in the future be essential to man's welfare. Smith certainly was either one of the strangest pathological types or one of the outstanding hoaxers of the ages.

Joseph found another master mind in Oliver Cowdery. May 15, 1829, an angel, John the Baptist, appeared to the two of them to confer upon them the priesthood of Aaron and ordered them to baptize each other. Later on, Peter, James and John conferred on them the Melchizedek priesthood and the keys of the Apostleship.

In 1830 the *Book of Mormons* was "translated" and published at Palmyra in New York. The last few pages carried the testimony of witness Cowdery and several others, who claimed to have seen the original golden plates and the angel caretaker. After Joseph translated the book and printed it on paper, he returned the golden plates to their secret repository, and the angel—it was claimed—took them back to heaven. Joseph now had a perfect alibi.

The revealed word of God blithely created a whole new race and a new geography.

"And now it came to pass . . . he truly did many miracles in the names of Jesus. . . .

"And now it came to pass . . . the thirty and third year had passed away, and the people began to look with great earnestness for the sign which had been given by the prophet Samuel, the Lamanite. . . .

"And it came to pass . . . there was terrible thunder . . . and the city of Zarahemla did take fire, and the city of Moroni did sink into the depths of the sea . . . ; and the earth was carried up upon the city of Moroniihah, that in the place of the city thereof there became a great mountain. . . .

"And it came to pass . . .

"And then behold, there was darkness upon the face of the land."

Quite the finest feature of the new sect was polygamy, introduced under the theory of "spiritual wives" and a mysterious system of unrestricted marriage called "sealing." Polygamy was a very sensible and realistic measure in a frontier country that needed quick settling and a rapid increase of population. Had the other American settlers not been under the influence of set doctrines derived from overpopulated Europe—doctrines and sex tabus which throughout the early history of our country prevented them from seeing all the realities of the America they conquered, settled and constructed—the Mormon sect would and should have swept the country merely on the basis of polygamy. That a Mormon America would be a much more jovial place in which to live we cannot doubt. In time the doctrine and practice of polygamy would have become unnecessary. Monogamy, boardwalk beauty contests, Hollywood and Reno would have satisfactorily taken its place.

Six members formed the first church at Fayette, Seneca County, New York, on April 6, 1830—with a declaration that "the ancient gospel had been restored with all its gifts and powers"—and missionaries were sent out.

The following year, the little band went west to seek more credulous converts and settled in Kirtland, Ohio, where adherents from many other states gathered. There the church was formally organized under its first presidency. But the queer financial doings of Smith and his leading associates, his unredeemable fiat money plus the constant hostility of narrow-minded neighbors, forced him to take those of his followers still loyal west to country adjacent to Independence, Missouri, where a small Mormon settlement had existed since 1831. There the new arrivals purchased considerable land and laid out a town. The Lord's Store was founded and thrived. At first the Mormons were well received, but soon again met with clodhopper hostility. The charge—a sneak charge, we prefer to believe—was concocted that they stole corn from the cribs of non-Mormon neighbors, that many hogs and cattle disappeared. When the Mormons finally printed a newspaper to set forth news and holy doctrines, frenzied neighbors—perhaps at bottom envious of Mormon industry and prosperity—after heated mass meetings, gathered in a mob, so typical still of the brute level of part of American life, and demolished the paper's machinery and materials and burned the building. Several Mormons were stripped, beaten, tarred and feathered.

The Mormons evacuated the town and settled ten miles west, concentrating their settlements to be able to prepare to resist. Deciding to take the initiative, they prepared an armed expedition to seize, sack and burn Independence itself. A fife and drum routed out every man, woman and child able to bear arms.

The non-Mormon neighbors got wind of the doings. Farmers poured in from all the countryside.

The two little armies met several miles outside of town. Surprised by so large a force, the Mormons surrendered without a shot. They were released on condition they leave the country without delay.

By the middle of the following month, November, 1833, not a Mormon remained in the entire county. Further west in Clay County they established the new town, Far West.

Trouble once more! Soon Governor Boggs, evidently an early Mayor Hague, issued a proclamation that they had to be exterminated or driven out, and the militia was used to eject them. They moved to

Hancock County, Illinois, settling in 1838 in the small town of Commerce, which they soon controlled and renamed "Nauvoo."

Here, for a time unmolested, they worked industriously, prospered and multiplied until they totaled over 15,000. Nauvoo, granted complete independence from the rest of the state, by 1845 had become the most important center, larger than Chicago.

But new trouble, by then, had again come to a head. Once more they were charged with evil doings: with harboring criminals who had taken on the Mormon cloak; with stealing horses and cattle. Disputes arose over land-titles; jealousies of Mormon prosperity and hatred for its creed and practices arose. In 1844 their prophet, Joseph Smith (Mayor of Nauvoo) and his brother and fellow patriarch, Hyrum Smith, were arrested and jailed in Carthage. There, despite the governor's assurances that the state militia would protect their safety, a mob was allowed to lynch them. Houses belonging to the Mormons were burned.

They decided to leave the growing city and wealthy agricultural region they had built up with so much patient toil. Through 1845-46 they worked desperately to prepare for their new migration—all the houses, even the temple, were converted into workshops. Twelve thousand wagons were built or made ready, and between February and May 16,000 Mormons filed out of their pleasant home and crossed the Mississippi which, during part of the first month, was frozen over solid. The initial encampment west of the river was hit by twenty degree below zero weather and a blizzard. They were on their way, as one leader said, "we knew not whither."

The various detachments floundered ahead through alternate snow and ice and gumbo mud. Orson Platt, one of the leaders, wrote in his diary, on April 9th, that part of the camp got about six miles that day, the others were "stuck fast in deep mud." They had to cut brush and tree-branches to keep their beds from disappearing into the mire. Bark and branches were the only forage for the animals.

Here and there, when spring finally came, fairly permanent camps —Garden Grove and Mount Pisgah—were laid out so that land might be sowed to grain and vegetables for those still to come.

About 1,000 old, feeble or ill were left behind the last detachment until better able to take up the journey.

The surrounding anti-Mormon population soon took advantage of this helpless remainder, and in early autumn attacked the place with musketry and cannon. The Mormons hurried into boats, carrying their sick, aiding the feeble, and were thus thrown upon the Iowa shore without beds, shelter or provisions to face the oncoming of winter. A large share of them perished miserably.

Thomas L. Kane, a steamship captain and Arctic explorer, describes the place the Mormons were forced thus to abandon:

Descending a hillside, he came upon a fine landscape. "Half-encircled by a bend of the river a beautiful city lay glittering in the fresh morning sun; its bright new dwellings, set in cool green gardens, ranging up around a stately dome-shaped hill . . . crowned by a noble marble edifice, whose high tapering spire was radiant with white and gold. The city appeared to cover several miles; and beyond . . . a fair country, checquered by the careful lines of fruitful husbandry. The unmistakable marks of industry, enterprise and educated wealth, everywhere made the scene one of singular and most striking beauty."

Rowing across the river, Kane landed at the chief wharf of the city. "No one met me there. I looked, and saw no one. I could hear no one move; though the quiet everywhere was such that I heard the flies buzz, and the water-ripples break against the shallow of the beach. I walked through the solitary streets. The town lay as in a dream, under some deadening spell of loneliness, from which I almost feared to wake it. For plainly it had not slept long. There was no grass growing up in the paved ways. Rains had not entirely washed away the prints of dusty footsteps.

"Yet I went about unchecked. I went into empty workshops, ropewalks and smithies. The spinner's wheel was idle; the carpenter had gone from his workbench and shavings, his unfinished sash and casing. Fresh bark was in the tanner's vat, and the fresh-chopped lightwood stood piled against the baker's oven. The blacksmith's shop was cold; but his coal heap and ladling pool and crooked water horn were all there, as if he had just gone off for a holiday. No work people anywhere looked to know my errand. If I went into the gardens, clinking the wicket-latch loudly after me, to pull the marygolds, heart's ease and lady-slippers, and draw a drink with the water-sodden well-bucket and its noisy chain; or, knocking off with my stick the tall heavy-headed dahlias and sunflowers, hunted over the beds for cucumbers and love-apples—no one called out to me from any opened window, or dog sprang forward to bark an alarm. I could have supposed the people hidden in the houses, but the doors were unfastened; and when at last I timidly entered them, I found dead ashes white upon the hearths, and had to tread a tiptoe as if walking down the aisle of a country church, to avoid rousing irreverent echoes from the naked floors."

Kane then crossed over the river and saw "the human creatures" who had been ejected, sleeping among the rushes, "bivouacked in tatters," folk "in the last stage of bilious remittent fever." One sick old man lay under several sheets raised tent-wise, and on a ripped-open straw mattress. "His gasping jaw and glazing eye told how short a time he would monopolize these luxuries." His wife and two little girls watched, sobbing and helpless. Almost all the group were "crippled victims of disease" for whom nothing effective could be done. There was no bread to quiet "the factious hunger-cries of their children."

Kane followed the trail of the vanishing folk clear across Iowa— the "Moravian Roads"—finding them "beaten hard, and even dusty by the tread and wear of the cattle and vehicles of emigrants laboring over them. By day I would overtake and pass, one after another, what amounted to an army train of them; and at night, if I encamped at the places where the timber and running water were found together, I was almost sure to be within call of some camp or other, or at least within sight of its watchfires." Whenever he tarried, he found "shelter and hospitality, scant, indeed, but never stinted . . . and always honest and kind."

Each of the high Council Bluffs, which were reached between June and July, was "crowned with its own great camp, gay with bright white canvas, and alive with . . . swarming occupants. In the clear blue morning air, the smoke streamed up from more than a thousand cooking fires."

From a single point, he counted four thousand head of cattle. Herdsmen drowsed. Sheep and horses, cows and oxen were feeding everywhere.

Women at the creeks, "in greater force than blanchisseuses upon the Seine," were washing "all manner of white muslins, red flannels, and parti-colored calicoes; and hanging them to bleach upon a greater area of grass and bushes than we can display in all our Washington Square."

Men were constantly at the forge, loom or turning lathe, said another witness. The cobbler, no sooner than each day's march ended, hunted for a lap stone to finish a previous boot sole by the campfire. Wool was sheared, dyed, spun and woven on the march.

There was music, too, of which the Mormons were ever fond; they "tooted, scraped and twanged" for festival and dance and religious service, or too often, a dirge for the dead.

Men and women got sick, got well or died and were then buried. They buried their numerous dead as they went, filled up each grave, "played the Miserere prayer and tried to sing a hopeful Psalm." Couples got married; children were born as the camp wagons creaked along or beside the night fires leaping skyward.

But through late winter snows and early spring rains and mud, on through summer heat, they toiled across Iowa, plunging into "one of the undistinguishable waves of that great land sea."

North of Omaha they took up "Winter Quarters," where they made a pact with the friendly Potawatomi Indians for a large acreage in the unhealthy Missouri bottoms.

All too soon the sound of hammer and saw, all the busy activities of the new settlers, drove the game out of the country, and the Red men, repenting of their generosity, and finding the Mormons unreasonable, appealed to the federal government to void the contract.

Once more the Mormons were obliged to seek a new place to live and worship. The blow fell at a most evil moment. The settlers were stricken with malaria, scurvy and pneumonia. Not enough hands were up to milk the cows, not enough voices to raise the Psalm on Sundays. The few who could "went about among the tents and wagons with food and water, like nurses through the wards of an infirmary."

Graves could not be dug fast enough, and in the open tents, women sat fanning the flies off their too long dead children or they merely sat weeping at night in the dim light from hollow turnips filled with oil and grease.

For a while they lived in provisional camps, then decided to abandon the boorish "land of liberty" entirely and migrate into Mexico.

Scouts were sent out, six men who went clear through to Salt Lake Valley. They came back with maps, a description of the soil and climate, and upon their recommendation, Salt Lake was solemnly chosen as "the Promised Land," the "Zion of the Continent."

On April 9, 1847, Brigham Young, the new prophet, left "Winter Quarters" for the Salt Lake Valley at the head of 143 men, three women and two children, with seventy-three wagons, a field-piece on wheels, thirty-six oxen, ninety-three horses, fifty-two mules, nineteen cows, seventeen dogs, and many chickens. In the party were mechanics, farmers, engineers, teachers, merchants, doctors and artisans.

Rigid rules were prescribed. At the five o'clock bugle, all had to rise and pray, tend the teams, get breakfast and be ready to leave by seven. All must start together and keep together. Each man had to travel on the offside of his team, loaded gun on his shoulder. The field cannon, in charge of a company guard, brought up the rear. An hour's halt for dinner. At night the wagons were put in a circle, the horses inside. The 8:30 evening bugle was the signal for all fires to be extinguished and for everyone to be at his wagon to pray.

After about a month, rigid discipline palled, especially among travelers not Mormons who had affixed themselves to the cavalcade. There was considerable dancing, card-playing, checkers, gambling, loud swearing and many quarrels. After enduring this for some time, Brigham Young threatened to punish all offenders so severely they would "never go back to tell the tale." Everybody took a solemn oath to behave himself.

Near the present town of Casper, they floated their wagons, lashed four abreast, across the Platte; and the first section of the train, pushing ahead because of sickness and six-weeks' lack of bread, on June 26th reached South Pass on the continental divide and four days later floated on rafts across Green River. By then they had been without bread for six weeks; many were ill with fever.

On July 19th, after toiling to make a difficult road up a canyon, the advance guard looked down on "the Promised Land." They "raised their hats, then swinging them," shouted. The cane brakes, on what became "Mill Creek," looked like inviting grain. July 20th they reached the Great Salt Lake and the very next day put in crops.

Other expeditions kept coming; by wintertime, the newly founded Salt Lake City had a population of 2,095 souls.

The following year ampler crops were planted, but millions of locusts descended from their Rocky Mountain breeding grounds and began devouring everything. Fortunately gulls from the lake came and devoured "the crickets"—this was considered an act of Providence for the special protection of the chosen.

News of the California gold rush drifted in, but despite numerous discouragements, the Mormons were not seduced. The head men of the church proclaimed in noble but most un-American language:

"The true use of gold is for paving streets, covering houses and making culinary dishes." The Lord, when they had raised enough grain and built enough cities, would provide them with all the gold they needed. "Until then let them not be over anxious, for the treasures of the earth are in the Lord's storehouse, and He will open the doors thereof when and where He pleases."

Their only bitterness was that their new home, as a result of the war with Mexico, promptly passed under the jurisdiction of the United States, which they had sought to escape, in which they had known mostly persecution and where they were to suffer more.

But the colony survived and little by little prospered. From 1847 on troops of people swarmed out to the Mormon settlement, many ill-prepared for the journey, lacking proper food, clothing and conveyances. Many perished. In 1856, in the late summer months, 600 men, women and children started from St. Joseph, Missouri, pushing handcarts with all their belongings, but in the Sweet Water country were overwhelmed by snowstorms. More than half of them dropped by the wayside.

Hearing of their plight Brigham Young sent out a rescue party led by Daniel W. Jones. In his *Forty Years Among the Indians,* Jones —not a Mormon—tells vividly of the terrible suffering and death, the bravery and folly of the Handcart Brigade:

"The weather was cold and stormy. We traveled hard, never taking time to stop for dinner. We began to feel great anxiety . . . we, strong men with good outfits, found the nights severe. What must be the condition of those we were to meet? Many old men and women, little children, mothers with nursing babies, crossing the plains, pulling handcarts. Our hearts began to ache when we reached Green River and yet found no word of them. Here an express was sent ahead with a light wagon to meet and cheer the people up.

"At the South Pass we enccuntered a severe snowstorm . . . two men were seen on horseback going west. They reported their company in a starving condition at their camp, then east of Rocky Ridge. . . . We started immediately through the storm. . . . On arriving we found them in a condition that would stir the feelings of the hardest heart. . . . They were out of provisions and really freezing and starving to death. The morning after our arrival nine were buried in one grave. . . . The boys struck out on horseback and dragged up a lot of wood; provisions were distributed. . . . Soon there was an improvement . . . but many poor, faithful people had gone too far—had passed beyond the power to recruit . . . many died after our arrival. . . .

"The greater portion of our company continued on toward Devil's Gate, traveling through snow all the way. . . ."

Jones there went out with another express. "After riding about twelve miles, we saw a White man's shoe track in the road. . . . We put our animals to their utmost speed and soon came in sight of the camp at Red Bluff. This was Brother Edward Martin's handcart company and Ben Horgett's wagon company. There was still another wagon company down near the Platte crossing.

"This company . . . in almost as bad a condition as the first one

. . . had nearly given up hope." Many were "worn out and sick."

They made the company move on a bit each day, their only salvation, but the handful of rescuers "among so many (some 1,200) could do but little, and there was danger of many deaths before proper help could arrive."

The rescuers went clear on to the rear to get the various other brigades to move on toward the lower valley. "The clouds were gathering thickly for a storm, and just as we were about to start, it commenced snowing very hard. The heavens were obscured by clouds, excepting a small place about the shape of the gable end of a house. This opening was in the direction of the valley, and the sun seemed to shine through with great brightness. The people . . . took this for a warning and soon started for their cattle."

The second day of travel, the rearguard and the rescuers overtook the handcart brigade going up a long muddy hill. "A condition of distress here met my eyes," says Jones, "that I never saw before or since. The train was strung out for three or four miles. There were old men pulling and tugging their carts, sometimes loaded with a sick wife or children, women pulling along sick husbands; little children six or eight years old struggling through mud and snow. As night came on, the mud would freeze on their clothes and feet. We gathered on to some of the most helpless with our riatas tied to the carts, and helped as many as we could into camp on Avenue Hill. This was a bitter, cold night, and we had no fuel except some very small sagebrush. Several died that night."

About the first of November, they finally reached Devil's Gate Fort: "The winter storms had now set in in all their severity. The provisions we took amounted to almost nothing among so many of them now on very short rations, some almost starving. Many were dying daily from exposure and want of food. . . . The men seemed to be failing and dying faster than the women and children. . . . All the people who could, crowded into the houses of the fort out of the cold and storm. One crowd cut away the walls of the house they were in for fuel, until half of the roof fell in."

They tried to cache the imperishable goods in pits, hardwares in one, clothing in another, etc., but the pits would fill up with drifting snow as fast as the dirt was thrown out.

"Cattle and horses were dying every day . . . finally one morning store rooms in the fort were cleared and about 200 wagons run in unloaded. No one was allowed to keep out anything but a change of clothing, some bedding and light cooking utensils. . . . The hand-cart people were notified to abandon most of their carts. Teams were hitched up and the sick and feeble loaded in with such light weight as was allowed. All became common property. . . . Next day all hands pulled out, most of them on foot."

After setting the camp in order, Jones followed up the train. Several miles further on, he came upon a lady sitting alone by the side of the road, weeping bitterly. She was elegantly dressed and appeared strong and well.

"This is too much for me," she complained. "I have always had plenty, and have never known hardships; we had a good team and wagon; my husband, if let alone, could have taken me in comfort. Now I am turned out to walk in the wind and snow. I am determined not to go on, but will stay here and die. My husband has gone and left me, but I will not go another step."

After considerable persuasion, Jones got her moving.

By constant assistance and encouragement, the immigrants, after much suffering, were gotten into the valley. Jones and his men then went back to Devil's Gate. Over 200 head of cattle had died in the vicinity of the fort, and carcasses were strewn along the route of each day's travel. Swarms of prairie wolves ate them and invaded even the camp, trying to attack the cattle. Even though the cattle were corralled at night, in a week twenty-five died or were killed by wolves, which had become so ravenous they even threatened to attack the people.

It was decided to slaughter the remaining fifty head of cattle for food, so that the men managed to live awhile without suffering except for lack of salt. Hunting brought little result, game was very scarce, so finally nothing but the hides was left. These were cooked and eaten without seasoning, and the whole company came down sick. They had plenty of coffee, but it palled. One man became delirious from drinking too much on an empty stomach. Though the hides made them sick, they continued to gnaw at them, swallowing glue and all. Next they ate the wrappings off the wagon-tongues, then old moccasin soles, finally pieces of buffalo hide that had been used for a foot-mat for two months.

Some of the boys, against orders, sneaked out and cut steaks from several carcasses of cattle which the wolves had not devoured. They became very sick. That was in February.

One sundown a Snake Indian came into camp. They gave him a piece of rawhide to eat and invited him to stay the night.

About eight o'clock they heard a loud noise and voices in an unknown tongue. It was swearing by French-Canadian mule drivers. Another group, the Magraw party, also came struggling up through the drifts, glad to reach protection and warm fires. They turned over all their provisions—just enough for supper and breakfast.

A Frenchman, with the mail company, and an Indian went out to look for game and came back loaded down with buffalo meat.

This lasted the party until March 4th. All they then had left was a packsaddle covered with rawhide. This would see them through for several days more. Just as they were soaking up the rawhide, six men with the Y. X. express came through. They brought with them another buffalo they had killed.

The group starved on through to the middle of April when a thaw allowed them to dig thistle roots. Even of these there were not many, and it was May before supplies reached them from Salt Lake City.

When Utah became part of the United States, Brigham Young was appointed Governor of the new territory. The old myths about the Mormons—thieving and other crimes—revived; a wave of ignorant hatred that anybody would practice anything but monogamy swept the United States. The Mormons became the goats for everything. Emigrants to the West Coast complained of suffering indignities; they even accused the Mormons of sicking the Indians on them to kill and rob.

In 1857 President James Buchanan removed Young as Governor of the Territory and appointed an outsider. The Mormons, now too numerous to migrate in masses, were so incensed they prepared to fight.

The war lasted nearly a year. The Mormons forced the first expedition back, seizing large quantities of supplies. A second federal expedition was outfitted. The supply trains alone, including customary graft, cost $15,000,000 and were described by Father Pierre Jean De Smet, the Chaplain, as being like "a fleet of vessels with all canvas spread." This expedition was also worsted.

Differences were then settled by agreement. A non-Mormon government was recognized by the sect, in exchange for promised non-interference, and for many years they were tacitly allowed to pursue their own customs unmolested.

But ignorant American hatred of non-conformity—always so pronounced in sex-matters—in due time came to life again, and in 1870, Joseph F. Smith, put on the mat, testified that he had six wives and forty-two children, but manfully told his persecutors:

"I would rather face the law than desert my family."

In 1889 Brigham H. Roberts was elected to Congress, but was refused a seat because he had three wives and twelve children by two of them.

"I have lived with good conscience . . ." he said to Congress. "You can brand me with shame and send me forth, but I shall leave with head erect and brow undaunted and walk the earth as angels walk the clouds." But by 1890 the Mormons did bow to the general antagonism to polygamy and proclaimed it no longer a tenet of their religion.

Despite all persecution, in a little over a century the Mormon Church increased from the first church at Fayette to 92 "Stakes of Zion," or bishoprics, governing 1,275 churches; from the six original members to 540,000, scattered over all but three of the states of the Union. Its missionaries—and every member must spend a period of probatory time in this work—now proselytize not only the United States, but almost every country in Europe, including Turkey, in South Africa, Canada, Mexico, South America, Australia, New Zealand and many Pacific Islands. Mormon agricultural colonies are found in Mexico and other foreign countries.

The Mormons, too, had their schisms, and at the death of Joseph Smith in 1844, a large group at Nauvoo even then renounced polygamy and founded the Reorganized Church of Jesus Christ of Latter Day Saints with headquarters now at Independence, Missouri. They have about 65,000 members. In 1938 the press reported the arrest of Mormons, belonging to "the United Order of Brethren," in the isolated Arizona village of Short Creek, for practicing polygamy.

Despite the country's unfair persecution of the Mormons, it owes much to them. By such as they was the land populated, developed, made rich. So was a nation founded and built.

Today the Mormon Church and Mormons are more prosperous than the nation as a whole. The Church owns vast properties and co-operative enterprises. It is one of the biggest participants in the beet sugar industry. Its members scorn to take government relief.

The Mormons were merely one of many sects torn loose from old moorings by the peculiarities of their beliefs and sent restlessly westward toward the setting sun, westward to find freer life, westward to found an empire.

CHAPTER IX

SETTLING UP THE COUNTRY

At least nine-tenths of the Colonial Americans were farmers. By 1770 only five cities claimed more than 8,000 inhabitants each, or only 3.8 per cent of the population.

Except for the first years and later in isolated frontier points, mere subsistence farming became less and less paramount. Almost from the start in America, agriculture, like industry, was a projection of the mercantile system. Almost from the start, markets for surplus produce—the *sine qua non* for cash crops in commercialized plantation agriculture—were at hand. In the early years a big outlet was found in the West Indies where the one-crop sugar system made necessary the importation—despite pirates—of most other food-stuffs, chiefly "flour and bread," but also, wrote Governor Cadwallader Colden of New York, "pork, bacon, hogshead staves, some beef, butter and a few candles," in return for molasses, sugar, logwood and cocoa.

Samuel Maverick, describing Massachusetts in 1660, notes that though in 1626 there were few domestic animals, within thirty-four years there were "great herds of cattle" and "Braue Flocks of Sheepe." Horses, "Neate Beasts and Hoggs" were being shipped to Newfoundland, Barbados, Jamaica, the "Carribe Islands," and other places.

Soon the rapid land enclosures in Europe, the expansion of the industrial system there, which drew more and more farmers into the new factories and caused a rapid increase in population, created an ever greater commercial demand for outside farm-products. Europe turned to America. Tobacco, rice, indigo, later cotton, became the leading crops of the South; in New England and the Middle Colonies, later in the Midwest also, corn, wheat, and other cereals, hogs and cattle. So long as our national economy remained agricultural, the South tended to outstrip the North in population; in 1770 it had almost as many people as the North and Middle Colonies put together, and it sold five times as much to England. In that year, agriculture export, including tobacco, totaled over $10,000,000. In addition, perhaps some millions more of produce were exported through clandestine trade channels to Spanish America.

One-crop systems led to quick soil exhaustion and on our Atlantic seaboard led to further land monopoly, also; and all three factors caused the westward migration of poorer discontented elements. Soil exhaustion sent even many of the well-to-do plantation owners following on their heels.

It was amazing how soon, after the first large migration to Kentucky and Tennessee occurred, the muddy streets of pine-board towns were filled with carriages of southern "aristocrats," making a brave show of snobbery and superiority and fine dress in that harsh, rough setting.

Our Revolution freed the American planter-trading classes from paying direct tribute to the English mercantile system. But the Revolution also represented a revolt of the men of small properties and of no properties against economic injustice. One aspect of Independence politics was the struggle between plantation-industrial-financial interests of the colonies (the Federalists) and the more liberal democratic forces (the Jeffersonians), not to mention even more radical elements.

Some of the first-named group had been Tories, who had opposed the Revolution and separation from England, but who jumped on the band-wagon only when victory was assured by the self-sacrificing Continentals, a third of whom, if General Greene's forces are a sample, at times were "entirely naked . . . nothing but a breach clout . . . the rest . . . ragged as wolves."

Whatever the quarrel of the wealthy New England merchants with England, which Horatio Gates called "an obstinate old slut, bent upon her ruin," the real efforts of the Revolution were exercised by the Committees of Safety and the new democratic legislative bodies, which had temporarily swept aside plantation-class rule. The Continentals turned churches into barracks. Unpatriotic merchants, hoarders of coffee and sugar, saw their goods forcibly taken into the public markets and dealt out—often by the women, who even mal-treated the owners.

The slogan was: "In the name of Jehovah and the Continental Congress."

Victory was pledged "about the flowing bowl," with toasts for "the success of Congress and the liberty and freedom of America." The revolutionists seized Crown lands and Tory plantations, something we now arrogantly coerce Mexico not to do, although the provocation has been greater there than in the Thirteen Colonies. The big estates of Lord Granville, McCulloh, Morris and Lord Fairfax were thus taken over. Also large estates beyond the Allegheny, irrespective of claims, were confiscated and settled. The laws of primogeniture and entail were wiped out. The Anglican Church was disestablished. Severe blows were struck at all sorts of privilege. At the same time, as many outside goods had been temporarily cut off during the struggle, new manufacturing sprang into being. But the cry and hope was for land.

For a long time, despite landlordism, access to the land was con-siderably easier for even the pauper than in any place in Europe. A large proportion of the settlers, especially in Pennsylvania and on South and West, were squatters with no absolute title. Some later paid up, others held their lands by force against all comers, others were later ejected.

After the Revolution many such squatters acquired title through successive grants by Congress, which was repeatedly forced to acknowl-edge right of possession. These laws, recognizing squatter rights, were equally utilized—often promoted—by dishonest land-stealing com-panies to seize vast areas of the public domain. In some regions, more squatters were injured than benefited.

But if real strides were made toward economic and political democ-racy, for the wealthier patriots the main need seemed to be the establishment of a strong centralism. The earlier Articles of Confederation were set aside and a document created, with due expressions of noble and disinterested principles, to put barriers to the further spread of democratic control, to throw obstacles, through the check and balance system, to the carrying out of the wishes of the people, and to keep the agrarian movement within bounds. The plantation and trading classes wanted freedom from England and more privileges for themselves but not for other elements in the population. They feared the new ideas of democracy, of land confiscation; they wanted to conserve their political control. The result was the American Constitution, to be sure, patterned on broad and fair principles, but modified to meet all the momentary and pressing conflicts and emergencies, and certainly never meant to become the rigid oracle that adoring descendants have made of it, but something to be further modified, amended and ever interpreted broadly and generously in accordance with expanding needs and new ideas. The leaders who made it were men of unusual minds, a group of thinkers who sensed the momentous nature of their task, and in a spirit of tolerance and loyalty to broad ideals, rose above their class origins, the selfishness they might have been expected to show in the heated passions of the time, to embrace concepts nobler than those they practiced on their own estates, viz., the rightful equality before the law and opportunities for all men.

They did love the status quo; they were afraid to see it changed to their own disadvantage; and so they put multiple checks on the too rapid fulfillment of democratic wishes; they even sacrificed efficiency by invoking in government, not the principle of unified administration and co-operation in all branches, but that of semi-independent powers for the three divisions, each to block in part the wishes of the other two. They feared concentration of power more than loss of efficiency. They had in mind, not modern dictatorships, but the monarchs of Europe, and the doctrines of Locke and Montesquieu. They were fencing against an imaginary king; they were fencing, like good aristocrats, against popular ignorance and immoderate mob desires.

In fencing against a mythical absolute monarchy, they established a broad bill of rights that is still to a great extent obeyed. In fencing against democracy, they sought moderation, checks, rather than absolute barriers to popular will. They were, even if "aristocrats" and wealthy traders, tinctured with the new middle-class concepts. Also they were still so close to the Reformation and the war on feudalism they did not feel entirely secure in their new rights without the aid of the populace.

Normal as all this may have been, liberal as was the Constitution, from the viewpoint of the mass of the Continentals, it cloaked a definite counter-revolution. This counter-revolution found expression in the work of the delegates—mostly of the wealthier merchant and plantation class—to the 1787 Constitutional Convention.

Effectively they did put more checks on the popular rule than on their own special groups—by the creation of a Senate not elected by popular vote but by state legislatures, a President to be named by a college of Electors, a federal judiciary with life tenure in office, and stiff and undemocratic procedure for amendment. A whole chain of vetoes was created to cool the tea of democratic fervor.

All the minority of seventy-three votes in the South Carolina Convention called to consider the new Constitution were Up-country men mostly of the small farmer and frontiersman class; those who approved it were the wealthier coast planters. They still had control of the electoral machinery, as did similar groups in most of the colonies. Voting was still a restricted privilege almost everywhere. Hence they reluctantly swallowed the more liberal compromise clauses of the Constitution, designed to attract those few colonies where democratic rights were more in vogue. Given all the extreme anti-democratic measures proposed by the closed-door Congress, it is amazing that the document turned out as moderate, liberal, democratic, with such a generous concept of human justice as it did.

But so cannily did the Founding Fathers work, so silken-gloved was their iron hand, that, except for brief periods, our federal government was kept to the shady super-conservative side. The Constitution provided an instrument by which the rich planters and well-to-do mercantile groups could retain much political control; it was equally successful as an instrument guaranteeing excessive control by later post-Civil War industrialists and in our own century by financiers.

But the way has not been barred to popular will. When aroused the people have made known their desires, have enforced them. If they have permitted too great wealth for a few and too great power to a few, it has been because of their faith in those few or because of their own slothfulness.

For brief moments a bit of the power has shifted to the Middle West farmers, but usually it has quickly shifted back to the industrialists and later financiers. All in all, the document was an eastern seaboard constitution that seemed to work well enough. But the more vital forces of the nation swept westward where developed new concepts more attuned to the real needs of America. Some of those have gradually been absorbed into our polity. Others are still to be heard from.

The numerous stresses that the Constitution might soon have had to undergo were put off by the westward movement. Not a new constitution, not new laws and attitudes, came to the fore, but new land. To the west lay opportunity, new life, Utopia. So long as there was plenty of land and men could move in upon it, the kind of Constitution did not really matter much. The wisdom embodied in it, however, is revealed by the easy manner in which it has since flung its ample cloak not over the little eastern strip of land, but over the restless and reckless men of a whole free open continent.

The English Crown had not intended to open up the western country to the rabble, but to nobles, favorites and creditors. The King had gotten rid of a bothersome debt to William Penn's father, by giving Pennsylvania to his firebrand son. The King and his successors hoped similarly to get rid of other obligations by parceling out the West in the same way. The Crown wished to buy loyalty and reward loyalty and take the edge off enemy conspirators by the lands of the American West. But the Long Rifles moved west anyway.

After Independence, the Founding Fathers, many of them engaged in land-grabbing and speculation, wished to control the western lands by a sort of proprietary system, such as had ruled the original colonies. They had similar objectives as had the Crown. It soon became evident that whoever had control of giving out the western lands could exercise a great political power. The politicians of no other new country and no old country have ever had such an enormous pork-barrel for patronage, for building up political following, and for self-enrichment as those who had charge of western lands. The extraordinary expenditures of the New Deal for political purposes are small change compared to the power involved in the settling of the West.

Even though this was true, in spite of political and legal restraints, all the new land grants to political grafters and insiders, the Long Rifles moved west even faster than in Colonial days. As Peattie put it, "there were men who without compass could line a grove across a hundred miles of unmapped prairie who yet were unable to read a proclamation!"

Very early, traders had threaded through the wilds over Indian trails that became the "traders' trace," and down the rivers. Early in the eighteenth century, explorers crossed the country. "Cowpens" were staked far out in the wilderness. Hog-drovers came through periodically to supply the East or new cotton country in the South; they sewed up the eyes of the hogs to keep them from running off into the wilds and drove them hundreds of miles. During the War of 1812, high prices caused thousands of cattle, as well as hogs, to be driven east over the Alleghenies from as far off as Ohio.

Migratory "pioneers," depending on quick haphazard crops, but mostly on hunting, handily wielding "musquett" or "fuzee," and tomahawks, pushed on from valley to valley, further breaking the hard edge of the frontier, their life incompatible with either complete wilderness or the lands settled and filled in behind them. Such daring ones were drum-majors for whole bands. They were the curling crest of a mighty flood of folk that swelled and swelled for a century, lapping into almost every valley and meadow, into every corner of the mighty land.

Folk went to escape a society already clogged with class prejudices. They sought economic and religious freedom; they felt the breath of liberty; they followed a gleam. They sang:

"Cheer up, brothers, as we go
O'er the mountains, westward ho,
Where bands of deer and buffalo
Furnish the fair.

"Then o'er the hills in legions, boys,
Fair freedom's star
Points to the Sunset regions, boys,
Ha, ha, ha—ha!"

The first part of the eighteenth century—despite Royal edicts trying to maintain feudal landlordism beyond even the actual settled Colonial borders—had already seen a cloud of Scotch-Irish and Palatine Germans, long rifles in hand, pushing and swarming up the Shenandoah into western Virginia and the Carolina Piedmont, on to Pittsburgh. In the Upper Piedmont in the South, they became "the Presbyterian aristocrats" of York, the Greenville Baptists, the Wafford Methodists of Spartanburg. They put up log cabins and lean-tos, made their own furniture, spun their own clothing, tanned their own hides for shoes and boots, ate corn from their own pastures and venison from the woods.

On their heels came lesser numbers of English, Welsh, and French Huguenots. The New York Germans pushed up the Mohawk. The Dutch, too, pushed upstream, over to Jersey and the Delaware River Gap and through Pennsylvania. The New England Puritans, who eddied into corners of Jersey, spread over northern Pennsylvania.

At first the great wedge beyond the Alleghenies was the Ohio Valley, where Washington earlier carried his ultimatum to the French to get out, and where Braddock, even in defeat, camped over the unknown mineral wealth of Pittsburgh. Here along the Ohio came Daniel Boone from the upland south into the rich Blue Grass country. Along the Ohio, settlers slid in between strong Indian confederacies, between the French to the north and the Spaniards to the south, and floated on easily to new homes. It has always been an intermediary region, even in prehistoric Indian days, and a great artery of travel and commerce. In a trickle then a tide and, after the Revolution burst all the legal and mountain barriers, in floods, settlers floated along, hurried along, rowing, with song, "the old boat along . . . Down the O-h-i-o."

Kentucky, Tennessee, the upper Ohio, were settled. Andrew Jackson crossed the mountains on horseback, in broadcloth and a Negro at his heels, though nary a penny in his purse. Tidewater Virginians and Carolinians moved in.

The 1785 Land Ordinance for the new Northwest provided the section and township boundaries which made location of each "forty" easy for newcomers. The 1787 Ordinance provided the framework of government, which was set up July 15th, the following year. Settlers came, squatted, claimed or bought land, seizing first upon those acres with rich alluvial lake deposits of glacier drift, fertile in loess and other rock powders. Few regions were ever richer in soil values.

In 1788 a band of New Englanders settled definitely in Marietta, Ohio. Ironically they named their settlement of new freedom after Marie Antoinette, but they opened up the Northwest Territory. They had to abandon their cherished clambakes, but they grew fat, many of them, on corn and pork and wild game.

Men from Connecticut settled along Lake Erie, giving birth to Cleveland and Youngstown. There came folk from Achter Kil and the lower Delaware. New Jerseyites, under John Cleves Symmes, obtained a Congressional grant, and Cincinnati sprang up. Virginians settled in an area which grew into Manchester and Chillicothe.

Into "Hoosier" Indiana came settlers from North Carolina. By 1820, Ohio, southern Indiana and Illinois, even southern Missouri, were being filled in. Yankees lumbered out in immigrant wagons. Kentuckians, among them the father of Abraham Lincoln, hacked their way into the Indiana woods and then those of Illinois—when Chicago was merely Fort Dearborn, a lonely military post in the wilderness. Virginians and Marylanders and folk from Massachusetts and Connecticut also seeped into Illinois—the state filled up "like a vase, from the bottom." Tennesseeans came seeking soil appropriate for slave labor. South met North. Flatboats, arks, rafts, keel boats, dugouts, canoes, drifted in with new settlers from many parts—along the Ohio, along the Wabash, the Illinois, the flat Rock, the Vermilion, the White, the Blue, the Sugar, the Wildcat, the Salamanie and the Kaskaskia Rivers. Plodding hooves tracked across the farthest reaches of the great American veldt, though often the wagons, in marshes and up steep mountains, would make only two miles a day.

Gone from the new scheme was the indented servant. It was every man on his own. It was the crude democracy of the strongest, the more daring, the more persistent.

Scotch-Irish Presbyterians, German Moravians, Carolina Methodists, New England Congregationalists, French Huguenots, English Quakers, Swedish Lutherans, caused a complex weave of customs and techniques, ideas and emotions, stimulated new activities, gave tonic to the blood-stream—a new outburst of creative energy, social endeavor and broader tolerance, of freedom and love of self-government. Even though soon many of the western immigrants came directly from Europe, the jostling mixture of creeds and ideas quickly made a new amalgam more typically American. All these varied elements forced even the East slowly to abandon thinking so much in European terms. The East along with the newer West had to turn to pragmatic American realities.

In good part the East had been settled up like so many separate beehives, each nationality and creed walled up in tight compartments. In the Middle West, nationalities, creeds, political opinions, were dumped into a jostling heap to shake and sift down as they could. Movement creates tolerance, destroys localism and narrow prejudice. New Englanders gone west had to slough off their Puritanical rigidity, their thin-mouthed dogmatism. Catholics had to hobnob with Holy Rollers. "Norskies" and "Yankees" broke their knuckles on each other's heads, but learned to live together.

Inevitably the invasion of the Ohio region obliged the newcomers to fight to obtain the region on up to the Great Lakes and the whole Mississippi Valley itself—soon to become, according to one Congressman, "the acknowledged seat of the empire of the world . . . bond of union made by nature itself." The Spaniards were obliged to sell us Florida. At the price of four cents an acre Jefferson purchased the vast Louisiana Territory, an empire as large as Europe. By war, we wrenched away half of Mexico's territory.

Carolinians presently spilled over into Georgia and Florida, later into Alabama, Mississippi, Louisiana, facing not only Indians but French and Spaniards and the "strangers feever," as the "Yellow Jack" was then called. The Gulf States were the Carolinians' Titanic offspring.

The far northwestern frontier was pushed out by eager immigrants and determined resistance was made to English claims. And the whole was taken from the Indians by cajolery, trickery, fraud, force and murder.

The greatest immediate expansion was made possible by the Louisiana Purchase, a step precipitated by Napoleon's need for cash to fight England and his desire to set a boundary to English New World ambitions. The plenipotentiaries exchanged signatures on May 3, 1803. Robert Livingston who signed for the United States waxed eloquent.

"We have lived long but this is the noblest work of our whole lives. The treaty we have just signed was neither obtained by subtlety nor dictated by force. Of equal advantage to both parties, it will transform vast solitudes into thriving districts. The United States ranks today among the powers of the first order, and England's exclusive influence over American affairs has passed, never to return. Thus one of the principal causes of European rivalries and hatreds has disappeared. . . . Through the United States will be established the maritime right of all the nations of the earth, today usurped by one alone. The instruments which we have just signed will cause no tears to be shed; they prepare ages of happiness for innumerable generations of human creatures. The Mississippi and the Missouri will see them succeed one another and multiply, truly worthy of the regard and care of Providence, in the bosom of equality, under just laws, freed from the errors of superstition and the scourges of bad government."

This was typical American optimism. He had not yet heard of Ma Ferguson or Bilbo. But in another sense he had a right to be optimistic. His forebears knew much of the technique of land-grabbing in new territory: his father was the wealthiest landowner in New York; his elder brother, after a scandalous defalcation by a subordinate in the customs, in 1804 went off to New Orleans where he grabbed land, sought to get hold of most of the river waterfront, and defended the pirate Lafitte.

Lausset, the last French Governor of Louisiana before the purchase, had already seen the handwriting on the wall and tells in the journal how the Kaintock (as the Creoles called not only the Kentuckians but all Americans in general) had secured the right, by the treaty of 1795, to a trading center in New Orleans. They now possessed Natchez, become a place of 8,000 people—and "What airs" they gave themselves there! "The General Assembly of Representatives of the Mississippi Territory"—one could "burst with laughing" at their "crude vanities," said Lausset.

But in the midst of his mockery, he reluctantly admitted admiration. He made copious notes about the Black Settlers, i.e., the American frontiersmen, and described keenly the processes of democracy, tolerance, boosterism, bluff, serious purposefulness and optimism that are still traits of American character:

"They set up their huts, cut and burn the timber, kill the savages or are killed by them, and disappear from the country either by dying or ceding to some steadfast cultivator the land they have already begun to clear. When a score of new colonists are thus gathered in a certain spot, they are followed by two printers, one a federalist, the other an anti-federalist, then by doctors, lawyers and adventurers; they propose toasts and nominate a speaker; they erect a city; they beget children without end; they vainly advertise vast territories for sale; they attract and deceive as many buyers as possible; they increase the figures of the population till they reach a total of 60,000 souls, at which they are able to form an independent state and send a representative to Congress . . . and there is one more star in the United States flag.

"Under the Spanish or the French a district is begun, discontinued, begun again, lost once more, and so forth, until its fate is definitely cast either for existence or non-existence; under the Americans a new-born state may advance with more or less prosperity, but one can be sure it will never lose ground, but will tend always to increase and consolidate itself.

"Imagination can scarcely conceive that these immense stretches of land, from the Mississippi to the Alleghanies which, forty years ago, had not a single man to cultivate them, are today sending by the Mississippi to New Orleans those abundant fruits of their harvest with which her markets are loaded."

The change in American life was reflected soon enough in national politics.

The New England statesman, when he returned home, went to his library to prepare metaphysical and hair-splitting discourses full of erudition and solemn Biblical injunctions. The plantation statesman went home to loll in a hammock, drink mint-juleps, hiccough, let a Negro slave fan the flies away, while he meditated on the sacredness of womanhood and banalities about high-born gentlemen. The western politician went home, spat on his hands and took hold of the plow.

But what the new settlements gained in freedom and boldness, they lacked in homogeneity and sometimes decency. Coarseness and strength and the slug on the jaw were more pronounced than thought, culture or artistic apperception—and the former criterion still holds large sway in our movies. The practical elbowed out even intelligent theory. Restless, nervous energy and ready invention produced great material returns, and often the spiritual counterparts, but they could hardly be expected to produce refinement, calm, or even wisdom. Costly trial and error predominated over planning and science. Energy seemed boundless, to be squandered easily like the resources of the land. Turner quotes Bryce, who found that the West reminded him "of the crowd which Vathek found in the hall of Eblis, each darting hither and thither, with swift steps and unique mien, driven to and fro by a fire in the heart. Time seems too short for what they have to do, and the result always to come short of their desire."

Ready movement, optimistic buoyancy and untrammeled freedom gave a sense of breadth and hope to life such as few peoples have enjoyed. One may smile now at the forlorn pages of *The Home Diadem* (as other ages for diverse reasons will smile over our ladies' journals of today) and other magazines of the time; at the naïvety, the crudeness, the lack of line and subtlety, but one can also regret that older simplicity. Above all, people had hope undying, faith and courage. People sang:

> "When we've wood and prairie land,
> Won by our toil,
> We'll reign like kings in fairee land,
> Lords of the soil."

Out from passing covered wagons floated the sad songs of the middle border, *Nellie Wildwood, Minnie Mintern, Belle Mahoney, Lily Dale*, and above all that air which became the marching song for a whole generation—*Over the Hills in Legions, Boys*. The singers were answered by the *boom boom boom* of the prairie cocks and the whirr of quail and the moan of pigeons. And among them the boy, Hamlin Garland, was marveling at "the flash and glimmer of the tall sunflowers, the myriad voices of gleeful bobolinks, the chirp and gurgle of red-winged blackbirds swaying on the willows, the meadow larks piping from grassy bogs, the peep of the prairie chick and the wailing call of the plover."

Soon plows bit into the thick "nigger-wool" and the wild buckwheat—"the epic breaking season." Acres of corn and wheat and rye spread out toward the golden horizon. Prayers were said over the johnnycake on the clean ash board; the tea-kettle swung from its lug-pole; and pewter spoons and basins clattered on the wooden benches. The spinning wheel wove cloth to be dyed with black walnut juice.

It was perhaps not a lofty or enlightened or a very understanding world that the frontiersmen created but, despite its violences, its ignorant cruelties, its restless get-ahead qualities, its boisterous slap-stick humor, it was on the whole a good, warm-hearted society— often generous. The folks' joys were mostly simple joys—though often these eventually provided significant contributions, some harmful, for the future psychology and customs of the nation: revival meetings, picnics, house-raising bees, harvest bees, barn dances, jigs and reels and songs:

"O wha will shoe my bonny foot
And wha will glove my hand?
And wha will bind my middle jimps
Wi' a lang, lang linen band?"

On far prairies the fiddle squawked out *Honest John* at boisterous barn dances—*"Lady lead to the right, deedle deedle dum dum."* And in Nebraska, they called:

"Gents bow out and ladies bow under,
Hug 'em tight and swing like thunder."

Charles Coleman Sellers, in his *Lorenzo Dow*, quotes a southern newspaper of a hundred years ago:

"The Reverend Mr. Blaney will preach next Sunday in Dempsey's Grove. . . . Providence permitting. Between sermons, the preacher will run his sorrel mare, Julia, against any nag that can be trotted out in this region for a purse of $100"—merely the Bingo touch of an earlier day.

Storytelling was also an art; folklore of all sorts blossomed, and that queer spirit of tongue-in-the-cheek exaggeration which measures so much of the humor of the hinterlands and spills over into Mark Twain. Nothing was better than for a bunch to sit around the stove, swapping yarns, as they chawed tobacco and spat on the stove to hear it sizzle. It was amazing how much pleasure could be gotten out of popping corn, or just throwing cane stalks into the hickory and oak fires to hear the hollow joints explode, loud as a pistol.

In time traveling entertainers came through on more traveled routes, and even side shows, with a mangy animal or two, and perhaps a lady to write autographs with her toes.

The rowdy elections around a whiskey barrel under the spreading hickory tree, Vigilante law, whore-house saloons, gambling, give us a less sweetly bucolic picture, but even those rougher activities were hale, reckless, vigorous, easy come, easy go. Naturally not all the settlers were God-fearing sorts, for along the line of the frontier was also washed up a lot of human scum: embryo criminals, desperados, bandits, Wallingfords, drunkards, sadists and degenerates. There were plenty of bravos, panhandlers, thieves, pirates on the rivers, gamblers. One early traveler going to Tennessee with his father to take up land on soldier's warrants, remarked in later years, "I remember . . . that the tavern-keepers and the few traders in sugar and whiskey were the only permanent settlers, all the rest being Virginia lawyers with a great air of gentility, and land sharks with a great air of benevolence."

Gradually some elegance did creep into town and city life: social affairs were pointing the way to a later Emily Post and best-seller books on etiquette—all a secret yearning for the snobbery the frontier folk despised. At a far later date in Chicago, the members of the City Council would come to open fisticuffs over the question of whether or not to wear white gloves at a reception for Queen Marie of Roumania. But in the old days, Chicago was already doing its best. Even by 1834 at social balls they were serving lobster and Regent's punch. In the quadrilles, though there were plenty of brogans and travel-worn riding dresses, there were also officers in full uniform, balancing tradesmen's daughters in fluffy short frocks and lace trousers—sort of exposed supernumerary drawers. "The golden aguilettes of a handsome surgeon flapped in unison with the glass beads upon the scrawny neck of fifty" dazzlingly bedecked. High buttons glistened on linsey-woolsey coats "in the *dos à dos*" with a partner with cinderella slippers and "raven locks, dressed à la madonna," over eyes of jet, "that told of a lineage drawn from the original owners of the soil." Such nut-brown beauties vied with those of "golden tresses, floating away from eyes of heaven's own colour, over a neck of alabaster," revealing "the Gothic ancestry of some of England's born." Trim and beaded leggings, inflated gigots, tall plumes—a motley to be sure; but, asked a contemporary observer, "Where the devil did all these well-dressed people come from?"

In 1841 the squatter claims under the general pre-emption law were legalized. 1861-62 was signalized by the Morril Act, the Homestead Law, the establishment of a Federal Bureau of Agriculture, the first Pacific Railway Bill, the Emancipation Proclamation—a revolution in agriculture, labor and transportation. The Homestead Act threw a goodly portion of the public domain legally open to new settlement—and to still greater land thefts. The dykes were down.

The cream of the soil, of course, went to land companies, in which high government officials often participated and became wealthy, later to the railways, the lumber, cattle and mining kings. Control of many vast areas was secured by federal grant, by fraud, by armed raids, by the murder of encroaching claimants and settlers. Even so, with the boom of expansion and a rapidly filling countryside, good crops plus increasing land-values for a time made payment relatively easy for the settlers, though with each succeeding financial crash it was soon evident that values had been falsely inflated, and marginal farmers, even many not marginal, were to go by the boards.

But these evils, ultimately to become more persistent, and today a menace to the stability of the nation, were concealed by repeated revivals, due not so much in many cases to American intelligence, as to conditions in Europe. There, industrialization and the expropriation of peasant communes created increasing demand for American farm products.

From the time of the first Virginia settlers up until 1870 we incorporated 408,000,000 acres into farms; then in three decades we added an additional 430,000,000 acres, or more than in the previous two and a half centuries. By 1870 there were 189,000,000 improved acres, representing the labor of American farmers since 1607, but in the thirty years following, 225,000,000 acres more became improved, in all only a trifle less than present cultivated area. Even as early as 1857, James Caird observed, the State of Ohio alone was manufacturing seven times as many reaping and mowing machines as all England.

Early in the eighteenth century, an irascible French Governor of Louisiana, Lamothe Cadillac—dismayed by the scandalous and poverty-stricken nature of his colony, envious of the gold and silver discovered by the Spaniards—decided to journey through the northern wilderness to find similar riches. The only gold, silver or precious stones he found was a bit of ore in the possession of persons who had gotten it from the Spaniards in Mexico. He suffered many hardships, the heat, the mosquitoes on the river, and finally came back empty-handed, raging:

"This country is a monster that has neither head nor tail!"

So must that endless flat expanse of plains, that tangle of mighty forest and lakes, have seemed. But within another century the better part of it had been seized by the American colonists (or rather by the English, Scotch, Irish, Welsh, Dutch, Swedes, Norwegians, French, Finns and Germans). They didn't even stop to see whether the monster had a head; they swallowed it head, tail and all.

In 1790, the Mississippi Valley region had 100,000 inhabitants (one fortieth of the whole population of the United States); by 1810, over a million (one seventh); by 1830, 3,750,000 (more than one fourth); by 1840, over 6,000,000 (more than a third), and before long was to have half the population of the country. Speculation thrived, but the country settled up by tens of thousands, by hundreds of thousands. Finally millions swept into the prairies, and set up their "straddle-bug" markers on claims.

"This gradual and continuous progress of the European race toward the Rocky Mountains," De Tocqueville remarked as early as 1833, "has the solemnity of a providential event . . . a deluge of men . . . driven daily onward by the hand of God."

It was not so gradual—except *in toto*. It was for given locales, for given years, a frenzy, a stampede, a mass emotionalism, a drunkenness of the collective and individual spirit. It was exalted greedy rush and grab. Then there would come a lull, a period of settlement and consolidation. Presently, however, the factors of economic pressure, religious antagonisms, cultural and class conflicts, would come to a head, a new railroad would open up and Europe and our own East would be bombarded with new John Law propaganda; a new millennial, almost hysterical optimism for the splendid opportunities of freer open country would seize the spirits of men feeling cramped, and in true revival spirit, with almost religious fanfare, a new wild rush would begin.

Gold in California swept men in a flood across the wilderness, around the Horn, through Panama, to the new Parker House and the City Hotel in San Francisco, with its canvas houses "pitched among the chaparral to the very summits" of the hills. The tent-shacks, transparent from the light within, the decoy gambling lights, the "magic lantern setting"—was like "an amphitheater of fire." It spelled romance, adventure, tragedy, comedy, greed, Vigilantes.

New Yankee settlers ranged through Michigan and Wisconsin, still echoing with Canadian boat-songs, still threaded by French voyageurs and fur traders. The newcomers hacked their way through woods and crossed the coulees. By 1850 Michigan had 400,000 inhabitants (among them my paternal grandfather). Another stream invaded Iowa (with it my maternal grandfather) and soon swept beyond, scattering themselves over the wooded tributaries of the Mississippi. They mingled with immigration from the South, folk who brought manners, easy virtue, and diverse creeds; and Yankees from the North bringing in the Puritan note, and both mingled with Germans and Scandinavians, many of them educated, forward thinkers, who came in by millions. Cincinnati, with its deep love of music, its civic pride, its well-organized community institutions, and Wisconsin, with its highly progressive tendencies, to this day bear strongly the German impress. Before 1900, according to Turner, the citizens born of foreign parents totaled: Nebraska, 42 per cent; Iowa, 43 per cent; South Dakota, 60 per cent; Wisconsin, 73 per cent; Minnesota, 75 per cent; North Dakota, 79 per cent.

By 1860 Nebraska had 28,000 settlers, by 1890 over 1,000,000. By 1870 Dakota had 14,000 settlers, by 1890, 510,000. Minnesota then had 373,000. Mining soon carried the torch to Colorado. "Pike's Peak or Bust" became the new moving slogan. The lure of precious metals soon carried men on to Montana and Idaho.

Railroads hurried across the land and "free land receded at railroad speed. As early as 1877 a Burlington railway land-selling pamphlet had pointed out that today there is but a small quantity of government land lying within reasonable distance from the railroad and fit for agricultural purposes, open to settlement." Soon so few acres were available in most places that by 1882, 20,000 settlers strained ready for the race into the newly opened Oklahoma territory for new lands.

As General Francis A. Walker remarked, "The course of settlement has called upon our people to occupy a territory as extensive as

Switzerland, as England, as Italy, and latterly as France or Germany, every ten years."

Even by 1860 Seward was saying of the trans-Alleghenian region, "When the next census shall reveal your power, you will be found to be the masters of the United States of America and through them the dominating political power in the world."

The sod house dugout, two thirds in the ground, with prairie grass over light ash poles, gave way to the log hut; the homespun coat to the product of the New England mills. Houses became constantly better, less barren and ugly, a new note of leisure and ease; yet Hamlin Garland mourned that "something sweet and splendid was dying out of the prairie. The wheeling pigeons, the wailing plover, the migrating ducks and geese, the soaring cranes, the shadowy wolves, all the untamed things were passing, vanishing with the bluejoint grass, the dainty wild rose and the tiger-lily's flaming torch. Settlement was complete."

Europe not only took more and more of our products but sent us a steady stream of impoverished immigrants, helped fill up the continent, made farming in America still more profitable. The proximity of other valuable raw materials, gold, silver, copper, lead, timber, and their prompt exploitation also helped populate the country. This non-agricultural population, close at hand, also demanded food in increasing quantities from the farmers. A large river system, and soon after canals, roads and railways, made the transportation of products easy.

Agriculture suddenly expanded into a form of mass production never before paralleled in the entire history of mankind anywhere in the world. The steam plow, harvester, and thresher increased man's productive capacity tenfold, a revolution in methods and magnitude that hastened the upset of all the economies of Europe and led to our own enrichment through a recurring surplus of food products for a vast, organized world market. Thus our average annual exports of wheat and flour jumped from 20,000,000 bushels in 1852-56 to 40,000,000 in 1862-66; 90,000,000 in 1877; 186,000,000 in 1880; and 234,000,000 in 1902. European agricultural production dropped phenomenally. It could not compete with the vast, free virgin lands of a whole continent. America thereby became a world power.

America was becoming not merely a power in the world, but also a unique experiment in human association, in law, culture and political democracy. It was a cloth of many, many weaves. Each new frontier had created something new, unique—different problems, different experiences—that reacted on the settled régime behind, bringing about a constant evolution of American political ideas, farming methods, customs, folklore and even language.

Each settler took something into himself from the land he claimed and that something became part of the woven fabric, part of the heritage of America. As Mari Sandoz has put it: "One can go into a wild country and make it tame, but, like a coat and cap and mittens that he can never take off, he must always carry the look of the land as it was. He can drive the plough through the nigger-wool, make fields and roads go every way, build him a fine house and wear the stiff collar, and yet he will always look like the grass where the buffalo have eaten and smell of the new ground his feet have walked on."

All this has gone into the making of America. All this was shaping man's relation to the soil of America.

But at the very peak of all this new creative power and prosperity, the new vital relation of man to the soil suddenly snapped. The course of empire changed. The rushing up-sap of the soil clogged in its course and all too soon ceased to nourish the American settler as it should.

CHAPTER X

OLD MAN RIVER

A good index of the filling up of the plains is the rapid growth of the Mississippi traffic. The importance of the inland waterways to the early life of the late eighteenth century, and after, cannot be over-estimated. They not merely provided the means for territorial expansion and the carrying of merchandise, but also served to promote unity, consciousness of empire, and the spread of culture, of political ideas and economic growth.

Farms distant from such waterways remained very isolated; up until the middle of the nineteenth century, largely self-sufficient, without much market. As late as the 'forties, even with the Erie Canal open, it cost twenty cents a bushel to get wheat merely from Buffalo to New York, and in 1840-41, the difference in price between wheat in New York and in Chicago was fifty-seven cents a bushel. People in interior Indiana, those years, were happy, after hauling their wheat ninety miles or more to Louisville, to be able to exchange a whole wagon load merely for sugar and coffee for winter needs. Thus the rivers alone made early inland trade feasible.

The French already the previous century had pointed the way along the Mississippi. French pioneers pushed down from the Great Lakes and up from New Orleans. By 1764, Pierre Laclede Liguest, a New Orleans trader, founded the fur depot of St. Louis. Bronzed French boatmen continued to row down from Illinois, already a granary, to Arkansas—where, in among the Indians, growing more restless and ready to revolt, dwelt only a dozen settlers and as many slaves. Below that, the river took the vessels past beautiful plantations sprinkled between vast stretches of forests into which the sawmills were slowly eating. These settlers dated back to the time of John Law's madcap colonization. Some had grown enormously wealthy. M. du Breuil had five hundred Negro slaves, indigo factories, silk factories, brick yards. Though an Indian massacre wiped the settlement of Natchez out of existence, a few years later it was flourishing again.

The Americans were equally active in the Ohio region and in through Kentucky and Mississippi. Little by little their produce trickled down to New Orleans, grew in volume, became a mighty flood of commerce.

As early as 1799 they took over the whole east bank, a region which two decades before had been scarcely settled and in which the French and English were then still dickering with strong native tribes for alliances.

Lausset, the last French governor before the Louisiana purchase, noted that at New Orleans one saw fifty-five American vessels as against ten of the French and Spanish. He asked the Citizen Minister to advise him how to handle the obstreperous Anglo-Saxons, for they constantly abused their privileges: "Under pretext of looking after their settlements on the east bank," he reported, "they flood the west bank with smuggled goods."

A good picture of all the busy river commerce is gleaned from eye-witness Timothy Flint, who traveled the Ohio. He describes all the "whimsical" varieties of water-craft, of every shape and structure: "the stately barge, of the size of a large Atlantic schooner, with its raised and outlandish looking deck, . . . [requiring] twenty-five hands to work it up stream. . . . Next . . . the keel-boat, of a long, slender and elegant form . . . generally carrying from fifteen to thirty tons . . . easily propelled over shallow water in the summer season. . . . Next . . . the Kentucky flats, or in the vernacular . . . , 'broad-horns,' a species of ark, very nearly resembling a New England pig-stye . . . fifteen feet wide, and from forty to one hundred feet in length." These carried from twenty to seventy tons. "Some . . . called family boats, . . . used by families in descending the river, are very large and roomy, and have comfortable and separate apartments, fitted up with chairs, beds, tables and stoves. It is no uncommon spectacle to see a large family, old and young, servants, cattle, hogs, horses, sheep, fowls, and animals of all kinds, bringing to recollection the cargo of the ancient ark, all embarked, and floating down on the same bottom. Then there are . . . 'covered sleds,' or ferry-flats, and Allegheny-skiffs, carrying from eight to twelve tons . . . [also] . . . pirogues of from two to four tons burden, hollowed sometimes from one prodigious tree, or from the trunks of two trees united, and a plank rim fitted to the upper part. There are common skiffs, and other small craft . . . 'dug-outs,' and canoes hollowed from smaller trees. . . . But besides these, in this land of freedom and invention, with a little aid, perhaps, from the influence of the moon, there are monstrous anomalies, reducible to no specific class of boats, and only illustrating the whimsical archetypes of things that have previously existed in the brain of inventive men, who reject the slavery of being obliged to build in any received form. You can scarcely imagine an abstract form in which a boat can be built, that in some part of the Ohio or Mississippi you will not see, actually in motion."

F. A. Michaux, canoeing down the Ohio in 1802, gave similar pictures—boats like "large square boxes," with tall sides, spinning every which way down the current. From within them came such a racket, he was puzzled enough to climb the high river bank to see what could be inside. There were "families . . . horses, cows, fowls, carts, ploughs, harness, beds, instruments of husbandry . . . furniture."

It all meant the eastern half of the Mississippi region was filling in ever more rapidly. Soon large stores in flat-boats appeared, the forerunner of our modern department store, a bit of everything. Seymour Dunbar, in his *A History of Travel in America* (pp. 305 f.), describes them vividly:

"There was a lack of . . . useful things in the earliest days of the river settlements, and a shrewd trader who fitted up his flatboat in the semblance of a rural drygoods shop . . . received an enthusiastic welcome at every community."

The approach was celebrated by "formalities worthy of such an important event." When within a short distance of his anchorage, "the Admiral of the department store mounted to the roof, and, striking a posture in which dignity and philanthropy were judiciously mingled, he announced his presence by repeated blasts on the familiar tin horn. It was a sound that by common agreement signified either the arrival of news or an important occurrence of some sort, and was sure to bring to the landing place a group that would scatter information of the arrival. Forthwith all the women folk of the little hamlet dropped their other affairs and hurried to the boat to enjoy again the almost forgotten delights of shopping, comparing patterns and buying the things they needed. A store-boat was fitted with shelves for the goods and counters for their display. The indefinable aroma of fresh, clean fabrics filled its creaking cabin, and the dignified Admiral of half an hour before, transformed into a smiling merchant with a huge pair of shears, snipped his calicoes, bargained with customers and told them the doings of the outside world. After he had accumulated all the money the population had on hand, he once more assumed his nautical rank, blew a farewell blast and disappeared down the river. The floating merchant . . . was the progenitor of today's universal emporium."

All this meant an expanding economic life, ever more settlers, more production, more trade. The diversity of agricultural and commercial activity is vividly etched by Flint:

"In the spring, one hundred boats . . . landed in one day at the mouth of the Bayan, at New Madrid." He tells of the "boisterous gaiety of the hands, the congratulations, the moving picture of the life on board . . . , the numerous animals, large and small . . . their different loads, the evidence of the increasing agriculture of the country above." He was greatly impressed by "the immense distances" which they had already traversed and "those which they have still to go," and added: "You can name no point from the numerous rivers of the Ohio and the Mississippi, from which some of these boats have not come."

Their products were correspondingly varied. "In one place there are boats loaded with planks, from the pine forests of the southwest of New York. In another quarter there are the Yankee notions of

Ohio. From Kentucky, pork, flour, whiskey, hemp, tobacco, bagging, and bale-rope. From Tennessee there are the same articles, together with great quantities of cotton. From Missouri and Illinois, cattle and horses, the same articles generally as from Ohio, together with peltry and lead from Missouri. Some boats are loaded with corn in the ear and in bulk; others with barrels of apples and potatoes. Some have loads of cider, and what they call 'cider royal,' strengthened by boiling or freezing. There are dried fruits, every kind of spirits manufactured in these regions, and in short, the products of the ingenuity and agriculture of the whole upper country of the west. They have come from regions, thousands of miles apart. They have floated to a common point of union. . . .

"Dunghill fowls are fluttering over the roofs. . . . The chanticleer raises his piercing note. The swine utter their cries. The cattle low. The horses trample, as in their stables. There are boats fitted on purpose, and loaded entirely with turkeys, that, having little else to do, gobble most furiously."

Americans kept pushing their produce downstream through New Orleans, forcing the Spaniards and French to grant shipping rights, threatening to oust them if obstructed.

The folk of New Orleans soon became accustomed to seeing Americans in their midst—as Benjamin Henry Latrobe describes them—"Kentuckians, dusty, savage and gigantic"; and the tough flat-boatmen in moccasins, coon caps and buckskin jackets, the frontier hunting knife dangling from the belt, were—as they described themselves—"half alligator and half horses."

The men who navigated the "Massassip" prided themselves on their toughness and their picturesque lingo. The prize example of this is found in Davy Crockett's memoirs:

One day he was sitting in the stern of his "broad horn," the old *Free and Easy,* taking a "horn of midshipman's grog, with a tin pot in each hand, first a draught of whiskey, and then one of river water." Who should float down past him but Joe Snag; "he was in a snooze as fast as a church, with his mouth wide open; he had been ramsquaddled with whiskey for a fortnight, and as it evaporated from his body, it looked like the steam from a vent pipe. Knowing the feller would be durned hard to wake, with all his steam on, as he floated past me, I hit him a crack over his knob with my big steering oar. He waved in a thundering rage. Says he, 'halloe stranger, who axed you to crack my lice?' Says I, 'shut your mouth or your teeth will get sunburnt.' Upon this he crooked up his neck and neighed like a stallion. I clapped my arms and crowed like a cock. Says he, 'if your a game chicken I'll pick all the pin feathers off of you.'

"For some time back I had been so wolfy about the head and shoulders that I was obliged to keep kivered up in a salt crib to keep from spiling, for I hadn't had a fight for as much as ten days. Says I, 'give us none of your chin music, but set your kickers on land, and I'll give you a severe licking.'

"The fellow . . . jumped ashore, and he was so tall he could not tell when his feet were cold. He jumped up a rod. Says he, 'take care how I lite on you,' and he gave me a real sockdogger that made my very liver and lites turn to jelly. But he found me a real scouger. I brake three of his ribs, and he knocked out five of my teeth and one eye. He was the severest colt that ever I tried to break. I finally got a bite hold that he could not shake off. We were now parted by some boatmen, and we were so exorsted that it was more than a month before either could have a fight. It seemed to me like an eternity. And although I didn't come out second best, I took care not to wake up a ring-tailed roarer with an oar again."

The river men were particularly proud of their hair, and the impressive beards and handlebar mustaches that waved over the bosom of the Father of Waters were astonishing. Major Elias Rector, U. S. Marshal of Arkansas, let his hair grow till it reached to his waist. Once a gang of roughs broke into a New Orleans ball, smashing the lights, and in the dark, taking Rector to be a woman, they let him go, thus giving him a chance to fetch the police.

The river men were all great tobacco chewers, and their expectoration must have greatly swelled the Mississippi crest. They took great enjoyment on being able to spurt forth a stream of brown juice fifteen feet with deadly accuracy.

They were, in short, a rough and happy-go-lucky lot. Many had a sweetheart at every landing, and they chanted: "I'm a salt-river roarer. I'm chuck full of fight, and I love the wimmen."

At overnight stations, remarks Timothy Flint, the hands visited together, went on shore, got roaring drunk to "raise the wind . . . became riotous."

In the French Creole sea terminus, as elsewhere, they raised the same Cain, got fighting soused and were occasionally jailed. If the river men didn't have the money to pay the bartender, likely as not, they would shoot holes through the whiskey barrel, then hold their tin cups under it, drinking up the liquor as fast as it streamed out. A favorite stunt was to shoot tin cans of whiskey off each other's heads. Only occasionally was their aim bad.

Lyle Saxon, in his *Fabulous New Orleans*, describes the river breed vividly:

"Gigantic rafts floated down the river, bringing their cargoes to the levee at New Orleans. The crews of these flat-boats—the rough and tumble American male, red of shirt and bronzed of face—lingered on the levee to drink and to fight, to terrorize the Negroes and to get gloriously drunk, there in New Orleans which they called 'The City of Sin.' . . . Then, penniless perhaps, they would strike out again along the overland trail which took them through hundreds of miles of forest and home again."

If they did not squander their earnings in the port, they were indeed lucky to get back up the river in their canoes, rifle in arm, to Natchez and beyond, without being drowned, robbed, or murdered by Indians or pirates, of which there were a goodly number. Often they quite merited their fate, for many, like wildcat Mike Fink, took pot shots at peaceable Indians or Negroes just for the fun of it. There are instances when Indians, abused or shot at by river boatmen, traveled a thousand miles or more through the woods and swamps trailing an offending boat and waiting their chance to take revenge. It was a free-for-all life, and free-for-all death was often the answer.

The imperative goal of the Americans became the mouth of the river—it drew them like a magnet; they swarmed there more and more of them. As Lyle Saxon describes it:

"The whole waterfront was astir. Negroes sang as they toiled, rolling the hogsheads, carrying the bales. Downstream came hemp, tobacco, flour, hoop-poles, staves, sugar—and the first bales of cotton, the beginning of the great cotton industry which was to develop. . . . Downstream from St. Louis came the important shipments of furs, destined for the markets of fashion-making Europe. . . .

"Plantations were being opened in the delta of the Yazoo-Mississippi. Trading posts were established up the Arkansas and the White Rivers. Farms dotted the shores of the Red River and the Ouachita. Memphis was a village. Vicks' Plantation was a settlement at the mouth of the Yazoo—later it was to develop into the city of Vicksburg. Natchez was a rich and thriving city. . . .

"Along the river, from Baton Rouge south to the Gulf, the country was dotted with vast plantations—plantations with great white-columned houses and wide fields, with Negro cabins in a long line behind the large house of the planter . . . orange groves, and vast fields of sugar-cane . . . cotton fields and acres of billowing corn. . . . Fortunes were in the making. Flush times were coming. The country was filling up."

And so New Orleans, thanks largely to Americans, became a considerable metropolis—in foreign hands. Society there, before the end of the eighteenth century, had become sophisticated enough to have a leper hospital and to give employment to a regular dancing master —who got himself killed by the Indians. By 1799 that city, numbering only twelve thousand inhabitants, was already a gay, wild place, full of flowering balconies, murders, convents, voodooism, yellow-fever, slave auctions, intrigue, Negro drums and dances on Congo Square, church-bells, lavish society balls and luxurious quadroon balls where then, and for long after, the "aristocrats" picked their mistresses. The City of Sin was not over-inclined to bother about literature, the arts, sex tabus, or race purity. *The Monitor* of Louisiana, founded by Carondelet, never succeeded in getting more than 80 subscribers even when the population reached 50,000. But Louisiana was to introduce still another important weave of customs, folklore, thought and law into the variegated American pattern of conduct and culture.

For, all the time, the upper valley dwellers pushed southward relentlessly, as an historian has said: "like a glacier," inevitably and steadfastly they sought the sea. But they went faster than any glacier.

In 1794 the Spanish Governor of Louisiana had already noted that the demand for free navigation by the Americans, "their mode of growth and their policy" were "as formidable for Spain as their armies." He noted their roving spirit and indifference to hardship. "Cold does not terrify them," and a "rifle and a little corn-meal in a bag are enough for an American wandering alone in the woods for a month." The American's hut of crossed logs made not only a quick home but "an impregnable fort against the Indians." The Governor saw little hope of resisting their advance and feared their ideas even before they advanced. Governor Estevan Miró, for instance, forebade the introduction of any boxes, clocks or other wares stamped with the American figure of liberty, but even so Spain, as did France, had to allow free navigation and customs-free depots.

New Orleans, said Wilkinson, was to the valley as the key to the lock, the citadel to the outworks. As American trade through New Orleans increased, American concern over control of the mouth of the river became intense. Various western leaders threatened at various times to descend on New Orleans and take it by force. Jefferson, toward the end of the eighteenth century, wrote Minister Robert Livingston in Paris: "There is one spot on earth and one only, of which the master must be constantly and inevitably our enemy. I refer to New Orleans. It is through this port that the products of three-eighths of our territory must pass in order to find outlet."

Economic expansion soon had even more pronounced political repercussions. Franklin disguised the profit-making motives of his Illinois land company, by saying that such a settlement would raise "a strength there which on occasions of future war might easily be poured down the Mississippi upon the lower country and into the Bay of Mexico to be used against Cuba, the French Islands, or Mexico itself." His modesty is revealed by his failure to mention the Falkland Islands.

When the eastern seaboard failed to heed western storm signals, failed to appreciate the anxiety of the Middle Westerners over New Orleans and the fate of their trade, on which depended their whole prosperity, bitter sectional feeling developed.

Rufus Putnam, a New Englander, observed as early as 1790 that should Congress give up her claim to the navigation of the Mississippi, the people in the West would leave the Union; they "would sooner put themselves under the despotic government of Spain than remain indented servants of Congress."

That the separatism of the American Middle West was then pronounced, and its desire for empire great, is also revealed by the plotting of Aaron Burr, who saw the strange mingling of French, English, Germans, Scotch-Irish, half-breeds of all stocks, bustling about in the new settlements, and felt out their hatred of the indifferent East and their hatred of the Spaniards blocking the river mouth. He was inspired by the mighty unity of the great stream: it "got into his blood, and reached for his heart cords."

The American Middle Westerners were determined to obtain New Orleans, even if they had to secede from the United States and live under French or Spanish rule. Or they were going to fight for it. If Jefferson had not made the 1803 purchase soon thereafter, the American Union would have been forced to war, or if the eastern seaboard had held back, the Union would have been split apart.

But no sooner had the prize fallen into American hands than a new mighty force—steam—came along to consolidate the new domain as never before.

In 1807 a small wooden sidewheeler, the *Clermont,* built by Robert Fulton, with English engine and boiler, whacked the water up the Hudson to Albany, belching forth black smoke—the first steamboat legally authorized.[1]

Those on the upstream bank, wrote H. Freeland, who witnessed

[1] For a hundred years previously such boats had been tried in Europe and for fifty years in America, with considerable success. In 1805, for instance, Stevens built a twin screw propeller, a boat fifty feet long and kept it running on the river until the following year. But it was Fulton who borrowed inventor Fitch's plans and sketched the machinery of a successful boat already operating on the Thames, and the diplomat landowner Robert Livingston who got a legislative monopoly and the publicity.

the sight as a boy, thought it a sea-monster; others declared it a sign of approaching judgment. But ambitious practical men saw wealth and empire suddenly near their grasp.

Fulton and Livingston, when getting their grant from the New York legislature, had talked lengthily of their lofty patriotic motives, but afterwards fought to maintain an unjustifiable monopoly on the Hudson, thus holding back the expansion of river traffic everywhere. A bit later they and Nicholas Roosevelt sought and obtained a similar monopoly from Governor Claiborne of Louisiana, hoping thus to bottle up the whole Mississippi traffic. Fortunately they failed.

In any event we are indebted to Nicholas Roosevelt for a magnificent effort at steam pioneering on the Ohio and Mississippi.

He first came out to the upper Ohio in the spring of 1809, with his bride—combining honeymoon with a dream of empire. He built a flatboat with tarpaulin and chairs and leisurely drifted down the river, talking to river men, getting the whole lay of the land, to find out if steamboats really could be utilized. His auditors, mostly skeptical, told of treacherous currents, low water, the Ohio rapids, warned him of Indians. But everywhere he saw new settlements rising, heard the sound of chopping axes. Clear to Natchez he floated, then went on in a pulling boat to New Orleans.

Convinced that steamboat traffic was feasible, he hurried north to New York by sea to help Robert Fulton organize the Ohio Steam Navigation Company. Fulton sent mechanics, lumber, engines, out to Pittsburgh, and Roosevelt started building. In March, 1811, the *New Orleans*, 116 feet overall with an extreme beam of twenty feet and of a hundred tons' burden, was floated. Sidewheels were supplemented with masts and sails, and high up forward was a pilot house. The vessel, by the standards of the day, worked beautifully.

Once more he and his young wife, with her relatives and servants, a pilot and crew of six, slipped downstream through the darkness. In the still forest night, they sat listening to the throb of the first moving engines the valley had ever known.

They had not the slightest assurance their boat would ever make the whole length of the river. She might ground, and they would be scalped by Indians. It might crack up in the rapids. For several months they merely idly cruised back and forth, perhaps steeling themselves for the ordeal ahead. They desired to seize an opportune moment when the river would be highest over the rocky rapids. Perhaps also they realized that failure might postpone inland steam-navigation for decades.

But like all good heroes, when the time came, Roosevelt did not falter, not much. In October they definitely set out on the long pioneer voyage they had planned. All went letter-perfect as far as Louisville. There, coming in at night, they let off steam, a thunderous sound, frightening sleeping folk, who stumbled out of bed and raced to the shore. At first they thought it must be a floating sawmill. The truth immediately stirred their imaginations to unbelievable heights, though perhaps not to the height of Louisville's actual twentieth century towers and smokestacks.

The leading citizens gave the couple a big reception. Roosevelt reciprocated with a dinner on board. In the midst of it, he ordered the vessel to start. His guests, thinking of the dreaded rapids below, left the table in fright. When the vessel, instead, went upstream, bravely throwing spray, they came back reassured to finish their meal.

Discharging his guests, Roosevelt drove back up the river clear to Cincinnati, and after some more threshing about, finally, in November, hardened his will and this time headed definitely down, straight for the rapids—make it or bust. They would go through or smash up. They would lose their lives or win success.

The feared fatal point was reached. They swept into the tossing rapids, churning foam. The boat quivered from stem to stern, pitched and shuddered. Every instant was an hour of anxiety. For a split second they hung in final doubt, then their spirits lifted when suddenly they eased into smooth water and came safely to rest alongside Sand Island.

They were not only safe, they had opened the waters of power, they had driven another mighty wedge into the heart of the rich continent. The wide Mississippi lay ahead, and a century of empire, a century and an empire that would swell with romance and echo with the names of Mark Twain, Andrew Jackson, Aaron Burr,

Lafitte, Abraham Lincoln, Captain Shreve, James B. Eads, mighty builder of bridges and levees, John Tripp, the wealthy gambler, Mike Fink, and John A. Murrell, the latter the founder of the dreaded Mystic Clan, which was to combine religion, desperadoism, thievery and murder on an imperial scale, all false-fronted by the best citizens.

January 12, 1812, the first steamboat, this same *New Orleans*, tied up with a load of cotton at the New Orleans levee—a Leviathan arrogantly pushing in between flatboats, wheel boats and hand-manipulated river craft of every description.

War with England came, but by 1817 the first steamboat anchored at St. Louis, and in two more years—the Roosevelt-Fulton monopoly by then had been broken in the courts—sixty steamers plied regularly.

In that year nearly two hundred steamboat arrivals from upstream were registered at New Orleans. The vessels carried nearly $17,000,-000 worth of goods.

Negro roustabouts, ebony chests gleaming with sweat, trundled freight and more freight and sang their chanties:

"De big wheel rolls, her head comes round;
    We're bound to go, 'less we take de ground. . . .
    Ah haah, de levee! Ah haah, de levee!"

By 1836 there were nearly 230 steamboats on the river. The floating palace arrived. Luxury came to the river craft in a monstrous gewgaw dream of beauty—gilt and tinsel decorations, scroll-saw work, wedding-cake fussiness, sparkling glass chandeliers. It was gorgeous and vigorously vulgar. The steamboat orchestra became an institution. Floating theaters and wax works and circuses plied the yellow rapids. Melodrama and classic feudal costumes thrilled the open-mouthed swamp yokels at isolated river landings. A mangy caged lion or two roared dismally. Side show monstrosities filled lost bayou settlements with awe.

Speed and more speed was demanded. In 1856, the *Grey Eagle*, "six hundred and seventy-three tons of marvel," raced at sixteen knots upstream from Dunleith to St. Paul to bring in the amazing news of the success of the new transatlantic cable. Queen Victoria had spoken to America! The *Grey Eagle* swept past the *Itasca*, one of the finest and fastest boats on the river, in a whimsical race, nip and tuck right up to the levee, crowded with cheering spectators. Captain Harris scribbled the world-shaking news on a piece of paper, wrapped it around a chunk of coal, and heaved it ashore, then he lashed the victory broom to the mast—he had swept the river clean. By 1870, the historic and magnificent *Lee*, 300 feet long, 44 feet wide, filled the river pioneers with new pride.

No more vivid picture of this buzzing world and all its excitements exists than in Mark Twain's *Life on the Mississippi*. Each afternoon numerous boats would pull out from the New Orleans landing. From three o'clock on they would begin burning resin and pitch pine, getting steam up to leave. They provided "the picturesque spectacle of a rank, some two or three miles long, of tall, ascending columns of coal-black smoke; a colonnade which supported a sable roof of the same smoke blended together and spreading abroad over the city. Every outward-bound boat had its flag flying at the jackstaff, and sometimes a duplicate on the verge-staff astern. Two or three miles of mates were commanding and swearing with more than usual emphasis; countless processions of freight barrels and boxes were spinning athwart the levee and flying aboard the stage-planks; belated passengers were dodging and skipping among these frantic things, hoping to reach the forecastle companionway alive, but having their doubts about it; women with reticules and bandboxes were trying to keep up with husbands freighted with carpet-sacks and crying babies, and making a failure of it by losing their heads in the whirl and roar and general distraction; drays and baggage-vans were clattering hither and thither in a wild hurry, every now and then getting blocked and jammed together, and then during ten seconds one could not see them for the profanity, except vaguely and dimly; every windlass connected with every fore-hatch, from one end of that long array of steamboats to the other, was keeping up a deafening whiz and whir, lowering freight into the hold, and the half-naked crews of perspiring negroes that worked them were roaring such songs as 'De las' Sack! De las' Sack!'—inspired to unimaginable ex-

altation by the chaos of turmoil and racket that was driving everybody else mad. By this time the hurricane and boiler decks of the
steamers would be packed and black with passengers. The 'last bells'
would begin to clang, all down the line, and then the powwow seemed
to double; in a moment or two the final warning came—a simultaneous din of Chinese gongs, with the cry, 'All dat ain't goin', please
to git asho'!—and behold, the powwow quadrupled! People came
swarming ashore overturning excited stragglers that were trying to
swarm aboard. One more moment later a long array of stage-planks
was being hauled in, each with its customary latest passenger clinging to the end of it with teeth, nails, and everything else, and the
customary latest procrastinator making a wild spring shoreward over
his head. . . .

"Steamer after steamer falls into line, and the stately procession
goes winging its flight up the river."

By 1840 the annual steamboat arrivals at New Orleans were 1,500
and the produce was valued at $50,000,000. Another decade and this
had almost doubled; and by 1860, 3,566 steamboats docked with
goods valued at $185,211,000. That is three times the value of all
the goods the whole nation now ships to Mexico, nearly eighty years
later.

And so is the story told of Louisiana—the soil of Louisiana added
to the soil of America. The lush growths of that region have had
their counterpart in a lush growth of human institutions and beliefs
which have in turn been woven into the bigger world we call
"America."

Symbolic of all has been proud New Orleans—the Crescent City,
a city of adventure and romance, a frontier city of gambling, much
whoring and every vice, "not a Puritan mother, not a hardy Western
pioneeress, simply a Parisian." But situated upon the crossroads of
the world, at the mouth of a great continental river, at the gateway
of Central and South America, it has also been the seat of colonial
conquest, the capital of empire, one of the main portals of the New
World. Into it have flooded French, Spanish, English and Yankees.
Here have eddied the cross currents of the migrations across the
American continent. Down the broad bosom of the Father of Waters

have drifted the explorers and trappers of Midwest America, all the way from Hudson Bay and the Great Lakes and the Northwest Territory and the headwaters of the Ohio in the Alleghenies. They have all ended up in the last port—New Orleans—to gamble away their fortunes or to win new fortunes on the turn of chance. The spirit of John Law survives. For every Mississippi bubble that bursts a new one is blown to larger proportions. From across the Gulf of Mexico have come Negro slaves and in more recent days the flotsam and jetsam of the tropics and ten thousand exiles from the petty tyrannies of the banana countries.

It has been the headquarters of a hundred soldiers of fortune, dozens of filibuster expeditions. A thousand revolutionary plots have been hatched in the Vieux Carré, and dozens of armed expeditions have slipped down the delta to overthrow the tyrannies in the lands from which much of the city's wealth is derived. Here the runty little tropic Napoleon, William Walker, of Nicaragua-and-Vanderbilt fame, once made his base of operations. From here big locomotive-engineer, Lee Christmas, went forth to make himself the uncrowned King of Honduras—for the banana companies.

Here, for a time, Narciso López, the Venezuelan who sought to free Cuba from Spanish rule, sought arms and ammunition before he finally was given the death *garrote* at La Punta, Havana. Here Benito Juárez, the Indian Lincoln of Mexico, sold peanuts and made cigars, waiting for the hour of his glory to sound. Here was one of the main bases of the United States in its war against Mexico, a center for supplies and troops, one of those gay moments of prosperity and abandon to wild carousal and gaiety that punctuate the life of the city and which have their annual expression still in the famous Mardi Gras.

Not the least of the soldiers of fortune to swagger its streets, at the head of his National Guards, was Huey P. Long, from the red scrub pine hills of the north.

But the city's real meaning comes from the great captive river that moves majestically past its doors. "On the map," wrote Louis Zara, in *Coronet*, "the Mississippi River is a slim tree, raising its gnarled trunk from the Gulf of Mexico up to its source somewhere in Minnesota." Its branches are the Arkansas, the Missouri, the Ohio, and a thousand lesser streams. Over those branches clambered millions of human locusts, devouring the leaves of freedom and personal enrichment, the leaves of death and of victory.

During the expanding years, ramshackle towns burned down and were rebuilt. Whole cities burned down and were rebuilt. Floods came and new piles were driven through the debris even before all the bodies were recovered; the great cholera and yellow-jack epidemics periodically spread their stench from New Orleans to St. Louis and beyond, but growth never halted. Those who fell by the wayside were stowed away in eternal sleep alongside Indian mounds where the Red man had been burying his kin for centuries. Although by 1842, St. Louis still had only nineteen steamboat arrivals, it already had bathtubs with running water—and that indeed was a swift consummation of what was to become a leading American fetish.

But whatever the great role of the Mississippi River in the conquest and settlement of the West, new forces were soon to change the course of empire and in due time to diminish the river's importance as an artery of travel. The most important transportation factors were the Erie Canal, roads and the railways. But for these later developments New Orleans would likely have become the mighty metropolis of the nation. As it was, Buffalo became a big center, in recent years surpassing New Orleans in tonnage; and New York City became a great international commercial market. The West was thus tied forever to eastern capitalism and forgot its agricultural solidarity with the South which previously had been its major market. The Mississippi region, instead of being unified, was split between North and South—the Civil War, in a sense, already was on. The Erie Canal—together with the network of inland waterways that soon spread over Ohio and Indiana—helped make a war, but also perhaps helped save the Union, bigger even than the Mississippi basin.

The towing of the first boat by a single horse over the first fifteen miles of the Erie Canal from Rome to Utica, took place "amid the ringing of bells, the roaring of cannon, and the loud acclamations of thousands of exhilarated spectators. . . . The scene was truly sublime."

Another spectator told of the embarkation of the governor and his party, with a roll of the drum and shouts . . . in the first boat, "sixty-one feet long and seven and a half wide," which "though literally loaded with passengers drew but fourteen inches of water."

Each new section of the canal opened called forth a similar delirium of bells, cannon, fife and drum corps, tooting of long horns, shrieks, fireworks, and "sweet smiles from the ladies."

In the 1823 celebration the dignitaries drank thirty-nine toasts, and it is reported that they were able to leave the banquet hall under their own steam.

American Memory quotes from the *Albany Daily Advertiser* (November 4, 1825) a description of the final celebration at the final opening of the waterway:

"At ten o'clock the *Seneca Chief,* with the governor, lieutenant governor, the Buffalo, Western and New York committees aboard, came down in fine style, and the thunder of cannon proclaimed that the work was done! and the assembled multitudes made the welkin ring with shouts of gladness. . . .

. . . "At 11 o'clock a procession was formed, under the direction of Welcome Esleeck, John Taylor, James Gibbons, Jr., and Francis I. Bradt, marshal of the day. . . .

"The procession, . . . very long and respectable . . . was headed by twenty-four cartmen, with their carts loaded with the produce of the west, each cart bearing a flag on which the articles conveyed in it were designated . . . wheat, corn, barley, flaxseed, ashes, butter, cheese, lard; a banner bearing the representation of Commerce; cotton and wool goods; peas and beans; beef and pork; water-lime, malt, lake fish; lumber; iron ores of various kinds; paper, glass, bricks; flax, hemp; maple sugar, beeswax, hops; wool; furs; whiskey, beer and cider; salt; flour; buckwheat; oats; rye. . . . Rev. Mr. Lacy gave thanks to the Great Ruler of the Universe for the blessings which we enjoy, in a fervid, solemn and highly appropriate manner."

By 1852 *De Bow's Review* was saying scornfully: "What is New

Orleans now? Where are her dreams of greatness and glory? . . .
While she slept an enemy has sowed tares in her most prolific fields,
. . . by bold, vigorous, and sustained efforts, has succeeded in re-
versing the very laws of nature and of nature's God—rolled back the
mighty tide of the Mississippi and its thousand tributary streams,
until their mouth practically and commercially, is more at New
York or Boston than at New Orleans."

America was settled and built precisely by smashing blows at
nature's normal ways and commands; and whatever or wherever its
mouth, the Mississippi Valley was destined to settle up and grow.
On the heels of the Erie Canal came railroads: in 1862, only 31,000
miles; a decade later, 66,000 miles; in two decades, 114,000; and by
1902, more than 200,000 miles, more than in all Europe, more than
in all Latin America.

Great cities arose. Pittsburgh, once a part of the uncouth West,
so feared by the East, became a citadel of iron and steel and nation-
making power, linked by bonds stronger than its own steel to the
financial capital of the East. Great factories arose beside the lakes
and over the plains. Wealth increased everywhere beyond the wildest
dreams. Graveyards, jails, asylums, schools, smoke, slums—the many
accomplishments of civilization—became firmly established.

By 1880 St. Louis had 350,000 inhabitants and was then second
only to New York and Philadelphia in manufacturing. Even before
1890 the manufacturing center of the nation, remarks Turner, had
swung to balance eight miles from the home of President McKinley,
the most outstanding political representative of the corporate wealth
the country had yet known.

Further west, now, was Populism and unrest, folk vaguely trying
to mold a changing world to their own futile dream of vanishing
freedom and individualism. The new proletarian unrest had not yet
arisen to the extent of becoming a challenge. The South was now a
region ruined by war, mired in ignorance and race-hatred. The Ohio
Valley belched forth smoke supreme.

Turner writes romantically: "The ideals of the Middle West began in the log huts set in the midst of the forest a century ago.
While his horizon was still bounded by the clearing that his axe had

made, the pioneer dreamed of continental conquests. The vastness of the wilderness kindled his imagination. His vision saw beyond the dank swamp at the edge of the great lake to the lofty buildings and the jostling multitudes of a mighty city; beyond the rank, grass-clad prairie to the seas of golden grain; beyond the harsh life of the log hut and the sod house to the home of his children, where should dwell comfort and the higher things of life, though they might not be for him. The men and women who made the Middle West were idealists, and they had the power of will to make their dreams come true. Here, also, were the pioneer's traits—individual activity, inventiveness, and competition for the prizes of the rich province that awaited exploitation and equality of opportunity. He honored the man whose eye was quickest and whose grasp was the strongest in the contest: it was everyone for himself."

And so by 1890 the entire land frontier was, except for a few small, less favorable pockets of the country, ended. By 1890 the land had been settled, the best taken up. Within 300 years of the coming of the first settler to Virginia, the President was calling the governors of all the states together to consider means to prevent exhaustion of the natural resources. They had seemed so bounteous and everlasting to the first comers. But by 1932 farmers were defending their mortgaged homes and eroded submarginal farms with pitchforks.

By 1890 the frontier was gone. In 1870 about half the population of the nation were still engaged in agriculture. By 1890 the tide had turned: considerably more than half had gone into other pursuits. In 1880, largely as a means of accommodating the freed southern slaves to the plantation system, a system of tenancy had sprung up, but already land-monopoly was cursing other parts of the country; already 25 per cent of the rural population of the United States were tenants. From then on the number of disinherited farmers continued to increase. Farm tenancy spread with ever-growing rapidity to nearly all parts of the country. By 1890, 28 per cent of the farm population owned no land and had to pay a half or more of the product of their labor to a landlord. By 1900, this had jumped to 36 per cent. By 1930 to 42 per cent, and from then on 40,000 new farmers each year have been dispossessed, forced to pass into the ranks of semi-

like tenants preyed upon by landlords, or into the ranks of a growing agricultural proletariat.

By 1890 the land was well filled in. For another decade our exports of wheat, corn, pork, beef, wool, continued to pour into Europe in an ever-expanding flood; and then they began to dwindle—except for the World War interlude—rather rapidly. By 1910 we exported only 87,000,000 bushels of wheat, or less than in 1877. By 1936 we actually imported more wheat than we sent out. Most agricultural products followed the same declining trend. We built up in record time the greatest agricultural plant in the world, and with equal swiftness we have seen our world markets dwindle, the plant thrown into partial idleness, bringing much calamity for our millions of farmers and for our country.

Supremacy in the exportation of grain and beef has passed to Russia, Argentina, and Australia, presently to Brazil also; of wool to Argentina, Uruguay and Australia. Now cotton goes the same road, as the supremacy passes to Brazil, Egypt, India and elsewhere.

Naturally farm values dropped. Even before our food-products export debacle, domestic evils had risen to plague us, and the Populist revolt spread. Even by 1893 credit froze, whole farm regions collapsed overnight; misery overtook a large sector of the American farm population, and still rules supreme in many places.

More and more we came to have great surpluses now with correspondingly low prices and the foreign market shrinking. In other words, since the turn of this century, without scarcely being aware of it, we have been undergoing one of the most tremendous economic revolutions that has ever afflicted a nation. The slack for a long while was taken up by industrialization, a new expansion that concealed the farm tragedies occurring. They were again concealed by the World War and the fever-flush prosperity that followed it. But that revolution is still with us; still, despite New Deal efforts, it grows more aggravated, increasingly acute year by year. It is a revolution in which most of our farming population has become disinherited.

CHAPTER XI

WHITE MEN CAN TAKE IT

In 1808 John Jacob Astor founded the American Fur Company which he soon sought to make a continent-wide monopoly. His early expedition to set up posts in Orgeon was temporarily blocked by the War of 1812, but he soon consolidated his empire. Through trading, in great part based on the illegal but profitable selling of whiskey to the Indians in order to swindle them, he caused the animals of the North American continent to be slaughtered off at a fiendish pace. In the process he also garnered in great tracts of land.

He bribed his way through state legislatures and the federal government. His officials were on his payrolls or had accepted emoluments from him. According to Gustavus Meyers, Secretary of War Lewis Cass, in charge of the administration of the Territories, received $35,000 from the company, and Cass was very effective in aiding Astor to pursue his ends. Other noble statesmen were paid off by their relatives being given juicy jobs with the Astor company.

Senator Benton, prominent Democratic leader from Missouri, Astor's legal representative in the West, fought his court cases and claims for him, and was rewarded with high office. Promoted to Washington, Benton spent much of his time getting bills passed, some of them drafted by John Jacob in person, to benefit the Astor empire and beat down everybody else.

Local and federal judges, themselves grabbing land, helped Astor cheat the Indians and obtain grants. The United States land agents were under his thumb. Those few, who were honest and obstructed him, were hounded out of their posts, their characters defamed.

Astor ruptured every effort, never too serious, by the government to protect the Indians.

His bootleg whiskey (sale of liquor to Indians had been forbidden by federal statutes since 1802) easily drew native trade away from the government trading posts, which had prevented him from gaining a complete monopoly. But not content, he compelled the abolition of the protective government agencies, ever a focus for exposure of his methods.

When the Indians themselves protested at being cheated, complainants were murdered. Reprisals would then result. Federal troops, ostensibly to put down the Indians, actually to protect Astor's far-flung fur-empire, were rushed out to slaughter the natives wholesale. By force, fraud, murder, among other things, Astor rifled a continent of its animal reserves; his partner was the United States government, which thereby lost its wealth, paid through the nose in addition, and blackened its reputation.

He appropriated enormous tracts in Wisconsin, Missouri, Iowa and elsewhere.[1]

In 1882 the unusually pious Christian Commissioner of Indian Affairs declared passionately: "Whiskey is furnished the Indians by disreputable White men who would sell themselves and their country for so many pieces of silver. Leniency to such men is a crime. Their homes should be behind bars, with never a human face to look upon, and never a sight of green earth or skies above, until, in solitary confinement for months and years, they have been taught the lesson that 'the way of transgressors is hard.' "

He was not, of course, referring to John Jacob Astor, long since dead.

---

[1] Typical is his attempted seizure of the 51,000 acres of the famous Phillips Estate in Putnam County, New York—"an unsavory business" described by Meyers. This highly improved tract, once belonging to the Tory Roger Morris and his wife, was confiscated during the Revolution by the State of New York. By the year 1809 some 700 families were on it, and it had become even then very valuable. Astor bought up the apparently worthless claims of the Morris heirs for $100,000, then sought to have the courts oust the settlers as trespassers. He claimed all their improvements made in thirty-three years. After much hullabaloo, in 1827 the legislature gave Astor $500,000. It was a cheap-souled but easily made profit.

Another early means used by many to grab land was to buy up worthless paper—government certificates and army land warrants—at a song, as the Washingtons did, and getting these validated at face value for the purchase of land. Enormous grants were given to Beverley, Borden, Carter and Lewis. As early as 1749 the First Ohio Company, of which George Washington's brothers were the leaders, had secured, partly by buying up depreciated soldiers' certificates, partly by political pull, 200,000 acres with a pre-emptive claim to 300,000 more. Later it merged with the Walpole Company, in which Benjamin Franklin was so interested. The Transylvania and Vandalia companies provided plenty of juicy investigation for later historians.

In 1769, the Mississippi Company, behind which were Lee, Washington and other large Virginia planters, put in their petition for two and a half million acres in the West.

General Rufus Putnam, one of the promoters of the Ohio Company of Associates (Boston, 1786), personally led out the first New England settlers. The company secured 892,000 acres, with depreciated government paper, etc., in addition to a free grant, by special act of Congress (April 21, 1792), of 100,000 acres. This land was sold to settlers at an enormous profit. The company's old land-office in Marietta, Ohio, is now appropriately owned by the Colonial Dames of America.

Numerous other land companies early stuck their fingers into the pie. Connecticut disposed of her rich holdings around Lake Erie to such a company.

All efforts of far-sighted persons to introduce some plan for intelligent and orderly development of the new region were brushed aside. John Quincy Adams declared that his proposed system of administration, which was to make the national domain the "inexhaustible fund for progressive and increasing internal improvement, . . . [had] failed."

People in all walks of life did not want scientific or thoughtful or conservative administration: they wanted land. The freed indented servants wanted land. The tenants wanted land. The disinherited of the eastern seaboard wanted land. The soldiers of the French Wars, the Revolution and the War of 1812, wanted land. The big land companies wanted land. The grafters, speculators, politicians, judges, Congressmen, wanted land. The South wanted more land for slavery, or were willing to trade the right to squander the public domain in return for non-intereference with their own system. For nearly a century the public domain became the football of politics, greed, intrigue; and our federal, state and local governments were thus corrupted from top to bottom. The country, in hit-and-miss fashion, was settled up, built up, made great, though we have no means of knowing whether it might have become greater by other methods; we do know that political demagogy was intrenched and a system of monopoly landholding eventually made possible, that wasteful farming methods were engendered which now menace the very survival of our republic.

Other land thefts were occurring in the South. In Louisiana, a public official reported to President Jackson that in seizing those lands the "most shameful frauds, impositions and perjuries had been committed." He described a notorious land-grabber:

"He could be seen followed to and from the land office by crowds of free Negroes, Indians and Spaniards, and the very lowest dregs of society, in the counties of Opelousa and Rapides, with their affidavits already prepared by himself, and sworn to before some justice of the peace in some remote county. These claims, to an immense extent, are presented and allowed . . . upon the evidence of the parties themselves. . . ."

In 1795 a special act of the Georgia Legislature, dominated by rich planters, sold most of the area now comprehended by Alabama and Mississippi to four new bribe-distributing companies for $500,000 —the famous Yazoo scandal. The subsequent electoral contest swept the corrupt legislators out of office one and all. The grants were rescinded as having been obtained "by improper influence." But the recipients of the land multiplied legal obstructions. The august Supreme Court of the land ruled that the grants, being a contract, once given, could not be rescinded by a subsequent legislature. "This," remarks Meyers, "was the first of a long list of court decisions validating grants and franchises of all kinds secured by bribery and fraud."

Finally, in 1814, though it had been repeatedly shown that the whole Georgia steal was fraudulent, the noble fathers of our country, under constant lobby pressure, granted $5,000,000—or 1,000 per cent over the original price—to recover the lands, which later, in good part, would be re-stolen.

Few of the millions of acres of lands then and later throughout the Union, sold on credit, were bought by bona fide settlers, but by speculators. Congressional report after report showed that at the public sales of lands, rich individuals bought up Land Office Registers and Receivers to defraud the government and rake in land. Such is the repeated story of the founding in America of what are known as sacred property rights.

Even five years before the lands in Wisconsin were open for legal registry, rich mineral properties were seized; and in 1840 the claims, filed by dummies, were dutifully allowed. "Honest men," the United States Senate found, "have been excluded from the purchase of these lands, while the dishonest and unscrupulous have been permitted to enter them by means of false oaths and fraud." In the Milwaukee district, though 6,441 claims had been filed on, by 1847 there were still only seven settlers.

The Federal Land Register of Garden City, Kansas, declared, in the 'eighties: "The rush for land . . . is unprecedented . . . a mass of humanity . . . press and excitement . . . fifty or more land agents or attorneys . . . make out the papers of hundreds." The mail and express packages with filings, from attorneys in all the little towns about, piled up. It was mostly "a real abuse of . . . the law." The majority of patrons "swept through by these land agents" never saw the land chosen, the whole "a scheme" to "defraud the spirit and intent of the law."

From the establishment of the federal government until 1839 the government bought from Indian tribes for money, merchandise or lands elsewhere, 442,866,370 acres,[1] for which it received from

---

[1] Meyers, quoting from Senate Document 616 (1840). In all the federal government has or has had for disposal 1,442,220,320 acres, of which 87.6 per cent has been given out. (U. S. Dept. Agric. Technical Bulletin, No. 357. May, 1933.)

new White owners a total of only $85,000,000 in money and merchandise, or less than 20 cents an acre! Little enough of it went to actual settlers; most of it was given away or sold for practically nothing to speculators, or just plain stolen. Land steals were usually rushed through by the Federal Land Office when Congress was not in session, showing that the federal officials were directly conniving with wealthy land-grabbers, railroads, corporations, etc.

One means of stealing land was by the creation of fake canal companies. The Erie Canal had been built at public expense for the benefit of all. But thereafter private companies, to undertake such work, were given huge subsidies, grants of land, and the title to the canals they built or did not build. In some cases the canal companies were merely given the right to buy land at $1.25 an acre. After taking over vast acreages on credit, often such companies would later slip through bills in Congress or corrupt state legislatures, to get the land for nothing. Often the canals were never built at all, the money simply pocketed. Often a mere pretense of building them was made. No water could flow through them; no boat could navigate them. The Portage Canal in Michigan, a worthless ditch and "full-fledged fraud," permitted those interested to survey and appropriate 400,000 acres. Half of this area was taken in prohibited or "interdicted lands," so that at least 100,000 acres of the richest copper lands were grabbed, lands which now comprise part of the sacred property rights of one of our respectable copper companies.

Land grants to such canal companies, mostly in the North Midwestern States, totaled four and a quarter million acres.

Prospective builders of roads and highways also got huge grants. Often the roads were not built, but the land was never returned. Between 1864 and 1869 several grants were made for such roads in Oregon. "In some cases no road had been built, although the governor had certified to its construction and completion," said the Federal Land Report. The Willamette Valley and Cascade Mountain road was never built. An inspector, for a hundred miles, could find no trace of road, but despite this published report, the company subsequently—in 1883—was granted 440,000 acres. The Oregon Capital Wagon Road, among other grants, was given 100,000 acres from an Indian reservation. Page after page is devoted in the Secretary of the Interior report of 1882 and other years to the minute description of the inspection and approval of surveying instruments and chains, but apparently far less attention to the character of the surveyors and still less to the validity of the claims for the lands actually surveyed, or the accuracy of the surveys themselves.

Another means of stealing lands was to get large grants, under the March 2, 1849 law, of swamp lands—of course to be drained and improved. The Swamp Act, incidentally, made no proper provision to protect legitimate established settlers.

The General Land Office report of 1885 states that up to the close of that fiscal year, 58,620,987 swamp acres had been given out and the disposition of about 16,000,000 more acres was pending. Often surveying was done during high flood season so that some of the richest lands in the country were thus given to such fraudulent grabbers and previous bona fide settlers shoved off. Diverse claims to the same land sometimes were made simultaneously under the swamp and the desert land laws!

Often no pretense at all was made of surveying swamp lands, but through connivance with corrupt officials, rich timber and mineral deposits were stolen. The valuable copper lands of the Hecla and Calumet Mining Company were originally obtained in 1852 through grants of swamp lands by Congress, grants upheld in the courts.

Another means of alienating the public domain was by grants to prospective railroad builders. Asa Whitney, original promoter of a railway to the Pacific, had a great dream of constructing such roads honestly in a way to benefit the builders, but so that the lines would become the property of the nation, thus helping both the government and the people. His plans were squelched, and "boodle" became the watchword of the day. From 1850 to 1872, the records show, not less than 155,504,995 acres were given in actual or future grants either directly to such corporations or to the states to be given to them. The 1914 report of the Secretary of the Interior stated that nearly 137,000,000 acres of lands in this total had actually gone to the railroads.

The railroads fraudulently surveyed in 10,000,000 extra acres over and above their grants. According to the 1885 Land Report the Winona and St. Peter Railroad would get 300,000, possibly 600,000 acres, in excess of the original legal grant; the Santa Fe, several hundred thousand acres over.

To boost quickly the values of land held by the proposed railroads, any number of "fanciful" routes—the Federal Land Commissioner so describes them—would be sketched one after another, and in each case, the public lands were withdrawn from settlement. Such areas remained—quite contrary to statutes—indefinitely withdrawn in order "to defeat settlement rights," often for twenty years or more.

This enabled the railroad to force settlers to buy its lands at gilt-edge prices while at the same time "selling land in large quantities to foreign syndicates at low prices"; or they obliged settlers to purchase railroad waivers or relinquishment of lands "to which the companies," according to the 1885 Land Report, "had not and might never have any color of legal right"; or it forced established settlers to abandon their holdings and improvements without recompense.

Settlers, trying to break through all these illegal barriers, soon discovered that their lawful claims went down under official decisions "as grain before the reaper's scythe." The "antagonism" to the rights of settlers, to their legitimate claims, according to the 1885 Report, "amounted to a crusade."

"The agents and attorneys of railroad companies were permitted to antagonize settlement claims at every point, . . . until it became cheaper for claimants to buy the land of the railroads than to pursue contests against them before this office and the appellate authority."

The railroads were allowed, by tracing such fanciful routes, "to appropriate the products of coal and other valuable lands; to dominate town sites and monopolize water privileges, and to devastate forests of their timber," often on land they had no claim to. Vast tracts "of the choicest woodlands of the public domain," to which the companies had not "the slightest legal or other claim," were thus stripped.

Besides these land grants, many railroads were privileged to take from the public domain without cost all materials such as stone, lumber, etc. In some cases they succeeded in having the lands from which they took such materials allotted to them in addition to those already granted. In any case they hastily used their permits, not only to supply their own needs, but to rape whole forests for public sale of lumber, shingles, etc.—all of it carelessly done with destruction of small trees, failure to dispose of brush, great loss through unnecessary forest fires, all told, "an enormous waste." The Denver and Rio Grande secured the right not merely to take public timber for construction but for perpetual repairs.

Often the railroad put in demands for compensation for relinquishing such claimed "fanciful" acreages in addition to the grants properly held. In Washington Territory the railroad company filed claims for indemnity on 637,928 acres, nearly double the area of land they were entitled to receive. Often several different claims for relinquished lands were carelessly allowed and paid.

Though railroad land grants specifically excluded mineral lands, later, amenable officials decided that coal and iron were not minerals. Special laws were often sneaked through to validate sub-soil ownership of copper, gold, silver, soda, salt, oil.

Taxation on railroad land grants was evaded by the little clause invariably slipped into such grants that final patent would not be granted until companies paid a small surveying fee. This became an established provision by the 1892 law. They would not pay this fee until they finally sold off the lands, hence often for years would pay no taxes. Farmers on adjacent property—for which they had paid the government or had bought from the railroads at inflated prices—got no such dispensation.

As the Secretary of the Interior put it in stilted official terms in 1882, the companies do not take out final patents and thus let "large bodies of land . . . grow valuable by the lapse of time and the settlement of the country, thus obtaining all the advantages of public protection and enhancement of values, without contributing to the maintenance of the public authority or of the common institutions of municipal organizations by the aid of which such enhanced values may be derived." It was the sort of taxation abuse protested against, some centuries before, by the townsfolk of New England.

In addition to getting free land, the railroad companies got direct monetary subsidies from federal, state, county and municipal governments. They secured heavy loans, then later slipped through legislation freeing them from all obligation to pay the government back. For the most part the brave railroad builders of America—most of whom knew nothing of railroads or construction, but were merely cunning speculators and politicians—received from two to four times the cost of constructing their lines. In addition they eventually sold more than enough stock to pay for the building. The costs were hidden by special construction companies run by the same directors of the railroads. The railroad stockholders did not get the benefit of these vast sums; in most cases the directors, in addition to fabulous salaries and bonuses, swallowed up the major profits. Railroad stocks and capitalization were written up to cover all these fantastic costs and more. The rates were then jimmied up to return handsome profits on all this water. Not only that, in most cases the initial construction was so slipshod that unnecessary wrecks took constant toll of life. The period is full of angry cartoons. One, entitled "How to insure against railway accidents," shows two silk-top directors lashed to the boiler of an engine. Most of the lines within less than ten years had to be rebuilt from stem to stern. This also meant higher rates.

The railroads, with little or no official restraints, promptly exercised an overwhelming influence and power over the economic and political life of the entire country, by which they continued to loot the land in many other ways as well. By suddenly boosting freight rates, the railroad insiders could and frequently did ruin a community, a farming region, some nascent industry, and thereby acquired additional holdings and industries at a fraction of their real value. They could destroy all rival enterprises.

The stockyards industry is replete with scandal after scandal of this nature. The railroads were often closely linked up with certain cattle and packing companies who got secret rebates or other favors, while independents were ruthlessly ruined. In good part, the Standard Oil built itself to power in this manner. In Wyoming in the early 'nineties, when many carloads of machinery had been installed for developing the soda mines near Rawlins, when the town of

Johnstown had "cast its sweetness on the desert air, when shafts had been sunk and timbered, and tons of soda had been taken out and freight trains were hauling it into the Casper station, the railroad suddenly put up their rates, and the whole enterprise went to rack and ruin. Johnstown became a ghost town."

The American public is still paying through the nose for all this fantastic thievery.

The railroads were really built by the taxes of the American people, and a goodly part of the public domain was thrown in to boot. The public then had to pay three to four times what it should have paid in freight and passenger rates for the right to ride and ship over the railroads it had paid for building many times over, but didn't own.

The Illinois Central, one of the first roads to get a public land grant—2,595,055 acres in Illinois alone, at a time when poor settlers had to pay from $5 to $15 an acre—by this means plus cash subsidies and stock-watering, provided its promoters and security holders, in addition to a full-fledged railroad cost free, a profit of nearly $2,000,000.

The Union Pacific promoters—after expending $436,000 in influencing government officials, including the highest in the land—succeeded in increasing their already generous cash subsidy and widening their land grant from a strip twenty miles to one forty miles wide, about 13,000,000 acres. A vast network of corruption, in which high government officials were seriously involved, among them Secretary of State James G. Blaine, the great father of Pan-Americanism, and James A. Garfield, subsequently President, was woven by the railroad's affiliated company, the Crédit Mobilier, the boodle gang of which pocketed about $44,000,000 by methods since then become even more respectable.

The La Crosse and Milwaukee Railroad—paying out $800,000 in bonds and money to influence Congressmen and state legislators—was granted 2,388,000 acres of public land in Wisconsin, land with valuable timber worth, as early as 1857, over $17,000,000. The company was exempted from taxation forever; the lands were exempt for ten years. "Wholesale plundering," said a post-mortem state investigating committee.

In 1854 Congress gave 900,000 acres of public land to the Minnesota and Northwestern Railroad. 14,000,000 acres of lands were released to the State of Minnesota to be given railroads.

John Blair, one of the inner lights of the Union Pacific, after stock-cuts in which high government officials participated, secured vast federal and state subsidies for railroads in Iowa. Railway land grants in that state totaled nearly 5,000,000 acres.

In California in 1862, the Central Pacific, in addition to huge cash subsidies (about $26,000,000), got 4,500,000 acres of land. Later the grant was doubled—all told, a profit by promoters of $50,000,000 in cash, $38,082,000 in bonds and $49,005,000 in stock. Besides that they took leases of their own lines for $3,400,000 annually. Proportionate easy money was made in connection with every new extension built.

The Texas and Pacific received 18,000,000 acres in various states. The Southern Pacific, for building a line from El Paso to San Francisco, got 5,000,000 acres. Huntington, spending more than $500,000 to influence legislation in mostly improper ways (some federal Congressmen, according to Huntington, were offered $16,000 a vote by the T. and P. agents), then got control of the Texas and Pacific and the 18,000,000 acres while getting around the necessity of building two lines. Before it was through, the Southern Pacific owned 105,-000,000 feet of standing timber, the largest single holding in the country.

In all Huntington received "hundreds of millions" in money, bonds and lands from the government, states, counties and municipalities. A shakedown all along the row.

Many of these railroad grants covered land already filed or settled on, but the individual holder, whatever improvements he had made and wished to save, rarely could fight the large railroad companies and was soon ousted.

By an 1857 land grant, the St. Paul, Minneapolis and Manitoba road, given large tracts—restricted, according to the ruling of the Department of the Interior to Minnesota—suddenly, after more than thirty years, laid claim to rich Dakota Red River country and, after getting a favorable Supreme Court decision (137 U.S. 528), gave abrupt notice to the farmers to vacate the lands. The numerous settlers, having long since received apparently sound titles from the United States government, over a long period of years had made it one of the richest agricultural regions in the West. Angrily they besieged Congress to save them from the railroad.

Our august solons hastened on February 28, 1891, to grant the railroad company other "non-mineral" lands in exchange. This enabled the company to get what its cynical directors really wanted: not only valuable timber lands in Idaho, Montana and Washington, but much valuable mineral land. Though all mineral deposits by then were well known, the land chosen was granted with the connivance of General Land Commissioner T. H. Carter. He was soon rewarded with a seat in the United States Senate.

In such ways Mr. James J. Hill, northwest railroad speculator, obtained control of 500,000,000 tons of iron ore, the richest and biggest deposit in the country. In 1864, by a series of financial maneuvers, he organized the Northern Pacific Railroad out of previous lines and companies, and was granted immense areas in Montana, Idaho and elsewhere; in all he raked in about 57,000,000 acres of the public domain. Later, attempts were made to recover the mineral lands, but the sacred Supreme Court got around this by a technicality. The railroad held on to its loot.

To this day railroads own enormous tracts of land, still for lease or sale, or merely held for speculation—in 1928, some 22,325,000 acres.

Another instrument for alienating the public domain was the Desert Land Law, by which a man could file on 640 acres. This was hailed as at last a boon to the bona fide settler; actually it did not require claimant-residence, so that it permitted the big cattle companies to seize still more lands. Vast areas were simply fenced in. All comers were held off at the point of the gun. Settlers had their homes burned, often were assassinated or lynched, until the cattle companies could get dummies to file up on all the fenced-in claims, or special grants could be pushed through Congress. In Arkansas Valley in

Colorado at least 1,000,000 acres were illegally seized. Similar thefts were made of whole counties from Texas north to Montana, enclosures ranging from 1,000 acres to over a million acres in single holdings.[1]

Corrupt Federal Land Commissioners and agents winked at all this, concealed the fact from prospective settlers that such cattle lands had not been filed on, and "accepted the flimsiest proofs of ownership" or obvious dummy filing. The Supreme Court, that great protector of our liberties, soon decided that no settlers could claim preemption on lands already fenced or improved by others. Thus large holders could with relative immunity seize the properties of poverty-stricken settlers, along with their improvements. Often by force the cattle companies established a pre-emptive claim.

The Henry Miller properties stretched for imperial miles in California, Wyoming and Texas; from well up in Canada, across the United States; and far into Mexico. Enormous Miller estates still survive, unsubdivided, undeveloped, barring roads, and travel.

The 1885 Land Report said: "A 'cattle king' employs . . . herders; 'cowboys' is the popular designation. . . . The herd is located on a favorable portion of the public lands, where grass, water and shelter are convenient, and each herder is . . . required to make a timber-culture entry of lands along the stream . . . all the watered lands in a township and render the remainder undesirable for actual settlement or farming purposes. . . . If a bona fide settler has located in advance of the cattle-man he is either bought off or scared off." The report tells how bona fide settlers, in one instance, were driven off by armed men, imported from a distant part of the state,

---

[1] According to the 1885 Land Office Report (pp. 318-320) Levinsey Brothers in Pueblo County, Colorado, illegally fenced in 62,700 acres; and nearly half a million acres in all that county were so enclosed. In Bent County, J. W. Powers illegally fenced in 200,000 acres; the Prairie Cattle Company, 1,000,000 acres; the Arkansas Valley Cattle Company, 553,000 acres; and these were only a few of those active. H. H. Metcalf fenced in 200,000 acres in Elbert County; the Brighton Ranch Company, 125,000 acres in Custer County; the Cimarrón and Renello Cattle Company seized 276,000 acres in New Mexico; Grayson and Birland, 100,000 acres. One steal alone in Kansas totaled 192,000 acres. Another in Utah, 128,000. These are just a few examples.

who did not even know the description of the lands they were supposed to file on. This was provided by the "cattle king."

"The best lands," continued the report, "and practically all the waters, are controlled by men who have no interest in the development of the country, evade taxation, and in many cases owe no allegiance to our laws and government. . . ."

The report goes on to describe how many "cattle kings," as soon as one batch of herders had filed up on lands, would rapidly successively hire new batches until a very "large amount of land would be gobbled up. . . . In other cases . . . the entryman was a myth, . . . the proof papers and deeds . . . were made out in the notary's office, fictitious names attached for both principal and witnesses . . . as though the parties had been actually present.

"It has been estimated that in Bent County [Colorado], . . . particularly adapted to the raising of stock, probably four-fifths of the land is illegally fenced, and the most desirable spots within the various large enclosures have been entered either fraudlently or in evasion of the Law."

Another great steal was made possible by the "Stone and Timber Act" of 1878; and an 1892 amendment made fraud even easier. The settlers could now get 160 acres of timber lands worth $100 an acre at $2.50. Big lumber companies at once rushed in whole train loads of dummy settlers and got vast areas. Southern lands, not affected by this act—some 40,000,000 acres of timber, coal and iron—were put on the market at $1.25, with no homestead provisions, and 8,000,000 acres were at once gobbled up.

The Coal Land Act permitted railroads and other corporations to seize half of the high-grade coal lands of the West, not less than 30,000,000 acres. Practically the whole coal supply of Oklahoma, Utah, and Wyoming—grabbed by making use of dummy occupiers, bribed at from $50 to $100 each—was monopolized by the Gould railway system. If any dummy settler later failed to turn over the property to the corporation, he and his family were ousted by force. Copper lands were also stolen by others in similar ways.

One recipient of valuable mineral lands in Wyoming, Charles A. Guernsey, found it useful to get introduced by a Senator to Land

Commissioner Thomas H. Carter of Montana, a politician during whose incumbency much of the public domain went up in smoke. The Senator laid his hand "on the commissioner's shoulder . . . [and] said sotto voce, 'He's one of our kind, Tom.' "

"Mineral claims were not granted to individuals by either Spain or Mexico," reported the Federal Land Commissioner of such fake claims in the territory taken from the republic to the south; but this was no "obstacle" to seizing sub-soil wealth under agricultural grants or by falsely extending the "claimed boundaries." Such fanciful claims were usually allowed by the courts.

It would be tedious to go on to recount the manner in which oil lands were seized. The corruption and fraud revealed by the Teapot Dome exposure, which made Senator Fall the victim, while the big boys went free, is still fresh in the minds of all.

No one thought of conservation or national parks. The only park we had for a long time was Yellowstone, but no timber reserves. When in 1890 Yosemite Valley, with its natural wonders and giant sequoias, after valiant efforts by John Muir, was declared a national park, this was done in the face of indignant private protests that such a step was dangerous interference with legitimate business; and when half a dozen years later President Cleveland proclaimed a national forest reserve of about 21,000,000 acres, "the wails of lumber, stockraising and mining companies reached such proportions that most of the land was quickly returned to the public domain"—to be stolen. But the idea of conservation was growing.

Its initial application was not entirely encouraging. In 1900 the high-minded Forest Reservation Bill was put through. By this act the government of course "protected the settlers" in such conserved ings for other public lands elsewhere. But the large owners pushed in a little clause "or any other claimant," and so the railroads were able to take advantage of it. Much of the land previously acquired by them was unsuitable for cultivation and containing no minerals, or else had already been ruthlessly denuded of forests. Now they were able to exchange snow-capped mountain tops, barren ice-bound stretches, empty lands denuded of timber, for millions of acres of more valuable agricultural, mineral and timber lands elsewhere.

And so in the name of virtue, another vast steal was arranged by our non-paternal government to bottle-feed our rugged individualists. After the steals had been consummated, a righteous hue and cry was raised; the act was then righteously repealed but not the thefts it had promoted.

Other vast land steals, besides the mineral rights already mentioned, were made by means of bribery and fraudulent titles in the new areas acquired from Mexico. Americans in Mexico have never lost and never can lose as much land and property in that country as Mexicans have already lost in the United States. In Mexico, lands taken from Americans since the 1910 revolution have been expropriated with promised compensation, in most cases for the social good. In the United States lands owned by Mexicans were, in plain language, in good part stolen outright, and the thefts subsequently legalized.

The Mexican law for the territory we wrenched away from her by armed conquest, had limited the maximum size of holdings to 48,000 acres; but as soon as these claims, bought or secured through chicanery by astute speculators, were established by the courts, then in connivance with corrupt local officials, millions of acres were surveyed and enclosed in single holdings, without regard for the Mexican owners, and by one skulduggery or another a big share of them was legalized. Our sacred Supreme Court easily found technicalities which enabled them to uphold the loftiest concepts of law, but permitted not only Mexican holders to be defrauded but the American people to be robbed of its patrimony won by war and death.

"The files of this government groan with the pitiful appeals of settlers to be protected against fraudulent surveys of private land claims"—reported the Federal Land Commissioner—but such appeals were without avail; they might as well have been "consigned to a fiery furnace."

In the case of the railroads "there certainly were grants," however prodigal, declared the 1885 General Land Office Report, but numerous so-called Spanish and Mexican claims were "wholly fictitious." The "encroachment upon the public domain by one claimant ceases only when it clashes with the pretensions of another."

The Cañon de Chama claim, originally embracing a single square league of land, was puffed up to more than a hundred square leagues by official survey allowed by corrupt agents. Stephen B. Elkins, an influential Republican Congressman from New Mexico, had his brother and another man named government surveyors, and when they got through surveying the 96,000 acres of the original Beaubien and Miranda claims, the acreage totaled 1,714,765 acres: valuable forest lands, the best farming lands in the state, rivers, towns, cities, villages, rich mineral deposits. The Federal Land Office promptly gave Elkins a patent for this enormous area. The sacred Supreme Court blithely upheld the grab.

"The missions had no title in perpetuity to their lands," besides "their possession ceased" when the missions were "secularized" by the Mexican government, but "vast estates have been conveyed upon pretexts of succession to mission claims," said a later Land Report.

And so, in these and other ways, the bulk of the public lands of America were corralled by speculators, promoters and corporations with no properly corresponding remuneration to the government or the people. General Weaver, candidate of the Greenback Party in 1880, in accepting nomination declared: "An area of our public domain larger than the territory occupied by the great German Empire has been wantonly donated to wealthy corporations."

Even by 1883 Secretary Teller reported that little land remained in the nation for the legitimate small settler. Farmers were obliged to take ill-suited lands, and some 15,000,000 acres of such early abandoned homesteads showed the futility of attempting to farm land improper for cultivation. Some 600,000 farmers today are on submarginal lands, lands from which they can't earn a decent living even in prosperity times. Many of these farms should never have been put under the plow, but folk were forced to try to till them often because of land monopoly.

All told, nowhere in the world, never in history, has there occurred —except possibly in the Spanish New World areas, and even there Indian titles were more extensively respected—such a colossal steal of empire as in the United States, such bare-faced theft of a nation's resources. The great fortunes which were thus built up were made precisely through control of government and through governmental paternalism on an epic scale. We speak of rugged individualism of Americans, of American business, but nowhere in the world has governmental paternalism been more extensively and constantly exercised than in our own country for the benefit of a special class. The great American fortunes, which now are concentrated in a few families that wield the economic power in our fair land, were built up not merely by individual initiative or ability, but by utilizing the government for the purposes of fraud, for open robbery of the public wealth. Politicians, Presidents, Cabinet-ministers, Supreme Court judges, Congressmen, Senators, Governors, legislators, government commissioners and employees took petty graft and favors to permit such individuals and companies to gain control of the resources of the nation.

As for that noble species of humanity, the American citizen, in order to make his own petty grab he was willing to let the powerful seize the key positions of control. Today his descendants are paying the piper. Even the Indians put up a better fight against losing their lands than did the American White man.

CHAPTER XII

REVOLT

When Lord Bryce said that if our western development had taken place more slowly, "it might have moved upon better lines." he was uttering what then was still a deep heresy.

The people who engaged in the western movement, whether mere pawns of the railroads or more independent, were swept by a fever of eagerness. Of course, they all hoped to find the promised land, the rainbow crock of gold, to get rick quick—and a small percentage of them did—but even more than that, it was one of those mass urges which overtake human beings; and few times in history has occurred such a magnificent upsurge of general human hope and excitement, such a sense of slipping off the leash of old confinements, of facing life hardily, with self-reliance, independent of everything—except wind, weather, wolves and Indians. It had in it, despite the mingling of crass motive, regardless of the particular sect to which people adhered, a mighty religious urge. It had the poetry of movement, of action, of adventure, of hope. Men's energies were released from treadmill tasks, and human endeavor swept together a civilization in a wilderness in record time.

It was the boom spirit. No limits were believed possible. Even the worst soil was expected to gush wealth. The theory was even held and promoted by scientific-minded professors (some of whom even in that early day may have received public relations fees from corporations) that if enough land were put into cultivation the very climate would change, that the increased humidity from upturned soil, irrigation of crops, and farmhouse trees would bring greater

rainfall and thus insure permanent agriculture in drouth-stricken regions. As a result, places long considered desert, during a span of
years when there was unusually heavy precipitation, were put into
crop-lands, and for a short while prospered. But false railroad pro-
motion-lies and God's trickery in sending rain at the moment of a
new great *putsch*, led the settlers into parts of the Western Mississippi Valley they should never have settled. Scientific long-term
weather observations were lacking. Faith—the stock in trade of the
pioneer—made up for such an unimportant lack. But faith without
knowledge, in worldly matters, however much it may serve for the
land beyond the sky, has a way of tripping people up. Now we know
the absurdity of some of those earlier expectations.

The people who engaged in the westward movement, that wild
scramble for land, fortune and the free life, were shaken up in a
new whirl of forces they little comprehended—indeed, even more
settled peoples rarely comprehend the forces that ring them round.
The frontiersmen, where everything seemed so hopeful, where the
great open spaces seemed illimitable, where there was apparently
room for everybody, saw few of the social and economic dangers
that would soon sweep upon them. They did not see that they were
the constant prey of more astute men; that their crops were valueless
unless they had an ample market; that for their crops to get to that
market, they had to move over the railroads which had drummed
up much of this westward movement; that they were at the mercy of
those railroads. A fly can buzz around in a big bottle and feel very
free, but its escape to real freedom is dependent upon the finger that
taps the bottle-neck opening.

There was no time to think of such things. The speculative spirit
ruled all hearts. With speculative madness, the railroads were built.
The reckless wine of greedy adventure pervaded everyone. Since
there seemed no limit to expansion, the common sense of economics
and frugality was thrown to the wind. The farmers, for instance,
saw no reason why they should not accept the mortgage money so
eagerly pressed upon them. The rise in land values, in crop yield,
the wealth generated by increasing population, would take care of
all obligations. The man who a few years before had come out penni-

less, suddenly found himself able to command extensive credit. He would have been less than human if he had not availed himself of it.

In the East, western mortgages were popular. Everyone wanted to participate in the golden flood of swelling wealth. If the bigger capitalist was careful to invest chiefly in municipal and state bonds, the medium-sized investor sought any sort of place to sink his money; and the western mortgages, "gorgeous with gold and green ink," seemed talismans of wealth and stability. They brought a good rate of interest, and for the mortgage companies they presented a profitable business. The companies translated them into a higher rate of interest for the farmers, and the difference, sometimes deducted at the outset from the total loan, made rich pickings.

The same process more or less existed during the flurry of our more recent Latin-American loan days. The banks cleaned up, but the American investor and the public in Latin America paid the piper. The West those days was our Latin-American finance frontier.

So flourishing was the business that in Kansas and Nebraska at one time, it was estimated that there were nearly 200 mortgage companies doing a thriving business. So ready were people in the East to put out their savings that they clamored for mortgages, and the loan agents sat on the doorsteps of farmers—as our bankers later did on those of Latin-American dictators—begging them to take money whether they really needed it or not. Loans were made up to the full value and more of the property on the theory that the value was bound to increase. In Kansas and North Dakota it was estimated that there was a mortgage for every two persons.

Such expansion of values did not seem unlikely. Farms in Kansas that had cost $5.00 an acre, in twenty years had become worth $200, even $250 an acre, and near some centers even more. Town lots often increased in a year or less 1,000 per cent in value. In 1887 the realty turnover in Kansas City was $13,000,000. In a year a town might double or triple in population. Plank sidewalks, Italian opera houses, court houses, jails, saloons, churches, and schools gave an appearance of organized social life. Real estate offices multiplied, and promoters, railroad land agents and similar ilk swilled in the gaudy bars, played "twenty-one," dandled hotsie-totsies in starchy lace-fringed drawers, and "leeched on the farmers' blood." In ten years a full-fledged city might even be born. "Double your money in thirty days," was a common slogan of the boom-minded.

John D. Hicks, who has written the authoritative history of the Populist movement, quotes a newspaper editor: "Nothing causes the Nebraska farmer more dismay than to return from town after spending a few hours there, and find that his farm has been converted into a thriving city with street-cars and electric lights during his absence."

He also quotes a jingle put out by the booming town of Beatrice, typical of the boom spirit in every hamlet:

> Beatrice is not dead or dying
> Real estate is simply flying.
>
> He who buys today is wise
> For Beatrice dirt is on the rise.

But in 1887 the bubble burst. Drouth came, and it lasted ten years. From then until 1897 for only two seasons was there enough rain to insure full crops. For five years there were practically no crops at all. Week after week the hot burning sun glared down from a cloudless brass sky.

Not only farming but the cattle industry was practically wiped out. The cattle barons went to the wall; their lands went into the hands of eastern bankers; their cattle were sacrificed at a song to pay accumulated debts. Cattle not sacrificed died anyway. The 1886 summer, hot and dry, as few summers had ever been, left the range grass bad; and the terrible 1886-87 winter, with its blizzards, huge snowdrifts and the endless glare of ice everywhere, with no chinook thaw, saw the herds perish in storms, and those that were saved grow lean and starve. The plains and hills were filled with the skeletons of dead cattle and rotting flesh. Even the wolves could not consume all the carcasses.

Money grew tight, mortgages were foreclosed. Men had to abandon their farms. A mighty exodus back to the eastern side of the Mississippi began. Whole districts were depopulated. Between 1888-

1892 fully half the settlers in western Kansas cleared out. Twenty flourishing towns were left without a single inhabitant.

Prairie schooners bore the wording:

> In God we trusted
> In Kansas we busted.

In 1891 it was estimated that 18,000 schooners crossed from the Nebraska back to the Iowa side of the river.

Manfully the editors of Kansas in 1887 cried to the world that the Kansas crop was a bumper crop. The Nebraska editors did the same and denounced the Kansas editors for their "painful effort," and shouted "for corn . . . come to Nebraska." Nebraska, though, was little better off.

The blizzards roared down from Canada; and in summer, the leaden heat shriveled the shoots of new crops and shriveled the skin of tender girls, growing gaunt and hungry, old before their time. With hope vanishing, the hardships previously endured with a smile as temporary, became bitter permanent realities. Then the flimsy cottonwood shack, unplastered, full of chinks, the roof warped and leaky, became a bitter symbol of defeat. Its single room, which for lack of shed or barn was crowded with family, harness, saddle, grain, seed, tools, became intolerable. Locusts destroyed what corn and wheat the drouth left, often taking all the miserable fodder as well, so animals died too. As one Kansas homesteader's wife said: "Those years . . . I wouldn't have given a snap of my finger for the whole of Kansas."

Hamlin Garland describes the scene out in Wisconsin: "Another dry year was upon the land, and the settlers were deeply disheartened. The holiday spirit of eight years before had entirely vanished. In its place was a sullen rebellion against government and against God. . . . Misfortune had not only destroyed hope, it had brought out the evil side of many men." Dissensions arose. Two neighbors went insane over the failure of their crops. Others skipped out on their debts. You could never tell when a good farmer those days was going to hang himself.

In addition to farm mortgages which threatened the farmers everywhere with being dispossessed, in addition to bad harvests and low prices for agricultural products, the towns, cities, counties and states were loaded down with exaggerated debts. The cry had been for a span of years: "Spend money like water; the increased population will take care of the costs of improvements; the improvements will bring population." Now the bubble had been pricked. Kansas, for instance, was staggering under a $75,000,000 debt for the building of railroads which it did not own, a debt the people had to pay in addition to their mortgages and high railroad rates. Eighty-five per cent of exaggerated local debts were also due to efforts to help railroad speculators finance new roads, many not even built, many not necessary. Little could be done about it, for Kansas was controlled body and soul by the Santa Fe Railroad.

Someone facetiously remarked that the goal of everybody was to get into the class that warranted his receiving a railroad pass. Politicians, preachers, business men, all rode free, but the farmers paid. The story is told of a poker game that lasted from Omaha to Chicago and back again—on free passes. "Half the people ride free," said one wag, "and the rest of the people pay double or triple fares." The world was thus divided into those who rode for nothing and those who bought tickets for more than they were worth. And it was amazing how a politician, puffed up with merely a free pass, would fight for the railroad rather than the constituents who had elected him.

Besides, the railroads controlled most stockyard facilities and grain-elevators and could charge the super-storage rates they pleased, thus making the farmers' plight still worse.

Hard times hit the entire nation, but particularly the rural districts in the West and South. In the South, following the Civil War when old plantations went under the hammer, people had ever since been buying farms on time payments. Now they were forced to the wall and had to sell out. The old plantation system lifted up its weary head and throve again—just as it is doing during the present depression with the help of the A.A.A. and other alphabet agencies. Banks, calculating landholders and speculators took in the farms, and people became tenants.

Signs of such farmer discontent had not entirely waited upon distress. As early as 1867 agitation caused railway rate legislation to be proposed, but it was buried by the proper pressure and fixing. "Fixing" was much cheaper those days. and the ones immediately following.

The Patrons of Husbandry, known as "the Grange" sprang up, and by 1873 had a membership of 1,600,000. It was the first sign of true solidity in the frontier farming class.

The Grange lodges had a lot of that circus mumbo-jumbo so dear to the American heart. General meetings were usually held in some large grove to which the various lodges behind bands marched under blazing banners with noble mottoes and guarded by marshals dashing to and fro in red sashes. The semi-military fol-de-rol was in itself a symptom of the passing of the aggressive frontier; now men could only simulate a former militancy. But the Grange helped to weld American country life, helped bring the frontiersman forth from his hut, his isolation, his exaggerated individualism, into a feeling of unity with his fellow man on a basis broader than any religious sect of the time could provide. The farmers began to read religiously the Guild publications with their pious admonitions on proper husbandry. But the Granger movement, by creating a feeling of solidarity, also provided a slight note of new economic interest in lieu of previous solely religious motivation or the occasional political tent-circus-anvil-popping campaigns.

Through Granger pressure some of the western states actually began regulating railway rates, a small enough gain, but an important wedge doubly significant because most of the state legislatures were controlled body and soul by the railroads. If need be, to defeat any given measure, the powerful lines would buy up whole Assemblies and Senates at so much a head. Still, angry public pressure brought about some reforms and paved the way for increasing state and federal regulations which later were to find expression in established railroad or public utility commissions in the states and as part of the federal government. All of these government bodies at times were partly or wholly under the control of the railroads; and if mostly, then and since, they have served the railroads instead of the people, providing a cushion to stave off further regulatory legislation undesired by the companies, even so they had to show some initiative; and now and then a few good men would get on them who would actually do something.

As early as 1874 the Greenback Party emerged and made its brief splurge in the 1876 campaign—the year of the Independence Centennial of the original American Revolution. It accomplished nothing, but it injected the currency question into politics for the rest of the century; and to this day the currency bug has bitten every reform group and government. Like the tariff, it is a nice issue to blind men to the real causes of their difficulties. But men greatly prefer to tinker with superficial rather than fundamental things.

Certainly the effects of inflation, though in turn due to other causes, were visible enough in the 'nineties. From 1865 to 1895 the dollar had increased in value threefold. A man who had contracted debt which had a goods-value of, say, 100 bushels of corn found that he would have to pay off, besides interest, with 200 or 300 bushels. He had only 10 cent corn, but had to pay 10 per cent interest. Cheaper money became the reiterated cry.

The Grange and the Greenback Party paved the way for the more radical Farmers' Alliance, which was a cry of real anguish from the starving farmers at a moment when the long trend toward destitution, loss of farms and tenancy was to set in to continue with only brief interruptions until the present day. The Farmers' Alliance became a militant crusading organization. Prohibition, religious righteousness, women's suffrage, single-tax, all the usual cure-alls, surged up to confuse issues with morals, God, personal conduct and Utopia, but by 1890 the Alliance had elected three Senators and fifty representatives. Small business men and incipient capitalists of the East gave it considerable support and together they forced through some middle-class anti-trust legislation; by 1890 twenty-three states had such laws. Now, of course, the passage of such laws is recognized as having been wasted effort, in fact reactionary, quite contrary to the inevitable economic lines along which America was to develop.

The following year the Populist Party was formally launched at a great mass convention in Cincinnati in a vain effort to unite the wage-earners of the East with western and southern farming elements. The famous Omaha convention followed the year after. The platform, assailing the old parties, demanded free coinage of silver, a graduated income tax, government ownership of railways and telegraphs, shorter hours, initiative and referendum, direct election of United States Senators, postal savings banks, immigration restrictions and the Australian ballot.

Even the mild-mannered Grange had provoked the cry in rich eastern circles that the foundations of property were being menaced by the wild men of the West. The Populists, now, were to arouse fury and fear. The grossest charges, the most bitter misrepresentations, the cheapest epithets, were to be hurled at them. Civilization was cracking.

It is hard, now, to see anything terrible at all in the Populist program, then considered so dangerous. Those reforms, many of them in vogue in Europe for a generation previous to the Populism, now are mostly an integral part of our accepted laws, are all such commonplaces that we no longer give them second thought. But the same sort of gibberish about anarchy and ruination is always hurled at any attempt to reform abuses or curtail dishonest profits.

"We want money, land and transportation," cried Populist Senator Peffer—a man with a cool head but searing voice and a long beard that would put Moses to shame. He insisted: "We want the abolition of the National Banks, and we want the power to make loans direct from the government." The last demand had to wait forty-five years until the day of F. D. Roosevelt for partial fulfillment. Not one of the important leaders who raised that cry in 1890 is today alive.

The Populists in Kansas tried to put across a program to halve the debts, a graduated income tax, homesteads free from taxation. It took nearly forty-five years and a worse crisis to win the first of these demands, through cheaper money; and by then farms had been lost, are still being lost daily.

The sacred Supreme Court repeatedly ruled the income tax to be unconstitutional so that it was not until the passage of the Sixteenth Amendment to the Constitution in 1913 that the tax became a reality. Some few states now have homestead exemption from taxes.

We get some of those Populist reforms only now. In the interim the ranks of pauperdom were increased; farm problems multiplied faster than they were solved. Whatever reforms were enacted or are being enacted, somewhere there was and is still always a finger ready to clamp on the bottle-neck.

About the only thing the Kansas Populists got across at the time needed was a bill prohibiting alien ownership of land, and that was a hollow victory. If it prevented individual absenteeism, it did not prevent mortgage companies, land companies, and banks from organizing Kansas subsidiaries. The Populists also tried to regulate warehouses, but were not successful; and now nearly fifty years later, something tangible—not much—is being done about that. In the meantime, there are more tenants in the nation, fewer property holders and, despite all, the trend is rapidly toward greater land monopoly.

Most of the Populist leaders had known only the frontier, were part of it, and their way of speech was seasoned with the soil. Their ideas, from whatever remote point they originated, were the authentic thinking of the prairie farmer. Senator Allen of Nebraska, president of the last convention, was born in Ohio, went to Iowa and Nebraska. He had seen the buffalo run and be killed off. He had grown up with the country. Peffer was right off the Kansas plains. Most of the Populists, largely Methodist in faith, were of American stock for at least a generation. Bryan's 1896 vote in the prairie states was practically the same percentage as the number of American-born persons. Dakota, overwhelmingly foreign, despite the similarity of its problems, went for McKinley. Though local leadership had something to do with that, perhaps the foreign-born farmer found himself so much better off, under any circumstances, than in Europe, that he had turned conservative, wanted no revolt. The Populists themselves were mostly ex-Republicans, i.e., they had left the Republican Party as soon as it had grown respectable and been captured by the eastern bankers. The Populists were the true sons of Paul Revere and the Continentals. They were the outer fringe that had once known the Leveler's philosophy of the Cromwellian armies.

Their grandfathers had harkened to the rebellious accent of the American Revolution.

Hence the farm revolt movement produced, besides Peffer and Allen, quite a group of picturesque and honest leaders, earmarked "100 per cent American," though the East called them plain "anarchists" and worse. James B. Weaver of Iowa, born in Dayton, Ohio, June 12, 1833, had been the Greenback Party nominee for President in 1880 and the Populist nominee in 1890. He served a term in the Senate, being elected as a Prohibitionist. He had a sort of U. S. Grant countenance, but a more genial, kindly expression and a more buoyant mustache. Even so he looked very solid and staunch. Not as good a speaker as many of the others, he was far more sedate in his platform manner, more restrained in his utterances. He is described in glowing terms by one of his co-workers, Mrs. Annie L. Diggs, as a person of "such symmetrical and harmonious development." In him, she said, "strength and gentleness" blended. And she adds: "The cannibalism of politics has snapped and bitten at him in vain." He was "severe while others are in tumult; clear while others are confused; secure in his orbit while others are erratic; certain while others are in doubt"—a rather different picture from the rabid crack-pot described by the eastern press.

Much more picturesque was "Sockless Jerry," famous Jerry Simpson of Medicine Lodge, Kansas, where I was born, a town also the haunt of Carrie Nation and very given to religious fervor. Jerry was a friend of my father, who was Populist District Attorney of Barber County and editor and part owner of the local Populist paper. Jerry, by birth a Canadian from New Brunswick, went to common school in Oneida, New York. For years he was a seaman on the Great Lakes where he rose to the captaincy of some of the largest vessels. Later he bought an interest in a sawmill and a farm, and served in the Civil War until taken ill. In 1878 he emigrated to Kansas, where he became a farmer and stock-raiser in Barber County; and from there, the seventh district, he was sent as Populist candidate to Congress.

Hamlin Garland described him at that time as about fifty years of age, slender but powerful, with abundant black hair, close-cropped mustache, touched with gray. Humorous eyes gleamed from behind old-fashioned glasses. He spoke in a crisp tone with a deep voice and usually with a decided western accent, had a sort of Whitcomb Riley touch, according to Garland, who considered him a remarkable speaker and a clear thinker. He had been an ardent Abolitionist, a Greenbacker, Single-taxer and Union Laborite.

In the campaign he dubbed his opponent, James R. Hallowel, a very well-groomed gentleman, "Prince Hal," a "user of silk socks." Jerry, himself, when dressed up, looked like a very respectable minister of the Gospel with a studious air. His glasses made him seem almost shy and deprived him of his rather hurly-burly western air, more apparent when he was rousting about in ranch costume. His opponent got back at him, however, by calling him "Sockless Jerry," saying he wore no socks at all. The story is told that when Jerry was in Congress, a fellow member, looking over his shoulder, noticed that in addressing letters, he had misspelled the name of his home-town "Medicine Lodge." Jerry retorted: "I can hire a fifteen dollar a week clerk to spell for me, but a fifteen dollar a week clerk can't get elected to Congress."

Jerry hated the railroads. He demanded government ownership. The Kansas roads had cost $100,000,000, Jerry claimed, and told the farmers they had paid for most of that amount. But the roads were capitalized at $300,000,000 and bonded for another $300,000,000. Thus the people, besides having built the roads for others, were paying interest on $600,000,000, which meant high fares and outlandish freight rates.

He flailed the Chicago grain gamblers who got all the farmers' profits: "If the government had protected the farmer as it protects the gamblers, this could not have happened." All the foreclosures and the money crises would not have occurred. Who today will say that he was entirely wrong?

"Man must have access to the land or he is a slave," declared Jerry. "The man who owns the earth owns the people, for they must buy the privilege of living on this earth."

But probably the greatest orator of Populism was Ignatius Donnelly—a Minnesota Irishman born in Pennsylvania, and known as the "Sage of Nininger." He had a short, plump body, monkish face and tawny hair. His speeches were full of wit and humor. He was ever ready to speak on anything at any time, and did, one of his favorite topics being the defense of Bacon as the author of Shakespeare's plays, so that he earned the nickname "Ignatius Donnelly Bacon." He too had been a Prohibitionist. He had led the Grangers in their war on the railroaders; he had gone into Greenbackism and was with the Union Laborites in 1888. Hicks quotes the *New York Sun* as saying at the time of the new party movement, when a get-together convention was being held, that a reform convention in Minnesota without Donnelly would have been "like a catfish without waffles in Pennsylvania."

Joseph Dorfman in his *Thorstein Veblen and His America* quotes an unsympathetic critic of Donnelly's opening address at the 1892 convention in Omaha for its "wild and frenzied assaults upon the existing order of things" and the resultant display of "social lunacy" by his hearers. The critic called it "a furious and hysterical arraignment, . . . incoherent intermingling of Jeremiah and Bellamy."

"Cheers and yells rose like a tornado from four thousand throats and raged without cessation for thirty-four minutes. Women shrieked and wept. Men embraced and kissed their neighbors, locked arms, marched back and forth and leaped upon tables and chairs in the ecstasy of their delirium."

It sounds pretty bad, but it is quite in line with frontier evangelism and the American convention-circus tradition, not so far removed even from present-day antics of our major party gatherings in the big tent every four years. The length of time people stand up and bray for their candidate is supposed to be a measure of his intelligence and a barometer of the future vote. However, the critic, mentioned by Dorfman, saw more back of all this Populist exhibitionism and "turmoil" than crop failure and poverty. "All . . . that summer week . . . the spectres of Nationalism, Socialism and general discontent" brooded over the city.

Nominated for Governor of Minnesota, Donnelly in subsequent addresses denounced "the horde of millionaires" trying to become "titled aristocrats." The farmers were "defrauded of a billion dol-

lars by an organized conspiracy of railroad men and grain speculators."

The best woman orator of the movement, with a deep trombone
voice, was Mary E. Lease of Kansas, wife of a Wichita druggist. She
had raised four children, managed a farm, studied law and got admitted to the bar, and still remained at the age of thirty-seven "tall,
slender and good-looking," though these later days, the picture of
her determined face, lifting above a high-boned collar, gives her a
formidable appearance that fills us with that slight uneasiness which
overtakes us in the presence of too insistent reformers. "Our Queen
Mary," General Weaver called her. One of her best bon mots was:
"What you farmers need to do is to raise less corn and more Hell."

"Wall Street owns the country," she averred in her Cassandra
voice. The United States no longer had a government of the people,
by the people and for the people, but "a government of Wall Street,
by Wall Street and for Wall Street." Wall Street was "master," the
people were "slaves." Monopoly ruled. Our Vice-President was "a
London banker." The West and South were prostrate before the
manufacturing East where money ruled. Our laws were the outcome
of a system "which clothed rascals in robes and honesty in rags."

She told of "the prairies of Kansas . . . dotted over with the
graves" of women who had "died of mortgage on the farm." People
wept.

She derided the idea of overproduction. Overproduction when
"10,000 little children . . . starve to death every year in the United
States and over 100,000 shop girls in New York are forced to sell
their virtue for the bread their niggardly wages deny them." A
dreadful enough picture, though she probably slightly exaggerated
the size of the market for shop girl virgins, and possibly also their
number. But people wept still more.

Miss Annie L. Diggs, the female Boswell of the movement, was a
tiny woman, weighing less than a hundred pounds. Her advent to
Populism had come, like that of so many, via Prohibition. In 1877
she had suddenly woke up to the fact that college boys of Lawrence,
Kansas, were being ruined by liquor. She also had the idea that the
silk-worm industry would do wonders for the country.

Mrs. Bethe Gay, a widow, cared for her own child and a big brood of homeless waifs she had picked up and mothered, managed her farm, spoke on women's suffrage, Prohibition, and Alliance reforms.

But Mrs. Eva McDonald Valesh of Minnesota was "the jauntiest, sauciest, prettiest little woman in the whole coterie" of the Alliance. She was equally at home, we are told, on the improvised stove-box platform as in a drawing room where she charmed by "radiating sparkling wit and repartee."

Though most of the leaders were thoughtful and well-read men, a great deal of fun of all sorts—and often justified—was poked at the hay-seed, jayhawk movement and its leaders, of wild "Coin" Harvey who stirred plainsman and mountaineer to frenzy over free silver theories; of Omer Kem, a candidate from Broken Bow, Nebraska. The latter name, because of its faint reminiscence of the Persian poet, provoked the jibing verse:

> "I cannot sing the old songs
> My heart is full of woe;
> But I can howl calamity
> From Hell to Broken Bow."

Of Bill Dech, the Populists themselves said he had "a heart as big as his feet and no shoe was ever made too big for him."

In the South, too, Populism had its leaders. South Carolina, which still in 1890 was 84.5 per cent rural and where 60 per cent of the farmers were already tenants, had its big Ben Tillman, who though from a wealthy landholding, slave-owning family, threatened to stick a pitchfork in "the big bag of fat" that was Cleveland. He was "an agrarian jehad," says one of his bitter critics, with—as Tillman put it himself—"a brass throat." He was fighting "oligarchy" and the "aristocracy," fighting the "bamboozled and debauched" state government, in behalf of the "woolhats" and the "clodknockers." For every contingency he had a quotation from Burns or Shakespeare or mayhap merely a nursery rhyme: "The girl . . . with a little curl . . . on her forrid . . . who was horrid . . ."

Tillman climbed up on farmer and poor-White unrest to political power, pushed through a reorganization of the Railroad Commission and a new system of county government, built up two farm colleges and a university—changes which seemed scarcely commensurate with all the hullabaloo he raised—then proceeded to sell the Farmers' Alliance and the Populist movement down the river to become a pat Democrat. The Bourbon cotton planters moved back into their briefly vacated seats.

In Georgia Thomas E. Watson, "a little, bony-faced man" with carrot-red hair, thirty-four years old, romped over the state, rousing the rural districts with the typical venomous lingo of Southern demagogues and wild shouts against the Jute Trust. One of the standpat opponents, Judge Twiggs, said Watson, merely "emitted the vapourings of a soured outlaw."

When interchange got too insulting, Twiggs challenged Watson to a duel. Watson scorned the challenge, but saved his dignity by offering to appear at a crowded fair ready to shoot on sight. The Judge did not show up. Watson went into the Senate, became a Populist die-hard, sticking to the sinking ship long after lesser species had scurried into fusion with the Democrats, then retired embittered to write a life of Napoleon. When he later swam back into the limelight, it was as a cheap demagogue, a "nigger-baiter," a Catholic-baiter, and a Jew-baiter. The brutal lynching of Leo Frank rests directly at his doors, as directly as though his hands were red with the boy's blood. He swept the ignorant yokels behind him in a frenzy of race hatred, bigotry and invective. His career is indicative of the highly individualistic sentiments that lay behind the Populist battle-cries, the ideas of rampant personal rights, and frontier liberties that were representative of a vanishing epoch, doomed before the regimented march of industrialization and corporate control.

But while it lasted, Populism was a great upsurge. It gave our plains the only authentic general intellectual leavening in their history. Besides their own papers, such as the *Nebraska Farmers' Alliance,* folk were reading Bellamy's *Looking Backward,* and Henry George's *Progress and Poverty,* and a few were dipping into Marx and Engels. There was a general scramble for knowledge.

Folk came to Populist meetings in hordes, many traveling hundreds of miles. Twenty or twenty-five thousand at a gathering was not uncommon. At Hastings, Nebraska, 16,000 teams came in. A four mile long procession of wagons and buggies entered Columbus, Kansas, singing and playing, and waving banners:

> WE ARE MORTGAGED. ALL BUT OUR VOTES
>
> DOWN WITH VESTED RIGHTS
>
> WE VOTE AS WE PRAY

Such gatherings gave opportunity for many hours of speechmaking, fireworks, races, band-playing, glee-club trilling, and mass song-singing. An Alliance song-book was ever at hand. The songs had the spirit of religious revival.

> "I work and vote and ne'er regret
> The Party left behind me."

> "I was once a tool of oppression
> And as green as a sucker could be,
> And monopolies banded together
> To beat a poor hayseed like me."

And they also sang "We shall meet in the Sweet Rye and Rye" which with different words was to grace the I.W.W. song-book twenty-five years later.

Naturally the movement was resisted by the badly frightened financial East. The East eventually won out. It spent $16,000,000 to defeat the terrible Bryan who almost won with a campaign fund of less than $500,000.

Populism was merely an aggravated intensification of similar short-lived frontier struggles, a conflict, which by the 'nineties, became acute because of the ending of the frontier and immediate disasters. Populism was a continuation of similar aspirations in other zones, of the early land-revolts in the Thirteen Colonies, of the Jackson revolt and the 1837 crisis. Jackson declared openly that he was fighting the war of democracy against "the moneyed aristocracy of the few" to prevent "honest laborers" from being made "hewers of wood and drawers of water." The currency system then also was the key to salvation.

But those prior revolts had soon lost their edge because of more lands on the frontier. The Populist movement, on the other hand, soon lost its edge because of rapid industrialization and increasing urbanization. The factory more and more was to absorb the disinherited and the misfits. Crime passed from the hands of frontier bad men into the saloons, brothels and gambling dives of the cities in perpetual alliance with politics. The acuteness of the American land problem could be largely ignored for another generation or so—while it grew still more aggravated and reached the generally dismal conditions of the present. Agrarianism, in 1896, deflected by the silver agitation, went down to a great defeat, from which it has never recovered.

But even so, Populism was also the beginning of a long ground swell of popular revolt that was to continue, though shoved into the shadow by the Spanish-American War and imperialism and thirty-odd years of prosperity and boodle—broken by not too prolonged periods of depression when boodle-gathering was even easier. In good part Populism was the forefather of the Socialist Party, the Farmer-Labor Party, the Share-croppers' Union, the I.W.W. and the C.I.O.; and on the milder side, the Bull Moose Party, the La Follette Progressive Party and the New Deal. The agrarian phases of the New Deal are a vague empty echo of Populism, for the New Deal blithely tries to save independent farms at a time when most of the farmers of the land are no longer free owners. The problems posed by the Populists—though many of their reforms were belatedly adopted—have never been solved. The problems have merely become national, more varied and more broadly social, not entirely sectional.

PART TWO

CHAPTER XIII

WARS IN WYOMING

The wind off the desolate upland Wyoming plains stirred up clouds of alkaline dust. The rodeo announcer, a tall bony man under a Texas sombrero, cantered up and down the field, megaphoning through his hands: "Eddie Livingstone coming out bareback on Bucket-of-Blood."

The corrals and runways were set back in a recession of low sandstone bluffs, making a natural amphitheater. The summit of the bluffs were thronged: men in shirt-sleeves and high boots, smoking black cigars; women in bright flowered dresses or riding habits. Indians from the Shoshoni Reservation squatted in bright blankets, scarlet neckerchiefs glowing. Solemnly they passed their communal pipe from mouth to mouth. Opposite the bluffs on lower ground, beyond a heavy rail fence, were parked the autos of other spectators, the wheels half sunk in sand and sagebrush.

"Eddie Livingstone. . . . Bucket-of-Bloo - - - oo - - oo - d," bellowed the announcer between gulps of dust.

The official clown with burnt-cork face, white-chalked eyes and watermelon mouth, unlatched the runway gate.

Bucket-of-Blood snorted into the arena, Cowboy Eddie clinging to the rope around the animal's belly. A series of jack-knife jumps and frenzied bucks carried the mustang clear to the fence. Eddie's black, broad-brimmed slouch hat popped high into the air, but he clung fast to the rope; his knees gripped the withers; man and beast seemed one being.

Presently, near the fence, Eddie took a header. His spur tangled in the rope end. He was dragged twenty feet.

Bucket-of-Blood dived through a break in the fence, scraped his flanks on the autos and streaked toward open country. Two horsemen scoured in his wake.

Eddie jumped up smiling, blood streaming down his face. He was limping a bit, holding his hand to his woolly "chaps."

"Hey, Eddie!" yelled a voice. "By God, you'll make the movies."

Soon the crowd dispersed, some to the baseball game, others to the various bootleggers, to drink corn whiskey or to stake their money on the green felt carpets of the various "twenty-one" games.

Such rodeos are not so brilliant as they used to be. The great free days of the open range have passed away. The rodeos are now merely a sentimental offering on the grave of a buried epoch. The years when the cattlemen were full masters of Wyoming are gone forever.

For a few brief decades they fought their way into the sun to found an economic and political dynasty. Even then the sheepmen were encroaching upon the range. Settlers came. Before long oil became more important than beef. New industries, new settlers, new trends. The heyday of the cattlemen is long since over.

But they did not submit gracefully to the changes. They did not relinquish their mighty rule without a long and bloody fight. It was glorious but futile. Despite its superficial romance, it was really merely another dull example of the blind selfishness of men in power.

Less than a century ago, Wyoming was still untamed wilderness, a huge empire in the hands of roving bands of Crow, Arapahoe and Shoshoni Indians. Even earlier, Washington Irving had predicted in his *Adventures of Captain Bonneville* that Wyoming and adjacent regions would forever remain a savage desert, the haunt of migratory Indians. Certainly those upland plains, bare of trees, save for willows and cottonwoods along the mammoth rivers, those bald crags and multi-colored bad-lands, those great eastern Rocky outposts, eternally snow-clad, were forbidding.

Here and there during the brief weeks of summer—only July is safe from frost—a thin coating of grass spreads over the loose soil. "When is summer?" asked a tenderfoot, shivering in early August.

"Don' know," replied Old-Timer with a spat of tobacco juice. "Been here go'n' on forty year, an' 'tain't come yet."

Soon enough blizzard after blizzard whirls the world ever deeper into winter; the thermometer drops down to thirty, forty, fifty, even sixty below zero. Thanks to the eternal winds, the plains are often swept free of snow; but elsewhere the drifts mount up, twenty feet or more. Men move to their tasks, icicles clinging from nose and beard. In very bad winters the range cattle get so thin that if you look at one sideways you see only ribs—"an old-fashioned wash-board"—and lengthwise—"a pair of horns at one end and a ragged tail at the other."

The salvation of the region is the occasional Chinook wind which for a few hours in the dead of winter brings southland warmth, a fleeting breath of spring. Were it not for this queer thaw, even cattle-raising and sheep-herding would be impossible; but when the feed on the range lies blanketed under snow, when the streams are a glare of solid ice, and sheep, cows and horses are starving, the snow miraculously melts.

Wyoming was the last great American empire to be tamed, and it still has spells of unruly snorting. In 1808 trapper John Colter split off from the Lewis and Clark expedition, pushed on into Wyoming to risk his life among the hostile Indian tribes. Strange aboriginal names echo through the account of his travels: Grey Bull, Shell Creek, No Wood, Little Wind Creek, Beaver Creek, Popi Agie. From the summits of Wind River Range, Colter crossed Snake River and Teton Pass to the Yellowstone, then on to the Stinking River country—finally drifted in a small canoe three thousand miles down the Missouri.

The first real invaders were the trappers and hunters. Some of these brought back hundreds of thousands of dollars' worth of furs in a single season—mostly for Mr. Astor. The American Fur Company took the bulk of their profits.

Hunter Ezekiel Williams passed by the bubbling Yellowstone springs, fought Indians, worked south through the Big Horn country and crossed the Laramie plains; Price Hunt trapped for the American Fur Company; Robert Stuart, overtaken by early winter below Fiery Narrows, put up the first White man's cabin in what is now Wyoming and ate raw buffalo meat to keep from starving; mulatto Jim Beckwourth became a Crow Indian chief and the hero of many marriages; Nathaniel J. Wyeth established log-cabin posts through the Snake, Green and Big Horn river regions; Thomas D. Smith had his broken leg amputated with a saw and hunting knife; "Parson" Williams was scalped.

By 1823 General William H. Ashley had set up a regular trading post and explored the Big Horn Mountains, stretching in a vast snow-capped arc from Montana south; he gave Sweetwater River, tumbling through Whiskey Gap and Devil's Gate, its name, and finally reached St. Louis with $200,000 worth of furs. Joseph Meek (1829) strayed into the Yellowstone wonders; Captain Bonneville (1832) made maps; Reverend Whitman and Father de Smet (1840) taught the Gospel to trappers and Indians. The latter carved his name on remote Independence Rock, an immense bow-shaped granite mound fifty-five miles southwest of Casper. John C. Frémont (1842), guided by Kit Carson, chiseled his name on the same rock, and defying warnings from Indian Chiefs Otter Hat, Breaker-of-Arrows, Black Night and Bull's Tail, moved on up the Platte, climbed lofty Fremont Peak, discovered Fremont Lake.

The first real shock of the westward movement came along the old Oregon Trail in the southern part of the state, where from 1840 to 1865, hundreds of thousands of men, women and children braved incredible hardships. Many an emigrant toiling over the bleak route of the upper North Platte and Sweetwater Rivers was shot down by Indian arrows dipped in rattlesnake poison and left his scalp to the Red men and his bones to the coyotes. The entire trail was strewn with the skeletons of horses and people.

By 1859 the Overland Stage Company started service; by 1861 the Western Union had strung wires clear across the Rockies.

Bad men came in. Stagecoach superintendent John A. Slade murdered Andrés Ferrara on a dare and cut off Jules Reni's ears for a watchguard after said Reni filled him full of buckshot.

The pressure of new settlers brought sharper conflicts with the Indians, jealous of their patrimony and embittered by our constant

treaty violations. The U. S. Army moved in; army posts were established. The date 1859 was written down as "Bloody Year" for both
sides. For nearly ten years brave Chief Red Cloud kept up the unequal fight.

Though for many decades large bands continued to roam the plains,
gradually most of the Indians were pushed back into the Bad Lands
Reservation of western Wyoming. Those who remained loose had
grown tamer. They gathered choke-berries and fished and hunted to
piece out their prairie-dog and maize diet, but often also stole ewes
and cattle, even attacked outlying ranches, stores or stagecoaches.

But by 1894 Chief Red Cloud himself was lodged in Casper jail,
was grossly and unnecessarily insulted, and had to sacrifice his horses
and wagon to pay his fine for illegally shooting antelope out of
season. October 20, 1897, the last Indian dance—fifty Shoshones—
occurred on the streets of Casper in front of the Odd Fellows Building (what a shift in folklore!). The Indians came now, not to sound
the drums of battle, but to collect a few pennies from the curious
bystanders.

"Falling Star," the boss buck, reported the local paper derisively,
"wore a crow feather on his head and a pair of moccasins on his feet
and that was about the extent of his clothing. Afraid-to-Ride-a-Horse
wore one feather in his hair and a V-cut pair of stockings. . . . Red
Crow and all the rest of the dancers wore paint on their bare legs
and low-cut moccasins and danced to the sweet music . . . [from]
an oil barrel turned upside down and half a dozen Indians pounding
on it with sticks."

This last Indian dance occurred but ten years after Casper, Wyoming's principal central town had been founded. June 1, 1888, John
Merrit had ridden to the present site of Casper and pitched his tent
in the sagebrush. He came fifteen days ahead of the laying down of
the tracks of the Chicago and Northwestern to that point. The railroad brought a hundred more settlers and set up land-offices. Soon
rows of flimsy wooden shacks and tents, stores, hotels, restaurants
and whore-house saloons, selling "forty-rod" whiskey, lined a dusty
street.

For a year or so Nathan S. Bristol, owner of the first grocery and feed store, and his employees had to sleep in the store, behind barri-cades of grain and flour sacks to keep off the bullets of drunk cele-brating cowboys.

The town was incorporated in April, 1889, and the federal census the following year—when "tin-horn" Black Dick rifled the monte table—reveals 544 inhabitants.

Already trappers were in the hills, miners had discovered gold, cattle were ranging far ridges. Casper became the rallying point for every human being for hundreds of miles north and west.

The successors of the trappers and hunters were the cattlemen. Undaunted by the cruel winter blizzards, unmindful of early hard-ships, with the help of the United States Army, they fought their way to security and wealth against the proud aborigines. After the Indians were pushed back into the bad-land reservations, the White man's stock roamed unhindered all along the far-flung Rocky ridges for hundreds of miles.

Rulings, provided for the Federal Land Offices in the state, per-mitted the rapid enclosure of vast areas of the public domain. The Wyoming cattle companies, under the Desert Land Act, were per-mitted "to prove up claims in the names of parties living in distant states . . . in evasion . . . of the law." (1885 Federal Land Office Report.) Often the notaries were merely the attorneys of the cattle companies.

Even so in the beginning there was room and a plenty for all newcomers. Towns sprang up to minister to the needs of the indus-try—wide-open places where the cowboys galloped down the streets in drunken glory, shooting at the stars, flinging away their earnings at monte and stud-poker games, carousing with the gold-teeth, flare-flounce girls of the gay 'eighties and 'nineties. Cheyenne became the fabulous cow town of the ages. Money flowed; so did whiskey. The cattle kings satisfied every whim recklessly, as Struthers Burt men-tions in *Powder River*, even to the extent of having hot-house flowers and fruit brought up clear from Texas over the Chisholm Trail. Even before the days of the New York Union Club, the Cheyenne Club was a swank wonder with a menu of unpronounceable names. Gam-blers, swindlers and painted women kept the place agog and aglitter.

For a time it helped the cattlemen to have fresh settlers. In the beginning they had had to drive their steers on the hoof three weeks or more for from 250 to 300 miles to Ogalalla, Nebraska. The animals got there thin as paper. But soon settlers brought in railroads; shipping points were closer. The founding of Casper was a godsend. Such new towns increased the cattlemen's wealth and power, augmented property values.

The new settler easily found a foothold. He pushed up some lost creek, hewed logs for a cabin under the cottonwood trees, slapped mud and straw on the roof, and was ready for business. Many such a nester started out with little more than a cow-pony and a rope, a Visalia single-cinch saddle, a round-up bed, a branding iron and an easy conscience.

During the 'eighties cattle rustling was popular, profitable, and not considered overly wrong. A little initiative, the stamping of a new registered brand on stray yearlings and mavericks, and within a few summers a cautious nester would have a nice little herd.

At first the big cattle outfits did not mind careless branding or the rounding up of the wild mares of the open range. But as the country settled up and the range became more crowded, strays were not so easily encountered. Soon the nester had to brand calves and shoot the mother-cows; or he botched old brands and drove the animals out of the neighborhood. The cattlemen invented new, more devious brands. Charles A. Guernsey stamped a nine in shoulder, side and hip, a two-by-four-inch wattle on the right thigh, and swallow-forked each ear. But the rustling continued.

The cattle barons became alarmed. The appropriation of livestock by nesters had gone far enough A new code of ethics and property rights quickly evolved to meet the changed situation. Rewards for arrest were posted; detectives were imported to gather evidence against rustlers. Many suspects were jailed.

But past practices were not so easily cast aside. The law remained lax. The rustlers had many friends in all the settlements, even among the cowboys working for the big outfits. Many people also protected the lawless elements through fear. For the rustlers, especially after steps were taken to curb their activities, became reckless men ready for any violence, quick to take vengeance. Even when the wealthy cattlemen were standing squarely on their lawful rights, popular sentiment was far from favoring them. More legitimate settlers were bitter because the powerful companies ruthlessly drove off farmers and the owners of small herds, monopolized the land, grabbed the water and stole the government range.

Despite the wealth of the cattlemen, sheriffs were often in cahoots with the rustlers, local judges remained largely influenced by the settlers; the courts had fallen into the hands of the newcomers who had no traditions regarding the sacredness of livestock as private property. The rustlers, like the modern gangsters, had extensive political connections. Despite unquestionably damning evidence, time and again rustler after rustler was turned free.

The cattlemen finally not only had to take the law into their own hands; they had to go into politics. They were forced to protect their economic power with guns and political power.

One of the first outstanding instances of private cattlemen's justice was the hanging of famous "Cattle Kate" and her paramour, Jim Averell, in 1889. Averell ran a saloon and small store in the Sweetwater country in Natrona County. "Cattle Kate," a gal of about twenty-five, clever and "far from bad looking," took up a nearby homestead on Steamboat Rock and ran a "hog ranch." There some claimed she was joined by a few questionable ladies to entertain cowpunchers. Averell's place was said to be a hangout for rustlers; and Cattle Kate was said to have accepted stolen cattle in payment for whiskey and other bills. She accumulated a considerable herd very quickly. But all this may have been merely publicity to discredit them, for their ranches interfered with the "cattle-kings'" domain.

Other reports paint them as respectable and honest. Averell certainly was a Yale graduate and a civil engineer. But whether disreputable or not, Jim and Kate represented the new economic force of the small settler, and what was worse for them, were conscious of the fact. April 7, 1889, Averell, in an open letter to the *Casper Weekly Mail*, called the cattlemen "land-grabbers" and "speculators under the Desert Land Act."

"They are opposed to anything," he went on, "that would settle and improve the country or make it anything but a cowpasture for eastern speculators. It is wonderful how much land some of these land-sharks own—in their minds—and how firmly they are organized to keep Wyoming from settling up."

He reiterated his points: "A poor man has nothing to say in the affairs of his country. . . . Most of these large tracts . . . so fraudulently entered now . . . ultimately must change hands and give the public domain to the honest settler."

He took a jab at land monopoly. "Is it not enough to excite one's prejudice to see the Sweetwater River owned, or claimed, for a distance of seventy-five miles from its mouth by three or four men?"

Change the irrigation laws and cancel the Desert Land Act, he insisted, and Wyoming would see orchards, farms and prosperity.

This letter spelled his doom. His homestead and that of Cattle Kate were located on land claimed by "the three or four men." A band of lynchers, including two of the big landowners, appeared at Cattle Kate's place, drove off her stock, and without giving her time to change her calico dress or moccasins, took her away in a wagon. Averell was then picked up. After some hot words, the two of them were hanged side by side to a scrub pine among canyon rocks. Kate gurgled, and her moccasins fell off.

The Casper deputy sheriff organized a posse, found the dangling bodies, cut the rope and buried them.

Averell's brother and Kate's father hurried to the scene, stirred up popular feeling against the cattlemen and raised a considerable fund to aid the prosecutor.

Fortunately for the land-grabbing cattlemen, a boy, who had witnessed the lynching, died of Bright's disease before the trial came up. The cattlemen bribed two other witnesses to get out of the state. Another witness was threatened, hunted like a wild beast, murdered, and his body burned up, people claimed, by one George B. Henderson, former Pennsylvania mine-policeman and strike breaker, imported range-manager of the big 71 cattle outfit. Still another witness mysteriously disappeared.

The lynchers had to be acquitted. The Averell and Cattle Kate homesteads were taken up by new parties who promptly sold them to one of the big landowners of the lynching party.

In 1892 the cattlemen gave an even bolder lesson to the settlers. On April 6th, in a special train from Denver, they brought in a crowd of gunmen and detectives, known as "Regulators." Three cattle cars were loaded with guns, ammunition and supplies. The cattleman, Major Frank Wolcott, Civil War veteran, commanded the "quick-on-the-trigger" party—a guy who "would go out of his way any time to fight bare-handed a mountain-lion, coyote or human wolf in sheep's clothing." He had, it seems, quite a few sheep togs himself. Sam T. Glover, special correspondent of *The Chicago Herald*, went along with the gang.

The fifty-two men of the expedition were guided by the foreman of the Western Union Beef Company to the KC ranch of Nate Champion, a settler on land claimed by cattlemen. He was also reputed to be a rustler.

Ducking low in the creek and the brush and taking posts in the stable, the Regulators surrounded the KC buildings. Two trappers came out of the house and were taken prisoners. A third, Nick Ray, was shot down. Wounded, he managed to crawl back inside.

Champion then came to the door and fired at the besiegers, then barricaded himself inside. Between shots he kept a notebook of what happened:

"Me and Nick was getting breakfast when the attack took place. Two men here with us—Bill Jones and another man. The old man went after water and did not come back. His friend went out to see what was the matter and he did not come back. Nick started out, and I told him to look out. . . . Nick is shot but not dead yet. He is awful sick. I must go and wait on him. It is now about two hours since the first shot. Nick is still alive. They are still shooting from the stable and river and back of the house. Nick is dead. He died about 9 o'clock."

There is something amazing, pathetic and brave about the lone defender, fighting off a little army of hired thugs, yet snatching time between shots to scribble down the events.

"I see smoke at the stable. I think they have fired it. I don't think they intend to let me get away. . . ."

The morning drags by. "It is now about noon. There is someone at the stable yet. . . . Boys, I don't know what they have done with them two fellows that stayed here last night. Boys, I feel pretty lonesome just now. I wish there was someone here with me so we could watch all sides at once. They may fool around until I get a good shot. . . ."

He was obliged to run from window to window to keep an eye on all sides at once. But he continues to record. "It's about 3 o'clock now. There was a man in a buckboard and one on horseback that just passed. They fired on them as they went by. I don't know if they killed them or not. I seen lots of men come out on horses on the other side of the river and take after them. I shot at the men in the stable just now; don't know if I got any or not. I must go and look out again."

He comes back to write: "I see twelve or fifteen men. . . . They are shooting at the house now. . . . They are coming back. I've got to look out."

All day he stood them off. "Well, they have just got through shelling the house like hail. I hear them splitting wood. I guess they are going to fire the house tonight. I think I will make a break when night comes, if alive. Shooting again."

But they didn't give him a chance to wait till dark. Presently he was to write down his last words before having to clear out. "I think they are going to fire the house this time. It's not night yet. The house is all fired."

But even with the flames crackling about his ears, he took time to write "Good-by, boys, if I never see you again." Stuffing his record inside his shirt, he dashed out through the smoke.

The Regulators had wheeled a wagon, loaded with hay and pitch pine, against the cabin to set fire to it. The flames soon spread from the floor over the whole north wall, finally enveloped the house. Clouds of smoke burst forth everywhere. A cordon of sharpshooters stood ready.

But the trapped man did not appear. He was writing in his little notebook "Good-by, boys."

"Reckon the cuss has shot himself," remarked one of the waiting marksmen.

Hardly were these words uttered than Champion, in his stocking feet, Winchester in hand, dashed out of billowing black smoke and headed for the ravine.

There, around a bend, stood two of the best shots in the Regulator gang, rifles leveled.

Champion's own shot went wide. He was hit in the rifle arm just as he pulled the trigger. He fell riddled.

The *Herald* correspondent, writing the affair up for the cattlemen, waxed eloquent with pathos. "Nate Champion, the king of the cattle thieves and the bravest man in Johnson County, was dead. Prone upon his back, with his teeth clenched and look of mingled defiance and determination on his face to the last, the intrepid rustler met his fate without a groan. . . ."

But he was not quite dead. The assassins pinned a card—"Cattle thieves, beware!" on the red stain spreading on his vest and rode away, leaving him there helpless, staring up fiercely at the night sky. Slowly the red stain spread; it soaked into his notebook, the notes he had scribbled down during that long, lonesome day of siege. Slowly he was bleeding to death. Hours later he died.

News of the attack had been spread. The man in the buckboard at whom the Regulators had fired had been "Black Jack" Flagg, delegate to the Democratic Convention (the cattlemen were mostly good Republicans). He escaped safely and hastened to tell other Democratic delegates assembled at a nearby ranch. They and various settlers scattered to get men together. By 8:30 the following morning forty-nine volunteers closed in on the Regulators at the TA ranch. There the Regulators—having heard of the approach of enemies— had built themselves strong breastworks.

Sheriff Angus of Buffalo, Wyoming, after having been refused aid by the Governor and the National Guard commander, who were little more than rubber stamps for the cattlemen, swore in six men and also started for the TA ranch. On the way his forces grew to forty men. He joined up with the Democrats and the settlers. By the following day two hundred and fifty men were under his orders. They prepared to smoke the cattlemen-thugs out.

But just as they were advancing behind portable breastworks, made of hind axles and bales of straw, to the attack, Colonel Van Horn, at the head of three hundred United States Cavalrymen, appeared on the scene.

He stopped the assault. Disarming the Regulators, he marched them prisoners to Fort McKinley. Among them were some of the leading cattlemen of the state, including Senator Tisdale, and their employees.

Nate Champion was buried as a hero by a large procession, his casket smothered in flowers. Reverend McCullim promised him justice, if not in this world, the next.

The Casper citizens armed themselves to the teeth to defy any new bands of Regulators. The townsfolk's interests were mostly with the wholly new Wyoming of settlers growing up. In assembled mass-meeting they passed a resolution regretting the distrust and fear aroused and reassuring the outside world that those who wished to invest in Wyoming and help develop its untold resources would be "perfectly safe" and reap "a plentiful reward."

Sheriff Angus demanded the prisoners in order to make short shrift of them, but the Army refused. Instead, cattlemen pressure having been brought on federal authorities, several of the leading landowners and cow-kings were released on parole. These hastened to Washington. There Major Wolcott tried to clear his friends and gunmen and frantically sought to have martial law declared to postpone civil action.

He wanted time so that the cattlemen could get rid of all witnesses. They had Colonel E. H. Kimball, editor of the Douglas newspaper, arrested for libel, and managed to keep him in jail thirty days. This prevented his newspaper from printing the facts when they were needed. A lawyer and a livery-stable man were hired to get the two trappers (who had first left Champion's house) out of the country— a thousand dollars each and expenses or death was the alternative given them. All efforts of the civil authorities to hold them as witnesses or get them back were thwarted.

The good Republican cattlemen easily won over the federal authorities to their side. President Harrison moved twelve troops of cavalry into the state. They were there, not to see justice done, but to save the cattlemen, who were on the hot spot.

The prisoners were taken to Cheyenne where the cattlemen completely controlled the courts and the government. On the excuse of preventing them from being lynched, really to give them considerate treatment, the prisoners were lodged, not in jail but in Keefe's hall. Shortly after, all were released on their own recognizance.

The gunmen immediately skipped the state. After feelings had died down, the court dismissed the case entirely. John Clay, president of the Wyoming Stockmen's Association, thereupon publicly congratulated the paid Regulators for having stood "shoulder to shoulder" under the most trying circumstances. So was another bright chapter written in American justice.

That fall Nate Champion's brother was also shot down. The court dismissed the case against the murderer.

Innumerable are the stories of the activities of the private gunmen hired by the cattle owners. Their contempt for the law was increased by observing that their powerful backers made their own laws and protected themselves and their friends from swinging for murder. Some of these gunmen eventually became the worst desperados, bank-robbers, and thugs of the community.

But after the war of the Regulators, any man who rustled cattle was definitely an outlaw. The cattlemen were from then on well intrenched in politics and the courts. If local town governments and judges eluded their control, the cattlemen still had the district courts under their thumbs, and as a final resort the state government and Supreme Court to carry out their wishes.

The decision of one judge in 1904, when sentencing horse-thief Tom O'Day to six years in the penitentiary, is an epitome of the whole shift of the region toward law and order to protect the wealthy but lawless cattlemen. Judge Craig said:

"In the early days of Wyoming it was the custom to rustle stock, and if a list could be completed of all the men who had gotten a start in life by this method, it would make quite a huge catalogue. But those days are past, and Tom, you ought to have quit when the rest of the boys did."

Those who from this time on defied the cattlemen and the law were really dangerous bandits who combined other crimes with rustling. The headquarters for the worst of these outlaws was "The Hole-in-the-Wall" in the Powder River country, a place famous in the annals of American brigandage. The Hole-in-the-Wall is a wide beautiful valley through which the Buffalo Creek flows for some thirty miles between great mountains and a high ridge known as the Red Wall.

From there, thieves worked their stolen stock north into Montana or south to the "Tex" ranch on South Creek. But it was difficult to get evidence. The country was rough and remote. The rustlers would stage a quite proper roundup, but would hold the cattle or horses in some secluded canyon until nightfall. Then one of the thieves would drive the animals hard across the mountains until midnight. The four-legged booty would be delivered to an accomplice, and the first man would return home to get to bed before daylight. The second man would be met shortly before dawn somewhere near his own home and would also hasten back to bed. In this way everyone concerned would establish an alibi. At the same time, the animals would be moved lightning quick across the state.

Bob and Al Smith and Bob Taylor, settlers in the Hole-in-the-Wall country, were supposed to be in "cahoots" with the rustlers. In 1897 Bob Devine, foreman of the big CY outfit, served notice on them through the Casper *Tribune* that he and his men were going to round up all the cattle of the CY, Keystone and Pugsley ranches found in the Hole-in-the-Wall. The following reply came through, signed by the "Revenge Gang" (quoted by Mokler):

"Bob Devine you think you have played hell you have just begun you will get your dose there is men enuff up here yet to kill you. We are going to get you or lose 12 more men you must stay out of this country if you want to live . . . we want one hair a piece out of that damned old chin of yours you have given us the worst of it all the way through and you must stay out or die . . . don't stick that old gray head of yours in this country again if you don't want it shot off. . . ."

Undaunted, Devine led his men boldly into the outlaw valley. Three miles above the Hole-in-the-Wall ranch, the Revenge Gang rode up to the invaders. Bob Smith pulled his six-shooter and shouted at Devine: "You damned old son-of-a-bitch, I am going to get you this time!"

The two groups began firing, careening back and forth on their cow-ponies, raising a cloud of dust and exchanging about a hundred shots.

When the smoke and dust settled, the invaders were in possession of the field, though Devine's horse was dead and men on both sides were injured. Bob Smith was found dangerously wounded. Al Smith escaped, though a bullet had ripped off his thumb, knocking his six-shooter out of his hand. Taylor was captured.

Devine started to shoot Bob Smith where he lay wounded, but a companion brushed his gun side. Taylor was brought into Casper with a noose about his neck.

The judge promptly dismissed the case against Devine.

Famous in the Hole-in-the-Wall country from 1894 to 1900 was the Currie gang, headed by Harvy Logan (alias "Kid Curry"), George Currie (alias "Flat Nose George") and Tom and George Dickenson (alias "The Roberts Brothers"). Early in June, 1898, they held up the store and post office in Wolton, escaped a posse, then held up the bank at Belle Fourche, South Dakota. In the get-away there, one of the gang, Tom O'Day, lost his horse and was captured. Taken to Deadwood jail, he soon escaped. Though O'Day was recaptured, the state's attorney had to release him for lack of evidence.

The rest of the gang swept through Wyoming clear to the Shoshoni Reservation and on into the wild Wind River country, four hundred miles in five days. Near the Canadian border, the posse surprised them in camp, but they leapt upon their horses' bare backs and escaped. Ten days later, doubling back and erasing their tracks, they were again safe in the Big Horn country.

Ere long a new menace confronted the cattlemen. They had won out against blizzard and drouth. They had disposed of the Indians. They had laid a heavy hand on bandits and rustlers. They had run out settlers blocking the water-holes and had temporarily won the battle against most of the nesters. They had fought their way to established power. They had won their way in politics and had gained control of the state machinery of government and the courts. Now they had to battle against the sheepmen.

In the early 'eighties, J. B. Okie had pushed a small herd of sheep into the Bad Water region, just south of the Big Horn basin, and threw up a little log cabin, the first settler in that section of the country, one of the first sheepmen in the state. As the big cattle outfits were fifty miles away in either direction, he was not at first disturbed. Gradually he built up his herd, until he was running fifty thousand head worth half a million dollars, which in normal years returned a $100,000 profit from wool and lambs. By the time of the World War, his sheep and other enterprises pushed his profits up close to the million dollar mark annually.

At Lost Cabin he started a saloon and store which in its palmy days returned a net profit of $40,000 a year; and he soon put in stores and saloons at other outlying points—Lysite, Arminta, Shoshoni, Moneta.

The nearest settled place of any size was at first Cheyenne, two hundred miles away, later Casper, ninety miles away.

When the freight for the store started north in the three large canvas-covered wagons drawn by eight or more horses, on their long struggle over the rough gullies and sandy plains, it was joyous news for the whole region; men came fifty miles or more from up in the mountains to lay in supplies; the youngsters would walk five miles down toward Alkali Gulch just to buy an apple. Okie also started a crack four-horse stage-line between Casper and Billings, Montana, with relays of fresh horses every ten miles. Occasionally it was held up by Indians or bandits.

By 1894 he established the first steam-shearing plant in the United

States. At 3:30 o'clock, Sunday, April 22nd, the engine was started, with a large gathering of sheep-owners, shearers, wool-buyers and business men present. The Casper newspaper announced: "Amid much applause the first sheep was sheared by Mrs. Okie, the wife of the man who was instrumental in initiating this method of shearing to the American people, and Mrs. Okie enjoys the distinction of shearing the first sheep ever shorn by this method in America, and she performed the task in less than five minutes."

Mrs. Okie swears to me at this late date that she merely ran the shears once over the sheep's head, but the enthusiasm of the local paper makes a better tale for posterity.

By that time there were many sheepmen in Wyoming. They were pushing in everywhere. In 1888 Joel J. Hurt had raised real fears among the cattlemen by driving 3,000 sheep right into Natrona County (a stronghold of theirs) and putting the herd on the open cattle range. These, and the sheep that followed, caused as much bloodshed as the arrival of the nesters and settlers. As the free pasturage areas shrank in size, the feuds became more and more bitter.

The cattlemen had become monarchs of all they surveyed. But now the sheep pushed off the cattle, ate the grass down to the roots, muddied the water-holes, threatened the supremacy of the great stock-raisers.

Powerful psychological factors also helped to precipitate violence. The cowboy was a wild, free dervish. He broke the fierce mustang, often as savage as any wildcat, and rode him, made him his companion, so faithful he would stand "hitched to a rattlesnake's tail or a dinosaur's third horn." Each horse he broke had a vividly different personality, presented a new problem. Even the wild steers required ingenuity, strength and bravery to handle. His work was fast and courageous; and he was as dashing and daring in his play as in his work. His dress was also debonair; red bandana, high-heeled boots, big roweled spurs, "chaps," six-shooter and cartridge belt.

In contrast, the sheepherder is a solitary individual, either morose or romantically moody, who moves slowly with his tinkling herd and astute dog. His dumb sheep are undistinguishable one from another. To tend them requires little but patience, a knowledge of weather, of good breeding and lambing ground.

The cowboys—with only contempt for the sheep business and the men who carried it on, and backed up in any and all aggressions by their powerful employers still controlling much of the political machinery of the state—never hesitated to commit any depredation. They would stand up calmly in their stirrups and with their rifles pick off sheep after sheep until their ammunition was exhausted. If a herder objected he also was shot. Oftentimes cowboys amused themselves by stampeding herds over precipices; or they drove a bunch of steers pellmell through the sheep herd, killing, maiming and scattering the bleating animals.

Though the range was all free government land, the cattlemen finally drew a deadline—and even that was a compromise. If any sheepman dared cross into cattle preserves, a gang would appear at night, murder the herder, kill the sheep and burn the camp-wagons and supplies. The cattlemen, so powerful politically, were immune from punishment. The sheepmen could get little or no justice in the courts.

On August 24, 1905, ten masked men visited the Louis A. Gantz sheep camp, some forty miles from Basin, and killed about 4,000 sheep, burned the wagons, shot a team of horses, destroyed grain and provisions. Even the sheep-dogs were tied to the wagons and burned alive. Though the men who committed this atrocity were well known, none was ever brought to justice.

But gradually the sheepmen became more powerful. There was far more money to be made out of their business than out of cattle. Okie's fabulous success was but one of many. Even some of the cattlemen themselves suddenly went into the despised sheep business. The Wyoming Woolgrowers' Association began to exercise definite influence in the affairs of the state. Going into politics, they soon influenced elections, getting a say in the appointment of judges. Like the cattlemen before them, they had to seek political power corresponding to their growing economic power.

By 1909 the sheepmen were finally able to secure a conviction for one of the numerous aggressions against them. On April 3rd cattle thugs made a night raid on a sheep camp in No Water Creek in the Ten Sleep country. A sheep-owner, his camp-mover and his herder were shot and their bodies burned. The wagons were destroyed and many sheep slain.

Thoroughly aroused, determined to punish the guilty parties, the Woolgrowers' Association posted rewards and secured arrests. Seven men were indicted. Two of these turned state's evidence; and all, despite the stubborn defense by their cattlemen backers, were given terms ranging from three to twenty-six years. This was the first real legal victory for the sheepmen. The same judge, though, condemned a Mexican sheepherder who had murdered a crooked gambler to life-imprisonment. But of course, besides being a sheepman, he was just a Mexican; and justice in America, as in most parts of the world, is often scaled to class and race lines.

From this time on the sheepmen gradually assumed the ascendancy and finally wrenched control of the state away from the cattle barons. Today hundreds of thousands of sheep range over the mountains and valleys.

By 1908 the prior bloody feuds with the nesters and rustlers were well-nigh forgotten. In that year Lee Moore, a cattleman, generously put over the grave of George W. Pike, who in his heyday had been a famous horse-thief, a slab with the following inscription (quoted by Mokler):

> Under this stone in eternal rest
> Sleeps the wildest one of the wayward west
> He was a gambler, sport and cowboy, too,
> And he led the pace in an outlaw crew.
> He was sure on the trigger and stayed to the end,
> But he was never known to quit a friend.

Lee Moore was putting up a monument to a vanished epoch.

I have not heard of a sheepman putting up a monument to any cowboy who destroyed his herds and killed his men; perhaps it is too soon yet; but the strange irony of today is that the leading participants in the rodeos now are rarely cattlemen but sheepmen. Wyoming is entering upon a new economic phase. But that is another tale.

The Indians, the Oregon emigrants, the trappers and fur-traders, then the cattlemen, not to mention the oil-drillers and miners, all wrote their epic stories into the pages of Wyoming history. The sheepmen who followed wrote a new page not yet completed, but soon to be turned.

CHAPTER XIV

THE END OF THE TRAIL

In all the vast empire of lofty snow-clad mountains and bleak upland plains known as Wyoming, until as late as 1901 gambling was a lawful occupation, almost as profitable and respectable as banking, cattle-raising, sheepherding, mining or oil-drilling. In all the villages, towns and what Wyoming calls cities, down on the dusty Cheyenne trail, over in Lander by the Twin Buttes of the Wind River Mountains, far up the Big Horn basin and clear to Buffalo and Crazy Woman Creek, games of poker, faro, monte and roulette were in operation night and day. From sheepherder to cattle baron the fever ran. Sums were flung away which, even in these New Deal days, would cause a gasp.

On February 18, 1893, the *Wyoming Derrick* reported of Casper: "The town is the liveliest in the state. Business of every kind is good, and as further evidence of our prosperity there are four stud poker games in full blast. There were two games at the Stock Exchange [Saloon] last week, the games continuing the entire night. A large sum of money exchanged hands and there was much excitement."

Gambling had to be above-board. Gamblers who "loaded" their roulette wheels or resorted to other shady tricks, if discovered, had to leave town hurriedly or go to jail or be lynched. But honest gamblers had the full protection of what law there was.

On a Sunday night in the fall of 1890, when the great snowdrifts swept down over the state in whining blizzards, "Black Dick," a "tin-horn and roustabout," seized the opportunity, when a thrilling poker game in the Casper White Saloon absorbed everyone's attention, to "lift" a sack of silver from a monte table. Captured by the sheriff at Big Muddy station when attempting to board an eastbound train, he barely escaped lynching and was sentenced to ninety days.

But Natrona County in central Wyoming did not boast a jail. Black Dick had to be sent over to neighboring Converse County. The whole state—though not a Kropotkin brotherhood—did not have a penitentiary. The occasional prisoner had to be farmed out in Joliet, Illinois. This was expensive. Thus it was quite a nuisance to try people in the courts. Usually offenders, if not strung up, were merely told to "skedaddle" fast. If they did not at once hit the high spots, punishment was apt to be worse than any prison term.

Toward the end of 1890 Casper began to feel the need of becoming more civilized, so it erected a jail—a one-room shack, iron bars across a tiny window up against the roof. This little dungeon lasted until Dr. Bender, the Town's physician, dentist, barber and confirmed drunkard, set fire to it to force the authorities to release him. Unfortunately they could not find the keys. For some time after that Casper reverted to the old "skedaddle" method.

When gambling was finally made unlawful, the tables merely moved into clandestine back-rooms of the saloons, to be utilized thereafter by less respectable gentry. Some of the old-time gamblers —the few who did not ultimately grace "wooden kimonos"—still float around the region. Ted Winthrop, whose antiquated Jesse James locks and massive white beard adorn the town of Lysite, now lives by panhandling, a chance game, cotton-tail stews and by selling home-brewed beer, and moonshine, raw as fire, sharpened with laundry soap and plug tobacco. He walks abroad with his elegant cane and handsome dog and cuts a venerable figure in his high boots, black-and-white-striped drill trousers, plaid shirt, and five-gallon hat.

Over the tables at Betty the bootlegger's, and surrounded by the penniless wrecks of the frontier days, he flips a deck of cards dextrously, hoping to allure anybody with real cash into a friendly game. With a glint of innocent blue eyes sparkling with malicious cunning, he tells you that before he was reformed and became a respectable gambler, he was a preacher. "For forty years I told the boys to save their money. I never took no man's money; he always give it to me."

Another old-time card-wrangler was Willie Moonlight, who now, thanks to his wife's cooking and washing, ekes out a living in a dusty cabin on the flats.

"Long Leather" of Lost Cabin saloon on Badwater Creek ended his days as a shotgun sieve. His right middle finger, because of a tendon severed in some fracas, stuck out straight and stiff; but under that mutilated digit he could snuffle in cards like an ant-eater and deal them out magically from any part of the deck. When sheepherders came down from the Big Horn range, their whole year's wages stacked up ready for a good time, Lon'—after plying them with Scotch—would inveigle them into a stud game and within a few hours would strip them to their socks. Then he would suddenly rise in bellowing wrath: "Get out, you bums; go crybaby that you've been robbed."

If they showed fight, Lon' was quick on the draw; but most of them meekly went out to weep over their "hoss's neck"—"Ze only friend I got in the world," and the next morning would plod off to their sheep wagons far up in the Sioux Canyon or Clear Water Creek to accumulate another sack of silver through the long winter of snow and ice—for Lon'.

"In timbered country, you can't keep the squirrels off the trees," the gambler would chuckle.

But the turn of the century not only marked a great break in the old gambling traditions, but the passing away of a whole era. The wild horses of the open range had all been rounded up and branded; and the wild men of Powder River and Salt Creek had been mostly hobbled to law and order. Cattle Kate and her paramour had been hanged. Driftwood Jim had been sent up; the Currie gang had been broken up; and "gentlemen horsethief" Chenoweth had been safely lodged in an insane asylum.

Morals also put on a more conservative dress. Casper, like other remote settlements, had been a hilarious center. The cowboys, hearty spenders, frolicked into town on their cayuses. Every saloon had its piano. Wild dancing compensated for the hardships of the roughnecks who carved out that western empire and whose sons and grandsons are now respectable members of the Rotary Clubs, Kiwanis and the Grand Order of Muscovites.

Gory thrills resulted from those early orgies. Lou Polk's notorious dance hall was the scene of many a fray. Lou and a consort, "Dogae Lee," ran the joint. Dogae, jealous of her flirtations, carried her off to the hills to horsewhip her. According to the veracious *Wyoming Derrick*, when he was about to be captured by the authorities, he sliced off her nose to disqualify her for any amorous successor. Noseless Lou came back to her dance hall, the lost member tenderly wrapped in a handkerchief.

She next hired "Killer" John Conway as official bouncer. Cowboy "Red Jack" of the F-1 outfit picked an unnecessary quarrel with inoffensive "Sonny," one of Lou's musicians. Conway promptly knocked unarmed Jack down with the butt of his pistol and shot him where he lay unconscious. Everybody ran shrieking out of the hall. Poor Sonny, butting into a pine tree, had his left eye gouged out—he might as well have had a good fight.

The sheriff had to smuggle prisoner Conway out of town in a baggage-car to save him from being lynched by the cowboys buzzing about with drawn six-shooters.

Not merely in the towns did such things go on. Up in the mountain stores and saloons, in shacks on Buffalo or Poison Snake Creeks or Powder River—especially during sheep shearing or annual roundups—the war-paints of the world's oldest profession set up temporary bars, gambling tables and back-room accommodations. If whiskey gave out, every grocery was well stocked with Peruna. Nothing was more ripsnorting than a good Peruna drunk. Up on Powder River, Big Jim had his throat slit from ear to ear during a Peruna jag and survived the jolting of a wagon bed for ten miles of the way to the doctor forty miles off.

As early as July 18, 1889, at the seventh session of the Casper town council, the city fathers became aware that public morals had to be rigorously safeguarded. It was firmly decreed that from ten o'clock at night until seven in the morning was time enough for whoring even in a wide-open town. Women were forbidden under penalty of a fine from five to twenty-five dollars to frequent any barroom except during those hours. Casper was to be made daylight pure. It was further made unlawful "for any woman to use any vile, profane or indecent language or to act in a boisterous or lewd manner, or to smoke any cigar, cigarette or pipe on any street in Casper." Even at this late date my gorge rises up at the idea of a "lewd" woman smoking a pipe on the streets.

By August, 1891, a Grand Jury in Casper demanded that the authorities lay a heavy hand on "ribaldry" which had "surpassed all limits." But not until 1898 on the eve of the war with Spain was the so-called "lewd" ordinance repealed, the town retrieved from the hands of the saloon elements, and a clean-up effected without benefit of law. Bad elements were ordered out of town; after a given date the authorities refused to be responsible for what might happen to them.

One harridan, on leaving, mounted the rear train platform and abused the good citizens in the depot "with the hardest, most blasphemous oaths the human tongue could articulate." The outraged Casperites telegraphed the Douglas authorities who brought her back under arrest. A heavy fine was then remitted if she would leave at once decorously. It must have been a touching sight to have seen the first citizens of the community nobly trying to teach a whore good manners and improve her diction.

The poor gal felt so shamed, she went to her room and swallowed laudanum. An emetic saved her. The boys stammered out remorseful conciliatory words; they had a few drinks with her all around; and she then left Casper presumably for all time.

Thus by the end of the century Casper was achieving those solid morals which now so feature our commonwealth as a whole. Not that violence died entirely or is yet dead. In 1902 Charles F. Woodard was arrested for killing the sheriff trying to apprehend him. In the night in the dead of winter, twenty-four masked men took Woodard from jail in a shrunken flannel shirt, "his nether parts exposed," and marched him barefoot through the snow to an improvised gallows—for the landscape was treeless. After many bungling attempts, they successfully hanged him, and when the "gurgling sound kept growing fainter" and life was extinct, a card was pinned to his shirt:

Process of law is a little slow
So this is the road you will have to go.
Murderers and thieves, beware!

Woodard died, but poetry was born.

By another five years even such episodes were almost unknown. Not even the opening of the brewery, July 26, 1915—built by subscriptions from the sound burghers of that later period—could bring back the old days, although cheese, sausages and "Wyoming Light Lager" was dispensed free with such gaiety that the opening was prolonged for a whole week. But by then Old Midwest Bar, Grand Central Bar, The Wyoming, The Buffet, The Stock Exchange, Elkhorn, The Inn, Parlor Car, and Burke's Place had already become decorous rivals of the Epworth League. Good Elks and Pythians stepped in to them to discuss civic improvements, Wallingford promotion schemes, and new school sites—over which more than one scandal of filth and graft emerged into the light of day.

Prohibition restored some disorder. The bootleggers who supplanted the honest saloon-keepers were sodden, unimaginative commercialists who could murder on occasion. Even so they had neither the frontier flare nor the romance of the Caponeites of the Loop or of the brass-knuckle brigades of our swank night clubs.

From its first days Casper had shown that it did not really desire to be unholy. Even before incorporation, when it had less than a year of life behind it and was still a huddle of shanties and tents, Mrs. Adah E. Allen enrolled nineteen pupils in a subscription school; and the following year a public school was set up in the Congregational Tabernacle. This and other churches struggled valiantly to save God's wayward children from the Dogaes and Lou Polks. Even the elements of darkness saw nothing very wrong in this religious invasion. They apparently considered that, up to a certain point, their own sinful activities were necessary in order to give righteous forces a justification for their efforts. When Reverend Bross conducted the first services in town—March 3, 1899, in the Graham Hotel office— the congregation was made up of devout business men, saloon-keepers, bartenders, gamblers, cowboys, and miners.

Very early, too, the town council became concerned over higher culture, and as early as January, 1895, remodeled the town hall to "make a first class opera-house out of it." This, said the local paper, would give Casper "the finest opera hall in central Wyoming."

The new drop curtain depicted "a mountain peak, a slough with huge cat-tails along the edge, a large lightning-splintered tree, and many other things that could be conjured only in the fertile brain of an artist and produced with a brush, paint and palette."

The town was also learning to carry on the political burdens of the great Republic.

In the early days of the Territory, political corruption in Wyoming was not even hidden from sight. The "Railroad Ticket" of company employees went openly on the ballot. Votes and jobs were openly bought. Candidates paid so much to get on a ticket. John Chase of the old Inter-Ocean Hotel in Cheyenne, used personally to take each employee to the poll, put the marked ballot in his hands to be delivered in his presence at the voting booth. Friends of candidates hung around the polls with currency of the realm in their fists, soliciting votes. Groups of United States soldiers from Camp Carlin and Fort D. A. Russell would march into town to sell their votes en masse to the highest bidder, often in open auction.

But before the turn of the century, the mechanics of such things moved into the back-rooms of the saloons.

In 1896 Casper valiantly helped save the day for McKinley and the Mark Hanna gang. Though as yet the Republican Party was much under the thumb of the cattlemen, Bryan was too much for the sheepmen, and they, too, were beginning now to fear new settlers. From the wool warehouse—for Casper was more in a sheep than a cattle region—Grand Marshal W. H. Dubling and the Douglas military band led an electoral procession of "ladies and men" in carriages carrying "transparencies, banners, torches and discharging fireworks." There were "many attractive floats": The "Good Ship Protection: Captain McKinley" (not for nothing had they started from the wool warehouse) was a large vessel under full sail. "The Campaign of 1896" float showed McKinley in the large end of the horn of prosperity and Bryan crawling out of the little end. In another float two ladies operated old-fashioned spinning wheels using Wyoming wool. Another showed a prosperous McKinley shearer busy taking the pelt off a Wyoming ewe, beside a famished ragged Bryan shearer.

Fifty-two decorated carriages contained each "from three to six ladies." After them came the Flambeaux Club, one hundred strong, burning red tableau fire and shooting off Roman candles. The procession wound up with the "Butler Brigade," one hundred boys carrying torches and blowing tin horns. Dwight Seely made the anvil roar; Jeff Crawford fired seven-inch cannon-crackers continuously; Jay Wilcox came along with his bear; John Ambruster with his big dog. Charley Hewes impersonated a hayseed. Uncle Sams were numerous; and further to emphasize democracy and prosperity there were many "kings and queens, gold men and silver men"—the last named, of course, scrawny caricatures.

In the hall those who could gain admission listened to the McKinley Quartette sing "Wyoming will be in Line." Judge Carey made "a most convincing argument," then everybody danced.

Wyoming was in line. For the entire country a new trend had set in. Colonel Torrey's Wyoming Rough Riders soon clattered off to the Spanish-American War and got as far as Jacksonville, Florida. The Wyoming infantry battalion, with a volunteer enlistment four times Secretary Alger's allotment, had sailed for the Philippines, had fought in the mythical Manila battle, and within fifteen months the survivors of tinned meat, syph and typhoid were back in Cheyenne ready to be honored by the state's $1,500 "Heroes' monument."

From then on there was to be no tampering with the gods of Big Business prosperity. In 1901 when McKinley was shot—certainly a jolt when God was in his heaven and all was right with the world and the better citizens—eight prominent Casper business men showed their civic righteousness by indignantly riding out of town on a 2 x 6 scantling a man named Wagner, who, deep in his Peruna cups, had ventured to remark, McKinley "ought to have been shot a year ago" —which at this late date strikes me as an extremely moderate statement.

The oil industry brought in a new type of resident. Early in the previous century Captain Bonneville had taken ointment from "great tar springs" for the backs of his horses and the aches and pains of his men. In January, 1889, the *Casper Mail* spoke of the Poison Spider, Rattlesnake, Popo Agie and Argo oil basins and mentioned three wells in the Popo Agie section with an aggregate 600 barrel flow a day. The first Salt Creek well was brought in in 1890; and by April, 1895, the first refinery was turning out 60 barrels weekly of refined engine oil. By 1900 the industry was really expanding, soon was brought under the control of the powerful companies. By 1923 the fires were started in the stills of Casper's third refinery, the Texas Oil plant, at the time perhaps the largest in the world. The Teapot Dome scandal came in due course.

And so colonial empire, far-flung trade, industrial hegemony, the Spanish-American War, marked a new era of Big Business, Mark Hanna pounding the drums. Oil and mining rounded out Wyoming's political controls, which previously, except for an occasional flare-up of the settlers, had been run by cattlemen and railroads and in a few places by the sheepmen. Gambling was now renamed "speculation"—some of our best bankers were whirling the new roulettes, for the most part "loaded." Gangsters were retreating from the sage-brush to the dives and brothels of our great cities. The twentieth century saw many an old frontier attitude vanish forever—swallowed up in the bigger and better America.

Prosperity brought other benefits of civilization. On June 12, 1900, at ten o'clock at night, Major W. S. Kimble quoted *Genesis:* "And God said, Let there be Light and there was Light. And God saw the Light that it was good; and God divided the Light from Darkness." Reverend J. H. Gillespie invoked the blessings of the Deity, and Mrs. Kimball pressed a button which flooded the city with electric illumination. All good citizens rejoiced, not the least realizing that they were helping to send our empire-builders to a new wild Wyoming to Bolivia to dig out wolfram; though a few of Casper's more prosperous deans, having later invested in South American bonds, perhaps now realize they are still paying dearly for their civic eagerness of three decades ago.

On March 22, 1902, forty-nine sets of Geneso-type phones were installed by the Rocky Mountain Telephone Company. The company put out elaborate instructions how to take the receiver off the hook and how to hold it to the ear. The exchange, located on the second floor of the Stock Exchange saloon, was in charge of "two female operators," who, though they worked in twelve-hour shifts, had "plenty of time between calls for rest and recreation." Although we have no documents to prove it, their joys probably differed from those of their predecessors, the barmaids.

By this time gun-toting by Casperites had become merely a gentleman's fetish, through membership in the Casper Gun Club. They at least made a simulacrum of the old days on May 11, 1903, when regular passenger service was inaugurated, by firing off their six-shooters and exploding powder on iron anvils—"Casper's joyful awakening"—so joyful several tenderfoot passengers hid under the seats and refused to get off.

And when the line was extended to Lander, 148 miles further northwest, and the inhabitants (October 17, 1906) celebrated the first train arrival, the new blessings were received with real but mixed emotions. Cora V. Wesley, editor of the *Mountaineer*, said: "Tears trickled down our cheeks and sadness crept over the household because the rural beauties of western life were to sink into the great abyss of the past. Real genuine tears of grief and joy chasing each other in confusion, trying to gain the victory."

That year the Fremont vigilante committee called upon the remaining "bad hombres" to leave the confines of the commonwealth. Lawlessness was at last routed—almost—even from the backwoods.

Today Casper is entirely a modern little city that has suffered badly from the depression. It is little different from a thousand other cities of like size strewn from coast to coast. Those interested in past romance may notice the single log-cabin, sentimentally preserved, or may hunt up the monument marking the old Oregon Trail, which is incorrectly located. Otherwise Casper has fallen into step with the best hundred per cent achievements of the Republic at large. It boasts the necessary allotment of schools with the latest gadgets, a Carnegie library, public hospital, county poor farm, sewer system, fire department, an airport. For a time it had the largest private radio-phone in the West. It has the customary movies, ice-cream parlors, hot-dog stands, garages, banks, stores and up-to-date hotels. The Y.M.C.A., Y.W.C.A., W.C.T.U., Salvation Army and similar uplift organizations pound the drums for financial support, lean these days. Churches of all denominations serve to make vague differences in social status rather than in Christian dogma, among the now dominant, uneventful and well-meaning middle class. The people are unusually good joiners; all lodges of importance are represented, not to mention specific professional and business groups: the Rotary Club, Kiwanis, Lions Club, Chamber of Commerce, Boy Scouts, Army Club, Grand Order of Muscovites, Masons, Elks, Pythians, Odd Fellows, etc., etc., each with its individual folklore, mumbo-jumbo, braid, parchment, bizarre titles—an adolescent hankering for a better life, distinction and snobbish superiority.

A fringe of the town is still a little tougher than any spots to be found in most small cities in more settled regions, but now the sheepherders, cattlemen and oil-workers take their joys furtively and only occasionally run amuck.

While I was there Crazy Jim, a very taciturn sheepherder who mumbles to himself, went in a wild drunk and knocked out three policemen before he was subdued. He spent the night in jail, but once sober was quietly freed—no charges preferred. It is an old tradition of liberty—and besides, the sheepmen, after a long season in the hills, scatter their savings generously among the local merchants. It is not good to have the sheepmen down on the place.

With the shift to more sedate enterprise, Mexicans, Filipinos, Negroes, Italians, have drifted into the region to work on the railroads, in the oil fields, or as sheepherders. The county governments are well controlled by the big sheepmen, who thirty years ago overthrew the state cattle dynasty, and these and the better elements in the cities keep the floating alien driftwood of our industrial development floating in the proper channels. When Mrs. Pearl Williams cold-bloodedly shot the Negro Robert Brown, with whom she had been flirting over the telephone, she was universally applauded. When A. J. Cunningham, President of the Casper National Bank, was shot accidentally in the arm by a Mexican stealing a pair of shoes, the

Mexican was sentenced to thirteen years and six months; and the city and county authorities, co-operating with the constitutional-minded citizens, rounded up two dozen Negroes and Mexicans, loaded them on a box car at the point of the gun and intelligently headed them—north.

The other violences of today are those which grace the headlines of our scandal sheets everywhere: petty larceny, jealous murders, hijacking. The violences of pettier crime and class and race discrimination have replaced the violences of empire building.

It is clear that now Casper, as well as other parts of Wyoming, faces the end of another epoch. The oil industry passed through its boom days and the Teapot Dome scandal, but now has shrunk; mining is at present mostly unprofitable; the wool industry routed cattle-raising, but is in turn now in the doldrums compared to old bonanza days. The gradual settling up of the more fertile areas is restricting the size of the herds. The lack of water, the very short summer, the uncertain climate, does not permit, in most places, the supplementing of sheep-raising with other large agricultural enterprises. The lawless competitive days of the sheep industry are now also over. Just as the cattleman was beginning to be menaced by the ordinary settler, so today the sheepmen are increasingly hemmed in by poor homesteaders in a grazing country ill-adapted to ordinary agriculture.

Wyoming's present and future resources have by now been parceled out. No pauper sheepherder now could come in with a few head of sheep—as did one thirty-odd years ago—and become a millionaire in a few short decades, build a mansion on the mesquite mesa, get culture, buy costly fad art now worth next to nothing, get rid of his wife for a young singer, who became lustful for his own son, and drive them both out at the point of his gun. The land is monopolized or tied up; the water-holes, which long ran red with blood, till titles were finally established, are now all closed in. And so still another of America's frontiers of enterprise has passed away.

The vast national problems of production, distribution, economic maladjustment, have struck all Wyoming beneath the belt. Casper's population has dwindled to half what it was in boom days.

Thus not only are the wild days of the open range gone, something else is now vanishing. The back-slapping optimism of the respectable promoters and the business joiners no longer suffice for the realization of the full possibilities of a wealthy commonwealth of free men. Wyoming is no longer a land of boundless opportunity. Nearly every activity is now more hedged about.

Even the big frontier barons, the new rough and ready aristocrats, are feeling the pinch and being mowed down one by one as their mortgages are taken up by eastern capital. The pinch comes everywhere.

Inevitably the new frontier, if there is to be one, must necessarily become that of social planning, a task for which individualistic Wyomingites are traditionally unprepared, but which cannot be long evaded.

A few Fourth of Julys ago, I was in Casper for the annual rodeo. Every man and boy in the city blossomed out in a ten-gallon black hat, edged with white, a red shirt, and a black tie. Conformity among the free souls of Casper could go no further in loyally celebrating the memory of its ancient non-conformities.

They are cherishing, thus, the tradition of the old cattle days which died three or four decades ago. They have not yet gotten around to such elaborate celebrations of the sheep-raising days or of the more recent business prosperity days. But the old trail is settled. Three eras have hurried past in a short time. What lies ahead on the new trail no man yet discerns. That it will be more significant and important than anything in the past, no man doubts.

CHAPTER XV

DON'T MONKEY WITH THE BUZZ-SAW

Enterprise after enterprise in America has come to an end, while the pioneer instincts of largess and freedom were—and are—still quick in the blood of our people. The closing of each frontier of effort narrowed the circle of free endeavor. The closing of the land frontier as a whole ended a great heroic age. The muscles and minds of men were forced by fire and effort to meet the hazards, the adventures, the fear of great spaces, to endure the wonder at the great arena that confronted them.

Then the great enterprises dwindled—like a bad joke of the gods. The dreamers saw the skyline fade before their eyes. Their coursing blood was choked back. Their ready muscles were tamed to tiddle-dee-wink tasks. The practical men of greed, of organization, of predatory power, held much of what was left.

For most of our citizens, routine quickly took the place of free mobile effort and migration. Men who carved a wilderness as free individuals became wage earners. The boundary of success became a job. The boundaries of conduct became fixed. And for millions, even the boundary of a job narrowed, during recent depression days, to a W.P.A. task, earmarked with charity lest it conflict with private industry.

In places, the wilderness was claimed in a quarter of a century. Within two decades or so the sod house gave way to the frame clapboard house; the acres were fenced in. Soon enough, barbed wire, through which at first the buffalo herds broke at will, wove a permanent arbitrary design on the plains. Life was tamed. The clouds

293

of pigeons no longer darkened the sky. The buffalo trail became U. S. 55; the water-hole of foxes became the First National Bank lot. A system of law arose far different from that known to the men who a few years before came lugging their firearms, their Bibles and their expectations over the Appalachians and along the river highways.

This whirling epoch and the change is exemplified in no enterprise more swiftly than in the lumber industry. Lumbering was a world of great exploits. Here towers the grandiose figure of Paul Bunyan, the great lumberjack, naturalized from a low-down Canuck, Paul Bonhomme, to a roistering American of the frontier who played at dice with huge square eggs of the gigantic gilly-grouse from the Big Onion River. Here rolled the great hoop snake, tail in its mouth, rolled and rolled all winter long. Once it struck a peavy handle causing it to swell so that Paul Bunyan cut a thousand cords of stove wood from it. One winter, that of the blue snow, Paul went off to an enormous cave where, with a whole pine tree for a pencil, he figured out greater deeds, bigger logging yields—a dreamer he was.

"Though Paul himself was a Canuck," writes Havighurst, "the loggers in the American pineries gave him his true properties.

"They gave him Babe, the great ox that measured forty-two ax-handles and a plug of chewing tobacco between the eyes. They created for him the fabulous logging camp with its enormous cook-house and the pile of prune stones darkening the window and the ax-handle hounds slinking over the campyard sniffing for peavies. They provided the chipmunks that feasted on the prune stones and grew so ferocious that Paul's men shot them for tigers, and the mosquitoes that straddled the rivers picking off lumberjacks from the log drive. . . ."

In such tales echo the grandiose exploits of one of the wildest breed of free Americans on the continent, men feeling their oats, men hard-muscled, powerful, godlike with pure physical exuberance.

Here also are the customary records of colossal theft, chicanery, political corruption and billions in the making. In the making of it all are left the scars of bitter labor feuds—that half-savage I.W.W. movement which battered two-fisted and reckless and futilely against the doom of an industry and an epoch, and whose leaders were herded to penitentiaries and jail during the war to make the world safe for democracy. Behind it all are the scars on the bosom of a great nation—the stump swamps from Alabama to Louisiana and Arkansas, the stump wilderness of Wisconsin and Minnesota, the brutally bare eroding slopes of the Rockies, the Sierra Madres, the noble crest of ten thousand skylines sheared and left looking like dandruff ads.

Out of all this haste and greed, a nation was hurriedly housed in grandiose super-shanty style (pending better building materials); a people, that in other places in the world would likely have sunk into brutish illiteracy, was provided with newspapers made from wood-pulp, newspapers which soon would make up in quantity, blatancy and size for what they still frequently lack in quality and bravery. A billion railroad ties anchored steel rails that end to end might reach many times around the earth.

Each week in the *New York Times,* which uses up acres of forest every month, is presented a graph of the lumber industry in the United States as a symbol of prosperity or depression. Its totals figure in with the business index of half a dozen industrial activities to provide master minds with an idea whether business is surviving in spite of the New Deal.

Those lumber statistics really mean but little with respect to true and lasting national happiness or prosperity. With conservation still lagging so terribly in our country, with lumbering so little controlled by any concept of future welfare, with so little regard relatively to the problems of reforestation, a rise in the index of lumber production means more land given to waste, more dislocated communities, more abandoned settlements, more bewildered folk crouching in abandoned shacks and lean-tos of collapsing communities. It means more drouth, bigger and greater floods.

My memories of the lumber industry go back to boyhood days. In California I climbed up alongside the miles of flues through the mountains; I swung my ax in the woods; I ate in the great kitchens; I helped run a bad Chinese cook out of camp, with a barrage of tin-cans and clods.

I remember the tough old lumberjacks coming to town after the season was over. They would march up to the bar, plant a boot on the rail, and sling down whiskey after whiskey, until their grip loosened and they keeled over backwards, dead drunk, to be heaved in a corner, their teeth in spit and sawdust. They wore out the boards of every small saloon; they staged mighty fights on main street—fights just for the joy of life, of strength, of good muscles.

They used to come into Eureka, their hobnails like grit on the rattly board walks of the town.

"Hey, kid, got a lop-offed dime for a timber wolf to get a cup of Java?"

In Wisconsin, Minnesota, the Northwest, the lumberjacks would gather in late October, outfitted with high leather boots, woolens, gloves, duffel-bags, mackinaws, a sky piece—as a rule, all they had to show for their last season's wages, their "hay," which had soon vanished in the saloons and with the bleazy, fat-bosomed ladies who followed the fringe of the cutting.

The swampers or punk-hunters went out in gangs over the pike to throw up the camps, bunk and cookhouse, machine-shed and the wanigan, or camp commissary. The overhead steam skidders were rigged up; the tote roads were sloshed with water to be slick for the slide.

And so, fifty miles from the nearest settlement, they would sleep in lousy double-decker "muzzle-loader" bunks, would work hours before "daybreak in the swamp" and until long after dark, hell-bent-for-chips and heavy on the see-saw cross-cut—all for a buck a day, six long greens a week, and their keep, which meant plenty of heavy, coarse food. Few had time or energy to sit on "the dream-seat" beside the bunk and read. More often this place was used on Sunday—"boiling up day"—to sew clothes and mittens.

Out on the job if a gazebo failed to hear "Timber down the line!" when the tree crashed, he might be lucky to get only a pair of cracked "stems" and be able to peddle pencils from then on out.

The fallen monarch was reduced to saw logs, branded with a double X or polywog cross-'n'-gaber to denote the company. These were dragged on the cross-haul by horses to the skidway, peavied into places by the "ground-hogs," who were ever careful not to gum them up by getting the ends out of line, skyhooked onto a load and clamped with chains on the log sled. The logs were then sent hurtling toward the river.

There, hardy log-straddlers, with pike-pole peavy, guided and "carded" the timber downstream, drives that went on and on day and night, and day and night it took often to pass a given point. With spurs on the soles of their shoes, the rivermen rode the plunging logs like cowboys on a mustang. Sure-footed, strong-muscled, quick of eye, they sorted out the logs, pushed them into place, broke tangles, coaxed laggers, kept them away from the off bank, poled them away from eddies. The log-straddlers were cannier than sheep-dogs with a flock of sheep. They were cats on logs, and if they survived nine log-drives, they really had something even on cats. It was no child's play leaping over that boiling white water, alive and growling with its thousands of pitching, churning logs. Sometimes jams piled up solid, acres of timber criss-crossed in chaos, dead corpses of the monarchs of the forest stood up, mightily and dripping, right on end, or were tossed up in heaps as if they were little straws. There they poised, motionless, "frozen" fast.

Find the king log, and a single thrust set the whole mass free, churning, roaring, pounding down, tens of thousands of trees, tons of trees that sometimes ground even logs to mash. They drummed and thundered—the sound reverberating for miles about, frightening the deer and the birds that rose screaming above the tops of the forest; and sometimes also, that mighty rush and hammer of wood, once set free, drowned the too daring, flinging them into the air, crushing their bodies to pulp. Swimming was useless. The unlucky one was ground under, rammed under, smashed under. The more fortunate would dance out "on a surging river of pine"; the less fortunate would ride 'er through, Death grinning behind them; right beside them; to right and left; Death in front of them. Tennyson would have written a good poem about it—but no better than the one the loggers sang.

The lumberjacks were a rough-and-ready lot, as a rule, uncomplaining unless grub got too God-awful. Usually if the mess-cook was at all worth his salt, they rushed ferociously hungry and hilarious "to put on the nose-bag." With shouts and jokes, their hobnails hit the floor for breakfast in the dark, and they drank tea that froze in their whiskers and ate beans that turned to ice and clinked on their tin plates, and crunched down "logging-berries"—prunes—frozen to black glass. They worked cheerfully in twenty-below weather. They fiddled, harmonica-ed, accordion-ed, built up fine poetry with gusto in it: bawdy and boisterous ballads, folklore from the very bowels of America, part of our rich heritage. Their feet hammered to fiddle and song, the *Pokegama Bear*, the *Little Brown Bulls*, *Devil's Dream*, *Monkey Musk*, *Big Ear Claire*, *Pop Goes the Weasel*.

It took an unusual "big push," or boss, to manage such men. The foreman had to be a beefy hulk, ready with tongue and fist, but also a natural born student of psychology.

Sometimes the men lost their lives in great roaring fires, fed not only by the timber stand, but also by the piles of slash and sawdust.

In one fire in Peshtigo 700 people were burned to death. The marshland was baked five feet deep. In a hardware store sixty dozen axes were melted to a jagged lump of iron.

One of the greatest fires was in August, 1894. It filled the sky of northern Minnesota with dense gray through which the sun was visible only as a dull copper disk. At night it blotted out the stars.

For three days the Great Northern trains were stalled as the smoke smothered river and town. As the fire swept closer, a wave of heat and flame was flung forward, fanned by a sixty-mile gale. The roaring blaze struck Hinckley sudden, and the fear-maddened populace stampeded, three hundred of them, aboard a south-bound train. It pulled out backwards, headlights boring the gloom over smoking ties behind, where danced the flickering silhouette of screaming, fleeing figures who had missed the train. The engineer's blue overall coat caught fire; his fingers seared fast to throttle. They roared over the wooden bridge of Grindstone Creek, converted into a slot of heavy fire, and never stopped for waving arms and uplifted faces. The ties were blazing now under the wheels; the coach-roofs were on fire.

The train whirled, a skyrocket of flame, right into Duluth. The engineer's hand had to be pried loose, but he and the passengers were alive. Behind him six towns lay in smoldering ruin; 418 people had missed the train; they had run over burning planking into walls of flame and had shriveled up like moths.

In terms of European dimensions, the American lumber industry has laid a whole empire low, has given a dozen kingdoms over to desolation.

But a short time ago—in 1655—Radisson and Groseilliers tramped over ice and snow and frozen tamarack swamps, through mighty virgin forests.

December 8, 1672, Louis Joliet covered 350 leagues by canoe, making fifty portages to reach the island of Michilimackinac and the thread of water between Lake Huron and Lake Michigan, in order to meet Jacques Marquette. Dedicating their voyage to the Virgin Mary, together, in their buckskin suits, they swung their paddles along the streams of wilderness, the haunts of the deer, the bear, the Chippewa. They crossed the "Wild Oats" territory full of wild rice in the clay bottoms, with flocks of turkeys flying over. Huge fish nearly overturned their boats. They kept on through great stands of timber for a hundred leagues. They were frightened by wild animals and grinning totem poles. Hopefully they brandished the feather calumet of peace and made friends with natives never before knowing outsiders. With buffalo skull spoons, they ate in the native villages and listened to native chanting. Finally they set out down the Mississippi.

After them came explorers on snowshoes, trappers, hunters, French traders, English settlers—marching hosts; and finally, tide on tide of Norsemen.

Those frontier days, the first settlers who turned to lumbering peddled their wood in the growing towns downstream. The first little logging camps were crude. Food was cooked over outdoor logs. Work was done by hand with the go-devil, the peavy and the ax. But by 1850 regular sawmill towns were springing up on all the rivers, and the rotary saw replaced the mule-saw. This technological advance, that cut twenty times as much lumber in a day's shift, did not matter with an expanding industry that in any case could not keep up with demand.

Irish and Canadian and Scandinavian choppers were busy; log drives had now quite succeeded the trading canoe. The more astute, busy leaders were men from the pine woods of Maine and Vermont. They became magnates and political bosses and even "statesmen."

Companies grew fast, rushed their "cruisers" out through the new country to report on the stands, and soon the spring rivers jammed up with a million, a half billion, a billion feet of pine. Soon little men were crowded out. Great powerful companies took the place of individual enterprise and of smaller concerns. The camps took on the aspects of industrial and business centers. The scramble for pine lands began.

The lumber men, as do all powerful folk, soon had dutiful politicians at their beck and call, men who for petty gain were willing to betray their trust and their country by falsifying the records. One such was Delegate Sibley, of Minnesota, who became the state's first governor, regent of the University, president of its historical society, and an LL.D. of Princeton.

He protested in sobbing tones against the restraints that were being put on the thieves of the public domain. The laws guarding the timber lands, he declared, should be "expunged as a disgrace to the country and to the nineteenth century." The man cutting down the timber had been "marked out as a victim." According to Sibley the lumber men were merely adding their "honest labor" to the "comfort" of their "fellow men," and as their reward, the poor chaps were "hampered by vexatious law proceedings."

But no law, no courts, no restraints, stayed the process of spoliation. There were plenty of Sibleys, plenty of lawyers, plenty of corrupt land-agents, judges, governors, Senators.

Already in 1854 I. W. Wallace, Federal Timber Agent for western Michigan, declared that there had already been shipped from there "more than 500,000,000 feet of lumber" in ten years of which "more than seven-eighths . . . [had been] plundered from the public lands." When the thieves were indicted, the lumber companies hired armed gangs to fight off the government agents trying to stop thefts, ousted honest officials, and the cases were compromised for insignificant sums. In 1854 also began the lumber steals in Minnesota; within three years six million acres of land were alienated by lobbied Congressional acts and by bribery.

I have already mentioned the "Stone and Timber" Act of 1878, which took the name of the "poor settler" in vain, and permitted the seizure by a relatively few parties of the lumber resources of the nation (land worth even then $100 an acre) for a miserly $2.50 an acre. The clever lumber syndicates had whole train loads of fake settlers to rush in and file on the land.

Jaid, an inspector, cited in the 1885 Land Report, states: "My observation has convinced me that entries of timber lands are made largely in the interest of mill men and lumber companies, their employees being used to perpetuate frauds. . . . Less than one-thirtieth of the claims taken in the Duluth United States land district are taken for actual settlement. . . . Less than one-tenth of the land . . . is now in the hands of the original claimants . . . 90 per cent of the entries are . . . purely and simply for speculation. . . ."

Special Agent Stubbs stated that "in the Vancouver land district, . . . three-fourths of the fraudulent entries . . . are promoted by unscrupulous parties of wealth, in order that they may obtain title to large tracts of valuable timber lands. . . ." Money was offered to irresponsible drifters, loggers, mill hands and sailors to locate on choice timber land.

"I am well satisfied," he remarks, "that three-fourths of the timber entries in Cowlitz, Pacific, and Skamani counties are of fraudulent character. . . . One-half the best timber lands . . . are held under these fraudulent entries."

Agent Cavenaugh reported that fully 50 per cent of the entries in the country west of the Cascade Mountains were "collusive, and therefore fraudulent." In all other areas he investigated, his estimate was that 90 per cent of the entries were fraudulent. He did not get these facts easily: he traveled more than 5,000 miles, "camped out, forded streams . . . was drenched to the skin . . . during long continued rain, [was] . . . lost in the forest, . . . and warned and threatened by men . . . evidently engaged in violating the law."

The new lumber barons soon ruled politically in the states and had invincible influence in national affairs; they personally won Senate jobs and cabinet posts in the federal government.

Even as late as 1901-08 nearly $60,000,000 of timber was rifled from the government. Eight million acres of timber lands were then seized for a song, not to mention the timber lands already lost or still later to be given to the railroads, in addition to the millions previously obtained, to be passed on to the affiliated lumber concerns.

It was a good thing to be a director on the railroads those earlier days, not so much to promote the interests of the stockholders or efficient railroading as to be on the inside of such profitable deals. The great Weyerhaeuser fortune was built on timber lands of Wisconsin and Minnesota, most of which were bought from the Northern Pacific Railway at $6.00 an acre. In 1900 a single block of 900,000 acres was so purchased, the choicest lands in the State of Washington. The Weyerhaeuser Timber Company alone came to control an empire of nearly 2,000,000 acres, and the family and associates had heavy financial interests in other lumber companies.

Under the 1897 Conservation Act and the 1899 Mount Rainier Park Law, railways and other corporations exchanged large acres of poor lands, or those already stripped, for fine timber lands elsewhere.

The report of the United States Commissioner of Corporations on the timber industry, for instance, states that the Northern Pacific relinquished over 500,000 acres, obtaining in exchange "free timber lands in other parts of the Northwest," of which at least 300,000 acres were sold to the Weyerhaeuser Timber Company and other companies in which the same family was interested. The elder Weyerhaeuser, reports Meyers, had a fortune estimated in 1915 at $300,-000,000. In spite of this, the railroads still possess large timber holdings.

For decades lumber companies controlled the politics of Wisconsin. They bought mayors, state representatives, Congressmen, judges, governors, directly or indirectly. And when the barnstorming elder La Follette finally broke their political power and cleaned up to make Wisconsin one of the few decently run states in the Union, the lumber companies were no longer much interested in keeping up the fight. They had skimmed the cream of the state's timber and were moving on to Minnesota, Washington, Oregon. They had made their pile and merely left La Follette to hold the bag and count worthless chips and stumps scattered across desolate fields rendered useless. Even so it took a long time to end the political corruption they had created and left behind them.

Nor was Wisconsin the only state so controlled. The Lumber Trust also reached into high federal quarters. A number of lumber kings became wealthy and therefore respectable and received high appointive posts, often in exchange for heavy campaign contributions. And, of course, capacity to get rich quick by rifling the resources of the government and the nation is considered by everybody a high proof of ability to run the government, a sign of superior political wisdom.

One of the millionaires made by this lumber speculation was Russell A. Alger, who as a result became Secretary of War in the McKinley boodle cabinet and was in charge of our military operations during the Spanish-American War. In spite of the glorious tales, or lies, related in most of our school textbooks, no army was ever handled more inefficiently; never was graft more rampant; never was a war conducted with more thievery, with more brazen disregard for the welfare of the soldiers. Despite repeated stuffed-shirt whitewashes, tinned "corn-beef" has become one of the jokes of the nation.

The State of Minnesota alone had timber enough, if cut with care and foresight, to have supplied the country for centuries. We preferred to gather a crop of millionaires and a semi-desert.

The lumberjacks, the pawns of this system, swept the hillsides clean; whole mountainsides were sliced off. Beautiful forests were ripped away. The great majesty of the mountains, the deep valleys of mighty pines, became harsh and empty, stripped bare.

In 1837 Franklin Steele and six half-breeds felled the first white pine in Minnesota. By 1926 the last great drive went down the historic river. Today the sawmills are quite boarded up in almost the entire state; many are in actual ruin. In the whole Duluth-Superior area, where once stood magnificent forest, there is today only one sawmill.

By 1929 Duluth went into tailspin that made the depression in much of the country seem like the tooting of the horns of plenty. Walter Havighurst vividly describes the end of the lumber kingdom:

"The long whistle wavering over the ruined forest was more than the symbol of the sawmill's end. It was the end of an empire, the brief and fabulous empire of logs. And when the echoes died away, loneliness settled down. Grass grew up in the streets, the saloons and dance halls decayed in the sun. Raspberry vines spread over the rusted rails of the logging line, the tote roads grew up in deer brush and aspen. The landing that had swarmed with teamsters, loaders and whistle punks became a burrow for muskrats. The vast piratic enterprise left its empty camps and its abandoned towns scattered over the ruined North."

If you wish to experience supreme melancholy, drive through that ruined stump country in late afternoon at the setting of the sun, when the pale yellow satin of the last light lies between the broken piles and all is desolate save perhaps for some flickering candle light from some shack of a bewildered lumberjack turned farmer on land never meant to be farmed. He, too, is economic waste. He costs the rest of the country hundreds of dollars annually to maintain him. His heavy muscles are needed no more; his face is furrowed with perplexity because in some way he cannot understand why he has fallen into a dark pit of uselessness. His productive powers are now almost nil; they are minus; they are lost. They are less than the Chippewas of old, less even than the scattered Chippewas who survive in their wigwams among the birches around Lake Itasca at the headwaters of the Mississippi and demand no charity.

Someone has said that that river is the most eloquent symbol of the scope and unity of America. But it is also symbol of the waste and the ruined heritage of America as its waters sweep off the rich top soil and every year go sweeping down, bringing flood and destruction upon those who remain in its path, a destruction in part unleashed by those great lumber pirates who swept its upper-reaches clear of timber and then left half a continent to its fate and its problems.

We do not even know our folly now, too late; even now we do so little to remedy it. Must we have plagues and famines and disaster on disaster before we will face the facts of a changed America?

There, at the very headwaters of the Mississippi, is the town of Bermidji (named after a great Chippewa Indian chief), the last of Minnesota's great boom towns. It is vividly described by Havighurst. Something of its romantic and majestic past, he tells us, is suggested by the odd wooden statue—nearly ten feet high—of the great chief long since gone to happier hunting grounds, a statue carved from a pine log by some unknown lumberjack. Its great size suggests something of the Paul Bunyan spirit, that idea of human spirit rising majestic as the trees that were conquered and brought low, save that in its conventional cigar-store pose of hand over peering eyes, the figure has some faint wistfulness of passing power. It was greed for lumber that ruined the last haunt of the Chippewas, and it is cut lumber that has, in the end, ruined much of Minnesota as so many other places of the Union.

As the Plains Indians prayed to their gods because of the sacrilege of making future dust-bowls, so the Chippewas prayed against the evil stripping away of the forests to leave a tangle of ruin and poverty. Today, thereabouts, the W.P.A. cuts no lumber, merely pathetically compiles a history of the ancient glories—not a dozen years old—of Bermidji.

In 1895, when the first settlers rocked through here in carts, pine trees covered Bermidji and trails around. But in twenty years the pines were mostly gone; in another decade the gleanings had been gathered; today one sawmill cleans up the remainders.

A few years ago all was fresh and exciting—railroads, sawmill camp and boom. Logging trains puffed out all through the twenty-four hours, right around the clock. Sawdust grew to mountains, faster than it could be burned. The slash stacked up like a gigantic game of pick-up sticks—a million feet of lumber a day. Big Business was working overtime, millionaires becoming multimillionaires. Parts of Bermidji are today spongy underfoot; the town rests on sawdust, on waste. So Havighurst tells the story of Bermidji. Today Minnesota imports lumber from Norway, Sweden, Finland and even the Soviet Union.

By violence, theft, fake documents, lobbies, high-powered lawyers, stranglehold control of key properties, by gunmen and murder, the lands were garnered in, monopolized and the patrimony of all America seized—and destroyed. The story of that destruction is part of the intrinsic relation of Americans to the soil of America. Out of it has grown some of our major farm-problems of today.

CHAPTER XVI

THE GREAT FLOOD

A young fellow, in high boots and a slouch felt hat, opened the foggy door of the little restaurant and let a gunny sack down softly in the middle of the floor.

"Lil' present fer yuh, Maisie," he said in clipped northern tongue.

The droopy, flat-breasted blonde, pretty and sullen, with stringy, lusterless hair and a cobweb complexion, showed a faint spark of animation. "What you-all got there, Larry?"

He dashed out again without replying. The girl stared at the sack half disinterestedly, then dragged out to the kitchen.

The restaurant was a dirty little place, smelling of dishwater and sawdust. Greasy fly-specked menus lay limply on the wooden tables that showed faint traces of a paint once light green. The packages of breakfast food on the counter shelves looked dingy; they sprawled about as though fallen over long ago with no strength to put themselves in order.

The blonde shuffled back, and as she listlessly dried dishes behind the counter, looked speculatively at the sack. It moved slightly. A puzzled expression almost crossed her cream-gray face. She came from behind the counter and poked the sack with an investigatory toe. A faint "meow" was the response.

She untied the string, and out walked three small kittens. One turned around at her, bristling and spitting, then dashed under a table, tail up. The second came readily into her lap. The third calmly explored his new habitat.

She put the kitten down, came back with a saucer of meat.

307

The young man burst in again. "Jesus! what a night!" he exclaimed.

He was one of the flood patrolmen pacing the nearby Mississippi levee, strained by the 1937 flood. The river was at its crest. The wind had driven spray over him. His coat was drenched.

"How yuh like the little devils? I got 'em off a roof-top. If I'd rowed along ten minutes later they'd 'a' been drowned. God knows what happened to the people. The whole hollow is under thirty foot of water—boiled up from under the levees."

The girl set two glasses of muddy water before us. "Ain't nothin' but veal or Brunswick stew."

So odd and tired was her dialect I couldn't understand what she said till she repeated it a second time. Having a prejudice against the great southern delicacy which disguises chipmunk meat, my companion and I decided on the veal.

"All the folks hereabouts been taken outta here," she explained, "I cain't get no food nowhere. Lucky to have this."

Beyond a flimsy partition, we could barely see the frayed elbow of a Negro, sucking loudly at his food.

Our veal stew came out of a big iron pot on cook range in a filthy kitchen. Though the concoction was a bit suspicious, possibly Brunswick stew after all, it was piping hot and seasoned hotter, which was good because we were cramped with cold. She brought us a torn hunk of stale home-made bread and poured coffee from a sooty pot, a thin straw-colored liquid, through a large not-clean strainer held over each cup. The big jagged lumps of sugar on the table were coarse and gray.

"Ain't no milk. Opened the last can this mawnin'."

"Where are we at?" I asked her.

"You-all's in Arkansas."

I had already driven my car three hundred miles since one o'clock, clear from the other side of Mississippi. I had to get to Oklahoma in a hurry, so all Sunday I had pushed hard across Tennessee to get past the river at Memphis before the authorities closed off traffic. Backwater floods were rising in all the country west. Now it was eleven o'clock at night, and we still had at least eighty miles to drive before we could get to a satisfactory place, safe to stay.

Late afternoon we had hit the Memphis bridge exactly at the moment the flood crest—boiling dark and tawny, with creamy dirty scum—had reached there. Upstream, Cairo was still in danger, and there and southward, a thousand patrols watched every foot of the sand-bag embankment. The waters were within a few inches of the top.

Memphis, on high ground, had nothing to fear. But the western side of the river was dangerous, so the police were stopping all local cars. Glimpsing my Connecticut license, they waved us on through.

The waters were boiling right up to the level of the bridge—yellow-brown waters—like a gathered-in flood of all the tobacco-juice spitting of a hundred years in southern lynch-law county courthouses. Broken roofs, whole trees, timbers, furniture, telegraph poles, privies, bales of straw, and an inflated inner tube came bumping along. An odor of stale earth and manure hit us coolly.

On the western side, the flood, broken over the first levee, had spread out in a silver sheen. Below our high causeway, a freight station was almost submerged; railroad tracks were covered; just the tips of the telegraph poles showed. Huge scummy uprooted trees were piled up against an embankment.

We were shunted along under the levees. Traffic funneled in here from a dozen states, for this was the only point one could cross except far south at Vicksburg or far north at St. Louis; and all the cars were hitting it up fast. No one quite relished driving under the levee at a time when the river was the highest in recorded history.

Homes on every side were empty, livestock gone, the people all evacuated. All that day trucks, filled with cows, steers, horses, mules, had roared past us going east into Tennessee. Little towns everywhere there and in Mississippi were knocking together refugee camps.

Now, half a dozen miles up alongside the levee we turned west on a gravel road, hit a bumpy road back south, and about dark came out again on Route 70 which had been closed at the West Memphis end. We mistakenly judged the flooded places were between this junction and there.

More truck loads of horses and cattle and refugees whirled past us going east toward Memphis.

Presently we noticed that the country was flooded on either side of the high-built road. It grew worse. In some places, the waters came up to the first stories of adjacent houses which sat low in marshy lands. We had to drive through shallow water for about an eighth of a mile. Before long, on either side of the road, there were not even any dry knolls now; everything was under water.

It had grown quite dark and uncanny. Lights were lit in the second stories of flooded houses. Here and there boats were taking people off. Lanterns swung with jumpy flickers. Voices came across the waters.

It became a bit frightening. But no one had stopped us or warned us not to go ahead. Evidently the road itself was in the clear.

Presently we forded a quarter of a mile of water. About a mile further on, we spied a big cluster of people. As we came closer, we saw they were farmers in work clothes, overalls, slouch hats—hayseed types. The women were bareheaded or with shawls. And here, the road dipped into water and disappeared entirely.

Several National Guardsmen regarded us curiously, indifferently.

"Can't we get on from here?" I asked one.

He grunted, something I took for a negative.

"You got a boat?" cackled an old fellow. "That's the only way you'll get across there, unless you got balloon tires that'll float you."

A big fat woman broke in. "There's eighteen miles of water out there; everything's under water."

"Did the levees break?"

"Naw, this is backwater on the St. Francis and Arkansas Rivers. Been better for us if the levees hadda broke."

Seated along the edge of the road, their feet almost in the water, was a huddle of refugees, a few of them with bundles, mostly with nothing. They regarded us indifferently. They looked cowed, apathetic, disregardful of their fate. They were just sitting there, waiting, waiting to be taken away. There were no Negroes. Perhaps Negroes weren't worth saving.

"Guess they'll come for us sometime," said the fat woman.

We heard the chug of a motor boat. It darted out of blackness, disgorged some more people. They climbed out stiffly, silent. As far as we could see, mile after mile, the far water was dotted with lights in second story windows. But nobody seemed very excited.

"Guess a lot of folk got drowned," said the old fellow, as though half-relishing the idea.

A shapely girl in overalls, with brown close-cropped curls, sauntered up. A three-year-old child barely toddled beside her.

"They took me and mah baby out'n a tree. Mah old man, he tells me to climb that tree, but I sez to him, 'I ain't takin' none of your sass.'

" 'I'll shore fan your fanny,' he yells. 'Climb, goddamn you, climb!' Ah shore clumb. That's the first time Ah evah let that no-account trash boss *me* aroun'."

The old man hee-heed softly.

With a jocular sort of fierceness, a slight catch in her voice, the girl added: "Ah, shore wish I knew where he wuz now. Ah'd jes' let him boss me all he wuz wishin'."

With some difficulty I got the car turned around on the narrow road—the water was almost on a level with the concrete—and raced back toward Memphis, now and then clipping through sprays of water.

Another road brought similar results. Why the devil didn't they have warnings out, or guards to tell one? There seemed to be plenty of uniforms back where they weren't needed, mostly doing nothing.

Once more we raced back. My gasoline got low. But all the gas stations were dark, the glass tanks of the pumps empty. A light showed from one little restaurant, its rumpy rear posts lapped with water. A gas pump stood in front of it.

Inside, a girl sat at the table with a National Guardsman. They were so very much engrossed in each other it took several honkings to bring her out.

"Theah ain't no gas 'long this road, Mistah. 'T's days since they delivuhed out this way." Then passion quivered in her voice. "Ain't this te'ble, simply te'ble. Ah don' know what we all gonna do, sho'ly don't."

We sped along the lonely road. Fortunately our gas just carried us back into West Memphis.

A guard there was noncommittal. He didn't know how we could get through.

At a gasoline station we were told that Route 61 was open clear through to Cairo. About 120 miles up, we could get a crossroad.

"Is it safe?"

"If the levee holds?"

It was uncanny running along in the dark. There were few cars now. It was growing late. And not a light anywhere. The whole countryside had been evacuated.

About fifty miles up, in a little settlement on higher ground, we finally saw a few lights and stopped at the little restaurant, with the tired looking blonde, the recipient of the kittens.

"Ah's wainheahfuyu," she said listlessly as we left.

"What!"

"You all come again soon."

We pushed on through zones of fuzzy fog and silent towns. In one place, in the dip of an underpass, we sloshed down over our axles. Men were pumping out the water as fast as it boiled up. Further on other boils flooded the road surface here and there. For long stretches water covered the fields off into the shapeless black night. Not a house had lights. The people had gone. Finally in Hayti—on high ground—a half dozen gas stations were shining brightly. After so much blackness, they seemed like the great white way.

The station man wiped our mist-covered windshield, splattered thick with mosquitoes and bugs.

He directed us west to Kennett. "The water's just gone down there," he told us. "Maybe you can get on through. Anyway there's a good road north from there."

We drew near Kennett about one o'clock. Once more the fields were flooded. The air tasted like wet wool. The town had been entirely surrounded by waters, but they had subsided considerably. We drew up to the ramshackle hotel.

"You're lucky!" said the lanky young fellow at the desk. "I've got just one room. Wouldn't have that but a guard officer just checked out. It's putty small and ain't got no bath. But it's about the only empty room in town. The place is cram full of soldiers and nu'ses and sick folk."

He padded ahead of us along the hall matting that raised dust.

We went out and found a small café. The bright light and warmth dazed us. All we could get down, we were so tired, was some coffee and rolls.

We looked over our maps. The best route was through Paragould —if we could get through. We asked the waiter.

"Some trucks just came through; the drivers were in here eating. Guess you can make it. They's a bus station on down the street. Ask there. They can give you the low-down."

We talked it over outside on the sidewalk. The air was wet wash; the mist was dank and heavy.

A National Guard officer, who had been scrutinizing us closely in the restaurant, came out and insolently looked us up and down, poking a toothpick at his yellow teeth.

We asked him about routes.

"Nobody ain't going through Paragould tonight. It's under water that way. You'll have to go up through Springfield, Missouri," he growled sourly.

That was more than a two-hundred-mile detour.

"The best thing you can do tonight is get some sleep," and he spat into the gutter.

We were up early. At a gas station we were told that trucks were still coming through from Paragould. It was pretty tough sledding, but it could be made. The road had been almost washed out last night.

A couple more trucks lumbered through, so we decided to make the attempt. If they could get through, we could.

Down the street, a guard stopped us. "Cain't go through the Paragould way," he said surlily.

"Trucks are going through."

"You ain't a truck. 'Tain't safe."

But he let me past to go to a gasoline station. From there, dis-

obeying his instructions, I swung around the block and started south-
east toward Paragould. Nobody stopped us.

In lower places the fields were badly flooded, but the road was
high, one half of it concrete, the other half macadam. South of Senath we saw more flooded country; and when we finally rolled into
Cardwell, the streets were caked soft mud, the stores were closed.
Men in high rubber boots were cleaning up the sidewalks and gutters.

We stopped at a clean little restaurant, run by a plump, good-
natured woman. I asked her what had happened there.

"We were under water here till early this morning. . . . Yes, you
can get on through. A few cars been getting through right along,
but 'tain't been safe. The road almost went last night. They wuz
workin' on it; been trying to save it for days now. You'll find a lot
of stretches under water, but you can make it."

When I inquired for a toilet, the woman led me out front and un-
locked the door of the drug store alongside.

In the back room of the drug store were sick men on cots and beds,
and in a corner a toilet set off by tattered cardboard. The men had
pneumonia, typhoid and diphtheria. They were flood refugees.

One was just getting over diphtheria, a young fellow about thirty.
He wanted to talk. He was worried about his wife and two kids.

"I don't know if they be dead or alive. I don't know why I'se
alive. I was too sick to move when the flood came. Mah wife
couldn't get no doctor. She'd almost given me up as daid. Then I
got a mite better, an' I told mah wife to git on out and save the kids.
But it was too late then. The first floor was all under water, an' still
acomin' up. Several times folk come along in boats but they didn't
have no room for sick folk, so my wife she dassn't leave me.

"Finally an officer said it was sure death to stay; she hadn't no
right not to save the kids.

"I told her to go but she wouldn't, till they promised her they'd
come right back to get me.

"I dunno know what happened next. I wuz there a whole day and
the water was right up under my bed, but I couldn't move. 'Last
some diff'unt folks come along an' found me an' drug me out. I don't

know how they ever 'spect I been there 'cuz when they shouted I couldn't answer.

"They tooked me off. I don't know if my wife and kids be daid or alive. If they ain't daid I reckon my wife's jes' 'bout killin' herself with her darn old conscience, worry'n' 'bout me. This here 'bout finished us. The crop's all gone now. We cain't live on hay, even if we had any."

"Who takes care of those sick men?" I asked the restaurant keeper.

"I sort of does," she answered. "I run in every chanct I git, with a little broth or something. The Red Cross nurse comes around every chanct she gits, but the town's full up with sick folk; and her on her feet night and day, it's the Lord's marvel to me she ain't in bed herself. We does the best we can, suh. There ain't nobody what ain't helpin every way he kin. The men folks all out savin' the road or somethin' and the women folk are lookin' after sick uns. I guess you gotta help people when they be in trouble. That's the way I sorta feels about it."

Beyond the town, we realized how reckless it would have been to have kept on the previous night. Here and there we had to ford short stretches. In many places workers had endeavored to sand-bag the road. But the sand bags had been tossed about, washed out. One lay in the road itself.

A little further on, the road had been undercut; the concrete on one side hung down at a forty-five degree angle like a kitchen fly-leaf table.

Further on, the water was still rushing over the road. Guards were directing one-way traffic. We waited for three or four cars and a bus to go by, then putting the engine in low, so it would not be splashed and stall, I went at a snail's pace for half a mile through water in places high as the wheels.

Around about, the whole countryside was under water.

The flood I was going through was that of the St. Francis River. We had seen merely the dirty fringes of it. Probably not one American in ten, outside of the immediate region, ever heard of the St. Francis River that rises in Missouri and, paralleling the Mississippi, flows down through Arkansas to enter the Father of Waters about seventy miles below Memphis. In the New York papers I noticed no mention of this particular backwater inundation.

The hardships this minor flood brought were a drop in the bucket compared to the vast damage done to Johnstown, Paducah, Cincinnati, and other cities, by the main Ohio River flood, in which in all nearly 300,000 families, over a million people, were left homeless. And yet this little St. Francis side show had caused the loss of many lives by drowning and many more by sickness. It had started epidemics; it had caused the hurried evacuation of tens of thousands of acres under water; it had destroyed crops, homes, livestock, farming machinery, millions of dollars' loss.

Here was the dramatic first-hand story of all men's recklessness and haste in America. Here is the great expectoration mighty Paul Bunyan let loose on the land. Here is the aftermath of denuded forests in Wisconsin, Minnesota, along the continental divide. Here was the oft-repeated spectacle of sad destruction of human lives and property. Here we reach a point where we have to turn back on our frontier steps, rectify the old waste of the hurried years.

Over the flood waters of some of our great cities floated millions of gallons of gasoline from torn-up tanks, setting terrible fires.

Why were our people not protected against such eventualities? Why are gas and gasoline tanks set down in the midst of dense habitation instead of apart in protected places? Is it the old story of profits being more important than human lives? Of saving for the companies a few dollars in piping and the loss of all for poor folk? Why, when flood danger exists, do people live under the shadow of such danger? Why, when it is over, do they go back to the mud-soaked houses to face it again another year?

Precisely because the rents are low; they can afford no safe place; nor can they afford insurance to protect what little they have.

And back of the story of floods is the story of the washing away of the topsoil of America, of 200,000,000 acres of land rendered useless, much of it never to be recovered in centuries; of 500,000,000 more acres already badly damaged. This is an Alexander's Empire we have indifferently tossed away. We have flung away the equivalent of the arable land of the four most powerful nations of Europe.

What we need is not less public spending but far more public spending—provided it really would promote the community welfare. We need to spend five billion dollars at once on flood relief: to re-forest our hills, where rapacious lumber companies, keeping their men in stinking camps, have sliced off the forests of the nation; we need dams; erosion work; dykes; the slicing through of sluggish turns in rivers, the straightening of courses. We throw away an empire, render it useless and unsafe, do not spend enough to retrieve it, but we protect it with battleships, more and more battleships.

In a few years we would have the value of our investment back. We would have farm-lands safe from future destruction; we would have lives safe from drowning; we would increase productivity incalculably, except that as things stand, increased productivity, despite people's need, also spells ruin. It is also quite idle even to imagine for a long time to come a thoroughgoing effort to control American floods. They follow the pattern of Mr. Wallace's crop-restriction methods, are even more effective than his. It is much better to throw away our soil and build battleships. That is really quite logical and proper, for our economic life is based on waste and scarcity. Only through scarcity, claim our great leaders, can prices be kept up—to benefit chiefly those who already have.

So long as we want such lowered production, waste and scarcity, there is no need for flood control. We should instead be glad to have nature help our politicians and grabbers destroy our patrimony; to increase the ruin of our fair land. Father Mississippi is on the side of Secretary Wallace, and doubtless the Secretary does not disdain so powerful an ally.

CHAPTER XVII

FUR EMPIRE [1]

Night is falling over the bayous and marsh region of southern Louisiana. Set between low sedgy banks, or bordered by gigantic live oaks draped with long trailing Spanish moss, the inlets are pale, motionless mirrors, here and there faintly yellow from the last rays of the sun. Heavy shadows darken the broad expanse of treacherous coastal morass. Dead stillness enfolds the teeming world of birds, animals, reptiles and insects, hidden in the swampy water and tall grasses—till the bullfrogs boom their lugubrious chorus. Almost invisible in the tangled gray moss, a wide-eyed owl peers stone-like.

Across the motionless water slides a pirogue. It draws up to a bleak clap-board shack. A splash of oars pulled in, a thud against the bank, and the occupant of the crude little boat—a raw-boned, leather-complexioned man—staggers ashore under a heavy load of pelts. His rubber hip-boots make a slushing sound in the mud as he walks to the shack. From its single window a kerosene lamp gleams dully. Casting down his skins, he pulls off his rubber boots with a grunt. He is clad in overalls and work blouse—almost like a factory hand.

"Not good at h'all, this day, no," he grumbles to his dumpy wife and two sons. "Yo' see, I pass at Bayou Manshac nex' week, no here'bout. Bot, 'bout cinq minute après fo', I cam'h'along side of one li'l lagoon, shape' around lak pond. . . ." So he describes his day's experiences, before setting to work on his pelts.

This tiny shack is like thousands scattered through the marsh

[1] Mr. Abel Plenn assisted in the preparation of this chapter.

country; this man is like almost any one of 30,000 trappers, the denizens of Louisiana's fur empire, mostly descendants of early French and Spanish settlers.

Many are "Cajuns," whose ancestors were Acadians deported from Nova Scotia in 1735, folk made famous in the legend of "Evangeline" and utilized in romantic literature ever since.

For the average American, Louisiana means sugar plantations, cotton-fields, Negroes, or a section of the U.S.A. where one Huey Long once held seignorial sway. Outside of the fur merchants and some zoologists and members of various Conservation Department staffs, few are aware of the fact that the southern part of Louisiana ranks alongside of Siberia as one of the world's chief fur preserves.

Most people have engraved vividly in their minds the exciting exploits of the Hudson Bay region and the Northwest, when millions of dollars of furs passed through the frontier post of St. Louis, and how the great Astor fortune was founded. But although the highest priced pelts, such as the precious silver fox, are found only in the far north, the beaver, which for a long time constituted the pillar of the fur trade in America, was trapped all the way from frigid Hudson Bay to the tropical sections of Mexico; for decades the tropics and sub-tropics have held important places in the fur industry. Today the beaver's place has largely been taken by the humble muskrat, the valuable coypu rat, or nutria, as it is known in the fur trade, and other important fur-bearing animals. The best habitat of these is the tropical and sub-tropical regions of North and South America. Because of the innumerable muskrats, the millions of grass-covered acres of semi-marshlands give Louisiana the distinction of being the greatest fur-producing commonwealth in the Union.

Parts of the swampy soil are literally honeycombed with burrows branching into underground tunnels—these lead to the banks and levees where the muskrats have built their houses out of cat-tails, bulrushes and other abundant grasses. Peaty humus and eatable sedge, the herbivorous muskrat's main foods, also abound in the Louisiana marshlands.

Thus the muskrats are the mainstay of the pelt wealth. In the grassy coastal marshlands of the southern part of the state—principally in the parishes (counties) of Terrebonne, Lafourche, St. Mary, Cameron—the animal has found conditions ideal for shelter, food, and mating. The richest lands are supposed to be on Delacroix Island in St. Bernard Parish, but Houma in Terrebonne Parish, sets itself up proudly as the fur capital of the United States—a brisk little city with shrimp, oyster and fish-packing industries, in addition to its activities as an outfitting center for trappers.

Before the World War, muskrats were worth very little, and American trade absorbed only 100,000 skins a year. But with the transfer after the War of the tanning and dyeing industries to this continent and the perfection of processes faster than manufacturers could erect plants and train skilled workers needed for one of the most highly specialized industries in the world, the fur trade in Canada and the United States grew by leaps and bounds. No branch of the fur industry benefited more by this change than did the muskrat trade. Thanks to new methods of treatment and the plucking of the animal's guard hairs, the lowly muskrat skin began to be converted into "Hudson seal," which even an experienced dealer often fails to distinguish from costly Alaskan seal that is actually less durable than muskrat. The muskrat's fur, the most useful of all furs for imitation purposes, it was found, could also be made into imitation mink and kolinsky, and through able utilization of the animal's silver belly, golden sides, and glistening dark back, into beautiful sleeves, collars, cuffs and wraps.

The muskrat thus makes it possible for the shop-girl and the waitress to strut around with furs that cannot be distinguished from those worn by millionaires.

By 1921 the American fur trade was already absorbing close to 7,000,000 muskrat skins a year to grace the shoulders of milady in northern metropolises, and prices rose as much as one thousand per cent.

During 1923 nearly 15,000,000 muskrat pelts were obtained in Louisiana—by far a world record in the history of muskrat trapping. In addition there were caught some 300,000 opossums, over 100,000 raccoons, over 50,000 mink, and varying numbers of otters, skunks, wildcats, foxes, even an occasional wolf, and other miscellaneous animals. Thus, Louisiana leads all our states in the yearly catch of minks, and is approached only by Arkansas in its annual contribution of raccoon and opossum pelts.

According to official figures, Louisiana, in an ordinary year (in 1934 production was halved due to salt flooding and a trappers' war), sends more than six million pelts to the world market. It is estimated that half as many more are bootlegged, with the connivance of crooked officials, to evade taxes.

Louisiana produces more pelts than all the rest of the United States mainland, more than Canada and Alaska combined.

The industry has been hard hit by depression, but in an ordinary year the value of pelts from the state is almost as great as the annual budget of Honduras; it is larger than that of all the gold and silver mined each year in Alaska, more than double all the fruits, vegetables and grains exported from Cuba.

Fur trapping in Louisiana is, like most imperial undertakings, a story of several centuries of adventure, hardship, and sudden wealth. It goes back to the glamorous days of the *voyageurs de bois*, the fur-trading forefathers who blazed a trail through the wilderness from northern Canada down to the mouth of the Mississippi, and from the Ohio westward across the Rockies. The first notable French fur trader, Iberville, who settled at Biloxi, Mississippi, outfitted *voyageurs* to compete with the English, all through the western country.

Following Iberville, Louis XIV granted seignorial jurisdiction over the region to Antoine Crozat, a Paris merchant. Crozat drove such harsh bargains with the natives and French colonists that the fur trade languished. Next came John Law with his *La Compagnie des Indies*, a great New World trading monopoly, including furs. But even after Law's swollen bubble burst, New Orleans remained an important fur center. Despite Indian wars and conflicts with the English, it was estimated in 1745 that 1,600 Frenchmen in the colony were engaged in the fur trade. The pelts stored at New Orleans that year were valued at 9,621 livres.

The trappers faced their dangers in the wilderness with a prayer on their lips to Saint Anne—the patron of the *voyageurs*—to protect them from wolves and hostile Indians. The friendlier Indians were given powder and rum in exchange for pelts.

Much of this trade was with the upper Mississippi, but experienced trappers soon settled in the lower regions, first in Mississippi, then in St. Bernard and Plaquemines parishes. When the colony was temporarily turned over to Spain, the Spanish settlers, especially Canary Islanders, promptly planted themselves on the Delacroix Isle and adjacent high ground and carried on the trade. A vast area was soon inhabited by "free" and "company" fur traders, many of whom were trappers.

Free and company traders alike carried off and raped Indian girls and cheated the Indians on every hand. A typical case: for 1,000 crowns' of fine beaver skins, some natives were given a small amount of gunpowder and told that it was a magic variety which, when planted, would produce as much powder as they might want! In those freebooting days, foolhardiness, braggadocio, lies, intrigues, theft and murder were the order of the day.

After the colony was turned over to the United States in 1803, and American settlers drifted in, fur trading more or less remained in the hands of the original French and Spanish descendants and the Cajuns. They roamed freely over the large expanse of trapping lands.

Thus Louisiana fur trapping involves the thrilling record of the conquest of a frontier, a story of cunning, violence and death. Today it is the story of the passing of one of the last frontiers in America, the ending of individual initiative, the rise of large companies, the establishment of a great monopoly—this, too, with violence and death.

What does this mean in human terms? If the glamor of northern adventure and the dangers of the trapper of the frozen regions have filled the pages of fiction, nevertheless today in this Year of Our Lord 1939, the trappers of Louisiana still lead a pioneer life, with risks as great, if not greater, than of their comrades in colder regions. Louisiana has no sub-zero weather and no blizzards, but there are other dangers. None but the veteran "marsh-walker" can penetrate, bent to the breaking point under his load of nearly 150 steel traps or as many furs, without sinking out of sight into the depths of gray ooze that are often bottomless, and which during the November to February trapping season are often bitingly cold—"cold as the winds through the Chilkoot Pass," the saying goes. The seven million acres of coastal marsh trapping lands stretch brownish gray with spots of "*terre tremblante*" to engulf the unwary, and even occasionally an expert trapper, trudging around his trap-line route, loses his step.

Only in the palmy post-war days, for the first time in decades, did the southern Louisiana trappers, many of whom had recently returned from overseas service, feel rewarded for the hardships in the swamps. Many earned as much as $3,000 that season. Most of this was clear profit, as their expenses were low. Outside of his necessary provisions, traps, stretchers, etc., practically the only other outlay a trappers had to make then was for a very small state license fee.

Just as his fathers had done before him, the trapper built his own shack among the marsh grasses where he stayed during the trapping season, accompanied by whatever sons were old enough to carry a few traps on their backs. He built his own pirogue—the light dugout hewed and burned from the solid trunk of a cypress—which he used to paddle over the stretches of open water on the daily visits to the traps. His wife and daughters, those brief prosperous days, were able to live in their cozy cottage on the mainland and made only an occasional necessary trip out to the shack.

The average trapper is a rough man, roughly clad, simple, hospitable, honest, often illiterate. His hands are horny and scarred from his harsh toil and the saline marsh water where he sets his traps and works. The trappers are a wiry breed, "like braided whipcord and rawhide." Though some are occasionally caught poaching during off-season or on the wrong lands, otherwise they are honest. A Conservation Commission official told me he had had no record of robbery among them for fourteen years.

By the middle of November the Cajun and other native trappers are prepared for their arduous labors. If they are not working for a company, by that date they have prepared their camp, a crazy plank shanty not much more impressive than the pile of mud and branches where the muskrats themselves nest. Occasionally, instead of such a hut, the trapper converts a raft into a houseboat for the two and a half or three months of the open season. The shacks are built on the driest ground possible, though often the bayous and streams rise and flood through them. Frequently the trapper and his family live ankle deep in water for days at a time. In the shack's interior, sometimes plastered with a few pictures cut out from popular magazines, are a short-length wood-stove, sometimes a kerosene or gasoline lamp, barrels for packing the furs, a cot or two, steel traps and wire stretchers. The diet consists of salt meat, flour, canned meat and vegetables. The coffee is dripped "black as a darky's heel, hotter than the hinges of hell, stronger than Arkansas religion." Red beans and rice complete the bill of fare. It is a rough frontier diet with plenty of calories, palatable after dawn-to-dark labor in the marshes.

On the first legal day he is up before daybreak and as the first light flickers over the marshes, he dons his rubber hip boots and sets out, bent half double under the load of a hundred and fifty steel traps, so heavy that most mortals could not carry them across the street, let alone thread the treacherous swamps.

Here and there bunches of tall reeds thrust up, or the rousseau cane, commonly called "rozo," which serves as a hint to the trapper of the haunt of the muskrat. He follows the trail of the animal and at convenient intervals in the vicinity of the nest of small clumps of dried marsh and twigs he sets out his traps.

The latest type of trap has two jaws, the first to catch the animal's foot, the second, more powerful, whips over to crush. Formerly the trapper found paws in the trap, and many rats escaped mutilated; now they are held and mercifully killed almost instantaneously.

No bait is used, and much depends upon skill with which a trap is placed and set. To anchor it, the trapper plunges a staff into the matted prairie vegetation; this also serves as a marker.

The following morning the grilling hard work begins in earnest. Up again before dawn, the trapper takes a swig of hot coffee, ties a lunch to his belt and is off. Clear cold days bring the muskrats out

best. "Ha! Zee first rat musque!" he cries. The jaws of the trap
are pried open, the animal extricated, and the trap reset.

The careful trapper carries his catch back to camp to be skinned
and treated. Those less ethical skin their rats on the spot and grind
the carcasses into the swamp under the heel of their boots—to gather
maggots and spread disease among the healthy live animals. But
the trapper who skins as he goes can bring in 200 pelts. The one
who properly returns with the dead animal, at most can carry a
hundred.

Long after dark, the trapper returns home, throws down his catch,
hurriedly eats his steaming supper; then, by the light of the flickering kerosene lamp, the whole family skins the animals. A swift
slash by the tail, a two-handed grasp of muscular fingers, a swift
jerk, and the skin comes off over the head like a nightshirt. Every
shred of fat or flesh must be carefully scraped off by dull knives so
as not to injure the pelt. The skins are then stretched on steel frames,
a U-shaped piece of very stiff wire.

Though it is late at night before the trapper can turn in, he rises
the next day at the same early hour to repeat the process. It is a
grueling labor which lasts without a single break for the seventy-five
or ninety days of the season. Some seasons there are frequent freezes.
There have been times when the ice did not thaw for a week. And
while the winter is the most healthful part of the year, even so the
trapper and his family are exposed to malaria, typhoid, pneumonia,
pernicious anaemia, hookworm and other dire diseases.

In the town of a popular muskrat district, boats and huts line the
banks of the bayous, as in a Venetian slum. The huts are on stilts because of the frequent flooding, often set among great live oaks festooned with gray Spanish moss. A few, if the soil is good, have tiny
gardens; perhaps a pig or two roots in the mud of a tiny pen. Down
the water lane, in the few places where the output is not yet controlled by the large companies, come the fur buyers in launches.
They bring the day's news from civilization or from other bayous;
they haggle over the prices and the grading of the furs.

The price, in the past, has reached the high water mark of $1.75
a fur; in 1934 the average pelt brought only 65 cents. In 1935 the

buyer was paid 85 cents for the tops, 70 to 75 cents for seconds, 20 to 25 cents for smalls and damaged furs, 5 cents for mice and pieces. These are re-classified for shipment to the outside market (which increases the buyer's profit) into ten groups: tops, seconds, mediums, flats, barebacks, smalls, kids, mice, No. 1 damaged, No. 2 damaged. In addition, the state collects a tax, which varies from one cent on muskrats, 'possums and skunks, up to 25 cents on an otter.

On the way north, where most of the skins are sent to be tanned, the muskrat pelt passes through the hands and warehouses of from five to seven commission men, each of whom adds a percentage to the cost.

Formerly the bulk of the skins was shipped to Europe to be finished, then returned to New York. With the War, new chemical, dyeing and tanning industries developed in this country, and large establishments sprang up, mostly in New York.

More recently efforts have been made, by such new companies as the Delacroix Corporation, to shift the finishing process to New Orleans. It is argued that there is no justification for shipping out the raw hides when work could be given to thousands near the scene of trapping operations. But most of the output each year still goes to northern fur centers.

After the season is over, the trapper brings the returns of his "take" home. When debts are paid, clothes and other necessities purchased for the family, plans are made to improve the house. But even before these things, the trappers in the various villages get together and hold a *fête* in some empty storeroom to celebrate the end of the season and the men's return. There, amid a mad jargon of French, Spanish and English, occasionally with a dash of Italian or perhaps Portuguese, they sing and dance, drink and eat plentifully, court, discuss plans for the young folks' education, recount experiences undergone during the season in the swamps, kid each other about the new-fangled thermos bottle or swanky-looking leather jacket one of them has bought the day before at Old Martín's or José's general store.

With the exception of the World War period when hundreds of French, Spanish and "Cajun" trappers were drafted and sent overseas with the A.E.F., the southern Louisiana marshland population had led strange isolated lives for decades, trapping in the winter, fishing and shrimping in the summer.

After the War, the life of the trappers began to improve remarkably. More houses sprang up in the mainland villages. Many of the people, even those who had never left their home village, were now able to visit New Orleans, a few hours away, Baton Rouge and more distant centers. Hygiene, schools, better roads, automobiles, radios, telephones, became topics of conversation.

Though their forefathers had carved huge areas of our country out from what was once a dense wilderness, for the first time they were becoming an integral part of the American population. Most important, their assimilation into the national American scene and the machine age was about to take place under extremely favorable economic conditions. The tragedy and bitterness of other peoples, over whom the machine age had ruthlessly swept overnight, was to be spared them. Literally speaking, many of them were about to ride into the twentieth century in limousines.

But suddenly the whole picture changed. The post-war expansion of the industry involved millions of dollars of profit, and cunning men soon saw ways to reap the harvest better by exploiting those who made this wealth possible.

The inhabitants had trapped, hunted and fished in the coastal marshes for generations, and it had never occurred to them this right would ever be abridged. It had never occurred to them that they should obtain titles or leases. Such a safeguard had never been deemed necessary. Who but those willing to trap and fish would aspire to own such otherwise useless territory? As far as they were concerned, anyone who wished to engage in trapping—and a good many came in during those years from different parts of the country—was welcome to range freely over the seven million acres of bayou lands.

But as soon as the new wealth of the fur industry was discovered, the whole region, little by little, was grabbed by various landowners and fur companies, who in a few short years established an almost iron-clad monopoly over the entire Louisiana fur trade.

And so, great corporations now hold what was once a public domain, and where even the private portions were freely trapped. Lease and purchase systems now dominate the region. Men now trap on shares or for cash rent. Naturally trouble has resulted just as when the cattle companies fenced in the far western range. Trappers' wars have sprung up. Men have been killed. Some have gone to jail. Trapping means no longer, now, a free roaming over the trapping fields, but almost an industrialized system.

A sturdy group of American citizens—in the kingdom of the late Huey Long—in the last few years has been driven into peonage. The story of this drastic change is one of chicanery, corrupt officials, crooked judges, strike-breakers, gunmen, battles, murders, jailings. Today three or four big fur companies have a monopoly of most of the land and have created a feudal situation similar to that so long existing in the soft-coal industry.

In about five parishes in western Louisiana, the trapping lands were acquired many years ago from the state by outside companies, such as the Miami Land and Exploration Company, The Louisiana Land and Exploration Company, the Castile Land Company, from ten to fifteen cents an acre, for timber, oil or sulphur exploitation, or purely for speculation. About eighty per cent of the best trapping land was in their hands, some two million acres. But anyone could trap on it.

After 1923 a few dealers and landowners started to lease land to the trapper for from $25 to $50 the season. By 1929 about fifty per cent of the landowners were doing this. In that year furs reached their maximum prices, and a few fur-dealers and owners then began leasing to trappers on a fifty-fifty share basis.

Monopolization of land and hence of the industry proceeded apace. In 1930 in western Louisiana, Morris Steinberg—a business associate of Senator Jules Fisher, a hand-in-glove man of Huey Long and at one time under indictment for income tax evasion—began to acquire more land. Steinberg and Company came to control sixty per cent of the best trapping land of Louisiana.

Another feature in western Louisiana is the leasing of the 230,000 acres comprising the four federal Rockefeller, Russell Sage, Singer,

Paul J. Rainey, and eight state wildlife reservations. Those of the lands under state control are leased to the trappers by a supervisor. The trapper must provide his own boat, traps, stretchers and materials and receives fifty per cent of the furs. Of the remaining fifty per cent, half goes to the supervisor and half to the state treasury. The supervisor's job is thus a rich plum, netting many thousands of dollars. He is usually a politician who knows nothing about furs, and farms out the actual administration for five per cent. Abuses in the grading of furs and of otherwise getting the best of the trapper have been charged.

In the rich trapping districts of St. Bernard, Plaquemines, also part of Jefferson Parish, i.e., eastern Louisiana, the trappers always worked freely until about 1924. Some owned their own lands. But several bad years and the sudden imposing of heavy taxes forced nearly all such to default, so the lands reverted to the state—this being maneuvered by a local official to favor a fur company.

About that year a district attorney, who was a prominent Huey Long man, prepared a cunning trap. He conceived the idea of organizing the trappers. Dues began at $10 a year, were raised to $50 and finally to $250, the money supposedly to be used for buying or leasing land. Instead, various trapping companies were organized behind which were fur interests, who soon squeezed out bona fide union members. Leasing the land from the state and from private owners, little by little all the land, mostly through trickery and fraud, was monopolized. Then the new companies began giving out trapping privileges on a fifty-fifty share basis, each trapper being required to put up a lease bond of $200, or $100 to $150 in cash.

The contracts with the trapper then and since in all parts of Louisiana have stipulated that the trappers' share of furs had to be sold to the landowners. The fur and land companies were thus able to name their own prices for the furs. In the majority of cases this was and is invariably much less than the open market price.

Thus actually the trapper now got only a fourth or less of the value of his actual catch. In addition, the fur buyer classified the muskrat pelts purchased in four categories of quality—a range of eighty cent difference in price—and by generally undergrading the trapper's catch pays the trapper from $100 to $400 less on several thousand furs. On reselling the furs, the merchant establishes nine or ten selling categories, so actually the loss to the trapper is even larger.

Naturally this growing monopoly of lands, the excluding of old-time free trappers and the importing of outside company men, led not only to the hostilities, but to a great deal of poaching in season and out. Every muskrat killed out of season means twenty fewer rats during the season. This and other factors by 1935 cut the value of the output by fully one-half, lower than any time in the previous twenty years.

Huey Long's satellites, closely tied up with the fur companies, put through a trespassing law so drastic that it is possible to arrest any outsider in the vicinity of company properties. An independent fur dealer characterized this law to me as "the most vicious statute ever put on the lawbooks of Louisiana."

Thus an iron-clad monopoly and control have been set up in the entire trapping region of the state. On the lands of most companies, imported guards, sworn in as federal deputies, keep watch over the bayous, and turn back all outsiders from the waterways, which theoretically should be freely transitable.

No one is allowed to get near the company trappers. Often no buyer can find a way to approach even the few remaining independent trappers, who thus must also sell to the same company. On streams so obviously public waterways that they cannot be thus arbitrarily controlled, guards stationed at all entrances trail every boat, and if an outsider puts foot on land, as is sometimes necessary, he is immediately arrested for trespassing. Most of the trapping lands of Louisiana have thus been converted into petty armed kingdoms with every sort of feudal abuse.

When the NRA spread its blue wings of hope over the land, several independent fur-buyers, also independent merchants, hard hit by the reduced living-scale of the trappers, helped the trappers to organize to form a code. After the trappers were well organized, the American Federation of Labor rushed in and pretended to complete the organization work. It merely appropriated thirty-five per cent of all dues, but never provided any leadership, legal advice or assistance. The trappers themselves, helped by Julius Dupont, a merchant of Houma, drew up a code and went to Washington. There they were confronted by an array of brilliant legal talent from the companies. Stormy sessions resulted, but a fairly liberal code was agreed upon, the chief safeguard to the trappers being that henceforth they were actually to be paid in kind, not in cash on company-determined prices, so that from then on they could freely dispose of their own share of the furs in the open market.

It sounded like brighter days for the trappers, but the companies never lived up to the provisions of the code. All the efforts of the trappers to get the federal "co-ordinator" to take action were met with a shrug. I could not find one single instance in which these provisions of the NRA code were ever enforced.

As a result of attempted unionization, the companies actively boycotted all local trappers, refusing to contract them; and outsiders, a large percentage of whom were mulattoes, were brought in under armed guard. The local men were left in a bad way, since they no longer had any land on which to work. As a result the independent trappers everywhere came close to starvation. Their earnings were used up.

They can, however, just survive by fishing, shrimping and oyster-hunting during the six months open season, but their highest return at such work is fifty cents a day. A recent shipment of oysters by one of the local men, also a trapper, brought him 23 cents a sack, from which he had to pay commission, transportation and refrigeration costs. Sometimes a fisherman goes into debt as a result of a week's arduous labor. A few cut broom straw at $22 a ton. This requires at least two days to cut, then it must be dried and baled. An unexpected rain ruins it. From the sum received, freight and commission charges are deducted. At Shell Beach I found people actually starving. In 1935 the Red Cross alone saved the Delacroix trappers from hunger. Since then the federal government has lent some assistance.

The trappers brought in from the outside leave no money in the community. The storekeepers are all very hard hit. "It hardly verifies to keep open," said one on Delacroix Island. All complained. Naturally their sympathies are with the trappers, for the company commissariats do not buy much from them. One storekeeper in Violet told us he had canceled three hundred trappers' accounts carried for three years, without a cent being paid on them. In that town the store which gets a little company trade is, as might be expected, run by the niece of the local judge who has done favors to the company at the expense of the trappers.

And so things have not been peaceful. In 1934 a company guard, known as "Big Boy," a Chicago gunman who boasted he was an Al Capone man, shot one of the trappers. In reprisal a group of un-known persons, undoubtedly trappers, evaded the network of the guards, and went into the marshes and tumbled several company camps into the bayous.

Federal deputy marshals thereupon appeared in the dead of night, terrorizing the trapper families and seizing those most prominent in the union or who had talked too freely. Twenty-seven trappers in all were thus arrested. Trappers called in for quizzing were vilely abused by the federal authorities, called "goddam liars" and put under arrest if they talked back. There was no adequate evidence as to who had upset the camp shacks, but nine trappers were indicted and held on $2,500 bail each for trespassing as compared to the $1,500 for the Chicago gunman who had attempted murder.

The raising of the trappers' bail was made unduly difficult. The federal commissioner refused to accept United States government bonds or any mortgaged property. Though well-to-do storekeepers and independent fur merchants came to the aid of the trappers with bond, it took them three or four days before they could produce property guarantees that would satisfy the commissioner. Some of the trappers were subsequently unjustly railroaded to prison, one a young fellow who was in New Orleans at the time of the raid.

The imported trappers have no bed of roses. They do not derive much benefit from the betrayal of their fellows. Contracted for the season on a fifty-fifty basis, they are taken out to company camps in boats. They must pay back the company hiring them for this trans-portation. They have no boats themselves and cannot escape if there is a flood. On one occasion, many families were taken off by fishermen after they had been standing on their beds for three days. The company made no effort to rescue them. Three or four families, men, women and children are dumped into a flimsy hut about the size of a small hotel room. To rent these shared shacks, each trapper must pay $25 or $30 a season. If a man must hire a dugout to get to his traps, he is charged $10 or $12 more. Food is brought out by the company, with 10 per cent added for delivery at already inflated prices. Our inquiries revealed that a $4.90 sack of sugar was sold to the trappers for $9 plus 10 per cent. Traps worth $2.75 a dozen were sold for $6 a dozen. Steel stretchers worth 80 cents a dozen were sold for $1.80. The company is supposed to provide water, but often forgets, and the people have to use the brackish bayou water to make coffee. I talked with one company trapper who had brought in the unusual number of 4,000 furs, worth at least $2,000 even at low unfair prices. By the end of the season he was $90 in debt to the company. A wizard of a trapper cannot any longer clear $100 a year, whereas when he was still free he used to be able to make several thousand dollars. Often the trappers have to wait weeks after the season is over before the company comes to take them off, and even longer for an accounting.

And so when milady puts on her soft fur coat, it is quite possible that it was once stretched out on the side of a shack in the Louisiana marshes by men little better off than the animals they hunt. Such is the vaunted individualism we are asked to protect as a sacred part of American life. Such is the ending of another free land frontier of America.

CHAPTER XVIII

BLACK ALABAMA

Washington County, Alabama, has achieved the supreme ridiculousness in race relations. Though local and county school funds in 1936 were sufficient to run its educational institutions only a trifle over a month, and though with its share of customary state aid, it was not able to keep them open even three months, nevertheless Washington County maintains an expensive three-way school system. The Whites —a pretty ignorant lot—won't permit either Negroes or Cajuns (Americans of French-plus descent) to attend their schools. Cajuns are supposed to have a little Indian, and in some cases, Negro blood. The latter they hotly deny and refused to attend the Negro schools, so separate schools must be provided for them. As yet, however, there are no Negro or Cajun high schools.

The hysteria that rules race relations in Alabama has stained the whole state a somber hue. Alabama, sodden, harsh and backward though it is, has its beauty and mystery of life, but it is like a black veil that makes the eyes entrancing but conceals the ulcered nose. Even the Ku Klux Klan, with its white hoods and flaming crosses, represents a variety of primitive religious experience, but it is an exhalation out of the black abyss of fear that permits cowardly men to cloak not only their bodies but their evil deeds in the mask of righteousness and anonymity.

Inevitably brutal oppression of the Negro has dragged down the living standards of the poor White, who in many sections is slightly worse off than even his Black companion in misery.

Economic slavery chains the master to the slave. The failure of

334

Alabama to provide proper educational facilities for the Negro has dragged down the intellectual and cultural level of even upper-class Whites. Just to be literate in Alabama provides one with superior economic leverage that contributes to slothful smugness. To be able to speak a grammatical sentence makes one feel himself an aristocrat.

Decatur, when the Scottsboro boys were being tried, was spending only $75 a month on its public library, an institution exclusively for Whites. (Negroes have scarcely any library facilities in the entire state.) This sum was for salary, new books, magazines, fuel and upkeep. Books on economics were never bought "because things are changing so," although two lives of Franklin Delano Roosevelt grace the shelves as well as a donated life of Herbert Hoover, which the librarian didn't throw out, "as most librarians in Alabama would"— a most exemplary though futile broad-mindedness.

Decatur is a small, frowsy, gangster-ridden city overfull of vicious elderly lynch-minded Protestant ministers. Yet even in Montgomery, capital of the state, the old proud capital of the Confederacy, a city considered a repository of culture, the public library contains no current official state or city publications. In it you can learn nothing regarding public education or social and economic facts in present-day Alabama. You can read some musty histories written decades ago with the full tang of Confederate patriotism. In 1936 the library contained only thirteen books on sociology, one of which dated as late as 1911; most were such things as reprints of Herbert Spencer or such profound studies as Theodore Roosevelt's *American Ideals*. The library contained exactly ten books on the Negro (mostly folklore) and race relations, three of which dated as late as 1911. It had a book of hoary date on labor.

Next to Georgia, for education Alabama spends per pupil less than any state in the Union. School attendance represents only 19 per cent of all White children of school age and 14 per cent of all Black children. Often for Black children, this signifies but from two to five months a year. If Negro schools keep open longer, it is because of sporadic help from northern foundations. Negro schools are inadequate and poorly situated, often being merely vacant tottering sharecropper shacks, without heat, running water, or toilet facilities. In

1934 the state spent $548,204 on the transportation of White pupils and $3,099 on Black pupils. The sum of $10,252,505 was spent on White schools; $1,282,680 for Negro schools. In 1932-33 the state spent $236,092 on new buildings for White schools and $17,813 for Black. The average annual salary in the counties for White teachers is $344, for Black teachers $147; in cities $957 and $579 respectively. The average monthly salary for rural Negro teachers is $31. Even the White schools were open less than 110 days.

There are very few public high schools for Negroes. Montgomery, the third largest city in the state, has none, though Negroes comprise 40 per cent of its population. Birmingham, however, boasts in all its literature of having the largest Negro high school in the world. It was built for 1,500 pupils and has an enrollment of nearly 4,000. It does not accredit to college as do the White schools. Montgomery has 22 public elementary schools, of which three are for Negroes.

The state does have a Division of Negro Education, run by two White workers, a part-time secretary and a colored state agent, but the cost of even this is paid by northern philanthropic agencies, not by Alabama.

Educational surveys of forty counties have been made; in three of them the authorities bothered to survey the Negro schools. Tuscaloosa County, where is located the state university (Negro students barred), is considered one of the better counties educationally, though it is a vicious Ku Klux Klan and lynch center. It has a population of 42,585 Whites and 21,568 Negroes. Daily White attendance, exclusive of private schools, is 55 per cent of the total school population; daily Negro attendance, inclusive of private schools, is 48 per cent. No colored children were transported until 1929-30. In 1931, 57 out of 3,134 pupils transported were Black. There were then 130 White public schools. The survey takes credit for a total of 50 Negro schools, but a small footnote mentions that only four are public schools maintained by the state. The rest are owned by individuals, communities, churches or foundations. Over 60 per cent of the Negro pupils in private and public schools were over age in the first grade; by second grade, over 84 per cent. First grade enrollment represented 50 per cent of all Black pupils. The previous ten years in the county the capital outlay was $204,181 for White schools and $22,873 for Negro schools. The survey, mimeographed in 1932, made extensive proposals. Those for Whites were largely carried out; those for Blacks scarcely at all, so that the racial discrepancy is today worse than ever. And this in a state where education is next to the lowest in the Union.

Even if proper schooling were provided, the economic status of most of the colored families is kept so low that most children do not attend school for lack of food, clothes and textbooks, and in nearly all cases remain out of school most of each year to help in the fields. More recently the state has tried to provide textbooks for the first grade. As usual the Negro schools have been sadly neglected, but are gradually being provided with worn-out books from the White schools.

The greater the race feeling, the fewer the educational and economic opportunities for Negroes. But in such places one invariably finds the largest number of Black churches. Ignorance, poverty and religion seem to walk hand in hand. Of the 93 churches in Montgomery, 67 are colored. If churches are a criterion of morality, then the Negroes are the best people in Alabama.

In nearly all places, the Negroes have no parks or recreational centers, no libraries. They are the pariahs, the untouchables. "Never fight a Negro with your fists," hit him with a stick or a gun is one of the local concepts of White manhood. "Bruised-knuckle" Harry, a Decatur policeman, is an exception. Every Saturday night he goes down to "nigger town" and breaks his knuckles on the heads and jaws of a few Negroes to be sure they know their proper places.

About the only civic rights the Negro has (approximately a thousand may vote if they care to be insulted and humiliated) are to pay taxes and be sentenced in the courts. Negro property is assessed slightly higher than White. Many towns have special, if unconstitutional, ordinances, such as no Negroes may park their cars (few have any) on the main street. In Decatur and other places no White person may remain under a Negro roof after nine o'clock at night.

As for the courts, the saying is: "An arrested Negro is a convicted

Negro." A slight exaggeration, but if the Scottsboro trial has been trumpeted around the world, dozens of Scottsboro cases never echo at all in the press. Lynch justice is common. The law does not protect the Negro against White violence and improper chicanery or against loan-sharks.

The Negroes, however, inadvertently serve to maintain the state political machine. Political power in Alabama centers in the Black Belt where Negroes are more numerous than the Whites. The Whites there are in an improperly favored situation. State appropriations are made on the basis of population; hence, in the Black counties, a handful of Whites, mostly plantation owners, have relatively enormous funds to spend and to graft and to cement their control on the rest of the state. Thus in preponderantly Black counties, since so little is spent on Negro education, the White schools are better than anywhere in the state, and in the Red Hill counties, where there are few Negroes, the children of White citizens are condemned to a Negro standard of education. Thus in Black Belt Sumter County, with 1,189 Whites and 10,190 Negroes, $53.75 is spent per White child, far above the state average, and $2.41 per Negro child (a fourth of the state average).

Occasionally city Negro clubs get up spunk to ask for something. The suggestions are often curious and bewildered, though illuminating. The South Side Community Welfare Association of Montgomery when I was there made the following demands, which they couldn't get printed in the city, except for triple price and with the right of censorship by the printer:

1. A playground.
2. Paved streets and proper sanitation.
3. Street lighting.
4. Negro high school.
5. Stop the law from beating up Negroes without cause.
6. White men to take off their hats when they enter our homes.
7. Break up illicit relations [raping] with White men and colored women.
8. Co-operation to stamp out vice and crime.

This gives a picture of Negro quarters in enlightened Montgomery. Conditions are mostly worse elsewhere. The Negro sections of Montgomery, as some poor White mill sections, have no paved streets, no proper street lighting, rarely any sewerage system. It is amazing in a city the size of Montgomery to see Negro privies standing in the back yards in almost the center of town, with consequent danger to the health of even the Whites.

The federal government there has been putting through a housing project for Negroes. Aesthetically the houses are uninviting, though at least they are of brick and cement, well lighted and sanitary. But the good White folk of Montgomery were furious at putting such ideas of well-being into the heads of "niggers," especially because the government is installing running water. "Now all the niggers will be wanting running water," which of course would put White landlords to some expense.

Economically, of course, the Negroes in Alabama, except for a few ill-paid professionals, are down below a Central American living scale, with fewer chances to obtain food, with a worse climate, far worse working conditions and less leisure. In most rural sections the gross so-called cash-crop return is not over $150 a year, of which they rarely see a red cent. The average monthly farmers' wage in Alabama is $17.25 as compared to the national average of $30.38 and the California average of $62. The average for share-croppers is naturally way below the $17.25 figure, and for Negroes is often infinitesimal. Mostly reduced to share-cropping, the Negroes live in rotting, tottering shacks, filled with holes, through which beat the wind and rain and snow. Even the few Negroes who own their own farms are located on such submarginal lands that they are as badly off as the outright serfs. In general, of the independent one-man farm owners, three Negroes to one White are on submarginal lands.

One of the very worst sections is right around the state agricultural college, the Alabama Polytechnic Institute, at Auburn in Lee County, an institution which for years, through agricultural instruction, has been working to improve rural standards. Yet the land thereabouts is badly cared for, eroded, gullied, and the shacks as small and dilapidated as anywhere. Going over the institution's publications, I discovered absolutely nothing helpful to a poor Negro cropper or farm-owner. It puts out nicely illustrated brochures on "The House Beautiful," with elaborate designs for baronial plantation homes; a booklet on fences, showing sketches of fancy modern wire fences and stone masonry gates. The Negro cropper or farmer can build a fence only of loose boulders or brush. Hopefully I opened a tiny folder on food suggestions to beat the depression. It contained such helpful items as imported Florida fruits and vegetables. The college does have a booklet of 4-H club girl songs about being industrious, the 4-H clubs being organizations promoted among poor people by the landlords of the reactionary Farm Bureau Federation.

Something, with considerable rhetoric, has been done by Tuskegee, the large Negro institute, established and run by northern funds. Of necessity its commendable, if very limited, extension activities are in the nature of pathetic social welfare work that cannot possibly cure the cancer. Its 1934 report showed the following Alabama achievements. In 33 counties 346 Negro farmers were encouraged to utilize 3,341 tons of compost or home fertilizer. It encouraged the establishment of the Bogue Chitto Milk Route in Dallas County: 18 farmers or so sold $225 worth of milk a week. Considerable health work was done among children of the Negro 4-H clubs. In co-operation with the federal authorities a self-help group was organized among starving Negro workers in a "busted" mill town. They received a loan of $68,431 for 35 years. A plot of 523 acres was bought from a lumber company and 93 Negro families housed in former mill shacks, etc. A piggery, truck-farm and cannery, dairy and poultry plant were installed. A federal land-use resettlement project was under way near Tuskegee, which had it finally been put through would have put 139 families, mostly Negro, on 9,000 acres; but resettlement work, of course, has been knifed out of existence by Secretary Wallace.

But aside from federal aid or Negro self-help, the Alabaman begrudges every cent of public money spent on the colored person, whom he considers a sort of wild animal, though it must be confessed that the outstanding animal traits are mostly displayed by the

Whites. One of the Morgan County deputy sheriffs told Roy Wright, one of the Scottsboro boys, prior to the shooting of Ozie Powell, that if he didn't do what he was told and get rid of his lawyers, he'd treat them "no better than a snake." Cullman County, though it has few Negroes, is a sweet place. Some years ago the L. and N. Railroad had to take Negro firemen off its trains because the Cullmanites stoned or shot them. There and in other places through the Red Hill district are big signs: "Nigger, don't let the sun set on your head here."

As a rule, the lynching or judicial murder of Negroes supposedly guilty of rape (though never the raping of Black women by Whites which is a White privilege) are highly publicized. But every year, about "settling up time," occurs a series of violences and deaths which never get into the press. In September and October, the White landlord, who has the entire right to sell farm products, settles with his tenants and croppers for the sale of their cotton. If any Negro objects to the landlord's terms or attempts to go to court, the plantation overseer is likely to kill him on the spot or presently a lynch party, which frequently includes the sheriff, drags him out, beats him or kills him. Many communities have a conventional Negro burier of such lynch victims, who for a small fee quietly takes the body out into the woods or swamps, no fuss or publicity.

While I was attending the Scottsboro trial at Decatur, a curious pamphlet fell into my hands. Attorney-at-law Woodford Mabry, the author, indulges himself in the most fantastic screed of race-hatred it has ever been my pleasure to read. It opens with a warning to the defense attorney for the Scottsboro boys to get out and remain away from Alabama, and contains direct incitements to lynching. It proceeds then in the most vicious language interspersed with pseudo-learning, childish anecdotes, "highfalutin" eloquence and phraseology, such as "unsullied Diana of the silent woods," to repeat all the current untruths about the Negro race, all the curious beliefs of the backwoods Red Hill dweller about Negro origins, anthropology, and character.

It calls upon the memory of the soldiers of the Confederacy, it drags God into the filth of the author's mind with such phrases as "vows to the Most High," and it exalts Caucasian civilization, which if Mr. Mabry is a typical product had better be destroyed the sooner the better.

I quote some of the gems: "We owe the Negro nothing. We found him a naked, snake-worshiping savage and conferred upon him all the polish of civilization that he is competent to receive." (Some African Negroes were savage; many were highly cultivated.)

"We must see to it that the Negro makes no Haitian hell of the United States." (Personally I find Haiti culturally and in many other ways a far more attractive place than Alabama.)

"The taxing of poor White people to furnish higher education for Negro wenches and sassy bucks is an outrage upon the White and an injury to the Negroes."

"God Almighty made the skin of the Negro black, climate did not do it, as is contended by some people, who have not studied the question. . . . The Chinaman lives under a sun as hot as Africa and he goes almost naked, as the Negro does in Africa; and yet the Chinaman is no more like the woolly-headed Negro than he was thousands of years ago." (Very deep anthropological observation!)

"The Negro can't be improved."

The American Negro, compared to his progenitors in Africa, "even of royal blood . . . is as much superior as a two hundred and fifty dollar Kentucky mule is to a Mexican jackass."

"The old-time darkey was the happiest being in the Lord's green earth."

"Has any radiant thought ever been born in his woolly head?"

"No idea of paradise was ever conceived by him."

We gave the Negro "liberty, property, free-speech, free press and freedom of conscience . . . that is all he is entitled to." (Since when?)

"Negroes with a suggestion of intellect are usually . . . mongrels in whose veins flow the blood of some depraved Caucasian."

All Negro women are "rotten with syphilis."

The White man is "the best friend the Negro has." (God help him!)

The Moses law of an eye for an eye is a "statute deep-graven on the heart of humanity by the burin of the Almighty." (What a lot of eyes the Whites will lose one of these days!)

The pamphlet reeks with such phrases as "the splendor of the manliness of the gentlemen of the South" . . . "Reverence" for "the mother and wife of the South" . . . "Anglo-Saxon superiority over the rest of mankind" . . . "veneration and respect for women" . . . and in a great burst of joy bright-boy Woodford ends up that *honest* people are welcomed to the South where "the mocking-bird warbles his sweetest song. . . . Here the queenly peach flushes with crimson when the Sun doth kiss her cheek. . . . Here the hills are festooned with tangling vines embossed with purple grapes that hang in clusters like a million crystal globes filled with blushing wine and the bananas with melting pulp of honey. . . . Here pomegranates hang like ruddy moons and lemons like golden globes and sometimes a nigger hangs way down in Dixie." A whole page of it!

He hurries on "to the Vestal Virgins of Rome" and cries out in real anguish of spirit: "Does the sacred fire burn low within me? Then woe unto me. . . ."

I quote this amazing pamphlet by this semi-illiterate with its extravagant phraseology because, apart from its language, it largely reflects the opinions of the mass of White people in Alabama. The election of Bill Graves on a Ku Klux Klan ticket was an open endorsement of lynching and race violence by the electorate of the state.

Let me turn to Mr. X., head of the Resettlement Investigation Bureau in the state, a federal officeholder, native of Tennessee. When in 1935 I asked him about the Share-Croppers' Union, he told me that it was made up of a bunch of "night-riders," and was officered by Negroes, who "dominate the poor Whites." When I asked him the reason for that, his reply was, "Well, if a nigger gets a little backing, he thinks he's important; if he gets a uniform he thinks he's a king; and if you give him a bugle, he thinks he's God Almighty." This came out of the mouth of a man supposed to be helping Negro and White share-croppers alike. (If Mr. X could get off *that* opinion without a bugle, what would *he* have been with a bugle?)

It is of course to be expected that the poor White share-cropper in the Black Belt and the Red Hill region, condemned to poverty, illiteracy, incest, degeneracy, and blind religious prejudice, should be unable to get the red clay and manure out of his hair or the cobwebs out of his brain. In fact to hate the Negro becomes almost a spiritual necessity. It is the one thing left to him that conserves his pride of not believing himself lower than everybody else. But the same opinions, a bit more refined, apparently rule 90 per cent of the White people of the state.

I have already described the generally low cultural level of the state. But note the following incident in academic circles themselves.

Not long ago Professor Cason of the University of Tuscaloosa wrote a beautiful book on the South, called *90° in the Shade*. It does not belong to the customary outpouring of romantic picturesqueness which customarily veils the evils of the South, but is a brave examination into the psychology, the life and the economic abuses. It is written by a native Alabaman, without a hint of sectional or race prejudice, with patent love for his state, with a deep sentiment, a calm spirit and in an attractive style. The day it was published, Professor Cason committed suicide. I talked to his best friend in Tuscaloosa who told me he had taken his life because he knew that he would lose his job at the university, that he would be ostracized by his fellow-professors and by his own family and social group. Yet it is a book that any civilized community would be proud to have written about itself.

When Samuel Leibowitz, the lawyer in charge of the Scottsboro defense, tried to engage a White Alabama lawyer to assist, even offering to step out of the picture himself, he could not find one courageous enough, open-minded enough, or sufficiently loyal to the better traditions of the profession to participate.

Strangely enough, when visiting Alabama, I have invariably felt myself more in a foreign country than I did in Turkey. Most of the things that I look to with pride upon as being basically American are not to be found in Alabama. Race-hatred has thrown a pall over the state. It has prevented the harmonious development of its human potentialities, Black and White. In spending so much effort to keep the Negro down, to keep him oppressed, to deny him opportunity, the White has been crippled himself. His energies have not been free to build a great commonwealth. The mass of the population rots in poverty and degeneracy.

These things have their explanations. One of the explanations is naturally the economic set-up, the inefficient semi-feudal plantation system, the share-cropper system, the tenant-farmer system, which had hastened the ruining of the land and increased the acreage of submarginal lands. The grinding down of the population over many decades to a starvation level, has prevented adequate state revenues, has blocked public enterprise, education, public improvements, the accumulation of new capital for industrial expansion. Most of Alabama's industrial capital is northern capital. The state is thus in the same position as other colonial entities, on the one hand held to backwardness by its plantation class, on the other by northern industrialism. In short Alabama is a semi-subjugated colony just as much as Cuba, Puerto Rico or Panama.

The agricultural decline began in some places by the time of the Civil War, in the Piedmont area as early as 1880, and in most areas as early as 1920, and now with the new mechanical appliances for the growing of cotton, the debacle will soon be complete, and the state will be faced with a stark ruin worse than that which now exists.

A species of Fascism came to Alabama soon after the end of the Reconstruction Period. Alabama at best has never known democracy, does not know it today. It is ruled largely by a small group of White plantation owners from the Black Belt, who themselves are terror-stricken because they too are caught in the web of collapse, and hence visit their own inner terror on their tenants. Alabama's Black citizenry are disenfranchised. A large part of its White citizenry are likewise disenfranchised. Politicians are at the beck and call of plantation owners.

And yet the morale of the political powers that be, despite their use of terrorism, their lynchings, their police thugs in the larger centers, their sedition laws, their childish fright of any ideas later than the twelfth century, seems to me cracked. They represent a feudal system that is doomed even in Alabama. They face one of the worst economic shifts that any region of any country has ever suffered. They are fighting a losing battle. They cannot hold up against the economic forces that are bound to shake their political control.

What will come out of it, I don't know. One of the brightest signs in Alabama which gave me some slight hope for even a state so backward and so benighted, was the Share-Croppers' Union, largely a Black union, but to which belonged many White share-croppers, and which in the deep South has held joint meetings of Whites and Blacks. It faced lynchings, terror, hunger, disaster. It was militant, unafraid to do battle for its rights, even with guns in hand. But it seems partly to have petered out.

One of the bright lights has been the determined struggle, and its increasing success, for civil liberties in Birmingham—a struggle carried on by Alabamans themselves.

A bright chapter has also been written by the brave, almost single-handed efforts of a former professor of the University, Dr. Joseph S. Gelders, who, despite threats and on one occasion a severe beating that almost cost him his life, has kept up an unwavering struggle for legality and the American Bill of Rights.

But the pall of darkness is thick indeed. I talked with some of the survivors of the five or more lynchings in Lowndes County in 1935. One woman told me how a mob of plantation owners and hirelings came to her house and hit her over the head with a gun, looking for share-cropper literature during a strike which demanded that wages be raised from 35 cents to a dollar a day for sun-up to sun-down labor. I talked with the young widow of a man who was strung up behind the landlord's house and a hundred bullets sent through his body. I talked with other survivors. Here is the picture and the exact transcript of what they told me, as nearly as I could copy it down.[1]

NOTES ON ALABAMA LYNCHING

Puffs of white spread in a flurry over the red hills and gullied land. It was cotton-picking time in Alabama.

But there were no Black folk dragging their bags between the rows,

[1] Names of persons and places have been changed.

no gnarled fingers clutching at the white fluff, no bright kerchiefs moving under the hot, glinting sun.

It was August, and the bolls were full, ripe and waiting, but no Black folk-songs came from the fields. The fields were silent. No Black babies lay in the shade of the furrow while their mothers bent over the low plants.

All the Negroes were huddled down in their broken shacks, with their rotting floors and gaping holes. There was a strike. The Black workers had not gone to the fields. They had been offered thirty-five cents a day for their sun-up, sun-down back-breaking labor. They wanted a dollar a day.

It was August, and they should have been happy after a hard winter full of snow and cold and sometimes sub-zero weather. Now there was no cold rain slanting through the holes of their flimsy cabins. But the folk were not happy. They were frightened. The cabins were hushed. And the dwellers in them were as tense as the brittle air. Even Black folk have nerves.

They had reason to be afraid. The sun was hot and round and looked smeared with blood. Death was coming, and they all knew it.

Sixteen of them died—murdered—and the papers said not a word about it. I talked with some of those who escaped and fled to Birmingham.

They were sitting dazed and mostly penniless in the broken huts down in Negro mill-town.

VIRGINIA GRAYSON (a middle-aged firm-voiced Negress with white hair, weazened face, very yellow teeth):

I belongs on J. W. Lakin's plantation. Dat Thu'sday, I wuz pickin' peas in de pea-patch on de hill when a White gang comes over de top of de hill.

I run fast as I could to de house. Four or five of de gang ran right behind me. "What'n hell yo' runnin' fo'?" dey yelled.

I don' have no breath to answer back, suh. I jus' wanted to advise de men fo'ks and chilluns. I come tearin' down de hill. I had on an old red hat, and I waved dat hat.

Mah fust cousin, Sam Hathaway and Laws Grayson, mah husband's nephew, dey got out. Three little boys done took out after 'em. Dat White gang up and shot at dem three boys.

"Laws, don' you-all kill him!" shouted Hassie Goodman [one of the boys' mothers]. She yells like she got a fit.

"We didn't kill the little nigger but we sho' shot hell out of Laws Grayson," dey said.

De gang caught up with me and come right on into de house.

"Where's yo' husband?" they asked me.

"The Boss man wrote for him."

"You're a goddam liar," they said, and Vaughn Dealer hit me in de head with a pistol.

De gang put me and my niece, Minnie Brown, and my sister, Hassie Goodman, and Lela Cohen and five children in the parlor. A man sat at the door with a gun. De man wuz Luke Carrion.

De ol' house we lived in had a parlor with a shed off it. On one side wuz an open place [a hall or passageway]. On de other wuz a middle room and fu'der back, stuck off a bit, wuz de kitchen. Dey wuz a plank from the middle room to de kitchen. We used ter git wet when it wuz rainin' and we crossed on dat ol' plank, and de rain would git on de cawn pone.

De gang left John Henry Gary sittin' in de middle room with a shotgun and dat man Luke Carrion sitting befo' our door.

Carrion wuz talkin' to us, sayin' dat anybody in de Union wuz gonter get hell, askin' us about it. But any time we said anything he tol' us to shut up our dirty black mouths.

Den I heard a shot.

"Did you git him?" asked Carrion.

"I don' know. I think likely," said Gary.

Gary shot at Jim Press Goodman when he come up between de middle room and de kitchen, when he put his foot on de plank.

Jim Press wuz at Henry Cassoway's and wuz carryin' on each of his shoulders two two-gallon buckets, some groceries, flour, meat, and on his back a sack of meal. He had a quart er syrup in his hip pocket.

Jim Press wuz shot in de hip with a shotgun just when he step up on de plank. De shot tore up de syrup and all. De pieces of glass from de bottle wuz drove right into his hip.

I wuz bleedin' so from bein' hit in de head with a pistol, I don' know nothin' what wuz goin' on. Dey brought Jim Press into de parlor.

He cain't stand up and mus' lie on his stomach. He ask for water, but dey don' let us git any.

I wuz bleedin' from de pistol and ask to lie down, but dey don' let me.

While Jim Press wuz lyin' on de floor on his stomach, Carrion ask him about de Union.

He kep' sayin' he don' know nothin'. He kep' sayin', "If a man don' know, he don' know."

"You niggers are so damn ignorant down heah. You-all better tell everything before Vaughn Dealer gets back heah. If you don' he's gonna kill de hell out of you."

Vaughn Dealer is de son of Ralph Dealer [the plantation owner], an' he wuz about twenty-five.

Gary keep on cussin' Jim Press out when he still say he don' know nothin' and call him a "bull-headed son-of-a-bitch."

CALLIE CASSOWAY (a Negress of about thirty, fairly buxom, good-humored, possibly more intelligent than Virginia Grayson):

Dat Thu'sday, de landlord, John Henry Gary, and a big mob or crew or gang, shot down Jim Press Goodman at Virginia Grayson's house. Dey wuz about twenty-five of 'em in de gang. . . .

No, I don' see Jim Press shot. I heard about it afterwards. All dat I seen is what de gang done at my house. Dey come down theah after goin' ter Virginia's house.

But I done hear how dey shot Jim Press. Dey all come into Virginia's house and put everybody in de front room. They wuz four women and eight chillun, but I hear how three chilluns got away. It's a four room house. Dey kep' de women shut up so dey cain't warn de fo'k dey was fixin' to kill.

Gary stay in de middle room with a gun. The rest of de gang come on down mah way.

Jim Press, dey tol' me after, he come out of de cotton patch right by Virginia's house, and he wuz shot down when he put his foot on de plank to de back door.

But de gang wuz all down to my house. I wuz theah with Mary Jane Goodman, dat's Jim Press's wife, and her seven-year-old gal.

Dey ask me where Henry, my husban', been, where he gone to.

He knowed dey wuz acomin' and light out. I tol' him he gone ter Wayland. He wan't theah, he done go somewhar else, but dat wuz what I tol' 'em. Dey said dey come lookin' for some "latitude" [strike literature].

I tol' 'em I don' know 'bout any "latitude," and Benny McArthur hauled off and hit me. He hit me right on de nose with his fist. Dey wuz a ring on his hand, an' he tore mah nose right open. I guess I mighty nigh los' half a gallon er blood. He knock me on de floor an' say: "If you don' shut yo' mouth, I'se gonter kill you."

Mary Jane wuz ahidin' behind de door. Putty quick they come on her. "Heah's one of de son-of-a-bitches we're lookin' for, heah behind the door."

Dey make her lie down on a chair, a cane-bottom chair, dat one right theah what you is sittin' on, suh, with her head down and on her stomach. Benny McArthur hol' her head way down and another one pull up her dress an' de others stood around. The worst of de gang hit her with a new plow line, I guess for about twenty minutes.

She don' tell nothin'. So dey hit her once mo' for twenty minutes.

She still won' say nothin' so dey throwed a rope over a j'st and put a loop on her neck and hanged her up. Her two feet wuz off de floor. She hanged theah five minutes and swung aroun' and aroun'. Den dey let her down. She fell unconscious fo' about five minutes.

Dey begin askin' her again about de Union.

'Las' she tell 'em she wuz in de Union, how it made her a leader but she don' never go to de meetings and don' know nothin' about it.

Dey make us shut up mah house and tol' me go on home with Mary Jane. Dey tol' us to stay home till dey tole us we cain go out, whether it wuz an hour, a day, two days or three days, or dey gonter kill us.

So we start fo' Jim Press's home. Mary Jane wuz feelin' bad, suh, but she don' say a word. Her place is a mile and a half away on Ralph Dealer's place. Jim Press wuz a wage hand theah.

We follow behin' de gang fo' about a mile. When we finally get over theah near home dey wuz about fifteen cars 'roun' Dealer's house.

We made our minds to take to de woods. Den we figured to go home ter notify Jim Press. We don' know he'd been shot. He wuzn't ter home so we took to de woods and went three or four miles on to de Pastor Place, beyond Jim Press's house, to Dora Dillard's. We stayed theah about thirty minutes, den went on up to George Josephson's place.

VIRGINIA GRAYSON:

De gang come back from Callie Cassoway's house. Vaughn Dealer and Benny McArthur come back with de gang. Dey ask Jim Press about some Union circulars. "You carried 'em aroun'," dey tol' him.

Jim Press wuz still lyin' on his stomach. He wuz groanin' when dey wuzn't talkin' to him. He tol' 'em. "I wuz gonter tell you 'bout dem papers yesterday."

"You black son-of-a-bitch. I'm gonter kill you." Vaughn Dealer drawed his pistol.

We women begged him not to kill Jim Press. We got to hollerin' around theah so he throwed his pistol on Hassie Goodman an' tol' her to git back outer theah.

Bing Lauder say, "All right, Jim, pull down your clothes an' let's see whar dey shot you."

He couldn't pull his overalls down so his sister Lela Cohen pulled 'em down.

"Dat ain't so bad, is it?" said Bing. "Dis nigger ain't shot, is you, Jim Press?"

"I guess you all knows what yo' talkin' about."

"All right, Jim Press, let's go up and go to de doctor man."

Vaughn Dealer, he said, "We got yo' doctor right heah." He shook his gun, but he don' kill him.

While dis wuz goin' on, Walt Goodman come nyar de house. De gang done shoot at him, but he took off.

Walt had gone ter town on a mule to bring me a letter from my husband who wuz away. He ran into a gang in town. Dey took de letter away from him and don' let him go. He say he want to go to de closet. Dey say for him to go into de bushes.

When he got into de bushes he keep agoin'. He left his mule and dey don' never give hit back.

After a while he come on ter my house an' look through de cornfield and seen de gang and lit out. He got up on de hill.

De gang spotted him theah, so he run down through de bottoms. Dey took twelve or fourteen shots at him.

He sure went through dat pasture an' left tracks dat long. [She held her hands wide apart.]

The gang come back inside.

Later dey went on over ter Walt's house and broke it open and smash' up de trunks, beds, 'bout everything.

Dey sho' tore up our house too. Dey throwed shoes and clothin' on de floor. Dey rip down all my dresses an' things.

"They's a gun in heah," somebody said.

"Any 'count?"

"Put a shell in it and take hit along."

So dey took down a single-barrel shotgun we had off de rack in de middle room.

When dey's all gone, Vaughn Dealer said: "Minnie Brown, you-all knows me. I ain't got mah face civered over, an' mah name better not be writ away from heah. Every goddam one of you better be heah when we git back."

Dey start to take Jim Press off.

He askt for a cane.

"Can I give him one?" I asked.

Dey says yes, so I give him a stick. He cain't hardly walk. Dey wuz a long long time gettin' out of sight. It wuz de worst time I ever had in all mah life, done near drive me crazy.

After dey go on off, de las' time, I, Lela, Minnie, Hassie an' de chilluns all leave and go on over de hill through de pasture whar we fin' Mary Jane Goodman's mother. De four of us went on over toward Minnie's house 'cause she say:

"I gotter go see 'bout my chil'."

I went with her 'cause I wanna git Mr. J. W. Lakin [he was a very decent plantation owner] and see a doctor to fix mah head.

Lela says to come to her house and put on a dress fust.

"No, I'se goin' in just what I got here," I said.

We gone up past Ralph Dealer's house [plantation owner, father of Vaughn Dealer]. They got Jim Press right behind de house. Benny McArthur's truck wuz theah in de pasture. Out in front wuz more cars dan you can count. Jim Press wuz sittin' on de ground against a post of de wire fence.

Benny McArthur askt us, "Where'n hell you all goin'?"

"We's gonter de store." [Nearby on the plantation.]

"You better git your goddam asses back down theah and git 'em out quick."

Benny McArthur and the others throwed guns on us, and we went on back.

Just when we got back to Minnie Brown's house we heard about a hundred shots. Of cou'se, dey claim de sheriff shot him [for trying to run away].

CALLIE CASSOWAY:

When we got ter George Josephson's place, like I tol' you, we heard 'em shootin' Jim Press, only den we don' know what de shootin' wuz. We don' know dey wuz killin' Jim Press.

Jim Press, like I tol' you, wuz shot in de hip, ground all up, a syrup jar wuz drove inter his hip, an' he wuz left lyin' dat way from 11 A.M. De gang tol' his sister, Virginia Grayson, dey gonna take him to his daughter. Dis wuz about twelve o'clock when de crew done gone back theah from mah house.

Dey took Jim Press up to Ralph Dealer's farm—to his house. Den dey hunt for Henry, mah husband. Like I tol' you, I let on he done gone ter Wayland to mill. Our boy Nathan come an' tol' him about de gang, an' he lit out toward Deedsburg so dey don' never find him.

Dey took Jim Press up on de hill near ter Dealer's house. Dey strung him up to a tree and poured a hundred shots into him.

After dey shoot him, dey throwed him into a ditch.

De gang went on ter Wayland. Dey sent a truck fo' Jim Press's body and brung it to Wayland. J. W. Lakin, he done raise Jim Press from a baby, so dey ask him if he want de body.

He say, Since de mob done kill him, dey can bury him.

So dey sent for Jake Daley, a colored man, to do de buryin'. He done it, an' took Jim Press out in de swamp. When Daley came back, he askt: "When you gonter have another nigger down theah to be killed?"

Jake, he does all such buryin' an' gits paid for it.

GLADYS GOODMAN (a very jovial slim Negress about thirty-five):

I'm Walt Goodman's wife. We live on Mr. Lakin's other place. Later on de gang come down theah and tore our house open. No one wuz home an' dey smashed everything up.

Before dat I wuz home. A man from Bu'mingham wuz theah on de porch to buy tu'keys so I look fo' Walt.

I start through de swamp fo' de store on Dealer's place—Benny McArthur runs it, but it belongs to Dealer. Dat's whar dey git de gang together, and Benny wuz de one who got hit up, I guess, 'cause Vaughn Dealer or his pa done tol' him to.

When I got theah, with some others, we seen de gang, an' dey cussed us out. Mr. Lakin wuz theah and tol' us ter go on off ter look for a mule.

"Yo' sho' dat's what you want?" I askt him.

He said yes, so we go on off. After a while we come back and I tol' Lakin, "We foun' de mule but whar's mah dah'key?"

Vaughn Dealer turn aroun' on Lakin and called him "a nigger-lovin' son-of-a-bitch."

Later on dey beat up Light Chambers, he's our preacher-man, and wounded him. He went to see Mr. Wales, de mayor, and so Wales, he go over to A. D. Zimmer's house [Zimmer was in the gang] and complain.

Dat sho' made Vaughn Dealer mad, so he come back with de others an' tol' Chambers to come along. He start to put some clothes on ter civer his wounds, but Dealer say, "You don' need no clothes."

On a little road off de highway, de one dat goes up to Laura Rogers', dey shot him and slit his belly open.

Poser Pastor, de uncle of Lughead Pastor (he own a big farm and wuz with de gang), said Lughead tol' him Light Chambers ast, he bein' a preacher-man, before dey kill him, he want a chanct to pray. Dey let him kneel down in de road an' pray, an' dey shot him right when he wuz a-prayin'.

"He wuz de hardest damn somebody to scare you ever did see," said Lughead.

CALLIE CASSOWAY:

De same gang met up with Light Chambers on de road and whip him so he cain't hardly walk, den dey turn him loose. He's our pastor, an' he wuz helpin' with de Union. He gone on home an' say he wuz goin' to see Charles Wales, de mayor.

Somebody tol' the mob crew, an' it went back an' dey tol' Chambers dey wuz goin' to take him to a doctor-man. Dey took him five miles out and slice his belly open. Dat wuz de same night of de day dey killed Jim Press.

Befo' he die—he's a Methodist preacher-man—dey made him pray. One of de gang say, "De damn nigger sure put up a good prayer befo' he die an' he don' be nothin' scared."

Mr. John Simpson, de mailman, foun' him dead de next mawnin'. De papers don' say a wo'd about it. He had a big family but dey wuz all married off.

Dey also got Norman Graves dat Thu'sday. He's an ol' man over eighty years old. Mr. Vaughn Dealer hit him in de head with a pistol. Graves, he put up his hand, so he done git his finger broke.

Dey foun' him at his home makin' baskets. Dey said he wuz with de Union.

VIRGINIA GRAYSON:

Norman Graves live half a mile back of Mr. Lakin's. He wuz eighty years old. Vaughn Dealer broke one of his fingers. He hit him in de haid. "You old gray son-of-a-bitch," Dealer said.

He took both Graves' shotguns. Dey tore up de bed.

Mr. Lakin got Graves' two shotguns back, but he cain't get ours back.

MARY JANE GOODMAN (a comely young Negress of about twenty-five, very quiet and intelligent):

Jim Press, my husband and I wuz down at Henry Cassoway's house 'cause we'd been tol' better not be home dat day. We live on Ralph Dealer's plantation, an' we wuz tol' if we ain't gonter pick cotton for 35 or 40 cents a day, we better not be home nex' day.

Nex' day de landlords come down ter Henry's house. Jim Press had gone up dat mawnin' to feed his chickens—he was afraid dey'd sta've—an' he stopped in at his sister's house. He wuz shot down theah.

But de gang, which come on ter Henry's house, didn't know dat yet.

Dey ask Henry's wife, Callie Cassoway, whar Henry wuz. Den dey asked who wuz theah with her.

He told 'em Mary Jane Goodman, her sister-in-law (dat's me), and mah little seven-year-ol' girl.

Willie Cruickshank, he said to Callie when he heard mah name, "Dat's de son-a-bitch we've been lookin' fo'."

Dey made us stand in de middle of de flo' and asked about Union leaflets. We told him they wuzn't any theah.

Benny McArthur hit Callie across de nose I guess with a pistol, but she never tol' nothin'.

Den he tore all de drawers out of de dresser and throwed everything on de floor. He pulled de civers off de bed an' ripped de mattress an' found some leaflets. He looked at them.

Dey asked me whar the leaflets come from an' who belonged to de Union.

I tol' 'em I don' know anything about hit.

Den he tol' me to take mah clothes off, said he wanted "naked meat."

Vaughn Dealer doubled up a rope four times, and Benny McArthur—he's Dealer's sto'keeper, held my head down.

Dey beat me fifteen or twenty minutes and asked me again.

I said I don' have nothin' to lie about. I don' know nothin'.

Dey made me lie down again and beat me again about fifteen or twenty minutes.

"See if you know anything about it now. Bet when we get through with you, this time, you'll know."

Dey undoubled de rope and tied it around my neck and threw it over a j'ist. Dey hung me up fifteen or twenty minutes till I wuz unconscious.

Den dey let me down, and mah mind come back.

"If you don' know nothin' now," dey told me, "de limb'll git you next."

I tol' 'em I don' know nothin' about it. I j'ined the Union but I don' have no part in it."

Vaughn Dealer said, "If you'd tol' us that to begin with we wouldn't 've beat you like dat."

"Come on, both of you, an' go on over to your house till we give you 'structions to leave. It may be half an hour or two or three days, but you be theah. We ain't gonter bother you, and we ain't gonter let no one else bother you."

Walking out of the house, Benny McArthur started to grab hold of mah little girl, den said, "Aw, what'n hell does she know about de Union?"

We went on home and stayed an hour and a half till we saw de gang leavin'. I tol' my sister-in-law I don' want to stay 'roun' hyar. Dey may kill us.

"But dey may kill us if we leave," she said.

I sent de little girl to mah aunt to stay an' den I and Callie went into de swamp. We stayed in de woods from an hour to a half hour befo' sundown. Other colo'd fo'k wuz theah.

Dey tol' us about Jim Press bein' shot. We went on out to Leedsburg an' tol' Mr. George Mason [White] an' he said if anything more happened to tell him. The sheriff done tol' him all wuz quiet, and they wasn't gonter do nothin' to de colo'd fo'k.

"I'm not going back out theah," I tol' him.

"If you're afraid, I'll give you a place to stay," he said.

They wuz guards all around Leedsburg, so we went to another friend's home and stayed. Friday morning we went back fu'ther towa'd home. Friday night we stayed in a vacant house, nyar de station. Callie an' her husband, Henry, met us theah Satiday, an' we all git on ter de train and come up hyar to Bu'mingham. Hyar we've been pickin' peas. We left everything. We ain't got anything now.

Callie Cassoway:

Saturday mawnin' the week Jim Press wuz killed, Henry an' I left the county, we left all we own behind, and come to Bu'mingham.

Afterwa'ds I went on back ter get de furniture. I wuz told we dassn't come back for two years. I had ter sell de cow for next ter nothin', suh.

HENRY CASSOWAY:

In de six months since I left I ain't managed to git maw'n five days' work. I couldn't pay de $6 a month rent on our shack, so we had ter move to this hyar shack. We ain't got no water hyar on de premises, and so I got to go a long way off to git some from our brother-in-law.

Every year in the South many such murders occur, and the bodies are dumped in the swamps, or they are buried by extra-official Black undertakers. No words of the crimes reach the press. No one is ever punished.

This is the story of men, White men, brave American men, so low and contemptible, they would murder human beings to keep from paying them more than thirty-five cents for a twelve-hour day, for bending over picking cotton in the hot sun of Alabama.

This is not Hitler's Germany. It is the U.S.A. This is not the heart of Africa. It is "civilized" America. To the Negroes we have been doing the same thing Hitler does to Jews and Catholics, only worse. Have the Jews ever lifted their voices up strongly for the Negroes? Have the Catholics ever lifted their voices up strongly for the Negroes? In the South the Catholic Church enforces the Jim Crow law in its temples—the only place in the world where that mighty institution makes human discriminations in the sight of God. A common penance for Whites is to make them go pray on the Negro benches. Hitler's mistreatment of the Jews is the passing story of a day. America's mistreatment of the Negroes is a story of generations. They too have few property rights, are ruled by continuous terror, are despoiled, beaten and murdered. America must come clean before she reprimands Hitler.

With variations, the story of Alabama is the story of the greater part of the South. The political and economic set-up is similar. The tragedy of race relations is similar. The degradation of the mass of the rural population, Black and White, is similar.

It is all part of the story of the American earth misused, and of the foul growths that spring from earth misused.

CHAPTER XIX

RED CLAY

Martha Mason, a millionaire heiress of Louisiana, owns, among other things, a big estate over near Lake Charles. She is a tall, slim, attractive woman, the embodiment of the best that southern charm implies, elegant, tasteful and modish in dress, cultivated in manners and in knowledge.

To spend Thanksgiving I motored with her and other friends across the southern end of Louisiana from New Orleans, over the fine concrete highways that spell out the name of Huey Long and political bossism.

Her tall, stately colonial mansion, with its baronial hall, stands in the midst of a luxurious garden. No note of ostentation, but good taste and cheery comfort pervade her establishment.

The Negro servants bespoke the gracious paternal family tradition of the South; they emanated an air of contentment and largess. The result was competence, friendliness.

A buxom and jovial Negress served breakfast to me in bed. Before taking later meals, we gathered in the little cozy sewing room to have a cocktail and chat; there we also had tea. Meals themselves, if formal, perfectly appointed, were animated affairs; none of the actual mechanics of the service intruded on one's consciousness. There was none of the parvenu, the *nouveaux riches*, which makes the table service more important than either the meal or human relationships. Dining there represented the same naturalness that marks equally the mealtime of the poverty-stricken or of the English aristocracy. If ordered with care, that care was partly that everything might be taken quite for granted.

Martha Mason's philanthropy is wide; she is one of the mainstays of one of the departments of a local university.

Interested in ethnology, she has organized expeditions which she has accompanied into the wilds of a number of countries.

Hardships, heat, primitive surroundings—these she accepted with the same naturalness as when presiding over her own dinner table.

The baronial entrance and wide hall, which swept the whole length of her home, carried still the aroma of the gaiety and ease of the Old South, now nearly everywhere utterly bankrupt.

Martha Mason is really considerably outside the old plantation group of the deep South. Her estate, which extends as far as the eye can see, is largely devoted to cattle raising, which in itself embodies all the old traditions of a free and easy America. On her property are numerous oil wells. Undeveloped salt mines and sulphur deposits also lie there. Thus, economically more varied, her estate has been projected easily into more modern activities.

Hence, here on the Mason plantation something of life at its idyllic best still survives unshaken. The estate is reminiscent of pioneering days in the first era of wealth and temporary stabilization. And the life represented by this estate happens in this wise to be one of the happy examples of a successful combination of the America of bold ambition and achievement, with wealth and true culture.

This was all made possible, not merely by the initiative of the Masons, but also by the very development of America, by the ascending curve of our civilization, of general material comfort and increasing population. In fact, it cannot be understood apart from the rest of America; it is an oasis in the desert of rural economic debasement in great areas of our country. It conserves its privileged position because it is considerable to one side of the march of forces that sooner or later are likely to shake this nation. At the same time it can be understood only in connection with what has happened to much of the land and the people in America, particularly of the South.

Most of the crumbling aristocracy of the deeper South has a pathetic refusal to face the modern world or its immediate realities, and, though frightened by the handwriting on the wall, will not accept the facts of depleted soil and narrowing economic avenues that lead to catastrophe. The plantation South lives in an economic world that is vanishing and a mental world that long since vanished. Often the plantation class now substitutes arrogance, narrow-mindedness and ignorance for its older values—for it refuses to admit its fear or to realize its own mistakes.

Mostly it is caught helpless in the backwash of modern industrialism, which represents northern absentee capital and which, instead of reintegrating southern society, introduces new ingredients of dissolution, throws the incapacity of the dying era into sharper relief, disrupts peaceful order, and introduces new dangerous forces.

Northern absentee capital reaches out inevitably to narrow the margin of profit of the plantation class. A few "aristocrats," it is true, have themselves turned industrialist, have learned to build factories and bridges. Even so, their industrial participation is mostly meager; it rests not so much upon personal ability as upon traditional political control, favoritism, graft; upon wealth and privilege rather than efficiency. These later days even that political control has been slipping into the hands of the demagogues, from Tillman and Watson down to Huey Long and Talmadge, mostly scrub-pine folk, who sway the ranks of the poor Whites but give them little but heavier debts, and secretly play the hand-in-glove game with northern industrialists. The southern plantation owners are in the same predicament as the older "aristocracy" of such colonial countries as Cuba, doomed to extinction, all but those few supple enough to become associates or instruments of modern capital

Let us turn to the other side of the somber picture.

It is raining in Alabama—all through the Black Belt—sluices of it day after day. The unpainted tenant-farmer shacks totter forlornly on the steep sides of deeply eroded fields or in red mud on the edge of loblolly swamps beyond the ragged stalks of the previous year's cotton crop—the crop that during the pickers' strike brought murder to a dozen counties.

We have come for miles along the slick cement highways, new but here and there already cracking up—down from Birmingham past blue and tan company huts of the iron and smelter workers, on into share-cropper country. Such a rarity is any halfway decent cottage with even a five-year-old coat of paint that we point and exclaim, like small boys counting white horses. It was the same dreary spectacle of unpainted broken-window shacks all the way down from Chattanooga to Decatur, where the Scottsboro boys were sentenced in an arena of ugly hate. It was the same from Decatur to Birmingham. It is the same everywhere we have been.

Now, further south, we pass through wretched towns with frowsy end-century brick buildings and clap-board stores with ugly high peeling foreheads branded with the sign of petty commercial Cain. A few blocks of smug little homes lift clean chins above the surrounding welter of unpainted hovels and privies, of squalor, garbage, dead dogs, mud holes and human degradation. Oh so red is the rose in Alabama!

We bump over the cobbled business streets of Montgomery, the one-time capital of the Confederacy and still proud of its fight to preserve human slavery. We circle drunken flimsy mill shacks, set on red brick stilts along foul ditches, broken privies a few feet from the back doors. Pale, anemic White children drag bare-footed through the mud. It is dusk now; snow is falling; faint kerosene lights glimmer through wide chinks in the walls. Snow, and the thermometer down to nearly zero! Blessed be the new industrial South!

It is raining again. We bump out past the old Capitol through the nice part of town, several long well-paved avenues of comfortable homes, an occasional white-columned colonial mansion. Then bump, bang, we bounce into red slush among shabby houses: this is the best "nigger" section, so why should the streets be paved?

We swing through the swank Cloverdale development, past baronial estates, past Kilby prison where for years the Scottsboro boys waited in the death house, and then, once more—the endless monotony of broken country shacks. Cement gives way to gravel as we reach Tallapoosa County; gravel gives way to slippery red mud. Soon our car is painted with it, as though bathed in blood. The shacks grow worse and worse.

We pass abandoned farms. In this section thirty-five per cent have been abandoned, a process that began over fifty years ago—a long story of agricultural decay, of social collapse, of human degeneracy, *Tobacco Road* style, with still worse to come.

On a steep hill our car sticks deep in the red mud. While our driver goes over the crest in the driving rain to get help, we read the *Montgomery Advertiser* that not so long ago called the Scottsboro boys "gorillas." The rotogravure section spouts sleek night club and actresses' legs and a whole page of succulent models displaying fashion changes in inner female garments, but of significant items about this region—torn by a five years' struggle, bloody and otherwise, between share-croppers and plantation owners—all we find are that as a result of a prize contest three suits of red flannels have been discovered in the little mill town of Opeleika and that in Auburn the Daughters of the American Revolution are to meet for bridge.

Share-croppers, holding a secret meeting in a large shack in the woods, came to pry us out of the mud. They have come from all over Talapoosa and adjacent counties in ragged clothes, mostly on foot through the driving downpour and bitter cold and ankle-deep mud; some will not get home till nearly dawn without having eaten all day. Some of them have hands and faces cracked and raw, ulcered and scabbed with pellagra.

We put up at the home of one of the most prosperous Negro farmers. His shack has two thin board rooms, opening on to an open-air center passageway—typical construction. The shed-like kitchen leaks. The fireplace is neatly whitewashed and there is plenty of fire-wood, but the cracks in the floor suck in the icy air; the cleated doors have holes. Everything, though, is spick and span. The three beds—a shotgun is racked above one and a red douche bag hangs beside another—have clean white spreads. On the plain board walls are a few commercial calendars and family photographs. Shabby clothing and neckties hang on nails. We spy a bottle of Hearts-of-Love hair-dressing, a hair waver, and two papier-mâché dogs on the mantel. There is an ancient sewing machine and an old-fashioned organ around which we later sing and dance. There are twig-broom, cane-bottom chairs, a shoe-rack, a weekly farm paper, a daily workers' paper, a Sears, Roebuck catalogue. A rusty cat yawns. Out in the yard are chickens, ducks, guinea hens, two cows, two mules, but no privy. Water is drawn hand over hand from a well, quite likely contaminated.

These folk eat twice a day, milk, corn-bread, sow-belly, fat-back and sorghum. Most folks don't have milk so they get pellagra. The place, humble though it be, is a palace of opulence compared to those of the poor White and Negro share-croppers round about. . . .

For Alabama is dying thrice over. It has suffered the lingering death due to the persistence of that social malady, the old plantation system, with its barely camouflaged feudalism and serfdom. It has suffered the malady of the depression, the temporary collapse of monopoly capitalism, worse in this colonial fringe of the nation than in many a truly industrial region. Birmingham was one of the hardest hit cities in the country. The breakdown of industrial feudalism aggravated the earlier agricultural breakdown. Even so, the state faces a third and more serious death: the breakdown of the cotton-growing industry. Already the cotton yield in this state is lower per acre than even in worn-out Georgia; it is far below the national average; and with new mechanical devices, such as the cotton-picker, coming into use, which demand large flat areas, with new rayon fibers coming into existence, with the foreign markets mostly forever gone, this whole central and northern region of Alabama faces the prospect of having its one important cash crop wiped out of existence, whereupon the existing chaos will become complete.

The present sad situation in the Alabama Black Belt, somewhat worse than that in numerous other rural areas throughout the country, is the product of a hundred years of agricultural "rugged individualism." Due here to the plantation system, slavery, land monopolization, many farms were early taken up which were incapable of yielding, under the most just of economic set-ups, a decent standard of living. And the plantation system has helped deteriorate even the good soil. The tenant has no incentive to terrace his land against erosion, to guard against soil exhaustion, or in any way to improve the acres he farms. He does not even take care of physical improvements. It is better to tear a board from the floor and keep warm for the moment, because he does not know when he will be kicked off. The Federal Resettlement Administration has stated that at least

75,000,000 acres of existing utilized crop-lands in the nation are utterly unsuited to agriculture, despite the great abandonment of farms and the increasing conversion of farmers into tenants and share-croppers. But perhaps the worst sores in the country are the submarginal cotton lands from Georgia to Arkansas.

This region faces an economic shift of such magnitude as few large regions of the world have ever suffered. To the present decay, despair and violence which characterize large sections of the South, will likely be added economic chaos of fearsome proportions, regardless of any recovery in the nation at large. This is what makes the struggle of the Share-Croppers' Union such a tragic uphill fight. This is what made the Resettlement effort in those parts, however admirable its intentions, seem so puny and futile.

Immediate rather than fundamental remedies have been mostly sought. Crop restriction helped temporarily to maintain prices and thus save the commission-men, speculators, and the banks, with mortgages on stored pools. Farmers were compensated for reducing the acreage cultivated, though in the South, in diverse ways, this compensation has all gone into the pockets of the large landowners, thus leaving the cropper and tenant in a more desperate plight than almost any agricultural population in the world, while at the same time buttressing up the existing unjust system, giving it improved powers of survival.

Though the Resettlement work of the government, the most effective and valuable federal undertaking, has been mostly abandoned, knifed by Secretary Wallace, it is still worth noting its purposes and the failure of its application in Alabama.

Three major purposes motivated the "land utilization" projects: the conservation and fullest use of land resources; the assistance of poverty-stricken dependents on unproductive land to sell out and obtain more profitable locations; third, to reorganize local public finances no longer able, because of the impossibility of collecting adequate taxes, properly to maintain schools and other public services.

Thus in Alabama four dots were put on the map where such resettlements were to be effected. Two of these were truly agricultural projects; that of Tuskegee, largely a Negro project, was certainly one of the most hopeful in the country. For this experiment it was planned to acquire a hundred thousand acres.

But soon the proposed area gradually shrank. After years of delay, option was finally taken on about 9,000 acres. But the permission to buy even this reduced acreage was not finally given.

Even had such a limited Hull House enterprise finally been carried to completion, it would have benefited only 139 families! Obviously this sort of piddling was not going to solve the problem of nearly two million people residing in rural Alabama, but at least it would have provided a good yardstick. It would have been a beginning for something that sooner or later—unless we wish bloody revolution—must be done.

Instead, stricken families, abandoned in the careless begin-and-never-finish of so many New Deal efforts, were put on to erosion work for $19 a month. Thereafter, instead of attempting to help the farmers cease being subjects of charity and become of productive value to the nation, we utilized them at less than coolie wages to improve plantation properties gone to rack and ruin that the owners might again secure tenants to destroy anew the land which the American citizen and forced labor were paying to retrieve. I use "forced labor" advisedly. It was, through poverty and exploitation, as forced as any with bayonets in the Soviet Union or Germany.

The more fundamental program—now abandoned—was evolved because of general rural destitution in the country. In 1934—and in most places in the South conditions since have not appreciably improved—a total of at least 4,500,000 rural inhabitants were being kept from starvation by handouts of local, state and federal governments or by rural rehabilitation work. The situation has not appreciably changed. Many of these are still migrating from place to place, camping out, living in frightful economic and sanitary conditions. This is particularly true of the Alabama Black Belt.

Immediate Rehabilitation—to bridge over actual starvation and ruin—soon proved to be largely another grim joke. In Alabama such rehabilitation got under way in 1934 by a federal commission "seriously interested in this Titanic struggle for existence which constitutes a dramatic chapter in our modern civilization." The commission was made up of Donald Cromer, one of the cotton textile kings of Alabama (an industry in which women's wages at times have been as low as $4.00 a week); H. C. Ryding, ex-president of the Tennessee Coal and Iron Company (and the coal and iron companies of Birmingham have terrorized workers with armed thugs to keep their wages down); and the president of Tuskegee, the Negro college (under whose administration two wounded Negro share-croppers, who showed up for treatment, were treacherously turned over to the police); and other industrialists and plantation owners. Actual administration was put in the hands of plantation owner R. K. Greene, who for his good work for the state, was later promoted to handle Rehabilitation in four states. The petty local officials, with this set-up, were naturally typically southern landowners, local rotarians, flat-tire Democrats, and others, some well known for their Ku Klux Klan activities and many of them in varying degrees responsible in part for the agricultural ruin and for the perpetuation of the system of human exploitation that had created it.

Under the Rehabilitation plan, the government became the landlord. It rented land from the owners and benefited them by paying them in immediate taxpayers' cash more than they had previously received after the end of the season and not usually for their best but their *worst* lands. This unfair rental, the government's new ward, of course, was required to pay back later. Thus the plantation owners, as a rule, got more ready cash out of it than tenants or share-croppers. The government, however, did then provide its tenants with food credits at the highbinder plantation stores, permitting them to survive, but again putting the fluid money into the hands of the owners and building up more unfair obligations against the croppers. Fortunately the tenant, though paying such prices, was not burdened with the customary twenty per cent interest charge. The authorities also bought him plow, seed, fertilizer and a work animal; for Negroes, a steer, and for Whites, all of whom refused to take steers, a mule. Naturally all these costs were charged up against the tenant, and if at times excessive, on the other hand, though he paid high rent, he was relieved from having to share his crop with the landlord.

The Negroes under this plan were known as "steer farmers." According to the official report, the steer is "the orneriest of all work critters," and doubly so because most were wild and too young to be of much use. They required more time breaking them in than in plowing. One poor farmer's steer bolted through two fences, plow and all, and was never heard of again. "But the acid test," declared the official report, "of the applicant's sincerity of purpose is his willingness to accept a steer." Just why the same "sincerity of purpose" was not demanded of White farmers, the report did not explain.

"I'd rather be in the penitentiary than be a steer farmer," one Negro rehabilitation tenant told me.

The steer farmer had to do triple the work, and many even mourned for the days when they were "furnished" and abused by the plantation owner; for Greene, in charge of this work, declared openly that the rehabilitation farmer had to be kept *below* the share-cropper level—and that was already close to the lowest level known among human beings anywhere on earth—apparently so as not to interfere with holy private initiative by plantation owners.

Through mud and rain I walked with Reece Graves to his miserable one-room shack with its gaping holes in floor, wall and roof. Graves was a big six foot, two hundred pound fellow from Chambers County. He can neither read nor write, but is intelligent and independent in spirit—a terrible handicap for a Negro in the South. A hard worker, he brought in bumper crops on the very inferior land the government temporarily provided him with.

During 1934, although Mr. Graves received a very young steer, he worked industriously to feed his family and pay off his government debts. The authorities took all his cotton, his government rent and parity checks under the A.A.A. acreage restriction. Though he never could get any exact statement, he was told he had cleared his debt. At least he had managed to feed his brood of nine.

In 1935 he got a bigger steer, some fertilizer and seed and for a few months a check for $6.00 and was given about eight acres of very inferior land for $15 rent, a conventional sum, to be advanced the landowner by the government. Graves also worked 66 days on the government erosion project to pay off the rent. During that time, he claimed he drew only $2.40 for victuals for himself and family, and the remaining $82.02 presumably paid his indebtedness; but presently a landlord, though the government was the renter, demanded $24 more directly from Graves for wood, water, pasturage and houserent, previously unheard-of charges. Such charges the landlords now tried to make stick everywhere, so that in some cases the rehabilitation farmer was made to pay twice and three times over merely in rent. The owners also stepped in past the federal authorities to impose imaginary debts and obligations. If the tenant became obstreperous, he was chased off, despite his contract with the federal government. The federal administrators, themselves often local well-to-do farmers or plantation heads, did nothing to stop such abuses. Many "rehabilitated" farmers, in accepting government help, merely exchanged one bad master for two worse masters.

Graves protested to the authorities against the extra charge (this necessitated a long trip), but was "cussed out," being told that "a nigger who won't pay his water rent, etc., is no account." Graves didn't have a cent, because the government had taken all his cash crop, his wages and his federal payments, but Negro neighbors, almost as poor as himself, gave him work to make an initial payment to the landlord of $9 so he wouldn't be evicted from government-leased land by the original proprietor.

Presently the Federal Farm Agent demanded that Graves sign a mortgage on all his possessions. Graves, believing himself paid up, refused. The agent next said Graves had ten days to get off the land, but that he would make "a fair settlement" by taking everything he owned "except his 'taters." Graves demanded an accounting. This he never got. His new boss, the U. S. government, treated him high-handedly just like the old landlord.

Previously Graves had sent various protests directly to government offices in Montgomery. Nothing came of them. On one occasion, he claims his letter never got out of Chambers County, for within an hour the farm agent, a typical southern White farmer, was "bawling him out" for writing, and also bragging to neighbors that "niggers" who protested wouldn't even be left with bed and chairs; and he told in chest-inflated fashion how unavailing had been even the special federal investigation of his own acts "by that sonnabitch of a northern man who came down here and looked into his business."

Ten days after the federal agent's notice, the sheriff came in the dead of night and took Graves' twin plow, two plow stocks, two steers, harness, two fifty gallon barrels full of syrup, a bale of cotton seed, 400 bales [pounds?] of fodder, 40 bushels of corn [this list I copied from the official order]: and, as Graves added, also "even the chillun's braid [bread]." Ten bushels of corn were left so Graves' family wouldn't starve to death during the next few days.

"If you don't like it, get yourself a lawyer," the sheriff told him.

"Me go hiring one of yo' men? How's I gonter pay him anyhow?" retorted Graves, which reveals he was a very uppish "nigger." Any southern Negro who acts like an independent human being is "uppish" or "ornery" or "a bad nigger" or "a no-account nigger."

Graves had to move his sick wife and eight children through snow and ice—the thermometer that day stood at 4 degrees—to a little thin-walled shack owned by a Negro friend. All his supplies for the winter were gone; his work animals gone; he had nothing. Before he was "rehabilitated" by the federal government he did have something. The authorities, however, were generous enough to offer him a job in Montgomery at $19 a month, five hours away by car.

At a reasonable estimate, the government took away from him at least $140 worth of goods; also it has made no accounting on his cotton, three bales totaling 1,525 pounds, which at the guaranteed 12 cents, would net him $183.

According to the official report, the average cost of rehabilitating a farmer was slightly more than $90. In this average was figured in the cost of White farmers, which often ran up to $180 or more, or less than merely the value of Graves' cotton, not to mention the work payments. What Graves actually got, I don't know. He could never get a statement from his new government bosses, any more than he could from the old White plantation owner. I had no access to his account. But undoubtedly the federal books were made to balance nicely, for the goods taken from Graves, if sold, would scarcely bring what they are really worth. In fact Graves' steers were sold at the first crossroads "to them Bradley boys," he does not know for how much. This was customary procedure. Then the government would go out and buy steers and other goods at market prices for another batch of farmers, in some cases perhaps the very same goods they just sacrificed at a song.

There were ugly stories about how local White farmers bagged the confiscated supplies of "the swept-clean" rehabilitated farmers at a song; how rehabilitation supplies, part of each consignment, were dropped off by the wayside at doors where they did not belong. In some counties, since getting their federal jobs, the farm agents, themselves hard-pressed previously, began buying up big tracts of land all around.

I asked Graves about others in the same fix. Did the authorities merely single him out because he was independent and a member of the Share-Croppers' Union? He insisted they had cleaned up practically all the rehabilitated farmers in his county in the same way. "Go ask Mrs. Otis Anders. She worked on the erosion project 66 days, she turned over three bales of cotton and half a bale of seed. Ask Ernest Holloway who got five children. . . . Ask Johnny Robertson. The sheriffs came in the dead of night, and he with a sick wife and kids and dey had no place to go, and she left sitting out there in the cold and the wides. They took every single thing he own and three bales of cotton. . . . Ask Mr. Robins who was looking for a month for a roof to squat under. . . . Ask Warren McDonald in Waverly across the railroad tracks. . . . Ask Mrs. Makins, she won't be flirtin' aroun' and rollin' her eyes an' bouncin', she'll tell you right straight what dey done to her."

I talked to some he mentioned and many others. In some counties, the process was less drastic, but essentially Rehabilitation, even when honestly administered, because of its adherence to old plantation abuses and other factors, as practiced in the Black Belt counties of Alabama, was a snare and a tragic joke. It was a pouring of water into a sieve. The well-intentioned bureaucrats who administered it apparently had no appreciation that the "rehabilitated" farmer in any case remained the prey of the old system which promptly took everything away that might not have been taken by the federal authorities; that this was even more certain to happen when local administration was left in the hands of local plantation owners and politicians, who at bottom hated anything done for the White share-croppers, and considered it even worse to do anything for the Negroes.

Toward the end of 1934 Federal Rehabilitation Administrator R. K. Greene boasted that 80 per cent of the farmers' federal debts had been paid—this in about six months' time! Shortly afterward he declared that not a single rehabilitation farmer in the whole state owed a dime. This was probably true, because those still in debt had been cleaned out, lock, stock, and barrel, in the style of Graves. Everything they possessed having been taken to liquidate their accounts, these unfortunate farmers were written off as "rehabilitated," and a new batch of human misery was fed into the mill. Such methods made the statistical record in Washington look better.

In any case the showing was truly remarkable. The gross cash income per family hereabouts rarely exceeds $150 a year; most families see not one red cent of this. One share-cropper to whom I talked was worried because in six months he had not been able to pay off his grocery bill of nine cents. A study of conditions in Gorgas in northern Tuscaloosa County, made by Dr. V. M. Sims and an associate of the state university for the Tennessee Valley Authority, shows that in this more favored hill settling the average gross income for White tenant families is $144 and for Negroes $148. Conditions are much worse in the Black Belt, and the rehabilitation farmers, almost without exception, got the worst lands—exhausted, eroded, stony acres which the landlords otherwise would have found it difficult to rent. The federal rehabilitation farmer had to work his head off for the little food credited to him at plantation stores—in amount and quality "scarcely wo'th the trouble to go an' tote it home"—and lived mostly on coarse unleavened corn bread and syrup. In return he had the doubtful privilege of coming to own an "ornery" steer and a plow, which in most cases, especially in Chambers County, he has had to turn back to the federal authorities or, the year following, to the landlord.

R. K. Greene described the rehabilitation policy as that of "learning to crawl before you walk." Most of his clients crawled with their bellies closer to the ground than ever. He boasted of his record in inducing successful belly-crawling. One glowing pap story told how a noble Negro farmer with nineteen in his family made a success by hitching himself to the plow and having one of his boys drive him. Another canned story concerned a poverty-stricken rehabilitation farmer who survived the first year and as a result would be able to have an evening meal of hot biscuits and syrup, after which he would "contentedly munch goobers" (peanuts). Hot biscuits, if not especially good for children, are a slight improvement over unleavened corn bread; and a peanut-muncher in Alabama is apparently considered the height of blessed prosperity. But there was something wrong when many rehabilitation farmers, though they produced a good crop and took outside work at every opportunity, faced the winter with a few bushels of corn and little chance of employment.

At the beginning of 1935 George Hawkins, a Negro share-cropper in Tallapoosa County in the Alabama Black Belt, was one of five tenants on a hundred-acre tract rented by the Federal Resettlement Administration from an absentee landlord and sublet in small patches at $50 a year each, three times the ordinary rent. The land, moreover, was the worst in the vicinity, full of ruts, stumps, and stones. Mr. Hawkins had to work hard indeed to put it in shape for planting. But if the land was bad and the rent high, he was to have the benefit of federal assistance.

No one had ever been concerned about the share-croppers before except the Share-Croppers' Union, and that had caused bloodshed. But now the family received $14 a month and had a ton of fertilizer, a sack of soda, a plow stock, and actually a mule instead of a steer. Hope was spreading its golden wings. Unfortunately the mule turned out to be "just ready to git home and die," which it did, and he was charged for it. Hawkins was then given a steer, too young to do much work.

Nor was an ordered budget easy to manage because after two months the payments from the government were cut to $10; after six months they abruptly ceased but were as abruptly renewed for October and November. Yet after all, $108 was probably more real cash than Hawkins had ever received before in his life in any single year. Out of it, it is true, he had to buy in certificates from specu-lators in order to sell his two bales of cotton. On the other hand, he grew sixty bushels of corn, which, if not taken away, would per-mit the family of fourteen to have its customary two-meals-a-day diet of corn bread and syrup.

The Hawkins family did not do so well, but the Federal Field Foreman told them he wanted them to stay on another year. Then, out of a clear sky, Hawkins received from the landlord himself a notice to vacate. He found a very dilapidated shack where he could begin farming on shares. Momentarily he expected the federal au-thorities to "clean him out." Hawkins' neighbors said he was thrown off because he was suspected of belonging to the Share-Croppers' Union. Fortunately, when he was finally evicted, he was generously provided with a temporary erosion job at $22 a month. Every day before dawn he had to walk eight miles in the mud and rain, and eight miles back in the dark. Hawkins didn't squawk; fourteen mouths to be fed. But Hawkins didn't feel very "rehabilitated."

Henry Mason, a Negro World War veteran in poor health, was also paying the excessive rent of $50 for a little piece of the same gullied land. He worked through 1934 under the Rehabilitation plan, then the government cleaned him out, taking his corn, plow lines, some fertilizer, fodder, so he would "git straight." He was told—and Greene also publicly stated—that his debt was cleared, though later it seemed there was still pending a charge of $54.

In 1935 Mason received some new supplies and $2.40 a week for his wife and five children. This continued for part of May and until the end of August, when they were "chopped off." They had received fertilizer, four "scooters," or plow-holds, an "old fifty-cent bridle," garden seed, ash potatoes, and every two weeks three to four cans of meat, "any ol' kinder meat," but "not enough ter walk after." They had also received an old mule, for which they were charged $60, but which "wuzn't wo'th $5." The Federal Field Fore-man promised he would see that they got a better one, but when an animal was most needed during plowing, he told them just "to scratch along." Since Mason by then couldn't work, his wife Callie, who was expecting a new baby, pushed the plow as deep as she could. The mule died in June. Callie didn't die because she is a strong woman and has magnificent courage.

After a while Callie and her husband stopped getting their living checks. The County Farm Agent had asked them to indorse their checks over to the Field Foreman in payment of debt. When they refused, since they needed the money badly, they were simply informed that the checks had never come. Suspected of being members of the Share-Croppers' Union, Callie and her family were ordered to vacate in October. But Callie fought eviction so strenuously, declaring she had a right to stay on the place until the end of the year, that the agent was "afraid to come around" to see her. Thereupon the farm administrator for the absentee landlord ordered her off, although it was the government that had paid her rent. Again she fought for her rights and stayed until January 1st. The place was then turned over to a man known to the Share-Croppers' Union as a stool-pigeon.

Just before Callie was evicted, her husband was taken to the veterans' hospital near Tuskegee. Callie herself was offered work on the erosion project at $22. She refused, pointing out that she couldn't walk eight miles to work and back with a nursing baby to care for. Her new place, taken on shares from a landlord—for Callie is known as a good worker—stood in a puddle of red mud, and while she explained these things to me in a quiet but intense monotone, her baby lay on the edge of one of her two ancient beds on which the rain was beating through holes in the wall. Callie did not feel "rehabilitated" either, but she was as cheerful as she could be with her husband in the hospital and only a few bushels of corn on hand.

She had to move all by herself on an icy day with the thermometer close to zero. That same day of her eviction, she received from F. N. Farrington, the Federal County Agent, with offices in Dadeville, a touching mimeographed circular. At the top was a picture of a sun rising over a hill and on either side were clusters of Christmas bells—rather unusual for a government communication. It read:

"Ring out the Old . . . Ring in the New . . . Happy New Year . . . Howdy and Happy New Year to Yours. . . .

"This beautiful Christmas season has been made happier for us by the thoughts of the fine friendships we have enjoyed among the farm people of Tallapoosa County."

Mr. Farrington worked hard to build up the landlords' organization, known as the Farm Bureau Federation. After the Share-Croppers' Union came into being, the Federation, amazingly enough, made a drive for Negro members, and even paid their $2 initiation fee for them. In Lowndes County, right after terrible lynchings, it even held a joint meeting of Blacks and Whites, to which a Negro speaker, a professor with a doctorate from Tuskegee, was invited. But when it came his turn to speak, he was merely asked to lead the croppers in "Swing low, sweet chariot." However, usually notices of the meetings of this organization carefully designated the race. On January 23, 1936, Mr. Farrington sent out calls for meetings, some White, some Black, to discuss legislation pending in the National Congress and to send wires to the President, Secretary Wallace, and Senators and Congressmen. The invitation did not state what the legislation was, though it was presumably to expand A.A.A. work. It was all a bit like a grocery man eating his own groceries.

Callie received a call to a meeting of colored people at Camp Hill, a site famous for its lynchings of colored share-croppers. She did not go. At the meeting Mr. Farrington and the local lynch-condoning landlords made speeches. Nothing was discussed from the floor; everything was passed upon by viva voce vote. Appended to the call that Callie received was one of Mr. Farrington's touching sentiments: "Usually after the darkest cloud the sun shines brightest, but sometimes the cloud lingers too long." Typical of Farrington's meetings was one at which the farm-measurement and apportion committee was chosen to determine the acreages for cotton-crop production. The farmers and share-croppers were presented with the names of four leading plantation owners, which were railroaded through.

Similar set-ups existed in all the Black Belt counties. The pattern, with minor variations, was as follows: the landlords controlled the federal acreage allotments; the "reduced" acreage they granted themselves was often far greater than any amount they ever cultivated. On the other hand, the acreage of the poor farmers and croppers was cut to the bone. Naturally the landlords then had more tax-free federal ginning certificates than they needed; the poor folk did not have enough for a crop to permit them to survive. Often the landlord also kept for himself the gin certificates allotted by the government for the croppers' minimum. The croppers then had to go to the larger landlords and buy, for from three to six cents a pound of cotton, certificates which had cost the possessor nothing and in addition to which he was receiving a bonus. Thus the planter often made as much as eighteen cents on part of his cotton, the cropper, only six cents.

The landlord had other advantages. The government was giving out rental checks of three and one-half cents per pound of lint cotton for the 40 per cent of production curtailed. These allotment checks went out at picking and selling times, and theoretically made it possible for the cropper to survive without exceeding his allotted acreage. At first the allotment checks were taken by the landlords; later when the checks were made out directly to the cropper, the landlord either forced him to indorse them over or simply forged his name. The government, of course, also guaranteed twelve-cent cotton, and sent out parity checks for any difference. These checks went the same route as the rental checks—into the landlord's pocket.

Will Wallace's new crop control bill, its administration left in the hands of local politicians and the dominant plantation owners, work any better?

The marketing of cotton is a White privilege and a landlord's privilege. The cropper has no say over the disposition of his crop, and only in recent years has he even dared be on hand to check up on the weighing of it. He has no means of knowing exactly when his cotton is sold, and he is charged fifty cents a month per bale for storage. The cropper rarely sees any cash, because the food and supplies he has been furnished at a 20 per cent interest charge usually eat up every cent.

With this arbitrary set-up the cropper has no chance to succeed. The land itself is nearly exhausted, eroded, and worthless. Still greater disaster for the cotton industry looms ahead so far as the Black Belt of Alabama is concerned. Even with the fairest economic set-up, even if the croppers were to receive the full product of their labor, they could scarcely make more than a semi-starvation living. The tragedy is that the federal government in its rehabilitation program adhered to all the old vicious landlord practices, and in fact strengthened them. Nor does the revised agricultural program of the government offer effective protection for the tenant farmer either. The New Deal has buttressed up the tottering, dying plantation system, the most destructive of all conceivable systems, right along the line. The poorer have gotten still poorer. Beggars' paradise has been temporarily sustained, the ultimate collapse merely postponed.

CHAPTER XX

GEORGIA: THE SWAN SONG OF UTOPIA

In no place has the American earth been more abused than in Georgia, the old utopia of Oglethorpe. No state east of the Mississippi River possesses more extensive land resources, and in no state have they been more wasted. Nowhere else has the depletion of the soil taken place so rapidly or so extensively. The ruining of soil has been paralleled by the deterioration of the people and the decay of social institutions, the breakdown of whole communities, the crumbling of education, group services, health, and much of the decency in many human relations. Nowhere else are ignorant race prejudices more pronounced. Orators love to talk about the decline of ancient Rome; our school teachers, instead of merely telling their pupils of the sad fate of Rome, should take them on a tour of rural Georgia, "the Cracker State."

The state has an area of 59,475 square miles, almost as large as the whole of New England, larger than England, and contains ten well-defined agricultural regions, each with distinct, if similar problems.

A very small section, mostly in Dade County in the far northwest corner of the state, part of the Cumberland Plateau, is of rolling sandstone cut by narrow limestone valleys and steep, rocky ravines. Difficult of access, not much used, the region has very shabby farms; income is low.

The rest of northwestern Georgia, the Valley and Ridge Belt (all or part of ten counties), is broad and low, with wide converging valleys between ridges and mountains. Farming is carried on in the residual and alluvial soils of the narrower valleys; the rough ridge land is

378

mostly too steep and broken up. Most of the farms are small, their proportion of land suitable for crops below average; few properties return a living to the owner.

The Blue Ridge region (all or part of fourteen counties in the northeast part of the state) is mostly mountainous with stony land so steep that the relatively good soils cannot be profitably used. Many people, scarcely able to survive, are stranded in this region.

Below this, extending nearly across the state, the narrow strip, known as the Blue Ridge Foothills, is very badly eroded and the incomes of the farmers are unusualy low.

The large Piedmont area, extending from border to border, is one of the most important agricultural areas of the state, but the one in which decline has been most rapid. The Upper Piedmont (all or part of twenty-two counties in the famous Black Belt), except where too steep, has good sandy and clay loams, the latter appearing wherever the sandy surface has been washed away. Bad erosion and soil depletion have caused great reduction in yield and extensive abandonment of the area.

The Lower Piedmont (thirty-five Black Belt counties) is steeper, even worse eroded, the surface soil mostly swept away, the whole badly cut up by gullies. Cotton, which must be planted later than in most places, is correspondingly more subject to boll weevil. Great abandonment of farm property has taken place.

The Sand Hills, an uneven Fall Line strip from border to border, has some productive sandy loams, among predominantly light-colored sands, but mostly it is wild land and forest, but little farmed.

The rolling Clay Hill area—a narrow ragged strip in the West Middle part of the state—is also very eroded, most of the surface soil gone, large tracts deeply cut by gullies. The major part of the region has been abandoned.

The Upper Coastal Plain with its light soils, though in places badly eroded, is still among the most productive parts of the southeastern United States.

The largest area of all is the Middle Coastal Plain, but though not so eroded, the soil has been so greatly leached out that constant excessive fertilization is required even to produce crops below the average yield of the rest of the United States.

The Coastal Flatwoods, a big lost corner area in southeastern Georgia, is mostly made up of deep swamps and tidal salt marshes and much soggy land requiring artificial drainage. Even then the land is rarely very productive. A turpentine country, mostly isolated, full of queer isolated folk, it is not important for agricultural purposes, though in some parts it has shown increased crop acreage. Negroes, desirous of independence, have there found submarginal lands which Whites do not wish to own.

Through Georgia runs part of the Black Belt, in which more than half the population is Negro, an area that strikes in a big crescent from Virginia to Texas, and which is described by Arthur F. Raper as that of "the richest soil and the poorest people." Here is the region of the White primary, Ku Klux Klanism, and Caucasian supremacy. The Negroes are disenfranchised, also a large share of the poorer Whites. The picture in Georgia, both in and out of the Black Belt, is such that one would have to travel far around the world to find similar decay. White supremacy in Georgia has little claim to be proud of itself.

When did the decline of Georgian agriculture begin? Hartman and Wooten, Raper, U. S. statistics, and several other reliable authorities give us the picture.

The maximum acreage and production in all Georgia was reached in 23 counties in 1880. During the next 50 years agricultural decline in those counties, declares Hartman and Wooten, varied from 64.6 per cent in Chattahoochee County to 10.6 per cent in Jefferson County. In all but 36 counties Georgia's peak agricultural development in crop acreage was reached in 1920 or earlier. In Troup County in the Lower Piedmont, on the border of Alabama, from 1900 to 1929, Raper tells us there was a 34.4 per cent decrease in the number of farms. In all but 40 counties of the state the peak had been reached by 1910. In only 36 counties was decline staved off until 1930. In only three counties (where the shrinkage of crop lands is due in part to the growth of Atlanta, Columbus and the establishment of the Fort Benning Military Reservation) can the retrogression be ascribed to other causes than the misuse of the soil, its exhaustion, its erosion, to the plantation system, or other agricultural factors.

Besides this general abandonment of farms or of crop acreage, at the present time more than three and a half million acres, some 37,000 farms, are submarginal, improper for farm use, incapable of returning a profit, let alone a decent livelihood, to those who attempt to cultivate them. And as the rural system grows harsher, as more people are robbed of a means of livelihood, they sneak into the swamps, the stony and waste land. "It is soil," remarks Erskine Caldwell, "that will not even grow a good crop of brown sedge."

Part of Georgia's difficulties has been due to the one-crop cash system. More than four-fifths of the harvested land in Georgia is planted to cotton or corn. But the cotton yield per acre, if not as low as in Alabama, is in most places below the average yield in the United States as a whole, while the costs of production, due in good part to the need of using fertilizer and also to ignorant and primitive methods, are greater than almost anywhere else in the United States. Georgia's inefficient production must compete not only with the productive, level areas of Texas, Oklahoma, Missouri and California, where highly mechanized production is in vogue and where soon the mechanical cotton-picker is to be used, but also with those still more productive areas in Brazil, the Paraguayan and Argentinian Chaco, Africa and elsewhere.

Corn is likewise an anti-economical crop for Georgia. The yield is lower per acre than any other state in the Union, well under half that of the United States as a whole. Costs of production, despite low wages, are higher than almost anywhere else.

A second important contributing cause of decay is the plantation system, with its tenantry and cropping, and all the adjuncts of class and race discrimination, economic privilege, and ruinous methods.

That system aggravates all evils. Its careless misuse of the soil, its inhuman exploitation, the Shylock credit practices which reduce the mass of tenant farmers practically to debt slavery, have led to ever-increasing human degeneration throughout most of the state. Absenteeism has been on the increase, and the amount of acreage coming into the hands of banks, mortgage companies and insurance companies has expanded.

The cash-crop system is further aggravated by the "furnish dealers." According to Moore, Giles and Campbell, the share-croppers and tenants in the two counties investigated had to pay 16 per cent on cash loans and 26 per cent on farm supplies, feed and foodstuffs. Purchases must be made at plantation stores—an abuse illegal in most civilized countries—where prices are jacked up to unreasonable levels.

In many counties the tenant is charged fifty dollars if he leaves a plantation, an amount practically impossible to raise (though he may be kicked off without notice and with no corresponding payment by the landlord). If he leaves without meeting his full debt (to which the fifty dollars is added) he is subject to imprisonment. Plain debt slavery. In no place, except in backward parts of Latin America or in darkest Africa, are such inhuman practices tolerated.

The result of all these conditions has been that the gross farm income for all crops sold or traded or used by the farm operator's family in 1928 with sixteen cent cotton, was less than $600 for 35.9 per cent of all farm operators in the state; this meant a net income of $300 or under. One can get an idea of the misery in the state those years when cotton has dropped to even the very excellent price of ten or twelve cents, and what it must be like in years of five cent cotton. Following 1928, even with high-priced cotton, the economic screws have been so tightened that tenants and share-croppers rarely get over $300. To aggravate natural difficulties, the boll weevil has also played havoc with much of the cotton production.

In Irwin County, 1924, the total value of farm crops and manufactured products was only $171.39 per capita. One person in 700 paid an income tax. In 1929, one person for every 1,743.

Though Montgomery County in the Middle Coastal Plain (Negroes 44.6 per cent of the population) has in Aley, a town of 400 people made up of plantation owners, merchants, and professionals, a place claiming to be one of the wealthiest towns in the country per capita, in 1924 the combined value of farm crops and manufactured products for the county was only $130.93 per person. In McIntosh County, in the Coastal Flatwoods (Negroes, 3,803; Whites, 1,258), the annual average per capita value of all farm, fisheries, and manufactured goods is only $95.46. Thomas County (Middle Coastal Plain, 48.9 per cent Negro), in 1930, had a per capita value of all products of $143.43; Greene County, $239; Macon County, $221.53, etc., etc.

As a result, tenancy and share-cropping have been on the increase; many former croppers have been crowded down into the day labor class; and in Georgia, the average rural wage, without housing or food, is but twenty-five to thirty-five cents. Only in parts of India and China and some other backward countries are such low levels equaled. More than two-thirds of all Georgia's farms are operated by tenants, and in large sections as many as 90 per cent. Nearly 60 per cent of these tenants are mere share-croppers. In Montgomery 70 per cent of all farmers in 1925 were tenants; among Negroes, 88.7 per cent.

Hartman and Wooten state in their *Georgia Land Use Problems:* "The prevalence of a one-crop system and large numbers of landless tenants and cropper farm operators with little hope of reward other than a bare subsistence living" is an index of the conditions resulting from "past and present land use practices," which bring about "seriously dislocated and disorganized rural communities in all parts of the State." They add: "The one-crop tenant and credit system is the curse of agriculture in the region. Landowners and owner-operators are by no means free from the crop lien and chattel mortgage, but practically all tenant cropper farmers are operating under this handicap. Furthermore, the tenants and croppers use a much greater percentage of their credit for living purposes than do the landlords and owners. Theirs is not an investment, but a stake to tide them over from year to year. This is not a business use of credit. It is a makeshift."

Another result of this brutal economic situation has been an intensification of racial discrimination.

The Negroes of Georgia are of Bantu and Sundan stock, among others, and are largely mixed with Arab (in Africa) and with Indians and Whites (in America). But, for his science, the average White Georgian does not go to anthropology but to the Bible. The prevalent

opinion is that the Negro is the result of God cursing Ham, turning
his skin black, and condemning him to perpetual servitude—"a servant of servants shall he be." If you attempt to argue that, even if the
Bible legend is accepted, it was Noah who, after his drunkenness,
cursed, not Ham, but Canaan, and that nowhere does the Holy Scrip-
ture mention that the cursed sons of Canaan are black of skin, the
Georgian will customarily retort angrily, as Raper observes, that he
doesn't want to have anything to do with anybody who does not
believe in the Holy Word of God. The average Georgian apparently
has sunk to a creature below interest in true knowledge, incapable of
reason, only of blind prejudice.

Such woefully ignorant folklore has been prevalent in Georgia for
a long time. We can judge of the cultural advance of the state during
the last century from the observations of William Howard Russell,
correspondent of the *London Times,* who visited there in 1861. From
supposedly cultured leaders of the state he heard the argument that
"the Bible says that he [the Negro] is a son of Ham, and prophesy
must be carried out in the rice swamps, sugar cane and maize fields of
the southern confederation."—Of course, to the profit of the Lord's
anointed, the White gentlemen of the plantations of the South. "It
is a flat blasphemy," added Russell, "to set yourself against it. . . ."
The southerners argued to him that "had cotton and sugar been
known, the Apostle might have been a planter," that St. Paul was a
slaveowner.

The average rural citizen of Georgia is such a poverty-stricken,
miserable and ignorant individual that the one attribute of superiority
to which he can still cling is his right to hate the Negro. The Negro
may be insulted with impunity, exploited, beaten up, without
White abuser, as a rule, ever being punished. Frequently the White
can even murder Negroes with impunity. Arthur Raper begins his
Tragedy of Lynching by pointing out that in 1930 more Negroes
were lynched in Georgia than in any other state. Even in the most
flagrant cases of White aggression, the mere fact of being White
is a great advantage in escaping due punishment. Raper tells of two
White men who attacked and murdered a Negro taxi driver and
wounded his companion. "At the trial the defense lawyers argued

that, being a Negro, the taxi driver was a potential rapist of White women. Capitalizing this and similar prejudices, they got the murderers off with a sentence of but five years each. One of these lawyers is now a Congressman, while the other holds an important county office."

All institutions deny the Negro opportunities even as minimum as those of the poorest, most ignorant White cropper. The whole financial, educational, social, political and religious set-up, all institutions, maintain the existing relationships, keep the Negro "in his place," and the whole weight of social organization is further emphasized by violence on the slightest provocation, or even lynching.

The Negro, denied suffrage, denied nearly all political and civil rights, denied all economic advantages, was in a less favorable position, even before decline set in in Georgia, so that with the recent depression—since he already had fewer defenses against bad times—his relative position has grown even worse. His relative inferiority has also been accentuated by the New Deal measures of farm recovery. He has been displaced in many lines by poor Whites, as in the mines of Bartow County, in the Valley and Ridge Belt.

Negro land ownership is very limited. In the old Piedmont Cotton Belt, 87 per cent of all owners are White, and 95 per cent of the land is owned by Whites. Sixty-six per cent of the acreage owned by Negroes is in units of less than 175 acres, nearly half of all Negro owners possess less than 50 acres each, and of course they must be content to take only such land that Whites do not want—almost invariably submarginal. In the Plantation Belt, a considerable part of Negro ownership is the result of earlier White benevolence, a large share of the Negro owners originally bearing the name of the White plantation head. In other words, they were the mulatto children by the Negro mistresses of White men. Negro ownership in the state, never great, reached its maximum about 1920, but since then it has greatly diminished, probably 30 per cent. In 1935 85.5 per cent of all Negroes in Georgia were tenants or croppers; but in Macon County this went up to 91.9 per cent.

Race and class discrimination exists in all phases of community life.

The largest farms are taxed the least per acre. The highest taxed farms in Georgia per acre are the small Negro farms.

Income is also sharply differentiated. Raper found that in 1934 in Greene County, the average cash income per White rural family was $301.26; per rural Negro family, $150.74; in Macon County, $872.21 and $299.56 respectively. Over a period of eight years, Negro income had dropped faster than White income. One-fifth of the Negro wage hands in Macon County received less than $100 a year, including relief!

In many places there are no accommodations for Negroes in public hospitals, or if they exist, they are inferior and unsanitary. The amount spent on education for Negroes, although in many counties they are more than half the population, is infinitesimal compared to that spent on Whites, which in turn is far below the average in the country.

In Georgia, as a whole, on each White child are spent $36.88 a year; on each Negro child, $5.07. In Jasper County, annual school costs per pupil were recently: Whites, $43.09; Negroes, $6.70; in Jones County, $43.96 and $5.21; Putnam County, $39.35 and $3.45; Montgomery County, $16.81 and $2.39 (1928); Thomas County, rural schools, $30.96 and $3.13, etc. In McIntosh, a very poor, sparsely settled county, expenditures for education for both Whites and Blacks are far above state average, but schools are very inferior, illiteracy worse than in the state as a whole. State funds are apportioned to the various counties in accordance with the population, which merely means that those counties with a large Black population, have the worst schools for Negroes and the best schools for Whites. Black teachers get infamously low pay, far below even that for the semi-starvation wages paid White school teachers.

Under the New Deal, racial discrimination has been perpetuated in distribution of benefits, in loans, and in relief. Though more Negroes needed relief than Whites, less of them got relief and they got less of it. In Greene County in March, 1935, as typical as any, 13.5 per cent of the Whites were on direct relief and only 8.7 per cent of the Negroes. Direct relief in Greene County in March, 1934, was $2.89 per month per White and but $2.30 per Negro. The C.W.A.

expenditures (six months, 1933-34) were Whites, $130.80; Blacks, $74. Skilled workers (all but two, White) got more. Often relief to Negroes was given, not in money as in the case of Whites, but in beef and rice. Under Rehabilitation, four times as many Whites were helped as Negroes, though results showed that of the five best farm-ers, four were Negro (all that were helped), surpassing all the rest of the Whites.

In nearly all cases in Georgia, as in Alabama, as in Louisiana, as in Tennessee, I found nearly all federal relief agencies controlled by the large planters. If their direct relatives were not in charge, some dependent or close political ally was. A little inquiry nearly always revealed the thread of connection. Relief has been patterned to tradi-tional abuse.

The result inevitably is political corruption and demagogy of the worst sort. The "red galluses" of Talmadge, who stormed with a plastered tail right out of the manure, for a time became a national legend. The result is the brutal, landlord-dominated sheriff system; politicians who shout of the wrongs of the people and sell out to plantation interests or northern industrialists; politicians who are lynch-provokers, Jew-haters, and howl at the Papal curse. Many times a large planter is himself the sheriff, or a relative, or someone thoroughly to be depended on to browbeat Negroes, evict croppers and tenants, not interfere with the flogging or lynching of Negroes, and perform other unsavory duties.

Political and economic degeneracy has resulted in a general break-down of community services and the failure of banks, the closing of schools, the deterioration of roads, the increase of town and county debt, the curtailment of health services, the increase of preventable disease and mortality. In many rural localities, for years now, prac-tically the only funds available to maintain community services have come from state or federal sources. In almost all the rural areas of Georgia, once-flourishing communities have declined in population. Oglethorpe, in Macon County, once having 20,000 people, now has less than 1,000. Bartow County, reached its maximum population in 1910. Screven County, in the old Plantation Belt, has shown a de-creasing population in town and country over a long period. Dislocated people have flooded into the larger cities, in turn frowsy and down at the heels, thus augmenting the severe unemployment problem. Railroads have been abandoned to weeds; roads to gullies.

Probably nearly a third of the rural population of Georgia lives in houses which, in comfort and sanitation, are inferior to those of the peasants of almost any part of Europe and are little better than those of savage tribes. Many are rotted and nearly roofless, and in parts of Georgia, winter weather often goes down to twelve below freezing, occasionally lower. Often all bedding is lacking to cover the cornshuck mattress. "Tenant shacks are rarely screened," says Raper in his *Preface to Peasantry*. "In and out of such houses, the children and flies, often the chickens and pigs—move at will. They are quite open; a mad dog can trot through one of them, or a tenant mother with a four-day-old baby may awake from an afternoon nap [as has happened] to find in her bed a snake attempting to nurse her full breasts."

In 1933, over 50 per cent of the deaths were due to entirely preventable diseases. Infant mortality is high, 67.2 per 1,000 for Georgia as a whole, but running up to 75 or 80 or even higher in rural districts. In Irwin County there is no health officer, no county nurse, no social worker, no recreation worker, no tuberculosis clinic, no county library, no city library, no Red Cross chapter.

Probably in few places in Europe is there such lack of medical care as in parts of rural Georgia. Many of the widespread diseases are merely due to lack of proper diet and clothing. Erskine Caldwell, a native Georgian and the author of *Tobacco Road*, wrote in the *New York Post*, February 18, 1935: "In parts of Georgia human existence has reached its lowest depths. Children are seen deformed by nature and malnutrition, women in rags beg for pennies, and men are so hungry that they eat snakes and cow dung . . . strip leaves off trees, dig roots out of the earth. . . ." When strangers come, in parts of Georgia, "folk hide their nakedness behind trees."

Raper states in his *Tragedy of Lynching:* "The propertyless rural Whites of Montgomery and surrounding counties are poor indeed. The Klan which they generally accepted as a way out, has failed them; cotton is cheap; there are no prosperous cities to run off to at will. Many of these men with their wives and children are emaciated in appearance, and look old beyond their years. One sees mothers with sunken chests and practically no teeth, little babies in arms with scabs on their heads and running sores about their ears, boys chewing tobacco before they are half grown and girls staring and popping their gum. Men, women, and children, dirty and unkempt, seething fatalism and pessimism, are not uncommon sights. Now and then an intoxicated fellow breaks the monotony and adds to the sordidness of the picture."

Crime has increased everywhere, especially among Whites, though in some places it has even decreased for Negroes. In Troup County, between 1921 and 1929, crime by Whites more than doubled; by Negroes, decreased over 30 per cent.

Is it necessary to quote Oliver Goldsmith?

> Ill fares the land to hastening ills a prey
> Where wealth accumulates and men decay.
> Princes and lords may flourish or fade,
> A breath can make them as a breath has made;
> But a bold peasantry, their country's pride,
> When once destroyed, can never be supplied.

It so happens that in Georgia, though class and race divisions yawn wide, general wealth is not increasing, quite the contrary.

Human deterioration has been paralleled in animal deterioration. Horses, cows, mules, steers, even chickens, have grown poorer in quality and fewer in number. Between 1920 and 1930 alone, there was a decline in the whole state of 86,217 milk cows, 374,675 head of cattle, 713,651 swine, and nearly 2,000,000 chickens. Between 1920 and 1926, in the old plantation Piedmont Cotton Belt, work animals decreased more than 30 per cent in relation to the area of crop acreage (which in that area in the same period decreased approximately 13 per cent).

In Morgan County between 1920 and 1932 the number of owners of work stock decreased more than 50 per cent. Probably over 60 per cent of the farm operators of Georgia have no work animals. In the state one rarely sees a double team plowing in the field; most of the farmers do not have a single animal to work with. In Thomas County (Middle Coastal Plain), the rural dwellers till the soil only with one-horse plows, many only with briar hooks or long-handled hoes. The productive process of a man with a hoe is curtailed at least 75 per cent. There has, in short, been no agricultural advance since 1880, better said only regression. Production in all lines in Georgia in general is below that in efficiency almost anywhere else in the Union. In Greene and Macon Counties one-fourth of all White families and half the Negro families were found to own no implements, not even a hoe. The rural economy of Georgia is mostly a hand-tool economy. In many places, it is not far above the pointed stick civilization.

"The New Deal, with its cotton restriction programs, its relief, expenditures, and its loan services, has temporarily revitalized the Black belt, has rejuvenated the decaying plantation economy," says Raper. But what has it done for non-plantation owners?

"The landless farmers, though able . . . to pay their rents and settle their accounts [which merely helped the plantation owners still more] are not only failing to escape their chronic dependence but are actually losing status. Many tenants are being pushed off the land while many others are being pushed down the tenure ladder, especially from cropper to wage-hand status.

"The tendency everywhere is for people who were poor in 1928 to be even poorer now, despite the federal money which has either gone through their hands or missed them."

In fact in order to get even larger federal benefits, and not have to share anything with croppers, the plantation owners, in many instances, have turned their tenants into wage hands. Security is lowered; a wage hand can be kicked off at any moment.

Wallace's farm policy and the A.A.A. have been highly satisfactory to most Black Belt leaders, i.e., planters, business men and professional people. But some hard-hit counties, where local owners could not control the federal plans, since acreage allotments have been rigidly based on depression production (sometimes a drop of 80 per cent below normal output), were penalized by the New Deal, permanently frozen into their lowest pattern of misery.

Tenants had a deep aversion to the plow-up, which to them represented labor started and labor expended to destroy the product of labor. The government rewards of $10 an acre practically all went into the hands of the landlord, rent in any case at once taking half of it.

Of the later tax-free cotton certificates, most also went into the plantation owner's hands, while the tenant to sell his cotton would usually have to buy such certificates from the landlord, sometimes above the legally set price of four cents.

By 1932 in Greene and Macon Counties, over 37,000 acres of farm lands were lost to loan companies. Various federal agencies appeared to provide rural credit: the Federal Land Bank, the Land Bank Commission, the Home Owners Loan Corporation, the Emergency Crop Loan Department and the Production Credit Association. Some of these agencies unfortunately have extended the chattel mortgage system still more widely, not only in Georgia, but in northern states where rarely practiced.

Even the tenant could get emergency crop loans, provided the landlord waived his prior rent lien to the government. This the planter was reluctant to do as it destroyed one of his powerful instruments of coercion, but when he saw a chance, even so, to pocket the tenant's loan money, he gave ready assent. Frequently the landlord promptly used this waiver to federal authorities to get hold of the loan check, charging the tenant a second interest still higher on the same money, plus government interest; or the planter took it all for granting supplies at customary credit prices. Though tenant interest on such loans was thus jacked up as high as 16 per cent or more, the planter was provided with big amounts of capital and could rake in interest on the government money he was taking care of for his cropper. Sometimes it all went merely to pay up back debts.

Government loans in good part also have kept to the traditional race hierarchy pattern. Careful examination of the figures for the various federal credit institutions shows that relative to Whites an insignificant number of Negroes have received loans, that loans to Negroes have been much smaller in amount, that in counties having more Blacks than Whites, the partiality to the ever-favored race is still more pronounced.

In November, 1938, Roosevelt and Ickes, in part a reprisal for political defeat, announced that all federal aid to the state would be cut off. Whatever the failure of the Wallace farm program in Georgia so far as the bulk of the population is concerned, the payments by other agencies merely for immediate human welfare or employment on public works have often meant life versus death. The state is in such misery that even a few pennies sometimes spell the possibility of further survival. Curtailment of relief means tragedy on a major scale. It is unfortunate that to punish disobedient politicians it is necessary to punish destitute Georgians, mostly deprived of the suffrage to chastise their unworthy rulers. Fortunately a partial compromise was worked out.

Did someone mention Rome?

CHAPTER XXI

MIGS: SHANTYTOWN ON WHEELS

The wooden panel on which the following was stenciled no longer encased an ice-making machine; it swung as a door on a shack of flattened oil tins, burlap, cardboard, and rags in the vast Hooverville jungle of Bakersfield, California.

UP   DO NOT TRUCK ON THIS SIDE

FRONT

FRAGILE

HANDLE WITH CARE

WARD'S DE LUXE ELECTRIC
REFRIGERATOR

MONTGOMERY WARD   USA

Before this improvised door and the tilted rusty smokestack poking above it, was a small bed of onions, withering in the terrific April heat of the inland San Joaquin Valley.

On a small box in the scant shade of a cottonwood tree sat a tow-haired girl of about eighteen, patching a pair of overalls, faded almost white from an incredible number of washings. Her round curves and silken corn-tassel hair made her seem fresh, but a lean hardness chiseled her face; she wore a loose, tattered calico dress and torn sneakers without stockings. At her feet, playing with an iron bolt, was one of her babies, tow-headed like herself, seemingly fat, but yellow and stinking with dysentery and covered with flies.

She and her family were fairly typical of several hundred others in this foul slough which stands on Bakersfield's main street, across from the trim lawns of the Chamber of Commerce Building. The Bakersfield jungle is typical of dozens of such places stretching across the land, particularly from the vast shambles in Oklahoma City out by the pig dump to Los Angeles, El Indio, Nipomo, Holtville, Cala-patria, El Centro, Brawley—to name but a few of those I personally have visited.

Out through the cotton fields, pea fields, vineyards, and orchards of New Mexico, Arizona, California, Idaho, Oregon, and other states, one encounters transient labor camps a step above the Hooverville jungles but almost equally deplorable with regard to health and broken lives.

One can easily imagine these haphazard camps: rows of tents, trailers, shacks, lean-tos, side-by-side close, with perhaps a single faucet for several hundred families, with half a dozen privies usually set in the very center of the camp. Imagine the lack of privacy, the misery of rain and sickness. It had been raining for two weeks when I visited the camps around Pima, Oceano, and Nipomo; the tents were literally swimming in mud.

The same month that I visited Nipomo, the public health nurse serving under the Council of Women for Home Missions, long active in this field, was also there and described the situation: [1]

"It was Holy Week in 1937 in the California County of San Luis Obispo. The pea crop was nearly ready to pick. Eight camps already had 1424 people, and other migratory workers were coming in daily by the hundreds. The rain was pouring down but migrants still continued to stretch their leaking tents over muddy pools. Many had no beds, springs, or mattresses; only wet bedding, leaking tents. Many had not had work for weeks, and those who had been employed had not been able to save any money. Now they must go to work at once— or go hungry. Many were both hungry and sick.

[1] *They Starve That We May Eat*, compiled by Edith E. Lowry.

"By the end of the week there were three thousand people in the pea district, ready to work. Many were starving—the rain was still pouring. Tomorrow would be Easter Sunday. . . . Peas to pick at Nipomo, but the peas were not ready to pick."

The most atrocious camps are those on the fringes of the large cities. In the countryside are camp sites provided by the large ranches —available, of course, only during picking season. These are perhaps the best. Smaller growers, unable to provide decent living conditions, get around the state laws by refusing to hire anyone who wishes to live on their land. Elsewhere camps are provided by farm agents and labor contractors.

The contractor camps, though the contractor must be licensed and must provide running water and a certain number of privies, are usually inferior to those provided on the ranches, and there is more exploitation. The contractors carry their workers over a few weeks until picking time. The goods are charged at double their proper value. The contractor also gets a cut on wages, usually about twenty per cent. He is, in a way, often a sort of labor "dick," for he guarantees the growers not only an adequate supply of labor but a group of workers tagged with the nonstrike guarantee. There are always more workers in the camp than are necessary in the fields—last year nearly two men for every job—and the contractor parcels out the work to those who show the most submissive deference.

Many colonies, however, are made up of roadside squatters. These impromptu camps are, of course, the very worst. Usually they have no sanitation whatsoever. One such had no water supply; the people used ditchwater. Another camp was dependent on water from a filling station, at five cents a bucket. Most are badly situated. One was on the edge of a malarial marsh. Official investigations have shown that the water used in camps is often contaminated. Dr. Omer Mills, regional economist for the Farm Security Administration, found in January, 1938, that of thirty migrant children examined in the Farmersville district in Tulane County, twenty-seven were defective through malnutrition. In another ditch camp, twenty-one of twenty-two children were defective. Conditions were even worse in Kem, Kings, and Imperial Counties.

Walter E. Packard, former Director of the Rural Resettlement Division of the United States Resettlement Administration, thus describes one camp:

"Migrants' camp, 765 individuals, and on the adjoining lot, 415 individuals. *Here was a small city, a city without order, a city of neglected souls.* The only sanitary facilities available were two rough, pit-type privies. The only water supply was furnished by a broken hand-pump. So great was the demand for space that tents were pitched wall against wall. Here and there a 'lean-to,' called 'hide-behinds' by the children, dotted the acreage, while on the outer fringe of it all, many had thrown their mattresses or bedding in the dirt and the sand, having abandoned all thought of hope or privacy. With the great variety of tents and housing facilities, the whole thing resembled a crazy quilt stretched out on a carpet of rubbish and debris, against a background of filth, and with an atmosphere of stench. Adding to the misery of it all, flies swarmed by the millions."

The dwellers in these places are the Migs, as they call themselves— migratory workers. They are part of the debris of the depression and are living symbols particularly of the drouth disaster in the Midwest. They are the "rubber tramps."

Lately I have been buzzing up and down the highways of the West, along the coast, through the San Joaquin, along the Salton Sea, through the citrus-fruit region, in and out of the Imperial Valley; and wherever I went, by main route 50 or 80 or 90 or the dustier side roads, I encountered these people in motion. They travel along in old hooded wagons, with bony nags, or in old rattly cars, sometimes with elaborate homemade trailers, or in light trucks. Each vehicle is stacked high with dirty torn bedding, cots, bedsprings, tents, a rusty iron stove. On the running board may be seen a battered trunk, a galvanized tub, perhaps a dog or an accordion. Each vehicle is crowded with children, grandfolks, aunts, cousins, neighbors. They all set a great store by kinsfolk.

In southern Arizona, I met a young Oklahoma farmer in a 1928 runabout, with his young wife and five children covered with sores, all their belongings stacked mountainously on fenders, running board, and hood. He was bargaining an old shotgun for drained motor oil and gas to get a little farther.

One such family I saw by the side of the road in the burning desert beyond Blythe. The woman was feeding her six children with flour gruel, made by scorching the flour in a pan and mixing it with water and a little grease. This and a dried prune apiece constituted their meal—all the food they had left. They were patiently waiting until the father should return. He had walked ten miles into town with a spare tire to try and trade it for some gas. The remarkable thing was that this woman did not feel set upon or hopeless. The Lord, she said, would help them; if He didn't, it was because in His wisdom He saw best to do otherwise.

Etta Pitchford, age 39, was one the Lord did not aid. She came to a tragic end in Carlsbad, New Mexico. Driven out of Antlers, Oklahoma, by the economic collapse of that region, though suffering from t.b., she gathered her three children together and got as far as New Mexico. There the last of her savings disappeared. She could not get on relief because she lacked the proper residence and she was too proud to beg—few of these people will ever beg. At last, in desperation, she gathered weeds and boiled them. As a result, she, Hanley Marion, aged 10, and Eliza, aged 8, were poisoned and died. Only Belle, aged 12, survived.

A storekeeper of Oceano, California, told me of another woman and two babies whom he found starved to death on the sand dunes.

Though many a tragedy is locked in the mystery of this strange twentieth-century migration of folk, it is surprising on the whole to observe their unfailing optimism, religious faith, and spirit of mutual aid. There is plenty of trouble, jealousy, and slander, as is inevitable in the crowded quarters of the camps, but on the whole the spirit of co-operation is far greater. Mostly is it share and share alike.

The newcomers are ineligible for relief, but I was in the San Luis Obispo relief agency when a special federal order was being carried out to distribute a few dollars per head during the lean week prior to the beginning of the pea harvest.

"Did you get everybody?" the head of the agency asked.

"Just about," said the field worker. "But, if I missed one or two, it won't make much difference. The funds will all be evenly distributed. They always divvy up on everything anyway."

In general, however, the migrant, since he must move from crop to crop, even from state to state, is at present outside the relief program, outside the health service, and often barred from local schools. He is, if anyone is, the forgotten man.

The worst sufferers are the children, and the families are usually larger than average. The smallest tots must labor in the fields beside their parents. Four-year-olds have been seen working in strawberry patches. Some must toil from four A.M. to six in the afternoon. Often they must attend half a dozen different schools a year, with all the painful psychological adjustment the child suffers in each new abrupt change of environment and the group hostility that each must face as the untested late-comer to the classroom. Their ragged clothes set them apart. Sneering epithets about "tramp kids" are merely part of classroom discrimination by more prosperous children, by teachers and by the state authorities. One observer quotes several Migs. "Residenters" look askance at "outlanders." Children are called "peapickers." "My children ain't raised decent like I was raised. . . . There was no rag houses then. . . ." The children everywhere, whatever their capabilities, in school and out must endure conditions that prevent them from ever acquiring the knowledge and techniques to get out of the class they are in.

This vast migration is an economic shift of great importance to the country, of large significance for the future. It is as dramatic in its way as the trek of Bedouins out of the Arabian desert upon the garden towns to the north, as described so vividly by Lawrence in his *Seven Pillars of Wisdom*, or some great movement of people out of central Asia. Those, too, were basically hunger treks. The Pacific Coast migration has not ceased; if anything, despite any return of prosperity to the country at large, it will likely be further augmented.

For though drouth and depression are immediately responsible, peculiar agricultural conditions in the Middle West and the Pacific States, among other places, point to the probability that these Migs are to become a permanent phenomenon of American life. They are apt to increase rather than decrease in numbers. They form a group already recognizable, with peculiar mores and, despite their low economic level and apparently hit-or-miss life, with rigid standards— moral, social, and otherwise. Among them is developing a distinctive lingo and folklore. In short, the Migs are in process of becoming America's permanent gypsies. They are, in fact, if the tendencies of the past fifty years continue, the typical rural American. For fifty years the number of farm laborers has been increasing in certain areas faster than any other element in our rural population. They are the next step down from the semi-stabilization period of tenancy and share-cropping. As a result the growth of the proportion of rural wage-earners will likely be much more rapid from now on.

This is a general trend of the country, but in the case of the California Migs special more immediate factors have augmented the movement.

As analyzed by Edward J. Rowell, of the U. S. Bureau of Labor Statistics, and others, about a fifth of them are Okies, i.e., from Oklahoma; three-fifths of them are from the drouth states of Arizona, Oklahoma, Arkansas, and Missouri; 80 per cent all told are from drouth areas. "They have been scattered like the dust of their farms, literally blown out." A small fraction is made up of traditional migratory workers from western and southern states; a still smaller fraction is drawn from the industrial centers of the Middle West, the East, and New England; and a still smaller fraction of them comes from the share-cropper states of the South unaffected by drouth.

Most of them, a few years ago, were share-croppers, tenant farmers, or independent ranchers. Most are men traditionally close to the soil, who turn instinctively to the soil, who are unhappy away from the soil, and who are quite unfit for industrial activities even could industry absorb them. There is even less prospect of agriculture's reabsorbing them on a settled basis; and the most extravagant plans of the resettlement program, even before it was whittled down to fragmentary welfare work, could scarcely have solved their problem. And so they bid fair to become a permanent gypsy class, for, as gypsies, there is a definite niche for them in the western American agrarian and economic scheme. Peculiarly enough, their disasters came at precisely the moment when more than ever there was a need for them in the migratory role which they were obliged to assume. And as roving gypsies their condition in certain instances has improved since the worst days of the depression.

Dr. Paul Taylor has made a detailed study of the migration statistics for California. These Migs had been arriving in a growing stream all through the period of the depression. The number of those in the Mig class who arrived by motor vehicle—excluding those who arrived afoot, by bus, or by train—totaled for the twelve months ending June 15, 1936, 71,047. It is estimated that more than 150,-000 Migs have become permanent denizens of California alone, without fixed address, mostly a roving horde.

As one camp denizen told me, with a proud laugh, "Oklahoma has captured California without firing a shot."

One can call these folks indigents, paupers, tramps—all the ugly terms which have been applied to them by the smug newspapers of California and elsewhere. But it is fair to remember that the American frontier was settled originally by folk who came West with even fewer resources than these latter-day emigrants—except that in the earlier days a gun secured food and the present folk have no such chance at nature, which has all been fenced in, less chance in fact than a Central American Indian. And they find no homesteads to clear at the end of the trail, no chance to build themselves up into comfortable citizens.

Such emigration has made the whole history of the United States what it is. Settlers have cleared the land, put in crops, built homes. When the land petered out, they moved west to new land. And so, in recurring waves, the frontier was settled. Of such emigrations, one can recall, for instance, the famous Mormon pushcart brigade, that strange expedition of folk who crossed pristine wilderness through northern snows, pushing their scant belongings ahead of them in carts. They, too, were in rags and tatters, and far more of them left their bones by the roadside than during the present migration. But they found the Promised Land. Today there is no Promised Land left.

If there is something of a definite frontier slant to these latter-day migrants, if like their predecessors, they are abandoning untillable lands, now they find no frontier waiting their industry; they arrive in the midst of a highly developed, industrialized agricultural system.

But they do have the appearance of romance novels or screen versions of another age. In the Oklahoman there is often something of the Hoosier: frequently one sees the ungainly Abraham Lincoln shape to the bodies, the same long hips and loose legs. Usually the Oklahomans have shorter torsos, little heads and hard, bony faces, with tight-creased lips in bitter half-moon curve; small, deep-set, boring eyes, pale, almost colorless; short, thin noses—a pushed-together, economical sort of face that seems to lift toward the sky looking for rain. The Texans have heavier bodies and legs, are thick of jowl, have fatter, open lips, as though about to drawl, a half-adenoidal expression—big men with simple, babyish faces; but they are more aggressive in spirit.

One gets to know the regional types. From parts of Texas come women with pioneer pink sunbonnets, drum-shaped, sewn with flexible cardboard stuffing that gives the appearance of staves, loose cloth flaps down the cheeks, and pooched with cloth at the back of the head. The men wear short leather jackets, big-brimmed felt hats, short boots with under-slung high heels.

Above all, they are a religious folk. This, too, is in the tradition of American migrations. The Atlantic seaboard was settled by folk who brought with them a stern, ever righteous God. The Mormons led another migration. The Moravians spread through Pennsylvania and Ohio. One still finds, scattered through the Middle West, old religious land colonies, with quaint communal customs.

The bulk of the present Migs are Pentecostals—the Church of the True Gospel. Their horrible camps are named The Angel, The Burning Bush, The One God, The Crusaders. The Pentecostal folk are a combination of Shakers, Holy Rollers, and Hard-Shell Baptists, and their emotional orgies often put an extravagant Negro sect in the shade.

The Pentecostal pastors circulate among the labor camps in Packard automobiles daubed with the words *Jesus Is Here*. Few of the harvest communities, despite their shifting population, are now without a small Pentecostal church. Weedpatch, Nipomo, Brawley, Holtville, harbor such churches. Elsewhere the itinerant pastor, the Moses of the migration, sets up a large brown tent which serves as a temple.

Interesting is the camp of Reverend Baylie Dudd. He, too, is obviously Oklahoman, except that he turned out shorter of leg, plumper of body, but with the same small, bony features topped with a big mass of blond hair. His hands, too, are big and bony. He leased a patch of ground near Bakersfield and rented out camp space at $3 a month. All the camp members, in addition, pay him tithes. The religion provides for frequent fasts, and in the hot harvest fields, where the temperature often reaches 110, the folk of his and other congregations will be found laboring in spite of carrying on an absolute fast for two, three, or even more days. In part this is unconsciously making holiness out of a necessity, for they cannot at the same time pay the tithes and have enough to eat.

The Pentecostals also quite conveniently leave everything to God, even health. Mostly they scorn the services of the nurses provided by charitable organizations and the relief administration. When a typhoid epidemic was in the offing, only seven out of Reverend Dudd's entire camp would submit to vaccination. The health authorities have tried in vain to segregate mothers with t.b. Soon all the numerous progeny are stricken with it. The Pentecostal beliefs will have little to do with modern science; but on the other hand they are rigidly moral. Though the Pentecostal music is sadistic and oversexual and their religious orgies in great part represent a form of sex sublimation and excitation, dancing is for them of the very devil. Any violation of the sexual code, if discovered, would likely result in an instantaneous hanging.

The Migs represent the first crumblings from the drouth and share-cropper areas. They fled from lands become gullies, land become fruitless. They fled from the whirling monster of sand that clutched at them as they slipped away from its parching death. But if those two factors, drouth and depression, created the immediate necessity to migrate, the makings of the exodus were under way long before.

Recent agricultural studies reveal that for certain parts of the South and New England, decline in soil fertility began before the Civil

War, in a still larger area as early as 1880, still more in the 'nineties, and that a definite decline set in everywhere, except in the Far West, around 1920-24. This tendency was concealed by the War and post-War inflation, which forced many submarginal lands into temporary use, but it was already an inexorable process over fifteen years ago. This partly accounted for earlier migrations from Virginia, Pennsylvania, the Carolinas, Kentucky, and Tennessee into Oklahoma, Texas, and Kansas.

This decline in soil fertility was due to unscientific farming, natural depletion, erosion, the plantation system in the South, the growth of intensive and industrialized agriculture in the North. The decline in soil or the expansion of technical agriculture requiring machinery and capital, was paralleled by an increasing disappearance of the independent small farmers. More and more, from 1920 on, the small rancher and little rural homeowner saw his possessions passing under the hammer, drifting into the hands of the banks, the large landowner. Thus the free farmer became a cropper. Simultaneously he had to battle declining crop returns and give a greater part of his yield to those who now owned the soil.

Thus the drouth and the depression merely accentuated a situation growing acute, which was in process before either of these two additional disasters appeared and which will be little remedied by a return of general industrial prosperity. In fact the ranks of the Migs are likely to be added to; more folk must leave the Middle West, and from the South at least 2,000,000 folk are apt to be uprooted unless the plantation system is modified or a new cash crop is found to substitute for cotton.

This appearance of the American rubber gypsy coincided with an economic situation in California and periphery western states which made the Mig the proper answer to the agricultural system devised there and which now tends to make him a permanent if not particularly happy American institution.

In California, improved land reached its maximum acreage back in 1889. Since then, the area cultivated has been declining. However, of this improved land, the proportion under artificial irrigation has steadily increased. Since 1885 the number of holdings in excess of

1,000 acres has increased 37 per cent, while those under fifty acres
has decreased. California has gradually abandoned dry farming and
extensive crops to grow intensive crops. In its day, the central valley
of California was the principal wheat granary of the world. The
blight of rust, the discovery of new hard varieties for colder climates,
and other factors forced a shift to other grains, finally to intensive
irrigated crops supporting a larger population through greater productivity. Whereas intensive crops (at first grapes and fruits, later
hops, sugar beets, cotton, truck gardening) had in 1879 provided less
than 4 per cent of the value of California farm products, by 1929
they provided nearly 80 per cent and were worth nearly $400,000,000.
This shift meant that, while in 1860 less than 40,000 persons were
gainfully employed in California agriculture, by 1930, 332,024 were
so employed. But, what is more important sociologically, California
has a larger percentage of farm laborers among those engaged in
agriculture than any other state in the Union. California agriculture
is run on a large-scale industrialized pattern.

Of large-scale farms, i.e., those having an annual product worth
$30,000 or more, California has 36.7 per cent of the total of such
farms for the entire United States. Compare this with Mississippi,
usually considered a large plantation state, which has only 0.4 per
cent of such large farms. Even in cotton, Mississippi's greatest product, California has 133 large-scale estates as compared to only 29 in
Mississippi. Within the borders of California in 1930 were 40 per
cent of the nation's large-scale dairy farms, 44 per cent of the large-
scale general farms, 52 per cent of the large-scale poultry estates, 60
per cent of the large-scale truck farms and fruit farms. Thus, with
the possible exception of the Soviet Union, the American tropics, and
parts of Africa, California represents the maximum development of
large-scale industrialized agriculture in the world today.

I visited the federal labor camp near Weedpatch, south of Bakersfield, where some slight effort has been made to provide a handful
of Okies and Migs with sanitary conveniences. I had driven there up
over the Coast Range, through one of the most beautiful valleys I
had seen anywhere in California, and saw in that rich, ample, and
fertile corner only one human residence—a gas station. I was travers-

ing part of the vast Miller estate of the Kern County Land Company, over 400,000 acres. This was just northwest of the primitive federal labor camp. Look at the map of California and you will see in that part a great stretch almost unmarked by towns or public roads. It is part of this estate. Above the Miller estate stretches the great Lux estate. Below it stretches the big Hoover ranch. All about the federal camp are the broad acres of Di Giorgio, subsidiary of the great fruit company in the Salinas Valley, where in the lettuce fields strikers were recently murdered, and terror reigned. And south of the camp, stretching as far as the eye can reach to the far mountains, are the broad acres of the Chandler estate.

The head of the labor camp told me that, even if a man should come into the region with $1,000 in his pocket to buy a modest five acres, he would have difficulty obtaining it. The federal authorities found real difficulty in locating ground they could lease for their camp, and were fought every inch of the way in their efforts to help out the Migs. But the local plantation owners and Vigilantes, once the camp was established, were afraid to raid it or shoot it up as they periodically do with other camps. Destruction of federal property is a serious offense. The owners feared they could not terrorize a federal camp as they do others, and so to get a foothold, the Weedpatch camp had to agree to forbid all union organization on the premises. To this extent the federal authorities had to submit to the prevailing system of lawlessness.

One fear of the owners was that residents would become permanent, thus increasing tax-costs. When their workers are kept moving they are ineligible for relief. Also permanent communities acquire solidarity, because, organized, they can demand decent wages. If the Migs are thrust out, they scatter; no permanent bands are forged.

Various other federal labor camps have been established since my last visit. They charge ten cents a day for camping site, the money being used for equipment to promote camp comfort and recreation. Entertainment is devised, a form of self-government is utilized, and those who do not abide by the wise, if strict, regulations, must leave. Something has been done, though but a drop in a big bucket, by the Farm Security Administration to promote health and sounder community living—about eight primitive but sanitary camps and considerable cash handouts.

A great deal, not only in California, but throughout the nation, has been accomplished for migrants by the Council of Women for Home Missions, headed by Edith E. Lowry. None of these efforts—though every person with humanitarian sentiments applauds them without any reservation—meets the basic economic situation. They are stop-gaps. They are in fact a species of subsidy to the growers who exploit this human misery.

The Council of Women for Home Missions itself recognized all this and presents a program for church and government, for "socially minded employers" and for community agencies. It admits that union organization—such as the one big union founded in July, 1937, by the C.I.O.—"seems to be the only practicable method by which the migrant can get a fair deal, unless national laws can quickly be passed to meet his needs."

The economic compulsives, the forces of world competition, the progress of techniques, of mechanization and industrialization, seem to override all other considerations. Large-scale industrial agriculture requires a numerous rural proletariat—at harvest season. It has little need for labor the rest of the year. Hence it needs a floating population.

Originally this seasonal labor supply was largely, but by no means entirely, furnished successively by Chinese, Japanese, Mexicans and Filipinos.

Each in turn has proved restive and has been discarded for cheaper sources. Thus for forty years migratory labor has been a feature of California agricultural life. The Wheatfield riots of 1914, the jailing of Ford and Suhr, the numerous bloody Vigilante acts, attest to the brutality of resulting labor-owner relations. Then stricter immigration regulations in 1929 limited the supply of such aliens. The depression here and improving conditions in Mexico caused the return of large numbers to the homeland. A depleted labor supply enabled the remaining Mexicans and Filipinos to organize. Bitter labor struggles ensued.

The remarkable thing is that such people, who should have been utterly hopeless, did get up spunk enough to demand better conditions, even though they knew they would be manhandled, beaten and killed by hired thugs, citizen Vigilantes and armed deputies. On the Pacific Coast more than forty rural strikes have occurred since December, 1932. In September, 1934, two hundred brave Vigilantes riddled a Filipino labor camp with bullets and set it afire.[1]

Now the Migs and Okies have made their triumphal way into the California agrarian system, in part by undercutting the previous wage levels of Japs, Mex, and Filipinos. The Okies are favored because they are religious and unorganized. But they, too, are now beginning to turn to unions.

Though California agriculture needs the Migs, a great hullabaloo has been raised against them both in and out of the state. The cities which must bear the relief burden during the off season naturally are wrathful. Los Angeles County arrogantly posted policemen outside its own borders at the state line to stop the influx. Imperial County also took a hand at stopping the Migs at the state line, but, when an unusually large harvest in the county and a short season made additional hands suddenly necessary, the big growers did not hesitate to rush agent contractors to bring in large additional cavalcades from Arizona.

In short, California really wants the Migs when the crops are ready to harvest, and she wishes they were in Timbuktu the rest of the year, for then they can only drift into the cities or into roadside slums, menacing public health, while they starve through to the next crop or through a year until they become eligible for relief. Relief is not so much a subsidy to the Migs as it is to the big growers, but this is not recognized. In the work season, therefore, the Migs are hailed gladly; in the off season, they are railroaded from county to county, jailed for vagrancy, and otherwise molested.

They are sneered at in the local press, called "riff-raff" and "moochers." They are jeered at in the more smug national journals. But in Walter Davenport's article in *Collier's*, he also pokes fun at the Californians for their long-standing ballyhoo about the land of milk and honey where "even the tears one sheds are tears of

[1] Cf. Lowry, *They Starve That We May Eat*, p. 28.

gladness." The tide of immigrants is part of the answer to the long era of boosterism that has featured the state since ninety years ago, ever since a man raced through the San Francisco streets, holding a bottle of yellow dust aloft and crying "Gold! Gold!"

These new folk have come, not with greedy hopes, but with hope— hope of earning their daily bread, a bare existence.

But, whatever the contretemps of their lives, they represent a dramatic population shift, they are part and parcel of a new economic development in the Far West. The only life they can lead is a gypsy life. They are the new American gypsies on wheels, following the crops from the early harvest in hot Imperial Valley, on up the coast to the pea harvest, over into San Joaquin for the grape harvest, finally the cotton picking. They have no homes; their children attend half a dozen or more schools during the year. Each year they become more definitely a group with cultural frontiers, less adaptable to any other kind of life. Most of them would no longer have any success as settlers. Once they were farmers; now they are nomads. They are agriculturists without roots in the soil whose wealth they garner.

CHAPTER XXII

LOST EMPIRE

In April, 1935, coming out of a movie one night in New Orleans, I was surprised to observe air filled with a yellow haze. It tasted and smelled of dust. The street lights were vague blurs. The parked automobiles seemed all to have turned rusty. Street and sidewalk were covered with a coating of fine red soil. The sound of my footsteps on the pavement was muffled.

I was treading upon a golden carpet. This was the rich top soil of America, blown south two thousand miles or more, from Oklahoma, Colorado, Kansas and the Dakotas, south over New Orleans, south into the Gulf of Mexico, forever beyond the reach of good one hundred per cent Americans.

Several years later, in Connecticut, I saw on the clean white snow, faint patches of the same red dirt, the rich top soil of America blown east into the Atlantic, beyond the reach of all good patriots.

In February, 1937, in Denton, Texas, I woke on a dull morning that remained so dark I had to turn the light on. Dust lay over everything; the air was thick with it. The sun was a pale, scarcely visible disk.

All day, going west, I faced that cloud of dust, the wind clawing at my car, at times almost lifting it off the road. Autos kept their headlights on, but even so were not visible more than fifteen yards away. Even with my car windows closed, the dust sifted in chokingly. The fine, granulated sand getting into my lungs gave me a cough that lasted for two months afterwards. My eyes smarted; the membranes of throat and nose dried up.

I was only in the fringe of the dust-bowl, but even so, many a village was ghostlike, half empty. On beyond, they told me, there were no human beings, no birds, no animals. The trees were gray with dust, hopeless-looking trees, and through brown fields ran big dry cracks; and over them sifted fine sand, finer than the sand of the sea, rippled by wind waves. Now and then little clouds of dust ran along the crest of sand ridges. Not so long ago this dust-bowl was full of cattle, not a Gobi Desert; it was the bread basket of the world. Now its top soil flies over a dozen states, even into the far oceans.

Area of the United States which has lost practically all top soil and is severely gullied, rendering it unsuited for further tillage, probably lost forever . . . .*51,465,097 acres*

> [More than six times the arable land of England and Wales; more than the arable land of Germany; more than the arable land of France; nearly as much as the arable land of Canada.]

Additional area which has lost practically all of the top soil, now of little agricultural value, includes much abandoned land, and much submarginal land, inappropriate for farming . . . . . .*105,594,229 acres*

> [More than twice the cultivated area of Germany; more than three times the cultivated area of Italy; more than thirteen times the cultivated area of England and Wales.]

Additional area which has lost one-fourth to three-fourths of the top soil, approaching the previous class but still can be saved if properly utilized . . . .*513,074,201 acres*

> [We have partially ruined, in addition to the 157,000,000 acres previously mentioned, an area more than eight times the arable land of Argentina, which exports three-fourths of the world's corn and nearly as much wheat as all North America, besides numerous other agricultural products.]

Additional area essentially destroyed for further tillage by wind erosion
                                                            4,443,849 acres

> [Twice the cultivated area of the Netherlands; more than the cultivated area of Belgium.]

*Area severely damaged by wind erosion, definitely injuring agricultural
value* .... *60,584,778 acres*

[Seven times the cultivated area of England; twice the cultivated
area of Italy; twice the cultivated area of the whole continent of
Australia.]

—Resettlement Administration and Its Work. Report,
July 24, 1935.

While other countries are trying to conquer new agricultural
regions by force of arms, we have busily thrown away an empire
larger than any of them will ever conquer.

This has resulted in an increasing number of our population being
stranded in regions and on land on which they cannot support themselves and hence becoming a heavy burden on the community.

I have seen such farms in corners of Connecticut, broken board
houses among the rocks; a tottering two-story home on a windy barren
hill in Missouri; I have seen their forlorn lights across the ruined
stump land of Minnesota; I have shared my lunch with hungry children of the stilt houses south of New Orleans, and followed the scrub-
pine trail to clapboard homes in the red hills of Louisiana; I have followed the blood-red roads of Alabama, my trousers flapping wet and
dirty, across the gullies of eroded hills in remote lynch counties. All
the statistics I present here from official sources are shot through in my
mind with the cracked and ulcered fingers and mouths of starving
pellagra sufferers, and house wives dragging to their doom with malaria down in the marshlands of Georgia and Alabama. These statistics tell of tattered children on the crossroads of Maryland, things
you rarely see on main concrete highways, Route U. S. 1 or 10 or 67
—at least not until you get into parts of the deep South or corners of
Illinois and Indiana.

Most folk don't believe it when you tell them of these things.
They are bounded by their own little sit-down world. They do not
follow off the beaten track, off the prosperous highways. To them
these things are merely quaint. They listen to them as of a world
that affects them not. They go to see *Tobacco Road* on the stage and
laugh at queer folk and their odd morals, and fail to realize that they

are looking on the lot of millions upon millions of 100 per cent Americans, and that the fate of those millions may yet pull their own comfortable homes down about their ears. So I put it all in figures, figures made by house-to-house canvass by census takers, by patient bureaucrats interested, not so much in human life, but in getting exact figures.

"Careful estimates of our Land Use Planning Section indicate that the number of families on land virtually incapable of producing an adequate livelihood through crop farming, ranges from 600,000 to 650,000, and that the aggregate area of the farms they occupy is more than 100,000,000 acres."
—Resettlement Administration, First Annual Report, 1936.

"There are between 6 and 7 million acres of submarginal land in New York. Nearly a million acres of such land are used for growing crops. . . . The State of Connecticut covers some 3 million acres. Of this, 1 million is . . . submarginal, another million . . . mediocre . . . or marginal. . . . The same story might be told of Rhode Island, of New Jersey, of Maryland, of Vermont, of Pennsylvania."
—Rural Rehabilitation in Region One, 1937. Farm Security Administration, U. S. Dept. of Agriculture.

"Less than half of the 55 million acres in farms in these four states [Georgia, South Carolina, Alabama and Florida] has been classified as physically suitable for farming purposes . . . in the cotton belt region [of these four states] . . . more than 111,000 farm families are stranded. . . . They are stranded on land so seriously eroded and depleted of soil fertility or otherwise so unsuited to farming, that even under normal economic conditions, they have little more than mere existence to hope for under old methods of land use."
—Resettlement Administration, Information Division Region V Headquarters, Montgomery, Alabama, 1935.

Depletion of the soil has led to increasing abandonment of land in all parts of the country, the uprooting of the rural population and forcing large sectors of it into lower economic levels. Soil depletion caused such abandonment long before drouth or boll weevil or other extraordinary disasters. People, without resources, cling to their unproductive land long after it can provide them a living. They have no place else to go. At least their shacks provide some sort of shelter. A few, with some resources left, do get out in time; most wait until death stares them in the face, but the day comes when willy-nilly they have to move. The eroded, leached land is abandoned. Abandonment usually causes its even quicker ruin.

"Figures issued at Cornell University indicate that approximately 100,-000 acres of land are abandoned annually in New York State, and that this process has been going on at about the same rate for 75 years."
—Rural Rehabilitation in Region One.

"Once paying farms [in New England, New York, Pennsylvania, New Jersey, Delaware and Maryland] are now raising potatoes and buckwheat, the last resort. Then follows the inevitable 'poverty grass' or 'white horse' and then shale out-croppings. At this stage the families die off or move off."
—Ibid.

In Georgia, the tillable agricultural land in 1920 was approximately 15,000,000 acres. By 1935 it had dropped to 10,700,000 acres, slightly less than in 1880 (despite the putting of new land into crops, land held in speculative reserve by large estates).
—U. S. Census 1880, 1920, 1935.

On top of this general decline in the soil resources of the nation, which in itself is sufficient to bring disaster upon many millions of our rural population, special tribulations have made the whole problem more acute. Floods, drouth, new pests such as the boll weevil, and much of Mr. Wallace's farm program, have brought added disaster. Although special groups among the farm population have actually benefited by all these evils, the majority of our rural population has been definitely injured.

We have already seen that, with the exceptions of Georgia and to a certain extent New England, New Jersey and Pennsylvania, the American Colonies were founded on the principle of land monopoly and in good part the plantation system. The land history of America reveals a race between land monopoly and the making of land accessible to the people. For a time the frontier seemed to outrun the effort to monopolize the land, but even in the days of the wide open spaces the effort was constantly being made to gain monopoly control of the new land resources, or to create an artificial scarcity that would increase the cost of land and the value of the larger holdings. By enormous grants, by artificial enclosures, by tax discrimination, efforts were made at all times to make the demand for land greater than the supply, and jack up prices. Only a fourth of the vast public domain of America was ever given out on homestead entries and a vast share of even those entries were corruptly made, were filed by the dummies of great corporations, were, in plain language, stolen from the American people.

The day came when land monopoly became a fact. With the closing of the frontier, it began to win the race. The ideal of the free farmer began to fade then. In 1880 the tide was already turning.

Thus, in addition to the blows of nature and of politicians, there have been added the unfair exploitation of man by man and the increasing concentration of land in the hands of the few, plus greater absenteeism, recognized in all epochs and all countries as one of the worst evils that can beset the agricultural prosperity of a people.

The market value of farm land owned by corporations in 1933 was approximately $770,000,000.
—Federal Bureau of Agricultural Economics.

[This did not include numerous farms in process of foreclosure at that time. It does not include the wholesale foreclosure since then.]

Though the farm population from 1890 to 1930 decreased in percentage of total population, in actual numbers it increased 35 per cent (not including wage hands). But the number of free, unmortgaged owners (exclusive of 276,819 free part-owners in 1930) has decreased 30 per cent and, since 1910, 40 per cent.
—U. S. Census, 1890, 1910, 1930.

"During the 40-year period for which complete census figures are available—1890 to 1930—the group of owner-operators free of mortgage debt steadily declined. Today they represent less than one-third of the total of farmers."
—House of Representatives. Subcommittee of the Committee on Public Lands. 74th Congress, 2nd session, 1936.

The small portion of unencumbered farms, 1,569,178 in 1930, in themselves represented a very wide range, from a few acres to millions of acres each. In this group are to be found vast plantations and industrialized estates, representing millions of dollars of capital, down to farms of only a few acres, and even submarginal farms. In any case farmers' net capital had shrunk from $34,390,000 in 1924 to $19,080,000 in 1933. This meant the average farmer suffered a capital loss of approximately $255 a year. This meant that the more marginal farmers were living off their own fat, were slipping backwards, were surviving only by using up their capital.

A large share of those farmers who do still own their own lands are mortgaged, often beyond the value of the lands. Because of debt the actual equity of operating owners is far less than the figures of farm ownership by themselves suggest. The smaller owners, who have mortgaged farms, are among the folk with the lowest income in the country and in the most treacherous position. They have a false psychology of independence, of superiority; they rank themselves with the small business man; they feel above other elements of the rural population and try to exploit them, but actually as a group they are worse off, in the matter of income, than tenants. By the time they have met principal and interest and all their other obligations, they have but little left for their families.

But here we are concerned with the actual numbers of them and their niche in the whole picture of rural life.

"The equity of operating farmers in their land is little more than one-fifth. Nearly four-fourths is in the hands of landlords and mortgage owners."
—Farm Tenancy Report of the President's Committee, National Resources Committee, Feb. 1937.

"Thousands of farm owner-operators are burdened with indebtedness contracted for amounts too large, at rates so high, or for terms so short that . . . they are likely to be forced to become tenants or croppers or join the ranks of migratory farm laborers or casual workers in other employments."
—Ibid.

The number of mortgaged farms, from 1890-1930, despite 35 per cent increase in farm population (not including wage hands), has increased 32 per cent, and if mortgaged part owners are included (not mentioned in the 1890 census) the increase is 71 per cent. The percentage that mortgaged farms hold to all full-owner farms (excluding small percentage not reported) has risen from 27.8 per cent in 1890 to 39.8 per cent in 1930; exclusive of mortgaged part owners.

—U. S. Census, 1890, 1930.

"Farm mortgages grew by leaps and bounds—from a total of slightly over three and one-quarter billion dollars in 1910 to nine and one-quarter billion dollars in 1930."

—House Subcommittee on Public Lands.

The general result of all these factors is an increasing exclusion of the bulk of American farm citizens from free access to the soil of their country, their defeat as self-sufficient human beings, their failure as productive units in creating national wealth. The farm population of America for more than 50 years has been steadily pushed down the economic ladder. Ever larger groups in the rural areas of our country have been steadily thrown into the propertyless class. In many instances the yield per acre gives a smaller percentage of return in proportion to the value of the property than the interest that must be paid on the mortgage. The mortgage, unpredictable weather, a series of bad crops, depression, soil depletion, control of the market by speculators, tariff discrimination in favor of industry, ever-mounting taxes, unfair railroad rates, all these and other factors force the free owner and the mortgage owner, increasingly to lose his land. Even where federal loans at lower interest are substituted, as has been done so widely, this has not greatly slowed up the process of foreclosures, it has by no means halted it, and it has in many instances extended the iniquitous chattel-mortgage system to northern states, putting such farmers in danger of losing absolutely all. A Department of Agriculture survey has shown 1,185,600 foreclosures in the nine years from 1926-34 inclusive. Foreclosures were greater in number under the first years of the New Deal than they had ever been before; in fact about half are found in the three years from 1932-34. Then and later the New Deal has not really stopped the general trend. The solution is not to be found in loans so long as the farmer, because of the general economic set-up, cannot become a going concern.

"In connection with the Elkhart County Farm Loan Association, with 1,005 members . . . (in 1933) with a total mortgage load . . . of $5,000,000 . . . up to that date over a period of ten years approximately 50 foreclosures had been executed. . . . Due to New Deal Legislation, March 4, 1933, the farmers were encouraged to reamortize their total loans [or take chattel mortgages]. . . . What good has this stay of execution about foreclosures been to the farmers of northern Indiana? The answer is today there are 15 members of the Elkhart Farmers Union Holiday Association . . . that in amortization, reamortization, the decrease in the interest rate does not solve the farm debt problem."

—Testimony of Mr. Lloyd J. Martin, of Goshen, Indiana. President of the Elkhart County Farmers Union Holiday Association before the House Subcommittee on Public Lands.

"Our foreclosures are running rampant . . . five . . . per week. . . . Some of the farmers—I expect most of them—have been running into a state where it [interest on Federal Land Bank Loans] has not been paid for 3 or 4 years, and the owner has either committed suicide or gone crazy or died. . . ." [Then the property became government property, the owner, if he survived, a tenant.]

—Testimony of Mr. Edwin Cornelious of Columbus City, Indiana, Director of the First Whitley County National Farm Loan Association, before the House Subcommittee on Public Lands.

"In Iowa over 10,000 farms are in the process of foreclosure and the Federal Land Bank is the most hard-boiled of the farmers' creditors . . . leads all private institutions in demanding its pound of flesh."

—Milo Reno, President of Farm Holiday Association, Radio address. Sept. 29, 1935.

What happens to the man who loses his farm? He becomes a tenant farmer or a wage hand.

"For the past fifty-five years, the entire period for which we have statistics on land tenure, there has been a continuous and marked decrease in

the proportion of operating owners and an accompanying increase in the proportion of tenants. Tenancy has increased from 25 per cent of all farmers in 1880, to 42 per cent in 1935."

> [The 1930 census figures give 42 per cent. Reliable estimates for 1934, show actually 49 per cent.]
>
> —President's Committee.

"An additional 10 per cent of all farmers were part owners. . . . These figures show that less than half of the farmers of the United States own all of the land they farm."

> —Ibid.

"Even now 3 million farm families are settling down to a social state of serfdom heretofore foreign to our great country.

"Almost 2 million more . . . struggle on under the burden of debt, hoping that a kind providence will save them from a like fate.

"Less than 2 million families of the Nation's once proud group of independent home owning farmers, remain, and their ranks are thinning every year. The independent home owner is rapidly vanishing."

> —House Subcommittee on Lands.

After the mortgage and lost farm the next step is tenancy, renting for cash, then on shares. Naturally tenants are obliged, as a rule, to use the worst acreages. Sometimes this is the result of a definite policy by imperial owners, by which they ruthlessly exploit both soil and other human beings. I have in mind a large estate in Illinois, in which crops are grown without regard to the ultimate fate of the soil, merely to reap the maximum immediate profit by means of mechanized methods and harsh utilization of day laborers. When this raping of the soil, usually after about five years, becomes less profitable, the abused land is turned over to tenants.

As a tenant farmer, the individual's economic defenses are still further lowered. He is less free in the choice of profitable land to cultivate. His costs of fertilizer are usually larger, his returns less. He is usually obliged to purchase at a company store at credit prices which are rarely less than 25 per cent above normal prices. In addition to this high price, if he is extended credit, he usually must pay from 12 to 30 per cent interest and even larger interest rates are on record. In addition he must turn over a large share of his crop to the landlord for rent. The result is that presently he wears out or loses his farm equipment and is unable to replace it. He then becomes a share-cropper, tied hand, foot and soul to the plantation owner.

"The cropper system prevails principally in the southern cotton and tobacco areas. Croppers operate 716,000 farms or over 10 per cent of all farms in the United States. They constitute 39 per cent of all tenants in the South."
—President's Committee.

From the standpoint of the conservation of the land resources of the nation, probably the worst form of agriculture is that of the single cash crop of the plantation system of the South. Although the human misery that it creates is, for the moment, perhaps not always so great as that in large industrialized agriculture, as in California, its waste of human resources is in general as great or greater than its waste of natural resources. The erosion of the soil finds its counterpart in the erosion of human character and of human institutions.

Farm tenancy, which is a form of agriculture pursued by over half our rural population, leads only to the increasing destruction of the soil and to increasing human bankruptcy. The farm tenant, who has no security beyond the will of the plantation owner, and who can be kicked off after any season, has utterly no interest in improving the land, no interest in conserving soil resources, no interest in any way advancing sound or scientific agricultural progress. If it is freezing, and he is cold, why not tear up a board from the floor and move on the next year? Chop down the privy if necessary. This also gives the plantation owner the chance to call him shiftless.

In the end, of course, the plantation owner is also caught in the web of the same disaster. Those plantation owners who attempt to be benevolent or efficient are merely placed at a great disadvantage alongside of those who harshly exploit their share-croppers and the soil. As the soil grows depleted and plantation productivity declines, the plantation owner can make a profit only by still further inhumanly exploiting his share-croppers. As the soil goes bad, as field after field is abandoned to gullies and brambles, the Big House itself—and this is to be seen throughout much of the Black Belt—goes the way that the share-cropper cabins have always gone: the paint peels off and can't be replaced: the roofs leak: the porches cave in. The system that brought this about is often called feudal, but it was rarely as decent in its human relations as feudalism was; and being based on commercial agriculture rather than pursuing the self-sufficiency goal of European feudalism, it has destroyed the soil in a way that Europe could never afford to do.

Realizing, though never admitting, that the plantation system is doomed, that cotton as a cash crop over much of the area is doomed, that his world is crumbling about him, the plantation owner is filled with panic. He himself is in part the prey of northern finance capital. His fate is dependent upon the fate of his products in the national and world market and upon industrial processes over which he has no control. His only solution appears to him to be to wring as much as possible out of his tenants: and since the level of existence has gone down so low and because his fear is so great, he can only rule by abuses and terrorism. His own lack of security, though relatively so much greater than those he exploits, results in a type of sadism and brutality that is typical of dictatorial régimes trying to prevent the establishment of popular rights and economic justice. Sooner or later, the plantation owner is converted into the outstanding prototype—Simon Legree.

The result of such conditions in the South and of similar, if as yet less aggravated, conditions throughout much of the nation has been to throw enormous numbers of the rural population into pauperism.

"The extreme poverty of one-fifth to one-fourth of the farm population reflects itself in a standard of living below any level of decency. . . . Over a million farm families have been forced into dependency in recent years."

—President's Committee.

"A total of 900,000 farm families on relief a year ago [1934] meant at least 4½ to 5 million rural inhabitants who were being kept from starvation by hand-outs of state, local and federal governments."

—Resettlement Administration, July 24, 1935.

It has been estimated that families on submarginal lands cost the government, local or national, at least $400 a year, merely in the upkeep of unnecessary schools and roads. This means that not only must such an anti-economical outlay be made, but that the country is deprived of the productive powers it might have were such people given access to proper land and to the knowledge to use it right. This estimate does not include actual government relief or the various costs due to human degeneration of people below the level of healthful subsistence, the proportionate cost of public hospitals, poorhouses, police, jails, prison, reform schools and insane asylums. It is not unreasonable to estimate the cost to the nation of submarginal farming at close to a billion dollars a year, an unnecessary burden borne by better-situated citizens.

The next step of such folk is to become a cropper or a wage hand. From the share-cropper and the tenant are splintered off the farm-wage laborers and the migrants. This is a process corresponding not so much to the plantation type of agriculture but is due to the economic difficulties of the cropper and the need for wage hands by the intensive and industrialized agriculture. This accounts for a proportionably higher number of wage hands in the North than in the South, for such a great number in California.

"In 1930 there were 2,733,000 paid farm laborers or 26 per cent of all persons gainfully employed in agriculture. In addition to the paid farm laborers, there were 1,660,000 unpaid laborers."
—President's Committee.

After I prepared the material on migratory workers, which appears in the previous chapter, "Migs: Shantytown on Wheels," and which, though here amplified, was published in *The Forum* magazine and republished in *Reader's Digest*, I had considerable trouble in finding an editor willing to publish it. One editor rejected it with the statement that I had missed the whole point of the American farm situation.

That I missed the implications of the migratory worker in relation to American agriculture, I seriously dispute. My conclusions, in fact, are not at all original. They are the conclusions of the President's Committee on Farm Tenancy, made up for the most part of very conservative authorities and technicians. The same conclusions are arrived at by the Council of Women for Home Missions which has been working in this neglected field under the leadership of Edith E. Lowry for many years. They are findings of all the reports of Rural Rehabilitation and of the Farm Security Administration. These conclusions are borne out by the findings of the Resettlement Administration. They correspond to the State Relief Administration Reports in California. They are borne out by the intimate and prolonged investigations of Dr. Paul S. Taylor of the University of California.

Another editor, avowedly interested in penetrating material which would get down to the roots of American life, returned it with the comment that these people are not typical of America.

This started me to thinking: What is typical of America? Is it the 41 per cent of our earners who have an income under $1,189 a year? Is it the 7,378,845 wage earners in manufacturing earning slightly over $1,000 a year? Is it the 7,400,000 farmers earning an average of $923 a year? In 1929, a year of prosperity and inflation, over 71 per cent of America's families were receiving less than $2,500 a year. Or are the men who receive over $10,000 a year, but 2 per cent of the population, a group to which my good editor belongs, more typical? How large a group do you have to have for it to represent something typical in American life? I fear the good editor was merely trying to create America in his own image.

Are the migrants in any way typical of American life? Let us summarize. Authoritative estimates have placed the number of migrant families at 350,000 or close to 2,000,000 people. In addition, official documents state that there are 650,000 families on submarginal lands, or approximately 3,250,000 people. These folks are frequently obliged to move from place to place. If technically they are not in the migrant class, they are likely to be in the migrant class, this year or the next, or the year after, and in any case their standard of living is little better, if any, than that of the migrants. There are several million more paid or unpaid farm laborers in the United States, who, though they may not move far, are for all practical purposes in the migratory class. These involve in all approximately 6,000,000 people. In the spring of 1935, according to the President's Committee, more than a third of the tenant farmers of the nation had occupied their present farms only one year—i.e., close to 900,000 tenant farmers, with families of close to 5,000,000 people. Probably the bulk of tenants do not remain on one plantation more than two years, but we will neglect them at the moment. But certainly a tenant who moves every year, even if not far, is a migrant. These migrating or semi-migrating groups provide us with a total of around 15,000,-000 people. Since when did 15,000,000 people cease to be typical of something important in American life? They are as well defined a group as almost any group in the nation. As a defined group, they are almost more numerous than any other definitely outlined group in the country.

The element in the rural population, classed strictly as migrant, follows distinct cycles of movement. One of the well-worn trails is that of the cotton harvests of Texas. As the season advances they move up into Oklahoma and the Panhandle. Later they return southward to work in the truck gardens and citrus orchards of the lower Rio Grande. Another definite circle of movement is by the families that move annually from the Southwest and Middle West to the sugar-beet fields of the mountain and middle-western states. Other groups of migrants from the deep South go into Florida for the winter fruit and vegetable seasons. Slowly they follow the berries, fruit and vegetable crops northward. One current eddies up as far north as New Jersey. There many Negroes engage in the oyster-canning season. Another current branches off west into Louisiana, Mississippi and Arkansas, picking grapes and berries, and ends up in Michigan picking peaches. The Pacific Coast has its own circle of migration. From the cotton and cantaloupe fields of the Imperial Valley, they move northward for truck gardening along the coast and into the San Joaquin Valley. The vegetable crops are followed north into Washington, some split off into Idaho for the bean and potato crops. They swing back for the grape harvest and later the cotton harvest of central California.

If many workers follow regular routes, season after season, depending upon "the lore of the open road" to guide them to casual employment, others go more hit or miss, depending upon employment agencies, labor contractors, stray newspaper advertisements, highway signs, the *padrone* or gang recruiter. All these systems are "hard on all concerned—farmer, laborer and the community."

"The growing number of recruits to the itinerating life too often enter upon it in great bewilderment as to distance, direction or destination. A map of the United States tracing the comings and goings of migrant workers would show some straight, clear paths, but there would also be an inextricable jumble of lines crossing and recrossing, weaving in and out of states, breaking off short, turning back on themselves."
—*They Starve That We May Eat*, Edith E. Lowry, Executive Secretary of Women for Home Missions.

Probably nearly half the rural population of the United States does not enjoy a standard of living sufficient for proper health, education, recreation; in fact, some of the most deplorable conditions exist on the richest farming land of the country. A good share of America's farmers who produce the food of the nation in super-abundance have insufficient food and improper diet, not to mention a lack of the other advantages of civilization. The overwhelming majorities of our rural population lacks what may be termed contemporary civilized standards. Naturally, your farm laborers, your migrants, your submarginal farmers, share-croppers and tenants have the worst standards. A 1938 survey by the Department of Agriculture shows average annual earnings among Negro cotton pickers were: females, $62; males, $178.

"Living and sanitary conditions are serious and irritating factors in the unrest we found in the Imperial Valley. . . . We inspected the temporary camps of pea-pickers. . . . We found filth, squalor, and entire absence of sanitation and the crowding of human beings into totally inadequate tents, or crude structures built of boards, weeds, and anything . . . at hand, to give a pitiful semblance of a home at its worst. . . . It is horrible that children are reared in an environment as pitiful."
—United States Special Commission on Agriculture Labor Disturbances in Imperial Valley, Cal., 1934.

"Of 775 migrant families which applied for relief, most of them had earned between $100 and $200 in 1935."

[This represented all income from which they had to pay for food, clothing and housing.]

—California Relief Administration, 1936.

Lest these facts seem to apply to merely one of the smaller, less-favored groups, let us turn to the submarginal farmers who occupy over 100,000,000 acres, equal to more than a third of the cultivated area of America, and more than a tenth of the total area in farms. We find the situation nearly as bad.

"Of the farmers in one poor area in the Lake States, 63 per cent were found to be receiving less than $100 net farm income per year. . . .

"In February, 1935, relief was being received by more than 30 per cent of all rural families in the more arid portions of the Great Plains. Total payments of all federal funds for relieving distress between April, 1933, and June, 1936, in many of the Great Plains counties exceeded $200 per capita of the total population."

—President's Report.

"In the case of more than 13,000 families living on the [submarginal] lands being acquired in the Land Use Program, the average gross income per family in 1934 was only $289, including $72 obtained from relief and other [outside] payments, while their average net income amounted to only $88."

—Resettlement Administration, First Annual Report, 1936.

Lest even this be considered a non-typical farming group, let us turn to the farm tenants comprising 42 per cent of the farmers in the country, utilizing 40 per cent of all farm lands and producing 41 per cent of the total harvest crops. We find, for instance, that in the State of Georgia, in the supremely prosperous year of 1929 with cotton at over 16 cents a pound, their average gross income was under $600 a year. Their income, when cotton is at 5 cents a pound, can be easily calculated.

"A study of 645 [southern] plantations representing over 5,000 families. . . . The average net plantation income above current cash operating expenses . . . was . . . $110 per capita. . . . On 12 plantations in

*the lower Mississippi delta, the annual net income averaged $46 per person.
. . . The average annual net income for croppers in this area was . . .
$38 per person, or slightly more than 10 cents per day.*"

[Practically no Mexican Indian, however primitive, has so small an
income.]
—President's Committee.

It is true that in many northern states the tenant farmer will in
some cases have an average income of slightly over $1,000 a year
and the average for the share-croppers in Texas (now thanks to
Wallace's A.A.A. largely turned into wage hands) was reported a
few years ago as $965. The average is raised there and in parts of the
Middle West by large-scale mechanized farming. But the small
tenant farmer in large areas is but little better off than his southern
cousin.

*The average tenant farmer throughout the entire United States in 1930
had a net cash income of only $21 a month. If his income dropped propor-
tionately to other farmer groups, in 1934 it amounted to only $14.70 a
month.*
—House Subcommittee on Public Lands.

But even lest tenant farmers be considered a too non-typical and
underprivileged group, let us turn to the farm-owners. On examining
mortgaged full and part owners—totaling in 1930, 1,457,766—we
find they are slightly worse off after paying interest than even tenant
farmers, their economic security even less assured.

*"After the average farm-owner has mortgaged his land . . . he is . . .
forced to meet interest and retirement payments . . . in order to prevent
foreclosure. In 1930 . . . his net cash income dwindled . . . to an
average of $15 per month. With this sum it is obviously impossible for the
farmer to meet his living expenses, which are just as great as they were
before he mortgaged his farm.*"
—House Subcommittee on Public Lands.

We have now included nearly 85 per cent of the farm population
of America. We will let Mr. Wallace look after the remaining 15
per cent as he has been so capably doing.

With these summaries it becomes possible for us to risk presenting some of the broader trends in American agriculture. The first of those trends concerns ownership and lowering of income and standards. Even the statistics heretofore given ignore the true picture of rural life because they largely omit the picture of the wage earner, also the worker who receives no wages and the migrant, from the final summary. What has been the change in status of our farm population? What has been the trend for different divisions?

1890–1930

Free owners	*−30%*
Mortgaged owners (excluding mortgaged part owners)	*+32%*
Mortgaged owners and part owners	*+52%*
Tenants	*+106%*
Wage hands [*since 1910*]	*+37%*

At the same time the value of all farm property increased 193%. The acreage in farms increased 59%.

—U. S. Census 1890, 1910, 1930.

All this shows clearly two things: increasing land monopoly and concentration of wealth in fewer hands, accompanied by increasing destitution and a propertyless condition.

Let us make a new classification of propertyless elements in our rural working population.

Wage workers	*2,733,000*
Tenants	*2,664,365*
Part owners (who must lease part of their land)	*656,750*
Mortgaged	*1,157,848*

Total of farm region operators and workers propertyless or in a very near propertyless condition *7,211,963*

—U. S. Census, 1930.

This means approximately 80 per cent of our rural population. It does not include 1,660,000 unpaid workers not properly classified by our census, many of whom are folk working for only board and room; others are members of owner and tenant and migrant families. They would, if we had proper information, undoubtedly add to our disinherited total, in fact might bring it up to 85 per cent. This means that at least 80 per cent, perhaps more, is in a state of pauperdom or near pauperdom, practically without any property. This is close to the average of dispossession which brought about the Russian and Mexican revolutions. Experience teaches that *no country* with such disproportionate ownership can maintain democracy or stability, and sooner or later faces revolution. In the case of the United States this rural population is much smaller in proportion to the whole, but such conditions are the prelude to the upsetting of all economic stability in the country, a loss of productive and consumptive power that cannot but help affect urban and industrial life adversely and little by little drag it down.

We chalk the warning up now, because we don't like revolutions, we don't like violence, and because we believe in orderly and just solutions.

Still other trends are obvious in all this: on the one hand, we observe an intensification and increase of feudal self-like conditions. On the other we see an increase in intensive agriculture, often with smaller units, but more mechanized, requiring greater capital, growing a larger output per acre.

On the one hand, the tenant and share-cropper are inhumanely ground down and the soil destroyed. On the other, the migrant wage hand is likewise inhumanely exploited and kicked about, but scientific agriculture mostly preserves the land.

But in either instance, the small independent farmer is competing with mass production. If one form is inefficient, nevertheless, by exploitation, costs are cut to the bone. In the other, low wages plus machinery plus efficiency also create lower costs with which he cannot compete. Though he owns his own property, free or encumbered, it means that he must cut his own personal profit down close to the coolie level. He is, so long as he competes in the market with commercialized products, unable to secure a decent livelihood.

Such conditions mean improper health care for more than half our rural population. Deaths from preventable diseases are high. Large areas are afflicted by malaria, a disease not difficult to control. A study of plantations near Vicksburg, Mississippi, by D. L. Van Dine, showed the average time lost from malaria was 14.4 adult days for each of the 74 tenant families. Another widespread rural disease, pellagra—the Red Plague—is due purely to deficient diet—semi-starvation, plus lack of greens, milk, eggs, etc. A purely vitamin disease, it is found in areas having some of the richest soil of the country. A compilation of data from the State Boards of Health from 13 southern states shows that of 121,388 persons examined, 28 per cent had hookworm, another quite preventable disease.

Such is the story of the plundering, the monopolization, the destruction of so much of the American earth. It is with sadness that we look back now upon the astonishing abundance that Mother America laid at the feet of American settlers. They forgot that it was a trust. They forgot that it was not merely to be thrown away in the spirit of a drunken sailor on a spree. They had so much religion, but so little religious kinship with the American earth.

Millions of lives are today being stunted, distorted, destroyed in America, more than all the airplanes of Mussolini ever blasted to death in the invasion of Ethiopia, more than all the Jews persecuted in Germany. The spirit of Hitler, cloaked in the greed for profits based on improper exploitation of human beings, rules vast areas of our country, pressing millions into economic slavery, into silence, into routine despairing existence. But it is easier to shout at wrongs across the sea and build a great fleet than to destroy Hitlerism at home, to give economic and political freedom, to guarantee civil liberties to all our people, Black and White. Where is the noble fatherland of our migrants, of the folk toiling so fruitlessly on sub-marginal lands, of tenants and share-croppers? Have they any reason to be worried about Naziism in far-off Germany? They cannot eat political democracy even if they had it. They are tinder for demagogues. They are tinder for the destruction of political democracy and the economic liberties still possessed by the rest of us.

"Farm ownership has been approved throughout our history as a primary means of attaining security. . . .

"The Committee's examination of the agricultural ladder has indicated

a series of groups of farm families whose insecurity is a threat to the integrity of rural life . . . half the total farm population of the country."
—President's Committee.

The President's Committee is here talking only of tenant families, not of farmers driven to the wall, not of mortgaged families, not of wage hands, not of migrants. The percentage, by adding these groups, is raised from 50 per cent to at least 80 per cent.

We have thrown away an empire, we have half-destroyed its agricultural value. While technological developments do not make this quite as serious as it sounds, in that process we have thrown away the security of millions, we have thrown away the decent life for them. Most of whole states have plunged into decay, and community life over large portions of the country is breaking down, despite New Deal efforts, before our very eyes. New technological discoveries will not, when applied, and least of all under present conditions, in themselves save the subnormal human elements now in ruins. In fact that new knowledge uncorrelated with economic and social controls may merely further promote misery and still greater uprooting.

If we wish to maintain a free country, before all else we must learn how to use our American earth wisely with the greatest possible benefits to all, with the purpose of creating a decent and happy existence for those who till the soil. In the American way of life, no industry which does not do that can long be allowed to continue under abusive mismanagement.

The New Deal, we claim, has failed miserably to meet this challenge.

CHAPTER XXIII

BEYOND THE LAST FRONTIER

In 1937 official optimism flapped its wings mightily over the increase in total gross farm income. That total had almost come against that of the first depression level in 1930. But for 1938, the Department of Agriculture was forced to admit that despite an increase of 11 per cent in A.A.A. payments, gross income would be off 12 per cent or about a billion dollars.

Blanket figures of total farm income have very little meaning unless broken down into the amounts received by the different rural groups. For the vast majority, no egg was laid even in 1937. Any surplus, above a very low level of poverty, is largely funneled into the relatively small unmortgaged farm-owner class, a small 15 per cent upper crust of "farmers."

The word "farmer" doesn't mean anything any more in America—not in a statistical sense. It may mean a feudal plantation lord or a gentleman farmer, a corporation, a bank, an insurance company. It may mean a man with 1,000,000 acres or with ten acres. It may mean a man with good land or with shale out-croppings that won't even grow tumble-weed.

It may mean a man with a mortgage bigger than the shrunken value of his farm.

It may mean a tenant farmer—42 (or 49?) per cent of our rural population. Most tenants are in a very bad way. And yet corporations can also be tenants, renting one big tract after another and quickly raping each of its soil values by mass mechanized production before casting it aside as useless acreage for poor tenants to starve on.

431

A farmer may mean a share-tenant, who works on shares. Or he may be just an ordinary cropper.

Gross farm income doesn't mean much, unless you break it down into definite classifications, which most statisticians, especially of the politician brand, engaged in great and noble policies, do not bother to do.

The economic control by our Kulak farmers and the class relationships in the farm areas are such that whatever profits might conceivably seep downwards are promptly siphoned back out of the low-earning reservoir. There is a definite social hierarchy in the farm population of America, and improvement due to federal aid has not extended even proportionately to the lower groups. Recent improvement in farm income, through the vast expenditures of the New Deal and 1937 bumper crops at guaranteed subsidies, has mostly given larger profits to that portion of our rural population which still owns farms unencumbered; above all, to the large landowners, those with most capital invested and most value of products per acreage, or those most exploiting tenants and croppers. This has been true ever since the inception of the New Deal, except to some slight extent during Rehabilitation, Resettlement and the earlier Conservation program, and except for those activities not aimed at agrarian improvement—relief and the W.P.A. Rehabilitation, pitiful at best, blew up; Resettlement went by the boards, except for a very limited Farm Security program now more ornamental than generally effective; and Conservation has been hitched up with the Wallace crop-restriction program, both pulling in different directions in a very one-sided teaming up.

Raper, a careful and accurate observer, investigating the effects of the Agricultural Adjustment Act of the New Deal in Georgia, came to the definite conclusion that it had helped save the inefficient, anti-economic and unjust plantation system. Rich planters were restored to relative prosperity, but practically all other farmer categories had lost status; therefore, in terms of possible social improvement or security, were actually worse off.

The study of Nourse, David and Black for the Brookings Institution concluded that in the country at large, the A.A.A. had caused considerable displacement of share-croppers, croppers becoming laborers, and, in contrast, a disproportionate increase in landlord's income. If the A.A.A. cannot be blamed for the long-standing acute situation of southern tenancy or for its getting worse, neither can it be said to have at all improved tenancy's condition or abolished it, except to create more wage earners, a lower status. A 1938 Kansas study, patronized by the state university and based on five years' investigation, regrets the concentration of farms in large units under the A.A.A. and the passing of the family farm. Like the Red Chess Queen, the A.A.A. has run hard—and slipped back a bit.

In a previous chapter, we pointed out the vast expansion during the last century of the American agricultural plant and of its new superior mechanical processes—a revolution brought about by rapidly expanding population, the industrialization of Europe and the opening up of vast world markets. The earlier agricultural development of the nation, never considered a problem at all, was that of bringing as much area as possible under cultivation as rapidly as possible, without particular regard for the scientific utilization of the soil and no forethought for the future.

The result was a tremendous waste of soil resources, although for a long time the line of soil exhaustion advanced too far in the rear of the frontier to be much observed or to cause undue alarm. But almost as soon as the frontier was more or less closed, then general decline, almost unnoticed, set in. Even certain areas of the new far-western states were affected.

The Populist revolt was in part due to the fact that enormous land areas had been settled up which never should have been put into crop land; even more, Populism was a symptom of the increasing subjugation of the American farmer to transportation monopoly and to unbridled speculation in farm products by others than the ones who produced them. That revolt told of the evils of public debt, of unequal taxation, of unbalanced tariffs, of the mortgage system, of improper railroad rates, of bankers' control of currency, and numerous other economic evils which have plagued the nation from that day to this. Populism was the last stand, and an unsuccessful one, of the independent farmer while he still represented a majority of the rural population. Now the word "farmer," as used in public discussions, means merely a small privileged minority.

Surplus land (despite depletion) and surplus farmers, the shrinkage of the European markets, new techniques, the replacement of work animals requiring hay and oats with traction requiring gasoline—these factors, among many other things, resulted in the periodic creation of enormous surpluses far beyond the purchasing power of the American people or foreign markets to absorb. The result was periodic crisis, loss of farms, destitution. The result has been a land revolution, which, though of great import, long went almost unnoticed because of the absorption of excess farm labor in manufacturing, mining, etc. Relative industrial prosperity long concealed the dilemma of the American farmer and permitted evils to become compounded without being properly remedied as they arose.

The decay of American agriculture and of the rural population was further concealed by the World War, which again called for great agricultural surpluses. Once more agriculture seemed to be expanding toward prosperity, almost as it had in the earlier frontier days.

But this was not a healthy expansion at all, for war is not quite a permanent institution; rather did the new boom resemble the dangerous over-exertion of a man suffering from high blood pressure and hardened arteries. It merely accelerated anew the evil practices of American agriculture, for much of the land was no longer capable of such increased non-scientific production, nor was the social structure of rural America strong enough (though this was not so apparent) to stand the strain of this false prosperity. The War unleashed all the hounds of speculation. It provoked anew the mortgage boom in the style of the early Kansas-Nebraskan days. Temporary high crop prices caused land to be drained still more quickly of its fertility. It caused new submarginal areas to be put under cultivation, which was merely to mean that in a few years still more people on such lands would become incapable of full self-support and hence a burden on the nation. Equally false was the post-War prosperity, which continued extravagant speculation and put off the consideration of the vital needs of American farm life, needs growing more pressing ever since the turn of the century. Over-expansion merely made resulting crises more severe.

The improper human and land tenure conditions have been sufficiently in evidence during all the past fifty years to preoccupy those patriots who thought of welfare rather than of glory and catchwords. But anyone who at all called attention to the plight of American agriculture was usually branded as a hare-brained nuisance. Now that so much of our top soil is at the bottom of the Gulf of Mexico, now that nearly half of our farm population is in abject misery, now that over 80 per cent of our rural population lives below a decent standard of comfort—below even a decent standard of shelter, health, and culture, we are wishing, as usually is the case, that we had listened less to the Fourth of July orators and more to the nuisances.

Today we openly witness the great social change of a disastrous nature that has overtaken one great branch of our productive life.

But that these agricultural problems have been solved in any fundamental manner, even by the New Deal, is open to serious question. Rather have the steps taken been those of political expediency, those of financial extravagance, those of promoting inefficient, not scientific production, those of benefiting a relatively small clique of landowners. It is a species of market-rigging. It has been on the well-known basis of treasury raids for a special group. It has resolved itself into petty pork-barrel hand-outs rather than a constructive program to pull agriculture out of the mire on to firm ground.

The tendencies toward decline have been and are more persistent, the evils deeper, than any question of mere prosperity—or depression-cycles—or drouth or flood. Increasing land monopoly, fewer free landowners, more mortgaged farms with a smaller farmer equity, owners worse off than tenants, increased areas of submarginal lands, more tenants and croppers, more wage hands, tell part of the story. Despite our vaunted soil conservation measures, more land even today is still ruined than saved by our belated reforms. Increasing acreage of submarginal lands, of eroded lands, of gullied lands, has meant an increasing number of folk on farms, even if they own them, incapable of earning a proper livelihood, whatever the economic prosperity of the rest of the country.

These long-range tendencies, not at all due merely to the depression, were, of course, so heightened by depression that evils, long maturing, suddenly ripened overnight and whole regions of rural America fell into dangerous near-collapse. One saw more families on the move, from drouth areas, from collapsing plantation regions, and also from many semi-agricultural industries, such as lumbering, which has left so much ruin, so many stranded folk in its wake. The whole agricultural population except about 15 per cent at the top began oozing down into the drain of poverty.

Much as we may be inclined to criticize the A.A.A. and subsequent Wallace programs, there is no need, of course, to belittle the brave efforts of the New Deal to salvage the broken lives of vast hordes of dislocated farmers from utter ruin. Relief measures were and are still being carried on on a big scale. This steady drain, unfortunately, does nothing to reshape American agriculture to a healthier pattern. It is a hand-to-mouth program, which, however necessary to prevent utter human desperation and stave off revolution, is a Sisyphus effort, with no end in sight. It provides no solutions. It gradually depletes the national wealth in a constantly narrowing circle. The long-standing sickness of rural life remains uncured, not only uncured but worse than before.

All told, the various New Deal activities present strange contradictions, so strange, in fact, that it is difficult often to tell in which direction our government really has been proceeding. Our crop and price control methods definitely promote inefficient agriculture and further soil depletion, and yet we greatly concern ourselves with soil conservation and for a time we tried to remove stranded folk from submarginal lands in order to make them produce more, though Mr. Wallace wants the nation to produce less. We continue to permit private lands to be destroyed, but T.V.A. plants 50,000,000 trees to prevent erosion. We curtail crop acreage but spend $500,000,000 on reclaiming new lands. We force farmers to quit producing because there is too much crop land, and we spend vast sums on new dams to open up vast new areas to increase our production. We fumble toward a proper land-use program, and set up 1,000 local and regional "Resources Committees," yet subsidize the wasteful southern plantation owners—but after all they do provide the Solid South vote.

Certainly one of the soundest enterprises undertaken by the whole New Deal was that of Resettlement. Here was a basic program— something that had been tried in various forms with great success in Sweden, Denmark and other countries—which would have retrieved a big share of our rural population from misery to make them self-supporting, hence an asset to themselves and to the nation. Badly as Resettlement was managed, much as it was hamstrung, little though it accomplished, the solution of this was not the destruction of the program but its improved application.

But Resettlement was also a thrust at the plantation owners of the South; it would have provided a striking contrast to their own slovenly methods, their tottering shacks called homes, their waste of the soil, their abuses. It might have made a few independent human beings who would have mocked the accusations of the upper plantation "aristocrats" that everyone in the social scale below them is merely shiftless. Here again the Solid South was not tampered with. Ruin plus votes was left in the seats of power. Resettlement was knifed.

Unfortunately, also, the principles of Resettlement ran directly counter to the political ambitions and agricultural aims of Secretary Henry Wallace, known to the boys as "King Korn Tassel," because of his deep interest in the genetics of dahlias. Jealousy between two governmental agencies saw the destruction of the one, which—if less comprehensive—was more valid, and which would have benefited a much more needy group. Instead 650,000 families in dire need and helpless to extricate themselves from present misery or to escape future disaster, were thus abandoned in order to further instead the cause chiefly of a million and a half full owners who mostly, if not in a bright situation, were able to survive and in many cases make large profits without governmental assistance. Resettlement was far more constructive than anything Mr. Wallace has put forward. But now, thanks to Mr. Wallace, Resettlement has been practically abandoned, whittled down to the Farm Security Administration, with a limited loan program able to take care, in a slovenly manner, of about 1,000 tenant farmers a year, when each year there are 40,000 new ones created. From beginning to end, Mr. Wallace has played the game of a relatively small clique of landowners. He has helped most those who already have, rather than those most requiring aid.

Mr. Henry Wallace has explained his aims fluently and capably with frequent oratorical mention of the Founding Fathers. Among other documents which he produced soon after taking power, is one entitled *America Must Choose*. One cannot quarrel with this analysis there put forward: his formulation of the aspects of American farm problems concerned with supply and demand and of European markets; but one can quarrel with his resultant proposals from the point of view of social organization, scientific efficiency, technical improvement, sound economics, sound agriculture and human justice.

The dilemma that Mr. Wallace so plausibly poses is the somewhat arbitrary one of isolation versus world trade. He thinks it doubtful that we can recover our former world market for farm products; in fact he properly envisages that we are doomed to lose even more of it. In an over-simplification, he points out that the opposite of this is to reduce American farm production to a point where we will abandon foreign markets entirely and minister only to our domestic needs. Thereupon, with a show of statesmanship, he chooses the middle course, which is the only course he could choose, or which anybody would wish him to choose, an outcome inevitable regardless of program.

His program, however, has caused us to lose more of that market than we needed to, though Mr. Wallace now blames Hitler for this. Actually the weather, which, good farmer that he is, Wallace forgot all about, should be blamed for part of this. As Nourse, Davis and Black, impartial investigators of the A.A.A., remark, "Compared with the effects of the weather, the contribution of the A.A.A. measures as they were applied was practically negligible." But they cost a *hell* of a lot.

Mr. Wallace's great contribution is to attempt to control adjustment to market conditions by governmental regulation, the aim being to help American *farmers* take the jolt more easily, and with the hope even of benefiting them or at least preventing still more of them from being forced to the wall. For a big share of the *farmers* of America this program is just forty or fifty years too late. There are relatively few free farmer owners left to help. The result of Wallace's efforts has been that mostly now it helps those who over the years have become the concentrated, wealthy landholding group. It is, in short, a purely Kulak program.

His program brings into play governmental regulation through crop pro-rating on the basis of past figures of production, by means of simultaneous subsidies and curtailment of crops. This, whether necessary or not, does not touch the basic problems of American agriculture at all. That restriction should be achieved at great governmental expense, in an artificial manner, without proper promotion of agricultural efficiency or community values, is very debatable. Wallace is playing speculator with the food of America, not with radios or Christmas toys. In any case, the Wallace program alone is no solution at all for the agricultural ills that beset us, ills that if not countered will rise up and eventually smite down a mere mechanical market-rigging stunt, as in fact they are doing right now, to Mr. Wallace's discomfiture. The Secretary of Agriculture is chiefly concerned with the good old stand-by of our classic economists: supply and demand. It is definitely a bankers' speculative approach, however much it may be camouflaged by such words as "social abundance," "parity income," etc. Quite realistically Wallace surveys the demand that normally exists here and abroad, and he then attempts to regulate supply to that demand.

But quite unrealistically he cannot take into proper account that other nations are not obliged to abide by his curtailment of supply either in production or in purchases. He has acted mostly as though the United States had a monopoly of such agricultural products. This is far from being the case. Other countries, fighting for the foreign market—in a world of too much foodstuffs where people are starving—rush their own products in to take up any slack we leave. The agricultural activities of other nations expand to the extent that we diminish our own output. And he was such a bad guesser on possible drouth and weather upsets that a few years back we actually had to import corn and wheat from Argentina when we had already paid our farmers out of the public treasury not to produce. The Wallace program, as much as anything, made possible the great expansion of cotton acreage in Brazil, India, and Egypt.

The 1936-37 world's cotton crop, outside of the United States, was 65 per cent greater than it was for the five-year average from 1928-32, just before our restriction schemes began. America's participation in the world market is constantly decreasing. By keeping up their own production, other countries can operate more efficiently, for this is a mass production world. The result is we are crowded out of foreign markets still more (especially as we are promoting high prices), and the only answer becomes still more crop curtailment, then still more loss of markets, still more federal subsidies, still more unemployment at home. This is precisely what has been happening, though it is fair to say that most alternatives are not rosy either.

Mr. Wallace has displaced land and labor, thereby encouraging enormous increase in the growth of cotton in other countries. We opened up by creating artificially high prices, markets to millions of pounds of new synthetic fibers, a development in large part unnecessary in view of our surplus of cotton.

Crop restriction also flounders constantly among the unpredictable bumps of international upsets and other outside factors.

Large areas of the world are so subject to dictatorial or imperial control that no dependable foreign demands exist. Wallace pointed this out himself to Henry Hazlitt of the *New York Times* (November 27, 1938): "The totalitarian states can, for example, shut off their imports from this country overnight, and as a result we are faced with grave economic problems." Not only that there are "interferences everywhere in the world with the flow of trade," there are "virtual embargoes on the currents of trade" by the dictatorships.

Mr. Wallace's own program cannot meet this situation despite the enormous outlays. Apparently it is quite proper to tinker with "supply," but only monopolists either in the political field, the industrial field, or the international field may tinker with "demand." Such monopolists, plus weather, whose monopoly as yet no man can greatly dispute, can run all supply-fixers ragged; they have already run Mr. Wallace ragged.

He is waking up to this now in 1938, after six years of unsuccessful experimentation. On November 18, 1938, he told Duke University, "It is just as important for the farmers and land-grant colleges of the South to study the significance of the trading methods of the totalitarian states, as it is to study the oncoming impact of synthetic fiber inventions." No one doubts the reality of the new German and Japanese trade moves, but like so many New Deal prophets who have seen their policies go down in ruins, Mr. Wallace, instead of admitting his mistakes, is now revealing that common psychological trait of blaming others. The goats for Mr. Wallace's failure to maintain prices and farm income, have now become Hitler and the rayon industry.

His program has given away much of the trade control to Hitler, and it has promoted synthetic fibers at the expense of cotton. In his speech he forecast almost the entire loss of America's foreign market in cotton, a loss he has helped bring about, and declared that he had abandoned his hopes for middle-course action—the thesis of his *America Must Choose*. This latest Wallace thesis means autarchy, a greater effort than ever to restrict American production. We are henceforth in agriculture to play the self-sufficiency game as does Germany, which really needs to while we do not. This means for us also an inevitable dictatorship of Fascist or semi-Fascist complexion. You cannot thus control the forces of production in defiance of human needs, without the help of the constabulary.

Naturally no Wallace-type program could be expected to work without complete international rationalization of a given industry. Country after country has found this out to its cost. The effort to keep up farm prices artificially—a substitute for a sound system of exchange and distribution and equitable landownership—has led to financial bankruptcy and political disorders.

Cuba found this out to her cost with sugar. An international arrangement then existed, in which she was falsely told that the United States adhered by sub-rosa "gentlemen's agreement." When this turned out not to be true, she was hit hard. Economic collapse and a series of political convulsions were the result.

Take merely one commodity. To fix the acreage of American cotton anywhere near a point to guarantee a given price and insure against governmental bankruptcy, Mr. Wallace would have to know:

1. The future weather in the United States.

2. The rapidity of new technological advance.

3. The coming productivity per acre, which varies widely from year to year.

4. The future antics of the boll weevil.

5. The future weather in Egypt, India, Brazil, the Chaco, etc., etc.

6. The probable acreage of Egypt, India, Brazil, the Chaco, Perú, etc., etc.

7. The acreage productivity in Egypt, Brazil, the Chaco, Perú, etc.

8. The amount of carry-over stocks in the world.

9. The possible subsidies to be granted in Egypt, Brazil, India, Perú, etc.

10. The possible tariff changes all over the world.

11. The possible new barter agreements all over the world.

12. The possible exchange control laws to be passed all over the world.

13. The thoughts in the brains of the heads of the cotton commission of Japan, in the heads of Hitler, of Mussolini, of the chiefs of the British textile industry, as to how much cotton they are going to buy next year in Brazil and Perú and how much in the U. S.

14. The possible needs of our textile industry.

15. Whether business is going to contract or expand.

16. Whether wages are going to rise or fall.

17. Whether the number of unemployed are going to increase or decrease.

18. Whether other departments are going to curtail relief and the W.P.A.

19. What Congress is thinking.

20. How much cotton the textile factories of Brazil are going to use.

21. How much cotton the textile factories of India are going to use.

22. The world market for our own textiles.

23. All the possible trade, barter, tariff, currency rigging, exchange controls for textiles in all the world.

24. The possibilities of the rayon industry.

Here are two dozen of at least fifty factors, most of them utterly unpredictable, which must be guessed right in controlling production for only one given farm product. Multiply this by other products, still more incalculable than cotton (a relatively easy one), and you pass quite into the realm of metaphysics. You have joined up with the priesthood and the Almighty. It must take a pretty vain man to want to do all this.

No wonder Mr. Wallace has thrown up the sponge. No wonder he wants to be done with foreign trade, so as to have a smaller laboratory in which to try out his theories. But the big bad wolf simply can't be shut out. International forces, even without trade, are too powerful; international price levels are too powerful. Only by means of an iron-clad dictatorship, as in the Soviet Union, could such steps have any hope of approximate success and then not over a long period.

The attempt to restrict crop-production in accordance with the law of supply and demand, when there is no stability in either supply or demand, when there is no possibility of forecasting it within a reasonable range of accuracy, is doomed chiefly to cause fantastic treasury outlays for meager results and sometimes near disaster. This is no argument against man's effort to bring order into his productive life, the contrary. Mr. Wallace merely introduces a new and dangerous element of disorder, his own desires, hopes and infallibilities. In a world largely controlled by arbitrary governments, with no free interchange of commodities, with our own life hedged about by land and industrial monopoly, the present Wallace program in the long run merely puts American agriculture, as in the past, subject to forces not only beyond our control, but now still further beyond our control, and this with no proper regard at home for scientific agriculture, efficiency or social needs.

In thus adhering to the classic formula of supply and demand, and ignoring real human needs, except as a pious hope they will be benefited, the good Secretary nevertheless had hoped to raise prices for crops so as really to provide the good life to farmers. He invented the pat phrase "parity prices." Parity prices were supposed to be those prices for American agricultural products which would bring to the American *farmer* [a few of the American farmers] an income commensurate with returns to industry.

The federal government has paid out much money to farmers to bring prices up to this rather mythical parity, payments which the good Secretary, with his flair for slogans which mean something different, often the opposite of what he is doing, called "the farmer's tariff." A subsidy, of course, is not even by poetic license a tariff. Any given tariff, however bad from the standpoint of sound economics, means treasury income; subsidy means treasury outgo. Both, however, tend to create monopoly, to set up higher walls against the free exchange of goods, a burden, benefiting a small minority at the expense of those least able to bear it.

Parity prices were defined in the 1933 A.A.A. act as those that would give agricultural commodities a purchasing power with respect to articles that the farmers buy equivalent to the purchasing power of agricultural commodities in the base period—for most products, 1909-14. The law does not elucidate whose agricultural products. It does not define the word "farmer." It cannot be said, however, that between 1909 and 1914 all farmers, even those who owned free farms, enjoyed their due share of the national income, far from it. Even so, those years with their sub-parity prices saw an unhealthy expansion of agriculture due to over-optimism because of rising prices, and to work on the basis of such prices now in a surplus production world upset by unpredictable control, meant that the government would merely shoulder staggering burdens that in the end could not be met. This, let it be repeated, is not the approach of efficiency, of equitable ownership, of sound production or of fair distribution.

The word "parity prices" greatly annoyed the dairy farmers caught between high feed prices and outside monopoly of distribution. It annoyed the consuming public. It hit the mass of poor workers hard, right between the eyes. The housewives of the country, counting their pennies, laid a curse on the good Secretary. So the phrase was hurriedly modified to "parity income," and Mr. Wallace himself now constantly denounces high farm prices and their burden to the consumer, while all the time trying to create them. "If prices were doubled," he recently declared, "of course, the poorer half of the population would be able to buy and consume only half as much dairy products, fruits and vegetables as before." King Korn Wallace has a genius for stating great issues and fine ideals, while in practice pursuing just the opposite policy. He has proposed loans of 45 cents a bushel on corn, is actually giving 57 cents, 23 cents above price (November 27, 1938), and wants the market price shoved up to at least 87 cents, which may or may not be a just level.

Which *farmers* are to get parity income? To what incomes in industry does the good Secretary refer? Is he referring to the ordinary wage earners in those industries? Or to highly paid managers? As in agriculture, so in industry there is a whole hierarchy of incomes. Does Mr. Wallace desire parity with the ill-paid textile industry? Or the better-paid automobile industry? Does he want parity with the average manufacturing wage of slightly over $1,000 a year? Is that the good life to which he so frequently refers?

The 1936 Soil Conservation and Domestic Allotment Act defined "parity income" as the re-establishment between "purchasing power of the net income per person on farms with that of the net income per person not on farms" that prevailed during the same 1909-14 period. The terms of the Act showed no definite way that even this unsatisfactory goal can actually be achieved. The proposals, improperly disguised as soil conservation, were for continued crop reduction.

Various categories of the farm population, as usual, were largely ignored under the provisions of the Act; this income would redound only to a very small percentage of the rural population. Actually, as Herbert Heaton has pointed out, the shift from price parity to income parity is a move from "an economically unwise ideal to a statistically indefinable one."

In spite of all the hullabaloo, all the cost and bureaucratic overhead, total *farmers'* income by 1936, by 1937, by 1938, had not yet reached the proportion of total national income it enjoyed in 1929; and even such totals as we have clearly demonstrated mean nothing with respect to equitable distribution of income among rural elements. In June, 1938, in spite of it all, cotton prices broke to their lowest level in terms of the gold dollar in all history. Nearly every commodity went down to the lowest levels of the depression.

The effort to raise farm prices artificially, rather than to create farmer income from efficiency, just land ownership, scientific soil use, prevention of speculation and monopoly, turns out to be merely playing the old death-game of scarcity. It is playing the game with food and human stomachs. It is politics used for market-rigging. It is the old bear-and-bull game artfully disguised, the game of stock market cornering. It does not create new values, or new wealth, or sound economic and social relationships.

Control of production plus scarcity in the market is the dream of all monopolists. Mr. Wallace's scarcity, high prices, hoarding, are a means of teaching more well-to-do farmers to act, in a petty way, just as do oil executives and the heads of the steel trust. Besides being producers, they are to become monopolist market-riggers and price-fixers. In a *very* petty way, we fear. Mr. Wallace has recently announced that (in spite of the high prices he forces the rest of us to pay, in spite of his huge ever-normal granary not made overly accessible to the people) the vast outlay of federal funds and his various devices will result in very unsatisfactory incomes. He has warned wheat farmers, among our relatively favored farmers, that they cannot expect more than about $300 to $400 a year net income.

This type of restriction of crops, which Mr. Wallace naturally prefers to call crop-control, merely results in freezing the present agricultural pattern of death in America in more or less its present mold. It benefits chiefly the large producer, those who still have farms, and for the most part has aggravated the condition of tenants and share-croppers, especially in the South. The wage earner is nearly out of the picture as a person to be protected. Mr. Wallace has never proposed a scarcity of wage hands to keep farm wages up. In no sense of the word is Mr. Wallace putting over a socialized control of agriculture. Clearly, despite occasional provisions for voluntary adherence, his program is a Fascist type of imposition, merely lacking the efficiency that ruthless, intelligent Fascist control gives. It hardens agriculture to the status quo; it bars new agricultural development; it blocks initiative, both individual and social. It establishes a rigid pattern, from which nearly all farmers' independence is erased. The modification of that pattern depends entirely upon bureaucratic policies administered by a complex bureaucracy, which locally is most often in the hands of those most likely to ruin any social value it might have because of traditional or selfish outlooks.

High prices for foodstuffs definitely increase the great burden on the producing classes of America, obliging them to spend a large amount of their incomes, already so greatly depleted by depression, on food. The great problem of overproduction of agriculture in America is not one of high prices and restriction at all, so long as the prior ones of landownership, proper food distribution and of mass purchasing power are not attended to. Those problems Mr. Wallace has never dared tackle.

Another favorite phrase coined by our good Secretary has been that of the "ever-normal granary." It strikes a ready appeal because it conjures up to us the old Biblical legend of providing for the seven lean years during the seven fat years. Its aim, according to the Secretary, is to increase farm security by providing a normal, constant and dependable annual income to the American farmer, or at least some of the American farmers, in defiance of drouth, bad weather, bad markets, Mr. Hitler and other contretemps. With his genius for calling everything by anything but its correct name, Wallace entitles this "Balanced Abundance," instead of "Badly balanced scarcity."

Just what is an "ever-normal granary"? Well-informed authorities have said that, barring excesses in certain crops, the American public as a whole, if it were to have the proper diet and could purchase food it really requires, would make necessary the doubling of our present agricultural output. Millions of our present farm population, not to mention our factory population, are suffering from diseases due to improper, faulty and insufficient diet. In other words, Mr. Wallace's ever-normal granary is really the same idea of scarcity sneaking in the back door. It is another high price maneuver!

This is to be achieved by market and storage quotas, plus crop reductions, subsidies and loans. He wants a carry-over of 350,000,000 bushels in farmer corn cribs, sealed by loans and federal agents. Many farmers cannot afford to build the necessary cribs, even with loans. Where is the cotton carry-over to be stored? Obviously in plantation or commercial warehouses, or at government expense. It is doubtful if there are a dozen ordinary tenant and cropper farmers in the South with facilities to store a single bale of cotton, or who can afford to store their cotton any length of time with others. The "ever-normal granary" is again a rigging up of the surplus for the speculator.

The 1938 Farm Act perpetuated nearly all the previous powers of the Secretary and added others. It mentions the granting of full powers to him 180 times. Wallace may determine acreage; he may determine payments to be made for acreage reduction; he may add payments for soil conservation practices; he may make loans to farmers in excess of the market value of the crops; he may purchase surplus stocks—to mention only a few of his manifold powers. If an intelligent control of farm production is desirable, that control is nevertheless impossible without a re-examination of farm ownership and the relative status of our farmers. All such controls tend merely to accentuate present discrepancies between the various farmer groups, to perpetuate unfair relationships, and to help those least needing it. It is a Kulak program.

Wallace's policies really represent nothing original at all—except for the magnitude of their application. In the last few decades a dozen countries have tried to play the uphill game of agricultural scarcity in order to maintain high prices for the wealthier producers. And in every case, in spite of all the controls, those countries have seen their treasuries drained of fabulous sums, their share in the world market diminished, their granaries filled up with the dead weight of surplus products greater than could be consumed. In any case they have not been able to withstand the general march of world prices. The cost to such governments invariably grew to staggering proportions. Countries trying such foolishness have seen augmented political skulduggery, favoritism in allotments to politicians and large growers, tenant and wage groups forced into lower income brackets. High prices mean fewer sales abroad; they mean accumulated stocks, pressing downward on price, resulting in ever greater treasury outlays.

Mr. Wallace drives ahead as though in a vacuum. He cannot control world supply, being constantly augmented (partly by his foolishness), and however much we seal up our borders, be it tighter than Russia or Germany, world price will still affect American price. It is a blind, dark alley down which Mr. Wallace has been heading, is still heading.

Already his program is collapsing and the consequences are already staggering. Despite all Wallace's controls America's cotton crop in 1936-37 amounted to 18,945,000 bales; the largest on record, brought about not by excessive acreage but by record yield; the wheat crop was the second largest on record. The fact is that with swiftly advancing technological process, acreage control is no sure guarantee of crop restriction. It does not even control the domestic supply. R. G. Daniell of Metter, head of the Cotton Producers' Association of America, has demanded of Wallace: "Why after six years of disastrous failure to make the cotton program work, does the Secretary insist on yoking it on the South for further trials?" It would, however, he predicted, be continued merely because of the "fears" instilled in farmers by Secretary Wallace and his aides.

Oscar Johnston, chairman of the National Council and former manager of the United States cotton pool, speaking recently in Memphis before cotton growers and processors, stated succinctly:

"We have the largest surplus of cotton in our history.

"We have the lowest world price in our history.

"Despite the fact that world consumption of cotton is increasing, world consumption of American cotton, both at home and abroad, is decreasing."

Under government loans made above market price, the government alone holds 9,654,000 bales of cotton, an amount equal to the entire 1934 crop; and it is still sealing up more cotton. According to the figures of the *New York Times*, in 1937, between August 1st and November 17th, we exported 2,236,000 bales (way below our normal export some years back); in 1938 in the same period we exported only 1,387,000 bales. Mr. Wallace has also been socked in the last few years by bumper wheat and corn crops, running up the cost of guaranteeing scarcity and high prices to fabulous amounts.

For years we have been digging up gold in Alaska, California and Arizona and burying it in Kentucky. It now seems we not only bury gold, we bury food and clothing. For some years we buried them right in the ground, plowing under cotton and tobacco, slaughtering six million hogs, letting California peaches rot on the trees. We now move our wheat and cotton into warehouses in increasing amounts. The scarcity program is a graveyard policy.

Mr. Wallace has tried to assume mastery in the face of world forces he could not control. He has done it at the expense of America.

We refuse to trade with countries practicing subsidized dumping, but oh, the dumping of American products, of American wealth—not to benefit Americans, but in a semi-gift to foreign peoples—that we are likely going to have to do! It will likely upset the economies of the world, not to mention our own. We are already subsidizing foreign sales of wheat and are likely to have to subsidize other surpluses, though we have paid so high for curtailment and for goodness knows how many other things. This sales subsidy is to benefit foreigners more than Americans. We pay out that foreigners may eat more cheaply than Americans. The winds have blown so much rich top-soil off into the Gulf of America. Mr. Wallace is puffing a lot more of it clear across the oceans. Not only that, but Americans must now pay to blow away that top-soil, drained into wheat grains, across the seas into waiting mouths abroad. I, for one, am on the side of the real wind—it charges us less than does Mr. Wallace's breezy airs.

Continued criticism of his policies has been made that high prices affect most harshly those on relief and the underpaid segment of our population. This has led the Secretary to state that the government now proposes to buy up at high prices, and further to maintain high prices, large quantities of foodstuffs for free or cheap distribution to the underprivileged—a two price system. Such was done with some of the livestock slaughtered off quite some years ago. Most of us are highly in favor of the mitigation of human misery, though the dole puts still greater drains on the treasury without solving the problem of the unemployed or of the disinherited rural inhabitant.

It does not help the latter in any way at all to achieve permanent economic security. In simple language, Mr. Wallace's crop distribution to the underprivileged is a process of using the United States treasury to subsidize growers and then to subsidize a large part of our population to buy the growers' product. To pay out government money to produce less and also to a large group of consumers to buy, seems to be cutting the circle pretty short. If you have to pay both producer and consumer, you are merely burning the candle at both ends. It can last only as long as the bananas of the treasury have not all dropped into the mouths of maimed producers and non-producers. It attests still further to the clogged nature of the American productive and distributive system.

Wallace's program achieves the charming inconsistency of making the American public not only pay higher for its farm products, but also pay through the nose, via taxes and the national treasury, in order to enable a small proportion of the farmers of America to charge us high prices. We pay in order to pay more. We also pay still another sum to permit another segment of the population to eat at all. Faced with further declining demand in foreign markets (in part due to the high prices brought about by making us pay to create the higher prices *we* must pay), he now further forces us to pay, via taxes and the national treasury, for a wheat subsidy (and other such subsidies are planned), in order that he may sell farm products in the foreign market (which he is progressively losing for us) at prices lower than we ourselves have to pay. In other words, we are to pay still further to create lower prices for somebody else, not American. We pay in order to pay more, then we are asked to pay again to give products free to those of us who can't pay; and then we pay still again so foreigners can pay less. All this is called patriotism and humanitarianism. This is why Henry Wallace is entitled to mention the Founding Fathers every time he speaks over the radio. By and large it is all just plain foolish.

Not only does Mr. Wallace make us pay coming and going—not only pay for creating high prices for ourselves, and pay to give products free, and pay for creating lower prices for foreigners—but increasingly he makes it more difficult for Americans to pay all of these bills.

For, by restricting crop production and at the same time paying out from the national treasury for lowered production, he thereby reduces the number of farm hands required, the number of ginners required to gin cotton, the number of men required to transport it, the number of men required to sell it; the number of wheat threshers, of grain-sackers, of truckers. The "dog-houses" of many harvesters are left empty. He decreases the demand for farm machinery, except for a manner we shall describe, thus throwing factory workers out of employment. By decreasing the quantity of agricultural products, while at the same time increasing prices, he is augmenting the profits of processors and middlemen, but at the same time decreasing the number of persons required on the distribution-end and the amount of salary paid out to such persons.

High cotton prices mean a terrific burden for our hard-hit textile industry, making it also less able to compete abroad. It has gone backward, while the textile industries of Germany, Italy and Japan have gone ahead. Our textile machinery has not been properly replaced. The efficiency of our industry has deteriorated. Today Japan has the most efficient cotton textile industry in the world, completely centralized and rationalized, with the most modern machinery. American textile workers are thrown out of jobs, consume less farm products— still another hurdle for Wallace's high prices and ever-normal granary.

And so it all boils down to our paying more to produce less to pay still more, in order that still fewer of us can pay more to produce still less. Then we must pay to keep alive those who are increasingly rendered unable to produce. Those who can still pay that more to produce less and buy at higher prices are merely forced to pay out more of their income to bring about this remarkable result. This in turn reduces general purchasing power. In the end, Mr. Wallace will have to restrict crops still more, at a still greater cost to the national government and to all of us, and make still more persons jobless and unable to pay out in order to make themselves pay more and help foreigners to pay less. In the end perhaps he will succeed in starving all of us.

The crop-restriction, high-price, crop-hoarding program of the New Deal accomplishes two laudable results: one, the largest subsidies and greatest benefits to those in the agricultural hierarchy who need it least; second, the subsidizing and stimulation of inefficient agriculture.

The maintenance of 12-cent cotton and later 10-cent cotton accomplished this very effectively. Experts have declared that on level areas of Texas, Oklahoma, and California, where highly mechanized production is possible, cotton can be grown profitably for from 4 to 5 cents a pound. But in eroded hilly districts of the old plantation area in the Black Belt, with low yields per acre and greater production costs per acre, cotton demands a 10- to 12-cent price if it is to be grown at all. As a result the largest payment under the Agricultural Adjustment Act and subsequent subsidy arrangements went to the large farms on the most fertile cotton land. The more insignificant payments went to the worn-out farms of the Piedmont and similar areas in the deep South. This has meant more soil depletion, still more inefficient agriculture.

This, let it be clearly stated, was no subsidy to provide men with the means of living nobly and fully; it was a subsidy for the poorest growers in the industry merely that they might barely survive while growing cotton at great expense where it should no longer be grown —cotton that nobody wants. It did not thereby provide any decent livelihood, it merely stabilized that decadent plantation area in misery and pauperdom—except for the greatly benefited plantation owners—while further promoting the exhaustion of soil resources.

It likewise promoted the misuse of even the most fertile land. On such land the wealthier growers, seeing the chance to reap richly at government expense, sought to make two blades grow where one grew before—the old abiding sin of American agriculture (when not accompanied by scientific care), thus endangering the fertility of our better cotton soils also.

The result of acreage restriction everywhere has been to increase unit production. This may or may not be conservative agriculture;

all too frequently it has meant merely leaching the soil. This, however, has tended to reduce employment and to bring about ever larger farms with technical equipment. The Kansas State College has sponsored a planning committee, which after five years' study has pointed out that the A.A.A. has definitely caused the displacement of family units. Enlarging farming units reduces the number of farms in a community, the number of families, the possibility of maintaining rural schools and roads, the number of users of electricity and customers for stores. It leads to rural depopulation and decay. One goes for miles on miles through this sort of concentrated farming in northern Illinois, where one fails to see a single house.

Despite this concentration of acreage which means a destruction of the self-supporting family unit, the demand for wage hands has not increased. Kansas, which used to require 50,000 extra wheat harvest hands, now, because of the new combined harvester needing only one man, warns all outsiders to keep away.

Two row, single-man machinery now plows, cultivates or plants 35 acres of cotton a day. Share-croppers were forced out, the larger grower taking all government benefits. In Texas, where a share-cropper a few years ago could make over $900 a year, a few have now been utilized only as wage hands, many of the rest sent on long treks to California, or to swell the ranks of the urban unemployed.

In the Corn Belt, a new mechanical picker, of which 65,000 are in use, now does the work of six men. Another machine taking care of silage displaces five men and two teams. Mr. Ray Murray, former State Secretary of Agriculture for Iowa, has declared that in the last few years a lost legion of 50,000 men has been displaced by such machinery in Iowa alone. Speaking of the 1936-37 crops (*New York Daily News*, May 30, 1938), Mr. Murray declared: "While we had one of the biggest and best crops in twenty years . . . we still had thousands of Iowa people, farm-trained and farm-minded, without employment."

The big producer, at the expense of all other farming elements, has been helped even more directly. Mr. Wallace has been called on the mat at various times because of the large payments going to such producers. One wealthy Florida sugar company, for instance, received over $1,100,000 in A.A.A. benefits. The largest A.A.A. payment in 1934 was made to a Mississippi company headed by Oscar Johnston, A.A.A. official, head of the Federal Cotton Pool, which got a rental benefit of $123,747.

One wheat grower received nearly $80,000. The prize example in the wheat industry is a Dakota grower who rented large tracts from an Indian Reservation for from 50 cents to $1.50 an acre, and received $7 an acre for keeping out of cultivation a large portion of this acreage upon which he would have lost nothing had he merely not rented it. Of this more than $50,000 hand-out received from the government, Indian croppers on the Reservation from which the land was leased, whom he had contracted, received in all less than $2,000.

Mr. Wallace, like a good politician, blamed this on the Republicans, who had caused so much farm land to fall "into the hands of corporations, absentee owners and larger operators." The A.A.A., he held, had "corrected this alarming development." The A.A.A., as a matter of fact, did not arrest this development. Mr. Wallace's argument is not even one of locking the stable-door after the horse has been stolen, but to put a few cows, chickens, pigs and what not in the stable to be stolen right along.

Here is the nub of a great deal of the difficulty in the various plans for crop restriction which does not enjoy international agreement or does not look to the sociological aspects of the problem. It is almost impossible to pass government benefits along to the tenant and share-cropper. Economically and politically, especially in the South, they are too much under the thumb of the large plantation owner to enjoy a share of these benefits. A large majority of them have never had any control over the marketing of their own crops. They are obliged to buy at credit prices at plantation stores, and pay huge interest rates. They can be kicked off after any season, or they can be held indefinitely under debt charges—virtual peonage, a form of debt slavery, similar to that which existed in Mexico three decades ago before the Revolution. Mexico has since become civilized enough to abolish debt slavery and make all plantation and company stores illegal. That would be too direct a step for Mr. Wallace to undertake even were he not handicapped by states-rights and the cumbersome ill-defined barriers between federal and state sovereignties. Rather has the Department of Agriculture, in most instances, tamely bowed to traditional southern abuses. The collapse of southern agriculture will do nobody any good, but it would be possible for the time being, until the system can be abolished, as has been done in Ireland, to regulate on a decent basis the relations between tenant and proprietor, guaranteeing a proper minimum of housing, sanitation, proper contracts, an ending of debt slavery, the abolition of plantation stores, and of the high interest "furnish dealer" practices.

In the administration of the crop-restriction plan, naturally the Department of Agriculture, in large part, has had to depend upon local agents. This is made to look very democratic. The farmers of a given community elect a committee of three; another committee of three is elected by the county. Mr. Wallace, however, appoints the state committee, and this operates through a system of federal farm agents who act as liaison officers. Usually they are able to determine the complexion of the local committees, and in nearly all instances that I have witnessed personally, they have played the game of the big growers.

Howard Kester, organizer for the Southern Tenant Farmers' Union, declared in the *New York Post*, February 10, 1936: "Tenants and croppers found the A.A.A. machinery, county agents, county committees were made up either of planters or their dependents. Tenants and croppers were cheated on their benefits, on their cotton gin certificates, and on the law's promise to let them have free farming and land withdrawn from cotton production. The planters were their own judges, and protests were of no avail."

In the Wallace set-up, politics inevitably have entered; and in the South particularly local politics are fully controlled in most places by the plantation heads; and they, as a rule, have been the very ones who still grind down the faces of tenants and Negroes. Long ago they brought disaster upon the South. They are the ones who dominated and ruined rehabilitation efforts, who determined and still largely determine the crop acreages to be allowed at the expense of tenants, and it is they who have largely distributed and received the advantages and lush federal outlays.

In Cuba, sugar-crop control resulted in exactly these evils: improper political influence, political favoritism, exceptions made for large growers with influence, bigger allotments for those swinging the votes, etc. It has happened here also.

Almost invariably the crop acreage for tenants and share-croppers has been more limited in proportion than that of the plantation owners. The latter, in control of the situation, have overstated their own previous crop acreages, have lowered previous acreage of tenants. In this way they have secured larger proportionate allotments, have gotten larger federal subsidies. I have found cases where their sowed acreage, after curtailment, was actually in excess of that previously cultivated and more than the owners ever dreamed of cultivating. This has enabled them to receive big rewards from the government, larger rental checks. I have already analyzed this process in Georgia and Alabama.

Practically all cash advances of the government to tenants and share-croppers, in addition to rental and parity checks, have gone directly to the landlord, or have arrived in his hands immediately afterward. Where the government rented land for the tenant (and usually the worst land at the highest price, which sum the tenant would later have to refund to the government), the money was invariably paid in advance to the plantation owner, who ordinarily would have had to have waited until the end of the season. When government credit was given for foodstuffs, it was almost invariably through high-priced plantation stores. If by some miracle any ready cash came into the hands of the tenant farmer or share-cropper from government sources, it was immediately snapped up for back debt, or by the imposition of fanciful charges.

There have been numerous federal agencies for farm loans, but whenever the tenant or share-cropper has miraculously received such loans, small in total in proportion to those granted to large proprietors, he has been obliged in many cases, if the sums have not been taken for back debts, to deposit the money at once with the plantation owner who for this service has charged 8 or 10 per cent on the tenant's own money, in addition to the 6 per cent interest already obligated to invest at interest, thus allowing him to get even a higher return than that indicated on money not belonging to him at all.

In none of the farm industries was the tenant more abused under New Deal regulations than in tobacco growing. Almost the entire reduction was saddled on them rather than on larger growers.

At one time President Roosevelt declared that while the A.A.A. was devised to meet an emergency crisis, he hoped that it would "prove as important in stimulating certain kinds of production as it has been in removing recent burdensome surpluses. . . . The benefit payments can be made on a basis that will encourage individual farmers to adopt sound farm management, crop rotation, and soil conservation methods."

But it was soon discovered that if the government persuaded the farmer to abandon growing cotton and turn to peanuts, presently the peanut surplus was too great, the price of peanuts was thrown entirely out of gear. A clamor rose from still another group.

Since substitute crops merely created new difficulties and dissension, restriction was changed to mean that only those substitute crops could be grown which had no cash market and would compete with nobody else. This may be aptly described as the crow-brings-apple-to-folded-hands-rump-moveless-on-rock policy; Mr. Wallace being the charitable crow, the American taxpayer the apple provider, and the farmer on the barren rock, the recipient.

This policy was jeered at so much, however, that without essentially changing it, Mr. Wallace now proposed that in return for crop-restriction benefits, the farmer should grow such non-marketable crops or grass coverage as would result in the improvement of his soil. Nobody in higher official circles, of course, can logically really want the soil improved because then it would merely become more fertile and more productive to grow crops it was desired to restrict. But at least this new program tied in beautifully with all the propaganda regarding our wasting of soil resources, the empire-we-have-thrown-away cry. The country had been pretty well terrorized by the drouth, floods, by fearful pictures widely distributed, during the short-lived Resettlement Administration, of the terrible things being done to our soil and the human wreckage resulting from it.

Soil conservation became the new cry. This was embodied in the Soil Conservation and Domestic Allotment Act of 1936. In crop-restriction itself there is no allotment of acreage on the basis of the character of the soil or the character of the farm operator. It is an arbitrary allotment dependent theoretically merely upon the amount of land or amount of crop previously cultivated. Thus the efficient and capable grower has been cut down along with the poor grower; the least efficient owner-grower has been promoted and has received benefits as well as the one most efficient. Soil conservation of unused portions (though no efficiency was enforced in the methods used for the crops actually grown) became the new answer.

While in many places, due to the activities of excellent technically trained men, especially in parts of the drouth area which were given special attention, much real work has been done in soil conservation, most observers are agreed that the grants under the Soil Conservation Act have been used largely to offset previous criticisms that only the higher ranks of the farming population have been very much benefited. Soil conservation payments have been used largely as widespread and fairly careless relief hand-outs to farmers, with little or no constructive purpose. No proper check-up on the farmers' carrying out the required conservation measures were made. As Nourse, Davis and Black put it, minor emphasis was placed in agriculture adjustment and "major emphasis on disbursing a very large amount of money to the maximum number of farmers." In good part they have resulted in anything but proper conservation of the soil. In short, this was in good part another demagoguish pork-barrel. Such hand-outs, without disturbing the proprietor-tenant, proprietor wage-hand relationship, may have kept a few folk from actually starving, but anything in excess of that could be squeezed out by those above.

In the long run, the lot of our farming population, whatever the immediate difficulties, must depend upon scientific and efficient methods of agriculture. In view of the obvious excess of production in relation to present limited demand, this statement may seem contradictory. It also seems contradictory because our problem is no longer one of attempting to produce enough to satisfy human wants; our technological advances take care or could take care of that easily—unless we keep on ruining so much soil, which is precisely what we are doing. This merely means that the pressing problem in connection with such efficient agriculture is that of the distribution to those who need and can use agricultural products, even though at present they are unable to purchase them; not by hand-outs but by restoring them to their rightful position as producing citizens. The problem is one of general purchasing power, of creating consumers, not merely of restricting supply, except as a costly stop-gap procedure. In seven years of existence, the New Deal has done nothing really to solve the unemployment problem, the most pressing and obvious of all requirements for increasing "demand" rather than curtailing "supply." Charity hand-outs, leaf-raking, etc., are neither a solution nor any great contribution to our national wealth.

Whatever the necessity of emergency legislation to meet the crop situation of America, that program, so costly, has not benefited the nation at large, nor has it protected the diminishing soil resources of the nation. At enormous cost it has favored a small, privileged group, above all, the 15 per cent of unencumbered farm owners, the smaller of which, in spite of being thus favored, have not been benefited in proportion to the great outlays involved. Whatever the emergency, the program has merely partly stabilized an evil situation. Thereby fundamental solutions have been choked back. The whole rigmarole of farm prices, parity income and the ever-normal granary camouflages the artificial promotion of scarcity and evades the basic problems, largely ignores the needs of the great mass of farm population. It is hocus-pocus to blind people to the things really at fault; a hocus-pocus to evade the problem of creating a domestic market by augmenting the purchasing power of the American people. It is a subterfuge for evading the problem of landownership, of land monopoly, of the plantation system, of tenants and share-croppers, in a land supposedly made up of free Americans.

More and more the course of action is determined by chiseling pressure groups rather than by any scientific planning for an agricultural system that will provide products to the consumers economically at low prices and create for all of the rural population, not just a small part of it, a chance to produce proper living standards and contentment. The fact is that crop controls, price rigging, storing up surpluses, are steps, which, to the extent that they are successful, merely perpetuate existing class differences and injustices—all the improper relation of tenant and share-croppers to owners, all the existing monopoly controls in agriculture.

Now we can understand better that contradiction which permits us to put out vast unrecoverable sums in order to restrict production, and other sums almost as vast to create new lands and reclaim lands at the same time that we are removing land from cultivation and permitting the continued destruction of the American soil. It is all a process by which we avoid treading upon the toes of big vested interests in agriculture; by which we avoid abolishing, gradually or immediately, the plantation-tenant system of the South. It is part and parcel of providing relatively miserable labor camps.

In a "foreword" to a recent pamphlet put out by Edith E. Lowry for the Council of Women for Home Missions, *They Starve That We May Eat*, which deals with the conditions of migratory workers, Mr. Wallace declares that their fate depends "upon the prosperity of agriculture generally." As we have seen, Mr. Wallace's concept of general agricultural prosperity is that of a program which, as it works out, benefits only a certain group that, however prosperous, will not distribute its profits downward because the lower ranks of the rural population are scattered, unorganized, weak, largely unable, except sporadically, to exert group pressure. He goes on to tell why the lower ranks of agricultural labor suffer. "If we have smug and complacent attitudes toward rural America," he announces, "they are likely to be extinguished by exposure to the problems of this disadvantaged group." He then adds, "It is important that books such as this be issued so that there will be a wider understanding of the problem. It will help speed the day when effective programs of action are directed specifically to the problem." He has recently expressed a hope of having a labor bureau in his present department of twenty-three bureaus.

His statements are pathetic confession that thus far he has not seriously concerned himself with the fate of the large mass of the farming population, a confession that in fact his program is designed to benefit only certain upper-crust groups.

Mr. Wallace has been Secretary of Agriculture for six years. The information about these elements in the rural population has piled up on his desk. He has been quick on the trigger to formulate colossal programs on the "scarcity" principle, while he has let other departments stagger on, doling out relief (and few migratory folk have access to relief), while various underprivileged farm classes have been pushed further down the ladder. In fact Mr. Wallace has fairly consistently curtailed all programs and expenditures, as he did for Resettlement, which sought to solve the submarginal human and land problems.

Our little circus federal labor camps in California—and I am glad that even that much is done—are in fact merely another subsidy to the large industrialized estates. The federal government, instead of obliging those estates to establish decent living quarters, foots the bill itself and at that in a casual, incomplete and haphazard fashion. Those camps are petty and miserable at best—not so different, we take it, from those forced labor camps of Germany and Russia—with a bit of sanitation for migratory workers, and on the other hand, permitting those same migratory workers to be beaten and murdered by Vigilantes and thugs when they have demanded of the big agriculturists decent standards and a living wage. Instead of seeing that these ill-treated migratory elements, in such a poor condition to defend their rights, are given an opportunity, either for fair wages or economic security or access to the land themselves, we stick up a few little shacks and a few screened in privies, then invite in the Y.M.C.A. to suggest nice recreation or hold musicals. It is like sticking a white lily on a manure pile and shouting, Look at the beautiful white lily I have planted—before it wilts.

New technological advances—though this is not the place to discuss them adequately—are likely soon greatly to transform American agriculture. I refer to the new science of agrobiology or chemical agriculture.

Some thirty years ago, following Mitscherlich's discovery of the basic laws of plant growth, a new science was born. Ten years ago, the discovery of the inverse relation of nitrogen to growth, led to the working out with scientific exactitude of the absolute maximum for plant growth and yield. Practical applications revealed the possibility of approximating very closely this maximum yield for any given crop on irrigated land, regardless of the properties of the soil. Dr. Gericke in California, by chemi-cultures, grows more than 200 tons of tomatoes or more than 2,000 bushels of potatoes per acre. Such developments may mean that in a short while no country in the world need fail to become agriculturally self-sufficient. It may also mean that if we now have a surplus farm population, before long we will have even a larger surplus and a larger percentage of farmers rendered useless. If so, technological unemployment on a scale never imagined by the wildest fears of the technocrats looms in our farm areas. Imagine the cutting down on acreage the good Secretary would then have to perform, the still greater unemployment he would have to assist in creating. King Canute, he is in any case, even now, futilely pushing against the wall of the rushing sea of technological change, rather than trying to provide a sound vessel in which we can ride out the storm.

Possibly the only way to bridge this coming disaster—for disaster it will be without economic and social foresight—is one, on the face of it, paradoxical, i.e., to put an end to land-monopolies, tenantry and share-cropping, and once more giving Americans free access to the soil as they once largely had.

In the very teeth of the growth of what efficient intensive industrialized agriculture we have (a type of production that now ruthlessly exploits migrant labor), we also behold the phenomenon of extensive, inefficient, wasteful plantation and tenant agriculture (with even worse exploitation), also expanding its acreage and its influence. Both squeeze the life out of the few remaining independent farmers. Nearly all new technical advances are featured by such parallel throw-backs. Now, to develop an agriculture which will bring happiness to those who engage in it and profit to the community, we shall need a still greater throw-back, one that for a time will parallel the new agrobiological development—not to protect privileged agricultural interest no longer able to produce efficiently and at a profit—but for humanitarian reasons; or, better said, since the word "humanitarian" arouses the ire of the hard-boiled, to conserve our citizenry, prevent economic collapse, stave off revolution, and keep industry and social system functioning without grave upsets.

In order to avoid overwhelming disaster to human beings and our country, we shall have to allow millions by free access to the land to get out of commercial agriculture and return to subsistence farming. Scientific agriculture, which is so promoting productive progress and commercial production as never before, requires capital and business methods. It brings success to the efficient, ruin for the haphazard (some of whom Wallace now protects at great cost). As a matter of fact today ninety per cent of our farmers are woefully haphazard. . . . But that is no reason for killing them off as we did the Indians. If for nothing else we may need them to fight wars.

Subsistence farming should not mean descent to large-scale southern serfdom, a further increase in our primitive feudal economics. We have plenty of that there now. Nor am I here romanticizing about the good earth—no poetizing of the village, no demand for a return to the simple life, as is advocated by the pre-Confederate southern agrarians, mostly worn-out intellectuals and poets. Primitive subsistence farming is a poor makeshift, something that brutalizes people in ignorance, cuts them off from proper human intercourse, removes them from the world of active exchange. It is no solution unless we want to turn ourselves into Chinamen, but we are doing worse than that now. The evil individual effects of such farming can, however, be partly mitigated by collective intelligence.

Until the mighty force of technological change can be adjusted to our social life, until we have more economic justice, subsistence farming will at least make men somewhat independent, self-sufficient, reasonably contented, able to survive. At least we will not have to pay millions of dollars to make millions of folk semi-producers along inefficient lines, and leave the rest to welter in complete uselessness for themselves and the country. Treasury drains would be greatly halted. We can well afford to promote more primitive subsistence agriculture in this manner during a transition period while the new agriculture provides its benefits to the country. This is in fact one of the few ways, unless we wish to increase by many millions our disinherited and starving proletariat and make even more fantastic drains on the treasury, and run the risk of revolution for us, to bridge the period until co-operative and collective farms, or agricultural unions, or proper social legislation are developed.

This naturally will require the abandonment of single cash crops in much of the nation, the abolition for a large portion of our rural population of the commercialized agriculture which has existed since the founding of our republic and which, because of improper methods, has led to the sad waste of resources we have described. Mr. Wallace, in fact, has been forcing just such abandonment, but with no corresponding constructive effort to give security or liberate our farming population, or to make it productive along more successful lines, or to provide any real cushion for the rapid development of intensive industrialized agriculture now on its way, agriculture such as will be promoted by T.V.A., the Arizona-Colorado ditch, the Coulee Dam, etc.

Some areas, such as that served by the T.V.A., can almost immediately, because of cheap electricity, abundant low-cost fertilizers, proper reforestation of submarginal lands, soil conservation, easy river transportation, and organized control, at once assume a proper place in the new style of agriculture. Individual, co-operative or other organized means of production can there be promptly worked out for the maximum benefit to those who produce. No blanket program for the whole country can work (that is part of Wallace's difficulty); various regions have their peculiar problems as to soil, social relationships, kind of crops, etc.

In any event, whatever the form of agriculture or its developments, the land of America must once more be considered a sort of public domain as it was before it was originally stolen and distributed —but not an idle domain. This difference must now come into play: those given access anew to the land can no longer, as of old, be permitted to destroy its fertility, through allowing careless erosion, the planting of improper crops, or other abuses. The farmer in America, whose cause I so advocate, by and large has shown himself incapable of properly preserving the land he farms. He can no longer enjoy his individual right to ruin it. The way of life of the American farmer —unless he prefers to semi-starve as a casual wage hand—cannot be respected merely because it is traditional. The holders cannot be allowed to wreak the havoc they have in the past. Land must henceforth be considered the patrimony of all America.

A great hue and cry has been raised up against Mr. Wallace because of so-called governmental paternalism and meddling with sacred individual rights of the farming classes. The unfortunate part of his invasion of so-called sacred individual rights is that it has been exercised basically not in any new fashion, but in the traditional way of helping one small privileged group at the expense of other groups and of the nation at large, of trying to make petty monopolists out of the more prosperous farmers. We may look upon it with some tolerance, because it represents special favoritism to a group which in the past has had less special privilege bestowed upon it proportionately than have many other groups.

The anti-economical features, the cost to the public at large, the relative discrimination against less-favored elements in the same field of agriculture, defects which feature the Wallace program, are of course not at all new in American history. My criticism of Wallace's program is specifically on the grounds that it so slavishly imitates the traditional pattern of paternalism to special groups—a racket of long standing, benignly accepted as "the American way."

His program is new merely in that it curtails production instead of promoting traditional agricultural expansion. It sets up a nonflexible pattern, rigidly sets an unchangeable class hierarchy, so that its implications are Fascist and authoritarian. This is not governmental planning, let alone social or community planning. It is merely meddling and, however disguised, arbitrary coercion. It is setting up, in a manner similar to that used by the decaying feudal class in France before the Revolution, of rigid controls over supply and demand and price. It is no constructive program at all. In every instance Mr. Wallace has mostly knifed sound programs of scientific land use, all effort to destroy monopoly controls to change the plantation system, to promote social justice and sound economics. These things have been shoved aside to further his short-sighted market-rigging stunts. The few constructive things have been done by others in spite of that program.

A government bulletin on technical land use has stated that the history of our country until recently has mostly shown only "haphazard settlement." Mr. Wallace's program may be called "haphazard de-settlement." What we need, perhaps, is scientific and controlled resettlement. A sound farm program should attempt to return to that more worthy tradition of America, that of economic expansion and abundance, the good life for all.

Instead of crop restriction, which has no moral validity so long as all Americans are not properly supplied, there should be control of abundance; the land should be regarded, not as something to be exploited or destroyed, or played with by a special group, but as a national patrimony to be used efficiently and to be properly conserved. Controls are of course inevitable (Wallace's slogan of crop control to cover a scarcity, petty-profit program, is an unfair use of the word) and should have the aim of seeing that no portion of our rural population is shoved down as at present below the minimum standards of food, clothing, shelter, health, education, recreation. Quite apart from humanitarian considerations, there is required a true land "use" program in accordance with social needs and scientific methods, not the previous land "misuse" practices of the nation or the present land "disuse and misuse" as promoted by our present Secretary.

Neither the burden of this book, nor the weight of history, nor the present crisis in American agriculture should be left upon the shoulders of Mr. Wallace. He has merely been caught in the down suction of a vanishing river of prosperity at the end of a historical process. He has sought manfully to face the tremendous problems involved. If I am in disaccord, both from a humanitarian and an economic standpoint, with the principles on which he has worked, I am not unaware of the marginal benefits of even a mistaken policy; and to the credit of the Roosevelt administration, it has been aware that the farm problems of America, so long ignored, are social and national, that upon the solution of them depends much of the happiness, prosperity and strength of our nation.

This book—if many historical aspects have been omitted—can be called the story of the relation of man to the American soil. That is the essential biography of a nation, of our nation, of any nation. In the last analysis, whatever the industrial development, whatever world trade is achieved, whatever the flowering of culture and the arts, the basic happiness, stability and prowess of any nation depends upon the sound and creative and health-giving relationship of the people to the land where they live. Upon that relationship depends the form by which property is held and men associate in their common tasks, the manner in which people are fed and clothed, the sentiments that nourish our whole being, our love of the earth that is our home—our nationality, our patriotism. The American earth is the ultimate source of our ideas, our poetry, our arts.

We have abused the American earth. We have destroyed much of it. We have denied men proper access to it, stunting their productive powers. We have seen vast numbers of those who still till the earth driven to low levels, so that they are denied not only a minimum with which properly to nourish their bodies and house their families, but have no access to leisure or culture. As in ancient Rome, we have created an unhealthy relationship between rural and urban life, choking the flow of goods and the reciprocal flow of knowledge. We have been greedy for the profits of a day, forgetting that the American earth is the greatest heritage we can pass on to our children, to our nation. It is our nationality.

Out of that abuse and haste have come millions of stunted lives, families dislocated, broken, cast down from the empire of prosperity that is America. Out of that abuse and haste have come dark fears and violence, the fears of those who still own land but see their prospects dwindling, and the fear of those who lack security, so that both are thrown into harsh conflict. Out of those fears have come class warfare, the ugliness of brutal farm strikes, of Vigilantes, armed thugs, lynching, of savagery between man and man. In many sections of our country, men have become merely dregs of that base conflict, not civilized beings living in peace, in created contentment as civilized beings, cultivating their nobler possibilities and attributes. And to that extent—by our lights—they cease to be true Americans. For if our nation has any meaning, it is not to be found in the spectacle of men reduced to snarling over a bare bone.

We come to the end of the trail along which we started. It started in the wide meadows of California, with its great sweep of open land and free men, its lofty mountains, its fertile valleys, its peaceful farms, its ambitious communities, the unlimited horizons on the last land frontier of America. Those horizons have not held. They have narrowed, and despite the herculean efforts of the New Deal, are still narrowing for the majority of the rural dwellers of America. In three score years the ineluctable march of our farm population down toward disinheritance, poverty and insecurity has continued. Of what avail are our advanced techniques, our expanding science, our machinery, our great dams and irrigation projects, if these things fail to bring more of the good life, if in fact life grows harsher for vast numbers, if opportunity and achievement are denied?

In spite of all this we can also count our great blessings. If this book has stressed evils and problems, and the breakdown in many directions of sound social and productive relationships, it is not thereby a pessimistic book. It is a book of hope and of faith. Despite our wastefulness, our nation is still wealthy in land resources and can produce an abundance for all. We are not crowded to desperation as some of the countries of Europe. The problem is merely one of proper use of our resources, the creating of possibilities for all men to produce without being unduly exploited. This cannot be achieved by a program of scarcity, of market controls, or of treasury hand-outs. That it can be achieved is shown by the experience of a few European countries, which, without menace to their neighbors, have created relatively active, prosperous and contented societies in the face of difficulties far greater than ours, with resources far more limited, with far less access to technical aids. Countries such as Denmark, Holland, Sweden, have achieved this in the face of enormous handicaps and international uncertainty. They have done so because they have worked more seriously toward the goal of abundance for all, security for all, the right of all to labor and receive proper returns from that labor.

They have worked for national harmony and balanced security in a spirit of social justice.

I am unwilling to admit that Americans are less intelligent, less able to plan their national welfare in terms of the right to work, decent living standards, human security, and justice between men and classes than are other nations. This is the challenge. It is a challenge that the United States of all nations should not fear.

BIBLIOGRAPHY

A Partial List of Sources

Adams, James Truslow, THE EPIC OF AMERICA, New York, 1931.

Alabama Polytechnic Institute, FEEDING THE FARM FAMILY IN THE PRESENT "HARD TIMES," Helen Kennedy, Extension pamphlet, No. 1, Auburn, Alabama.

American Historical Association, ANNUAL REPORTS.

Amlie, Thomas R., THE INDEPENDENT FARMER, *Common Sense*, September, 1935.

Anthony, Irwin, PADDLE WHEELS AND PISTOLS, Philadelphia, 1929.

Ball, William Watts, THE STATE THAT FORGOT, Indianapolis, 1932.

Baxter, W. P., MIGRATORY LABOR CAMPS, U. S. Resettlement Reprint from *The Quartermaster Review*, July-August, 1937.

Beecher, Lyman, AUTOBIOGRAPHY, etc., New York, 1864.

Beston, Henry (Ed.), AMERICAN MEMORY, New York, 1937.

Bowman, Isaiah, THE PIONEER FRINGE, American Geographic Society, New York, 1931.

Burt, Struthers, POWDER RIVER, New York, 1938.

Caldwell, Erskine, and Bourke-White, Margaret, YOU HAVE SEEN THEIR FACES, New York, 1937.

Calverton, V. F., THE PASSING OF THE GODS, New York, 1934.

Carmer, Carl, STARS FELL ON ALABAMA, New York, 1934.

Connor, L. G., A BRIEF HISTORY OF THE SHEEP INDUSTRY OF THE UNITED STATES, American Historical Society, Annual Report, 1921.

Dunbar, Seymour, A HISTORY OF TRAVEL IN AMERICA, New York, 1937.

Dwight, Timothy, TRAVELS: IN NEW ENGLAND AND NEW YORK, 4 Vols., New Haven, 1821-2.

Fisher, Sidney George, THE MAKING OF PENNSYLVANIA, Philadelphia, 1896.

Forbes, Allan, TOWNS OF NEW ENGLAND AND OLD ENGLAND, New York, 1920, 1937.

Garland, Hamlin, THE SON OF THE MIDDLE BORDER, New York, 1914, 1917, 1923.

Goodrich, Samuel Griswold, Recollections of a Lifetime, Auburn, N. Y., 1856.

Graves, Ralph A., Louisiana, Land of Perpetual Romance, *The National Geographic Magazine*, April, 1930.

Guernsey, Chas. A., Wyoming Cowboy Days, New York, 1936.

Hader, J. J., Honk Honk Hobo, *Survey Graphic*, 1928.

Hartman, Sadakichi, A History of American Art, 2 Vols., Boston, 1901.

Hartman, W. A., and Wooten, H. H., Georgia Land Use Problems, Georgia Experiment Station, Bulletin 191, May, 1935.

Heaton, Herbert, Agriculture: The Decisive Factor, *Political Quarterly*, London.

Havighurst, Walter, Upper Mississippi, A Wilderness Saga, New York, 1937.

Hibbs, Ben, The Dust Bowl Can Be Saved, *Saturday Evening Post*, Dec. 18, 1937.

Hicks, Clifton, Upheaval in the Corn Belt, *Harpers Magazine*, Oct., 1934.

Holbrook, Stewart H., Holy Old Mackinaw, New York, 1938.

Hubbart, Henry Clyde, The Older Middle West, 1840-1880, New York, 1936.

Johnson, Alvin, Homesteads and Subsistence Homesteads, *Yale Review*, March, 1935.

Kester, Howard, Terror Stalks Cotton Belt Again, *New York Post*, Feb. 10, 1936.

King, Grace, New Orleans, the Place and the People, New York, 1934.

Kruif, Paul de, The Rise and Fall of Pellagra, *Country Gentleman*, Aug., 1937.

Lathrop, Elise, Early American Inns and Taverns, New York, 1937.

Louisiana, Dept. of Conservation, Division of Forestry, Classification and Uses of Agricultural and Forest Lands in the State of Louisiana and the Parishes, Bulletin No. 24, Vol. II.

Lowry, Edith E., They Starve That We May Eat; Migrants of the Crops, Council of Women for Home Missions, New York, 1938.

Mather, Cotton, Magnalia Christi Americana (1702), Hartford, 1853.

McLellan, Elizabeth, HISTORY OF AMERICAN COSTUME, 1607-1870, New York, 1937.

Meyers, Gustavus, HISTORY OF THE GREAT AMERICAN FORTUNES, New York, 1907, 1936.

Mitchell, Jonathan, THE FARMER IS FINANCED, *New Republic*, June 30, 1937.

Mokler, Alfred James, HISTORY OF NATRONA COUNTY, WYOMING, Chicago, 1923.

—— TRANSITION OF THE WEST, Vol. I, Chicago, 1927.

Mussey, Barrows (Ed.), WE WERE NEW ENGLAND, New York, 1937.

Nourse, E. G., Davis, J. S. and Black, J. D., THREE YEARS OF THE AGRICULTURAL ADJUSTMENT ADMINISTRATION, Washington, 1937.

Nichols, Thomas Low, FORTY YEARS OF AMERICAN LIFE, 1821-62, (1864), New York, 1937.

Odum, Howard W., SOUTHERN REGIONS OF THE UNITED STATES, Chapel Hill, 1936.

Oudard, Georges, FOUR CENTS AN ACRE, New York, 1931.

Owen, Thomas M., ANNALS OF ALABAMA, Birmingham, 1900.

Parker, Carleton, THE CASUAL LABORER AND OTHER ESSAYS, New York, 1920.

Peattie, Donald Culross, A PRAIRIE GROVE, Boston, 1938.

Phillips, Ulrich Bonnell, GEORGIA AND STATE RIGHTS, American Historical Association, Annual Report, 1901, Vol. II, Washington, 1902.

Pitzer, Robert Claiborne, THREE FRONTIERS, Muscatine, Iowa, 1938.

Raper, Arthur F., PREFACE TO PEASANTRY, Chapel Hill, 1936.

—— TRAGEDY OF LYNCHING, Chapel Hill, 1938.

Russell, William Howard, MY DIARY, NORTH AND SOUTH, Boston, 1863.

Rowell, Edward J., DROUGHT REFUGEE AND LABOR MIGRATION TO CALIFORNIA IN 1936, U. S. Dept. of Labor, Washington, 1937.

Rhyne, Jennings I., SOME SOUTHERN COTTON MILL WORKERS AND THEIR VILLAGES, Chapel Hill, 1930.

Rister, Carl Coke, SOUTHERN PLAINSMEN, Norman, Oklahoma, 1938.

Saxon, Lyle, FABULOUS NEW ORLEANS, New York, 1934.

Sewall, Samuel, DIARY, 1674-1729, 3 Vols., Boston, 1878-82.

Stephenson, George M., JOHN LIND OF MINNESOTA, Minneapolis, 1935.

Stewart, Maxwell S. (Ed.), FARM POLICIES UNDER THE NEW DEAL, Public Affairs Committee, 1938.

Tate, Allen, THE MIGRATION, *Yale Review*, Sept., 1934.

Taylor, Dr. Paul S., AGAIN THE COVERED WAGON, *Survey Graphic*, July, 1936.

—— FROM THE GROUND UP, *Survey Graphic*, Sept., 1936.

—— MIGRATORY FARM LABOR IN THE UNITED STATES, *Monthly Labor Review* (U. S. Dept. of Labor), March, 1937.

—— SYNOPSIS OF SURVEY OF MIGRATORY LABOR PROBLEMS IN CALIFORNIA, Resettlement Administration, San Francisco, 1936.

—— UPRISING ON FARMS, *Survey Graphic*, Jan., 1935.

Taylor, Dr. Paul S., and Vasey, Tom, CONTEMPORARY BACKGROUND OF CALIFORNIA FARM LABOR, Reprint from *Rural Sociology*, Vol. I, No. 4, Dec., 1938.

Turner, Frederick Jackson, THE FRONTIER IN AMERICAN HISTORY, New York, 1920, 1937.

United States:

Dept. of Agriculture, Agricultural Adjustment Administrations, Mimeographed circulars issued by county agents, Dadeville, Auburn, etc.

—— BUREAU OF SOILS, SOIL SURVEY OF OCONEE, MORGAN, GREENE AND PUTNAM COUNTIES, ALABAMA, Washington, 1922.

—— FARM SECURITY ADMINISTRATION, REGION IX, Bulletin News Release, San Francisco, Dec., 1936.

—— FARM SECURITY ADMINISTRATION, RURAL REHABILITATION IN REGION I, 1937, Washington, 1938.

—— STATE LAND SETTLEMENT PROBLEMS AND POLICIES IN THE UNITED STATES, Tech. Bull. No. 357, Washington, 1937.

—— YEAR BOOK OF AGRICULTURE: 1937, Washington, 1938.

Dept. of Commerce Census, 1880, et al.

—— CENSUS OF AGRICULTURE, 1935.

—— RELIGIOUS BODIES, 2 Vols., Washington, 1936.

Congress, House of Representatives, Report of the Subcommittee of the Committee on Public Lands, 74th Congress, 2nd Session, HOMES FOR ACTUAL FARM FAMILIES, Final Print, Washington, 1936.

Federal Farm Board, ITS GENERAL POLICIES AND WORK IN HELPING AGRICULTURE, Circular, No. 3, Washington, March, 1931.

General Land Office, Commissioner of Annual Reports, 1885, etc.

Sec. of the Interior, Annual Reports, 1882, etc.

Dept. of Labor, Bureau of Labor Statistics, DROUGHT REFUGEE AND LABOR MIGRATION TO CALIFORNIA IN 1936, Washington, 1937.

National Resources Committee, Report of the President's Committee, FARM TENANCY, Washington, 1937.

Resettlement Administration, First Annual Report, 1936.

—— Information Div., Region V Headquarters, Montgomery, Alabama, 1935.

—— STATEMENT OF REGIONAL OFFICE ON HOUSING OF MIGRATORY AGRICULTUAL LABORERS, Presented at California Conference, Santa Cruz, Nov. 18, 1935.

—— RESETTLEMENT ADMINISTRATION AND ITS WORK, Departmental Bull., July 24, 1938.

Van Woodward, C., TOM WATSON: AGRARIAN REBEL, New York, 1938.

Wallace, Henry, AMERICA MUST CHOOSE, Washington, 1933.

—— BALANCED ABUNDANCE, *New York Times*, Nov. 14, 1937.

—— DEFENDS THE "FARMER'S TARIFF," *New York Times*, Nov. 3, 1935.

Wertenbaker, Thomas Jefferson, THE FOUNDING OF AMERICAN CIVILIZATION: THE MIDDLE COLONIES, New York, 1938.

Wilcox, O. W., AN ABUNDANCE PROGRAM FOR AGRICULTURE, *Common Sense*, March, 1938.

Wilstach, Paul, HUDSON RIVER LANDINGS, Indianapolis, 1933.

—— POTOMAC LANDINGS (1920), New York, 1937.

INDEX

A.A.A., cf. Agricultural Adjustment Act
Abenakis of St. François, 44
Abolitionists, 249
Acadians, 319
Achter Kil, 185
Adair, James, 30
Adamites, 140
Adams, John Quincy, 221
Adventures of Captain Bonneville, 260
A.E.F., 327
Africa, 58, 342, 357, 381, 382, 383, 404
Agricultural Adjustment Act, 243, 367, 375,
  390-92, 426, 431-67
Agriculture, 196, 217, 238-39, 367-470
  absenteeism, 100, 118, 381
  decline of, 345, 380-83, 403, 409-30, 434
  Federal Bureau of, 192, 193
  machinery, 193, 196
  methods, 128, 404
  products, 404, 438
  U. S. Dept. of, 412, 416, 431, 456, 462
Agrobiology, 462
Alabama, 53, 55, 69, 152, 153, 187, 222,
  295, 334-70, 380, 381, 387, 411, 412
Alaska, 60, 66, 321, 450
Albany, 102, 207
Albany Daily Advertiser, 215
Alger, Russell A., 287, 303
Aley, Georgia, 382
Alkali Gulch, 275
Alleghenies, 51, 60, 83, 120, 179, 183, 189,
  200, 213
Allen, Senator, 247, 248
Allen, Mrs. Adah E., 285
Allen, Col. Samuel, 100
Alligators, 28, 30, 92
Almanac, 117
Alsop, Geo., 30, 78
Altadena, 9
Amadas, Captain, 45
American Federation of Labor, 330

American Fur Company, 219, 261
American Memory, 55, 215
American Ideals, 335
America Must Choose, 438, 441
Amsterdam, Classis of, 149
Anabaptists, 140, 158
Anarchists, 157, 248
Andrews, Missionary, 44
Anne, Queen, 107, 144
Antinomianism, 148
Anti-Sabbatarians, 158
Antlers, Oklahoma, 397
Antony and Cleopatra, 143
Apostolic Faith Mission, 152
Appalachian Mts., 294
Arabia, 398
Arabs, 383
Arapahoe Indians, 260
Arapooish, 26, 27
Arctic, 75, 166
Argentina, 218, 381, 410
Argo Oil Basin, 288
Aristocracy, 92, 103-8, 113-15, 120, 138, 139,
  143, 178, 180, 181, 250, 252, 254, 358-
  60
Arizona, 59, 84, 153, 176, 394, 396, 407,
  450, 465
Arkansas, State of, 152, 153, 198, 203, 205,
  295, 308, 324, 399, 423
Arkansas River, 214, 311
Arkansas Valley, Colorado, 231-32
Arminta, Wyoming, 275
Army, U. S., 263
Arnold, Matthew, 18
Art, 18, 37, 38, 88, 143
Articles of Confederation, 180
Ashata, 34
Ashe, Thomas, 29
Ashley, General William, 262
Asia, 398
Astor, John Jacob, 219-20, 261, 319

477

Astor, John Jacob (Cont.)
  expedition of, 161
Atlanta, 380
Atlantic Ocean, 136, 409
Audubon, 32, 339, 362
Australia, 85, 175, 218, 411
Autarchy, 441
Averell, Jim, 266-68
Aztecs, 66, 106

Bacon, 250
Bacon's Rebellion, 118
Bad Lands Reservation, 263
Bad Water Creek, 275, 282
Bakersfield, 393, 394, 403, 404
Baldwin, Abraham, 107
Ball, William Watts, 92, 119
Baltimore, Lord, 104
Bandits, 273-75
Bantu, 383
Bank-ers, -ing, 104, 142, 280
Baptists, 122, 140, 155, 158, 184, 401
Barbados, 121, 177
Barber County, Kansas, 248
Barlow, Captain, 45
Barter, 442, 443
Barstow County, Georgia, 385, 387
Bartram, John, 88
Baton Rouge, 205, 327
Baxter, 142
Bayan, 201
Bayard, Nicholas, 101
Bear Pan Mountain, 57, 102
Beatrice, Kansas, 241
Beaubien land claims, 236
Beavers, 30, 31, 33, 34, 77, 319, 322
Beaver Creek, 261
Beckwourth, Jim, 262
Beecher, Dr. Lyman, 112, 117
Belgium, 410
Bellamy, 253
Belle Fourche, 274
Bellomont, Governor, 100, 124
Bender, Dr., 281
Bent County, Colorado, 232, 233
Benton, Senator, 219

Berks County, Pa., 99
Berkshires, 101
Bermidji, 305, 306
Beston, Henry, 55, 64
Bethlehem, Pennsylvania, 14
Beverley, Robert, 109, 111, 146, 221
Beverly Hills, 10
Beverley Manor, 105
Bible, 48, 49, 50, 93, 156, 161, 189, 294,
  383-84, 447
Bienville Jean Baptiste Le Moyne, 96
Big Ear Claire, 298
Big Horn Country, 261, 262, 275, 280, 282
Big Muddy Station, 281
Bilbo, 187
Billings, Montana, 275
Biloxi, 321
Birmingham, 336, 346, 360, 363, 366
Bishop Hall, 36
Black, J. D., 432, 438, 459
Black Belt, 338, 344, 360, 363, 365, 371,
  372, 375, 376, 379, 380, 390, 419
Blackfeet Indians, 59
Black Hawk War, 52
Black Night, Chief, 262
Black Warrior River, 69
Blaine, James G., 229
Blair, John, 230
Blake, William, 136
Blue River, 185
Blythe, 397
Bodaka Creek, 53
Boggs, Governor, 164
Bolivia, 288
Boll-weevil, 382, 413, 442
Bonneville, Captain, 48, 57, 262, 288
Book of Martyrs, 93
Book of Mormons, 162
Boone, Daniel, 32, 35, 127, 184
Borden, 221
Borden, Mary, 28, 29
Boston, 49, 90-91, 114, 122, 124, 139, 216,
  221
Bowels Opened, 93
Boy Scouts, 290

Bozrah Manufacturing Company, 142
Braddock, 46, 184
Bradford, William, 59, 79
Branford, 148
Brasford Manor, 104
Brazil, 218, 381, 440, 442
Brawley, 394, 401
Breaker of Arrows, Chief, 262
Brent, Margaret, 104
Breuil, M. du, 199
Brewster's branch, 131
Brickell, John, 31
Broken Bow, Nebraska, 252
Brookings Institution, 432
Bross, Reverend, 285
Brotherhood of the White Temple, 12
Bryan, 247, 254, 286, 287
Bryce, 189, 238
Buchanan, President James, 174
Bucks County, Pennsylvania, 99
Buffalo, 26, 27, 30, 33, 34, 36, 59, 68, 69,
    174, 247, 262, 293, 294
Buffalo, New York, 198, 204, 215
Buffalo, Wyoming, 270
Buffalo Creek, 273, 280, 283
Bull Moose Party, 255
Bull's Tail, Chief, 262
Bunyan, John, 93
Bunyan, Paul, 294, 305
Burlington Railway, 195
Burns, 252
Burr, Aaron, 207, 209
Burt, Struthers, 264
Burton, Nathan S., 263-64
Butler, 121

Cadillac, Lamothe, 193
Caird, James, 193
Cairo, 309
Cajuns, 69, 119, 322, 323, 326, 334
Caldwell, Erskine, 381, 388
California,
    Relief Administration, 425
    State of, 9-25, 35, 42, 85, 152, 153, 159,
        170, 194, 230, 295, 339, 381, 393-408,

California (Cont.)
    419, 421, 422, 423-25, 450, 453, 462,
        463, 469
    University of, 422
    University of, at Los Angeles, 10
Calpatria, 394
Calvert, Leonard, 104
Calverton, V. F., 143, 146
Calvin, John, 74, 139, 140, 155
Calvinism, 88
Calvinists, 48
Cambridge, Vt., 128, 131
Cameron Parish, 320
Camp Hill, 375
Campbell, 382
Canaan, 384
Canada, 34, 129, 175, 195, 232, 242, 248,
    320, 321, 410
Canadians, 300
Canals, 196, 198, 215
    companies, 224
    Erie, 224
Canary Islanders, 322
Cannasateego, 43
Canoes, 61, 77, 83
Cape Cod, 104
Capitalism, 136, 141-42, 143, 157, 345, 360,
    420
Capitalists, 240, 245
Cardwell, 314
Carew, Bramfylde Moore, 109-11
Caribbean, 177
Carlin, Camp, 286
Carlsbad, New Mexico, 397
Carmer, Carl, 69
Carolinas, 23, 30, 91, 115, 119, 158, 185,
    186, 403
Carondolet, 205
Carson, Kit, 262
Carter, 105, 221
Carter, T. H., 231, 234
Carteret Grant, 145
Carthage, Mo., 165
Cartwright, Peter, 156
Cascade Mountains, 224, 301

Casiques, 106

Cason, Professor, 344

Casper, 59, 229, 262, 263, 264, 265, 271, 273, 275-76, 280-92

Casper Weekly Mail, 266, 288

Cass, Sec. of War Lewis, 219

Castile Land Company, 328

Catalina Island, 10

Catholic Church, 73, 86, 136-40, 143, 387

Catholics, 81, 122, 150, 152, 157, 158, 159, 186, 253, 357

Catholicism, 136-41

Catlin, George, 59

Cattle, 104, 117, 125, 165, 173, 177, 178, 183, 193, 200, 202, 221, 232, 241, 261, 264-80, 328, 359, 389
    "Kings," 64, 233, 266-68
    men, 260, 264, 265-80, 286, 288
    raising, 280
    rustling, 265 f.

Cattle Kate, 266, 282

Caughnewagos, 38

Cavaliers, 121

Cavalry, U. S., 47, 51, 271, 272

Cavanaugh, Agent, 301

Census, U. S., 413, 414, 416, 427

Central America, 212, 339, 400

Central Pacific R. R., 230

Chaco, 381, 442

Chama, Cañon de, 236

Chamber of Commerce, 290, 394

Chambers County, Alabama, 367, 368

Champion, Nate, 268-72

Champlain, Lake, 130

Chandler Estate, 405

Charles, Lake, 358

Charles, King, 106, 118

Charleston, 106, 138, 143

Charleston News and Courier, 92

Chase, John, 286

Chase, Stuart, 90

Chattahoochee County, Georgia, 380

Chattanooga, 361

Chenoweth, 282

Cherokee Phoenix, 55

Cherokees, 43, 53, 55-56, 57, 67

Chesapeake, 104

Chester County, Pennsylvania, 99

Chesterton, 122

Cheyenne, 264, 272, 275, 286, 287

Cheyenne Indians, 62

Cheyenne trail, 280

Chicago, 165, 185, 192, 198, 243, 249

Chicago and Northwestern Ry., 263

Chicago Herald, The, 268, 270

Chichen Itza, 66

Chickasaws, 43, 53

Chillicothe, 185

China, 383

Chinese, 342, 406

Chinook wind, 241, 261

Chippewa Indians, 299, 304, 305

Chisholm Trail, 264

Chivington, Rev. J. M., 47

Choctaws, 45, 53

Cholera, 214

Christian Dictionary, The, 142

Christianity, 37-38, 44-45, 47, 49-51, 58, 79-80. Cf. Missionaries.

Christian Socialists, 157

Christmas, Lee, 213

Church of England, 50, 138, 158, 179

Church of God in Christ, 152

Church of the Nazarene, 152

Cincinnati, 185, 195, 209, 216, 245

C.I.O., 255, 406

Civil Liberties, 20-21, 342, 385

Civil War, 91, 92, 107, 108, 120, 182, 214, 243, 248, 268, 345, 402-3

Claiborne, Governor, 208

Class Conflict, 14, 35, 90, 91, 116, 118, 120, 125, 381, 385-92

Clay, John, 272

Clay County, Missouri, 164

Clear Water Creek, 282

Clermont, 207

Cleveland, Ohio, 185

Cleveland, Pres., 234, 252

Climate, 26, 28-9, 75, 242, 260-61, 275, 322, 323, 325, 339, 342, 361, 416, 438, 442, 447

Coal, 64, 233, 328

Coal Land Act, 233

Coates, 102

Colden, Governor Cadwallader, 114, 177

Collier's, 407

Colonial Dames of America, 221

Colonists, 73, 89, 97-98, 104, 113, 119, 194

Colorado, 47, 152, 153, 195, 232, 233, 409, 465

Colter, John, 261

Columbia River, 26

Columbus, 19

Columbus, Georgia, 380

Columbus, Kansas, 254

Columbus City, Indiana, 417

Commerce, Missouri, 165

Committees of Safety, 179

Communalism, 140

Communists, 89, 139, 145, 157

Confederacy, 339, 341, 361

Congregational Holiness, 152

Congregationalists, 121, 145, 149, 186, 285

Congress, U. S., 43, 175, 179, 199, 221
    Committee on Indian Affairs, 57

Connecticut,
    State of, 33, 41, 82, 90, 101, 102, 117, 129, 148, 185, 221, 409, 411, 412
    Valley of, 46

Conservation, 217, 234, 432

Conservation Act (1897), 302

Constitution, U. S., 20, 64, 180, 181, 182

Continental Congress, 179

Continentals, 178, 179, 181, 247

Converse County, Wyoming, 281

Conway, John, 283

Cooper, James Fenimore, 60

Copley, John Singleton, 90

Copper, 196, 225, 227, 233

Corn, 30, 76, 77, 83, 118, 126, 131, 178, 190, 202, 215, 218, 242, 245, 251, 369, 373, 381, 410, 450, 454

Cornelius, Edward, 403

Cornell University, 413

Cornwallis, Thos., 104

Coronet, The, 213

Cotton, 59, 60, 178, 218, 253, 319

Cotton, 345, 346-47, 357, 360, 363, 364, 369, 373, 376, 379, 381, 382, 384, 385, 389, 390, 391, 394, 404, 412, 419, 424, 425, 440, 441, 442, 443, 446, 448, 449, 450, 452, 453, 454, 455

Cotton, John, 74

Cotton-picker, 381

Cotton Producers' Association, 449

Cottonwood, 27, 67, 265

Coulee dam, 465

Council Bluffs, 167

Council of Women for Home Missions, 394, 406, 422, 424, 461

Cowboys, 276, 282, 283, 285

Cowdery, Oliver, 162

Cowles, Julia, 90

Cowlitz County, Washington, 301

Craig, Judge, 272-73

Crawford, Joan, 18

Crazy Woman Creek, 280

Crédit Mobilier, 229

Creek Indians, 53

Crime, 22-23, 109, 123, 191, 255, 281, 338, 357, 389

Crockett, David, 202

Cromer, Donald, 366

Cromwell, 247

Crop-restriction, 317, 364, 367, 375-76, 390-92, 432-70
    surpluses, 218, 461

Crow Indians, 260, 262

Crozat, Antoine, 321

Crusaders, 137

Cuba, 206, 213, 321, 345, 360, 441, 457

Cullman County, Alabama, 341

Cumberland County, Pennsylvania, 99

Cumberland Plateau, 378

Currency, 245, 246, 254, 255, 433, 443
    exchange controls, 442, 443

Currie, George, 274

Currie gang, 274, 282

Custer, 61

Custer County, Colorado, 232

C.W.A., 386

Czechoslovakia, 53

Dade County, Alabama, 378
Dadeville, 374
Dairy farming, 122, 404, 444
Dakotas, 36, 247, 409, 455
Dallas County, Alabama, 340
Danes, 125
Daniell, R. G., 449
Daughters of the American Revolution, 27,
    362
Dauphin Island, 96, 97
Davenport, Reverend John, 142, 148
Davenport, Walter, 407
Davies, Marion, 12
Davis, J. S., 432, 438, 459
Day, Clive, 141
Dayton, Ohio, 248
Dearborn, Fort, 185
De Bow's Review, 215
Debts, 243, 246, 368, 367-74, 381, 382, 387,
    414, 415, 416-18, 433, 455, 456, 457
Decatur, 335, 337, 341, 361
Deck, Bill, 252
Dedham, 100
Deerfield, 100
Di Giorgio, 405
Delacroix Corporation, 326
Delacroix Island, 322, 331-32
Delaware, State of, 31, 413
    River, 98, 184, 185
Democracy, 23, 71, 74, 92, 104, 106, 107,
    116, 121, 139, 156, 180, 181, 186, 188,
    197, 254, 295, 428, 429
Democratic Party, 253, 270
Denmark, 437, 469
Densmore, John B., 23
Denton, 409
Denton, Daniel, 29
Denver and Rio Grande, 227
Descartes, 144
Desert Land Law, 225, 231, 264, 266
De Smet, Father Pierre Jean, 33-34, 175, 262
De Soto, 69
De Tocqueville, 194
Devil's Dream, 298
Devil's Gate, 171-73, 262

Devon, 110
Dewey, John, 94
Dickson, John, 88
Dictatorship, 157, 158, 180, 443
Dictionary of American Biography, 59
Dietrich, Marlene, 18
Diggs, Annie L., 248, 251
Diseases, 325, 362, 387, 388, 394, 395, 428,
    429
Dissenters, 146
Divine Science, 152
Doddridge, Reverend Joseph, 46, 83
Dodge, David L., 142
Donnelly, Ignatius, 249-50
Dorfman, Joseph, 250
Douglas, Wyoming, 284
Dover, 122
Dress, 34, 77, 83-84, 90, 184, 401
Drouth, 152, 238-39, 241, 242, 275, 399,
    402, 403, 409-11, 413, 435, 436, 447,
    459
Ducks, 31, 34, 35, 196
Dudd, Reverend Baylie, 402
Duke University, 441
Duluth, 298, 301, 303, 304
Dunbar, Seymour, 49, 200
Dunbar's War, 47
Dunkards, 146
Dunleith, 210
Dunstable, 100
Dupont, Julius, 331
Duquesne, 70
Dustin, Hannah, 46
Dutartres, 148
Dutch, 31, 72, 77, 78, 79, 102, 184, 194
Dutch Calvinist, 158
Dutch Lutheran, 158
Dutch Reformed Church, 72, 119, 149
Dutch West India Company, 101
Dwight, Timothy, 77, 108, 116, 123, 124-28,
    135, 143

Eads, James B., 210
Eaton brothers, 142
Eblis, 189

Education, 53, 61, 116, 144, 146, 285-86, 327, 335-38, 342, 378, 386, 398, 421, 454

Edwards, Jonathan, 118

Egypt, 218, 440, 442

Elbert County, Colorado, 232

El Centro, 394

El Indio, 394

Eliot, John, 50

Elizabeth, New Jersey, 145

Elizabeth, Queen, 100

Elk, 27, 30, 33

Elkins, Stephen B., 236

Elks, Order of, 285

El Paso, 230

Elvin, Rhodam, 154

Emancipation Proclamation, 192

Emergency Crop Loan Department, 391

Emerson, 18

Engels, Frederick, 253

England, 28, 29, 31, 37, 73, 74, 77, 78, 89, 101, 102, 108, 119, 120 138, 139, 177, 187, 192, 193, 196, 210, 378, 410, 411
    King of, 182
    Queen of, 40

English, The, 69-70, 72, 73, 77, 79-89, 184, 186, 194, 199, 207, 212, 299, 321

Enthusiasts, 140

Epic Plan, 12, 22

Episcopalians, 87-88, 119, 138, 143, 147

Epworth League, 285

Erie, Lake, 61, 68, 185, 221
    Canal, 198, 214, 216, 224

Erosion, 339, 360, 371, 373, 374, 379, 381, 402, 409-13, 419, 435, 436
    wind, 410, 411

Estates, 99, 101-10, 113-19, 405, 416, 462

Ethiopia, 429

Eureka, California, 296

Europe, 37, 45, 62, 73, 74, 75, 83, 86, 87, 91, 93, 103, 112, 136, 137, 148, 175, 177, 186, 193, 194, 196, 205, 207, 216 218, 247, 316, 326, 388, 433, 434, 438, 469

Evans, Captain John R. N., 101

Exports, 178, 196. Cf. Trade.

Fabulous New Orleans, 204

Fairfax, Lord, 179
    estate of, 105

Fairfield County, Connecticut, 33

Falkland Islands, 206

Fall, Senator, 234

Fallen Timbers, Battle of, 52

Familistic Sects, 140

Farm Act of 1938, 448

Farm Bureau Federation, 340, 375

Farm Bureau of Agricultural Economics, 414

Farmer-Labor Party, 255

Farmers, 104, 117-19, 164, 177, 181, 182, 193, 196, 217, 236, 240, 242-44, 247, 249, 255, 304, 364, 408, 418-70
    income, 415, 422
    revolt, 238-55
    cf. Income, Tenant farmers, Share-croppers, Labor, Wages, etc.

Farmers' Alliance, 245, 252, 253, 254

Farmersville District, 395

Farm Holiday Association, 417

Farming, 364-76, 378, 404
    dry, 404
    fruit, 404
    large-scale, 404
    machinery, 428, 452, 454
    truck, 404, 423
    cf. Land, Labor, Agricultural Adjustment Act, Rural credits, etc.

Farmington, 90

Farms, 236, 240, 243, 244, 255, 363
    free, 415
    foreclosure of, 414-18
    mortgaged, 415, 416-18
    submarginal, 217
    cf. Land, Plantations, Estates, Dairy industry, Cattle-raising, etc.

Farm Security Administration, 395, 405, 422, 437

Farm Tenancy Report, 415 f.

Farrington, F. N., 374-75

Far West, town of, 164

Fascism, 345
Fascists, 89, 157
Fayette, 163, 175
Federal Land Bank, 391, 417
Federalists, 178, 188
Feke, Robert, 88
Ferguson, Ma, 187
Ferrara, Andrés, 262
Feudalism, 71, 98, 101-10, 113-20, 136, 139, 141, 143, 184, 363, 428
Fiery Narrows, 262
Filipinos, 15, 290, 406, 407
Fink, Mike, 204, 210
Finland, 306
Finns, 194
Fish, -ing, 26, 31, 34, 35, 77, 103, 125-26, 215, 320, 331, 383
Fisher, Senator Jules, 328
Fisher, Sidney George, 98
Fitch, 207
Fitzhugh, William, 105
Fitzpatrick, Mayor Thomas, 161
Flat Rock River, 185
Fletcher, Governor, 101
Flint, Timothy, 199, 201, 204
Floods, 28, 307-17, 413, 435
Florida, 106, 153, 186, 287, 412, 423, 455
Flour, 196, 202, 215
Folklore, 191, 197, 290, 294, 298, 335, 399
Fontleroy estate, 105
Food, 35, 117, 308, 340, 363
  products, 196, 215, 218
Ford, 22, 406
Foresters, 82, 124-35
Forest Reservation Bill, 234
Forests, 194, 227, 233, 234, 236, 295-98, 300-06
  fires in, 298
Fort Bennington Military Reservation, 380
Fort D. A. Russell, 286
Fort Orange, 114
Forum, The, 421
Forty Years Among the Indians, 171
Four-H Club, 340
Fox, J., 93
France, 96, 97, 99, 196, 206, 410

Frank, Leo, 253
Franklin, Benjamin, 206
Free Church of Christ in God, 152
Freeholders, 112, 119
Frémont, John C., 35, 262
Fremont Lake, 262
Fremont Peak, 262
French, 70, 96-97, 158, 174, 184, 186-88, 193, 194, 195, 198, 199, 202, 204, 207, 212, 299, 319, 321, 322, 326
French Calvinists, 158
French-Canadians, 174
French Wars, 221
Freud, 29, 155
Friends, 140
Frontier, 23, 25, 59, 74, 83-85, 149-60, 161-217, 218, 239, 255, 288, 292, 293, 298, 322, 400, 413, 414, 433
Frontiersmen, 127, 146, 150, 153, 155, 181, 188, 189, 239
Fulton, Robert, 207-8, 210
Furs, 23, 30, 54, 101, 103, 215, 219, 261, 262, 318-31
  traders in, 279
Furnish dealers, 382, 456

Gable, Clark, 18
Gall, Chief, 59
Gambling, 191, 192, 210, 255, 260, 264, 280-83, 285, 288
Game, 43, 126, 174, 185
Gangsters, 288
Gantz, Louis A., 277
Garden City, 223
Garden Grove, 165
Garfield, James A., 229
Garland, Hamlin, 33, 125, 190, 196, 242, 248-50
Gates, Horatio, 78
Gay, Bethe, 252
Geese, 31, 34, 196
Gelders, Joseph S., 346
Geneva, 74
George, Henry, 253
George I., 31
Georgia, 55, 107-8, 118, 153, 186, 222, 223,

253, 335, 364, 378-92, 411, 412, 413, 425, 432

Georgia Land Use Problems, 383

Germans, 39, 89, 125, 146, 150, 184, 195, 207

Germany, 121, 138, 196, 236, 357, 365, 410, 429, 441, 449, 452, 462

Gerónimo, 59

Gericke, Dr., 463

Gerrard, Gent., Thos., 104

Giles, 382

Gillespie, Rev. J. H., 288

Glover, Sam T., 268

Gobi Desert, 410

Godfrey, Thomas, 88

Gold, 67, 78, 97, 193, 194, 196, 227, 264, 408

Golden Books, 108

Golden Gate, 22, 23

Goldsmith, Oliver, 389

Goodrich, Samuel Griswold, 33, 116

Gorgas, Alabama, 371

Gorges, Sir Fernandino, 100

Gould railway system, 233

Governors Island, 111

Graft, 225-31, 237, 303, 360

Grand Isle, 131

Grand Order of Muscovites, 283

Grange, The, 244-46

Granville, Lord, 106, 119, 179

Grass, John, 59

Graves, Bill, 343

Graves, Reece, 367

Great Lakes, 186, 198, 213, 248
  states of, 425

Great Northern R. R., 298

Great Salt Lake, 170

Green River, 32, 170, 171

Green River, Wyoming, 262

Greenback Party, 236, 245, 248-50

Greene, General, 178

Greene, R. K., 366, 367, 371, 373

Greene County, Georgia, 383, 386, 390, 391

Greenville, 184

Greenwich Village, 16, 60

Grey Bull, Chief, 261

Grey Eagle, S.S., 210-11

Grindstone Creek, 298

Groseilliers, 299

Guatemala, 108

Guinea, 81, 105

Guernsey, Charles A., 265

Gyles, James, 39-40

Hague, Mayor Frank, 21, 27, 164

Haiti, 342

Half Moon, 98

Hancock County, Ill., 165

Handcart Brigade, 171

Hanna, Mark, 286, 288

Hans Breitmann's Ballads, 89

Harmonie, 153

Harmonists, 141

Harper's Magazine, 28

Harris, Captain, 211

Harrison, President, 272

Hartman, 380, 383

Harvey, "Coin," 252

Hastings, 254

Havana, 213

Haverhill, 130

Havighurst, Walter, 36, 156, 304-06

Hawkins, George, 372

Hawthorne, Nathaniel, 44

Hayti, 312

Hayward, Nicholas, 105

Hazlitt, Henry, 440

Heaton, Herbert, 445

Hecla and Calumet Mining Company, 225

Hempstead, Robert, 122

Henderson, George B., 267

Hicks, John D., 241, 250

Hicksites, 149

Hill, James J., 231

Hinckley, 298

History of Travel in America, 200

Hitler, 122, 357, 429, 438, 441, 442, 447

Hogs, 32, 36, 117, 126, 177, 183, 389, 450

Hole in the Wall, 273

Holiness Church, 152

Holland, 98, 158, 469

Holloway, Ernest, 370
Hollywood, 10, 12, 163
Holmes, Obadiah, 122
Holtville, 394, 401
Holy Rollers, 186, 401
Home Diadem, The, 189
Home Owners Loan Corporation, 391
Homestead Law, 192
Honduras, 213, 321
Hookworm, 325, 429
Hoosiers, 401
Hoover, Herbert, 88, 335
Hoover ranch, 405
Hooverville, 393-4
Horses, 28, 177, 200, 202, 262
Hortado, Antonio, 80
Hot Springs, Arkansas, 152
Houma, 320, 331
Hubbel, Seth, 129 f.
Hudibras, 121
Hudson, Hendrik, 98
Hudson Bay, 213, 319
Hudson River, 98, 101, 102, 104, 111, 207
Hudson River Landings, 103
Huguenots, 107, 184, 186
Hunt, Price, 261
Hunter, Governor, 111
Hunters, -ing, 23, 32, 34, 37, 68, 125, 128, 264, 299
Huntington, Collis P., 230
Huron, Lake, 299
Hurt, Joel J., 276
Huss, John, 139
Hutchinson, Anne, 148
Hyde Park, Vermont, 129

Iberville, 321
Ickes, Harold, 392
Idaho, 58, 59, 153, 167, 195, 231, 394, 423
Illinois, state of, 152, 164, 185, 202, 206, 229, 281, 411, 418, 454
    River, 185
Illinois Central R. R., 229
Illiteracy, 344, cf. Education
Immigrants, 89, 111, 116, 187, 196
    restriction of, 246

Immobile, 96
Imperial County, 395, 407
Imperial Valley, 396, 408, 423, 424
Imperialism, 255
Income, 339, 371, 382, 386, 415, 424, 425, 426, 431, 432, 444-46, 460
    tax, 246
Independence, American, 105, 112, 119, 144, 178, 182
Independence, Missouri, 164
Independence Rock, 262
India, 58, 218, 383, 440, 442
Indian Affairs, Commissioner of, 58, 220
Indian Lands Bill, 53
Indian Territory, 53, 58
Indians, 37-64, 237, 238, 279, 299, 305, 464
    abuse of, 97, 187, 204
    agriculture of, 455
    Americanism of, 60
    art, 38, 58, 60, 65
    astronomy and, 66
    buffaloes and, 34-35
    Christianity and, 37-38, 44-45, 47-51, 58
    Confederacies of, 184
    conflicts with, 261-63
    cruelty, 38, 40, 45, 46, 51
    culture, 34-38, 48, 55, 58, 60, 65-69
    customs, 83, 126
    dances, 58, 59, 65
    danger from, 128
    defrauding of, 45-46, 49, 54, 62, 101, 321-22, 187, 219
    depredations of, 275
    destruction of, 23, 59, 263
    dress, 83
    drunkenness, 41, 45, 60, 219, 220
    Dutch and, 97, 98
    festivals, 65, 66
    food, 30, 31, 34, 35, 37, 83
    French and, 70
    generosity of, 42
    Guatemalan, 108
    handicrafts, 60, 65
    honesty of, 38
    hunting, 174

Indians (Cont.)
  intermarriage of, 262, 334
  lands, 37-64, 222, 223, 224, 225, 236
  lands stolen, 53, 54, 55-59, 62, 187
  literature, 65
  magic, 65
  massacres, by, of, 42, 47, 199, 205
  medicine, 40, 67, 83
  Mexican, 108, 426
  migratory, 260
  morals, 58
  mounds, 27-28, 214
  Pennsylvania, 98
  population, 61
  prisoners of, 38-40, 46
  Quakers and, 86-87
  religion, 38, 44, 45, 65-69, 136, 262
  revolts, 108
  robbery by, 157
  rum and, 37
  scalping, 83, 208
  soil, relation to, 26, 27
  temples, 66
  trading, 31, 129
  trails, 37-44, 50-51
  travelers and, 42
  treaties, 51, 52, 98
  Whites and, 37-64
  United States government and, 43, 47, 52-59
  warfare, 37-64, 83-87, 112, 120, 151, 161, 321
Indiana, 141, 152, 153, 159, 185, 198, 214, 411, 417
Indiana Centinel, 49
Indigo, 119, 178, 199
Industrialists, 182, 360
Inquisition, 121, 138, 144
Interior, Secretary of, 225, 227
  Department of, 230
Iowa, 159, 195, 220, 230, 242, 248, 417, 454
Irish, 117, 157, 194, 300
Iron, 61, 231, 360
Iroquois, 47, 48, 70
Irrigation, 238

Irving, Washington, 260
Irwin County, Georgia, 382, 388
Italians, 290
Italy, 196, 418, 411, 452
Itasca, S.S., 211
Itasca, Lake, 304
I.W.W., 254, 255, 294

Jackson, President Andrew, 185, 209, 222, 254
Jackson, Mrs. Andrew, 83
Jackson, Helen Hunt, 60
Jacksonville, Florida, 287
Jaid, Inspector, 301
Jamaica, 177
James, William, 94
James VI, 139
Jamestown, 40, 76, 104, 143
Japan, 441, 442, 452
Japanese, 15, 406, 407
Jasper County, Georgia, 386
Jefferson County, Georgia, 380
Jefferson Parish, 329
Jefferson, Thomas, 37, 206
Jeffersonians, 178
Jennison, Mary, 38, 50
Jersey City, 21
Jesuits, 105
Jews, 158, 253, 357, 387
Johnson, Vermont, 129, 131
Johnson, Sir William, 50
Johnson County, Wyoming, 270
Johnston, Oscar, 449, 455
Johnstown, 229, 316
Joliet, 281
Joliet, Louis, 299
Jones, Daniel W., 171-73
Jones, Evans, 56
Jones County, 386
Joseph, Chief, 75
Juárez, Benito, 213
Juet, 98
Justice, 337-38, 341

Kalm, Peter, 45
Kamaiakan, 59

Kane, Thomas L., 166-68
Kansas, 152, 153, 159, 223, 232, 240, 242,
    246, 247, 248, 251, 254, 403, 434, 454
    State College, 454
Kansas City, 240
Kaskaskia River, 186
Keithites, 149
Kem, Omer, 252
Kemper County, Mississippi, 53
Kentuckians, 185
Kentucky, 32, 34, 105, 126, 150-51, 152,
    158, 178, 185, 188, 342, 403, 450
Kennett, 312
Kern County, California, 395
Kern County Land Company, 405
Kester, Howard, 456
Kimball, Col. E. H., 271
Kimble, Major W. S., 288
Kings County, California, 395
Kirtland, 163
Kiwanis, 283
Knox, John, 48
Kropotkin, 281
Ku Klux Klan, 138, 334, 336, 343, 366, 380,
    388

L. and N. R. R., 341
Labor, 15, 22-23, 124, 192, 246, 335-47,
    365
    agricultural, 111-13, 115, 117, 404, 406-
    08, 415, 417, 422, 433-35, cf. Migrant
    labor
    camps, 404-06, 461, 462
    child, 111, 142
    female, 111
    feuds, 294
    indentured, 104, 108-13, 118
    unions, 406
Labor Statistics, U. S. Bureau of, 399
La Crosse and Milwaukee R. R., 229
Lafitte, 188, 210
La Follette, Robert, 255, 302, 303
Lafourche Parish, 320
Lancaster, Massachusetts, 100
Lancaster County, Pennsylvania, 99

Land,
    canal company, grants of, to, 224
    cattle, 231-33
    coal, 233
    companies, 193, 206, 221
    conservation, 419
    confiscation of, 179
    copper, 233
    cultivated, 193, 403-04
    depletion of, 402, 409-30, 434
    exploitation of, 72
    forest, 233-34
    frontier, 255
    grants, 96-120, 224-25
    Indian, 236
    Mexican, 234-36
    mineral, 226-27, 233-34
    monopoly, 96-120, 184, 236, 328, 330,
        413, 427, 435, 443, 460, 463
    owners, 100-10, 113-15, 119, 187, 271,
        383, 385, 435
    ownership, 252, 255, 385, 414, 427, 429,
        441, 460
    Portage Canal grant, 224
    public, 191, 195, 221-25, 226-31, 233-35,
        417
    railroad, 225-31
    religion and, 136
    revolt, 119-20
    road grants, 224-25
    settlement, 96-120
    speculation, 223
    Spanish claims, 235
    submarginal, 236, 304, 339, 364, 381, 402,
        403, 409-30, 435, 436, 462
    surveys, 227-28
    swamp, 225
    theft of, 179, 187, 224-25, 226-31, 236,
        266-67, 301-02, 306, 327-29
    titles, 51-52
    use, 340, 364, 412-70
    war for, 37-64
    cf. Westward movement, Indians, Soil,
        Plantations, Agriculture, etc.
Land Bank Commission, 391

Land Commissioner, Federal, 226, 231, 232, 233-34, 235
Land Office, Federal, 224, 225, 236, 264
  report of, 235, 301
Lander, 280, 289
Landgraves, 106
Landlords, 112, 117, 118, 125, 179, 184, 217, 340, 341, 372, 374, 376, 383, 391, 415-20
Laramie plains, 261
Lasselle, Stanislaus, 42
Latin America, 47, 60, 85, 178, 216, 240, 382
Latrobe, Benjamin Henry, 202
Latter Day Saints, 153
Latter Day Saints Reorganized Church, 176
Laughing Boy, 60
Lausset, 188, 199
Law, 82, 126, 144
Law, John, 19, 96-7, 194, 199, 213, 321
Lawrence of Arabia, 398
Lawrence, D. H., 65
Lawrence, Kansas, 251
Lead, 196
Lease, Mary E., 251
Leavenworth, 58
Lee, 105
Lee, Dogae, 283, 285
Lee, S.S., 211
Lee County, 339
Leet courts, 103
Leibowitz, Samuel, 344
Leicester, 100
Leisler revolt, 120
Leland, Charles G., 89
Lemoille River, 131
Lennerson, Samuel, 46
Levelers, 140, 247
Lewis, 221
Lewis and Clark, 261
Liberal Catholic Mennonites, 153
Life on the Mississippi, 211
Liguest, Pierre Laclede, 198
Lincoln, Abraham, 185, 210, 213, 401
Linnaeus, 88
Lions Club, 290

Little Brown Bull, 298
Lives of the Loyalists, 103
Livingston, Robert, 102
Livingston, Robert (descendant), 187, 206, 207, 208
Livingston Manor, 111, 113
Locke, John, 106, 180
Logan, Chief, 47
Logan, Harvey, 274
Logan County, Kentucky, 151
Lollard movement, 138
London, 78, 103, 105, 109, 114
London, Jack, 22
London Company, 104
London Times, 91, 384
Long, Huey P., 213, 319, 328, 329, 330, 358, 360
Long Island, 29, 102
Looking Backward, 253
López, Narciso, 213
Lords of Trade, 100, 114, 124
Lorenzo Dow, 191
Los Angeles, 9, 11, 12, 15, 21, 394
Los Angeles County, 407
Lost Cabin, Wyoming, 275, 282
Louis XV, 321
Louisburg, 87
Louisiana, 96, 152, 187, 188, 193, 205, 206, 208, 212, 222, 295, 318, 319, 320, 321-36, 358, 387, 411, 423
Louisiana Land and Exploration Company, 328
Louisiana Purchase, 187, 199, 207, 322
Louisiana Territory, 186
Louisville, 198, 209
Loundes County, 346, 375
Lourdes, 152
Lovestonites, 157
Lowry, Edith E., 394, 406, 407, 422, 424, 461
Luke Island, 106
Lumber, 77, 193, 201, 208, 227, 233, 293-306, 328, 340
Luther, 139
Lutherans, 146, 149, 150, 186
Lux Estate, 405

Lyman, Caleb, 46
Lynching, 53, 81, 119, 231, 253, 267, 272, 309, 336, 338, 341, 345, 346-57, 375, 384, 411, 468
Lynn, 122
Lysite, 275, 281

Mabry, Woodford, 341, 343
Macaulay, 121
Macon County, Georgia, 383, 386, 387, 390, 391
Madison, Mrs., 83
Magón brothers, 12
Maine, 55, 82, 100, 153, 380
Maize, 30, 67-68
Makka, 69
Malaria, 325, 411, 428, 429
Manchester, 185
Manila, 287
Manon Lescaut, 97
Manors, 102-04
Manufacturing, 179, 193, 216, 251, 360, 382, 383, 422, 433, 445
Mardi Gras, 213
Marie, Queen, 192
Marie Antoinette, 185
Marietta, 32, 185, 221
Marquette, Jacques, 299
Martin, Lloyd J., 417
Marx, Karl, 253
Maryland, 30, 104, 105, 108, 110, 115, 122, 411, 412, 413
Marylanders, 185
Mason, Henry, 373
Mason, Martha, 358, 359
Mason, Van Wyck, 111
Mason and Dixon line, 92
Masons, 290
Massachusetts, 41, 100, 108, 118, 121-22, 124, 141, 148, 157, 177, 185
  Assembly of, 46
  General court of, 73, 100, 101
  Governor of, 44
Massachusetts Bay Company, 100, 116
Massacre Island, 96
Mather, Cotton, 49, 59, 80, 81, 142

Mather, Increase, 49, 59, 80
Matthews River, 106
Maverick, Samuel, 177
Mayas, 66
Mayflower, 104
McIntosh County, Georgia, 382, 386
McCulloh, 179
McKinley, President, 216, 247, 286, 287, 303
McNamara brothers, 12
McPherson, Aimee, 12
Medicine, 40, 67, 83, 151
Medicine Lodge, 248, 249
Medicis, 23
Meek, Joseph, 262
Melville, John, 139
Memphis, 205, 308, 309, 316
Mendon, 100, 118
Mennonites, 140, 146, 155
Mercantilism, 92, 115, 177, 178
Merchants, 99, 114, 137, 138
Merrimac Valley, 100
Merriam, Governor, 22
Merritt, John, 263
Mestizo, 60
Methodists, 140, 151, 155, 156, 158, 184, 186, 247
Metter, 449
Mexicans, 12, 15, 17, 235, 278, 406, 407
  lands of, 235
Mexico, 66, 72-73, 108, 138, 169, 170, 175, 179, 186, 193, 206, 212, 213, 232, 234, 235, 319, 406, 428, 455
  Gulf of, 75, 205, 206, 213, 409, 435, 450
Meyers, Gustavus, 103, 111, 219, 220, 222, 223
Miami Land and Exploration Company, 328
Michaux, F. A., 32, 200
Michelet, 97
Michigan, 152, 153, 159, 195, 224, 300, 423
Michigan, Lake, 299
Michilimackinac, 299
Migrant Labor, 393-408, 415, 421, 422-26, 462, 463
  camps for, 393-97, cf. Labor
Miles River, 109

Mill Creek, 170
Miller, Henry, 232
Miller, Joaquin, 22
Miller estate, 405
Mills, Dr. Omer, 395
Milwaukee, 223
Mining, 193, 195, 280, 434
Minnesota, 153, 195, 214, 230, 249, 250,
    252, 295, 296, 298, 300, 301, 302, 303,
    304-06, 316
  University of, 30
Minnesota and Northwest R. R., 230
Miranda Claims, 236
Miró, Governor Esteván, 206
Mischerlich, 462
Missionaries, 31, 37, 50, 56, 58, 236, 262
Missionary Church Association, 152
Mississippi
  Basin, 36
  Delta, 426
  River, 68, 97, 98, 165, 187, 189, 195,
    198-218, 241, 299, 304, 305, 308, 309,
    315, 321, 322, 378
  State of, 19, 152, 187, 199, 219, 220, 222,
    321, 404, 423, 428, 455
  Territory, 188
  Valley, 186, 194, 216, 239
Missouri
  River, 26, 168, 187, 214, 261
  State of, 152, 153, 164, 170, 185, 315,
    381, 399, 411
Mittleberger, 109
Mobile, 96
Moctezuma, 106
Mohammedans, 137
Mohawk Indians, 37, 42, 44
Mohawk River, 184
Mohonk, Lake, 102
Molinos, 144
Mokler, Alfred J., 27, 60, 273, 278
Moneta, 275
Monitor, The, 205
Monkey Muck, 298
Monogamy, 152, 163, 175
Montgomery, 335, 336, 339, 361, 368, 369,
    412

Montgomery Advertiser, 362
Montgomery County, Georgia, 382, 383, 386,
    388
Montesquieu, 180
Mooney, Tom, 22, 23
Moonlight, Willie, 282
Monroe, President James, 53
Montana, 57, 153, 195, 231, 232, 234, 262,
    273, 275
Moore, 382
Moore, Colonel James, 119
Moore, Lee, 278
Moquis Pueblo, 58
Moravians, 49, 140, 149, 153, 155, 186,
    401
Morgan County, Alabama, 341, 389
Mormons, 41-42, 140, 153, 161-76, 400, 401
Morril Act, 192
Morris, Roger, 179, 220
Morse, Jedidiah, 43
Mortgages, 239, 240, 249, 251, 254, 292,
    414, 415, 416, 417, 418, 426, 427,
    433-35
  chattel, 383, 416, 417
Mount Pisgah, 165
Mount Rainier Park Law (1899), 302
Mount Vernon, 105, 113
Mount Wilson Observatory, 12
Mountaineer, 289
Moyamensing, 33
Muhlenberg, 29, 31, 150
Muir, John, 35-36, 234
Munich, 53
  University of, 89
Murray, Ray, 454
Murrell, John A., 210
Muskrats, 30, 34, 304, 319-36
Mussolini, 429, 442
Mystic Clan, 210
Mysticism, 138, 144, 157

Nantiquas, 40
Napoleon, 187, 253
Nassau, Long Island, 102
Natchez, 188, 204, 208
Nation, Carrie, 248

National Resources Committee, 415
Natrona County, 27, 60, 266, 276, 281
Nauvoo, 165, 176
Nazis, 89
Naziism, 429
Neal, John, 82
Nebraska, 153, 156, 191, 195, 240, 241, 242, 247, 252, 254, 265, 434
Nebraska Farmers' Alliance, 253
Neff, Mary, 46
Negroes, 15, 41, 53, 69, 71, 78, 81, 89, 92, 97, 107, 113, 114, 115, 117, 119, 158, 204, 290, 291, 319, 334-57, 358, 362-63, 364, 366-77, 380, 382-91, 401, 424, 429, 456
  free, 222
  labor, 205, 210
  religion, 154
  slavery, 189, 199, 213
Nesters, 265 f., 278
Netherlands, 410
New Amsterdam, 114
Newark, 149
New Brunswick, 248
New Deal, 183, 218, 255, 295, 365, 377, 385, 386, 390, 416-70
New Echota, 55
New England, 50, 56, 91, 92, 99-100, 115-17, 122, 123, 141, 145, 178, 184, 185, 186, 189, 196, 199, 221, 227, 378, 399, 402, 413
New England Company, 99
Newfoundland, 177
New Hampshire, 100, 101, 112, 117, 130
New Haven, 123, 142, 148
New Jersey, 30-31, 111, 115, 124, 145, 148, 149, 152, 184, 413
New Jerseyites, 185
New Madrid, 201
New Mexico, 232, 236, 394, 397
New Netherlands, 101
New Orleans, 96, 97, 187, 188, 189, 198, 199, 202, 203-16, 321, 326, 327, 331, 358, 409, 411
  Vieux Carré, 213
New Orleans, S.S., 208, 210

New York City, 158, 198, 208, 214, 216, 316, 326
  harbor of, 102
New York State, 41, 42, 77, 81, 100, 102-05, 108, 111-15, 120, 122-24, 146, 153, 158, 159, 162, 163, 177, 184, 187, 202, 208, 215, 220, 248, 412, 413
New York Daily News, 454
New York Observer, 55
New York Post, 388
New York Times, 295, 440, 449
New Zealand, 175
Nez Percés, 48, 57-58
Niagara, 27, 68
Nicaragua, 213
Nichols, Thomas Low, 112, 117
Ninety Degrees in the Shade, 344
Nipomo, 394, 401
Northampton, 49, 118
Northampton County, Pennsylvania, 99
North Carolina, 31, 106, 119, 153, 185
North Dakota, 240
North Guilford, 112, 117
Northern Pacific R. R., 231
North Platte River, 262
Northwest Territory, 32, 185, 213
  Land Ordinance of (1787), 185
Norwalk, Connecticut, 129
Norway, 36, 306
Norwegians, 36, 156, 157, 186, 194
Norwich, 142
Nourse, 432, 438, 459
Nova Scotia, 319
No Water Creek, 278
No Wood, Wyoming, 261
NRA, 330, 331

Oceano, 394, 397
Occoquan River, 105
O'Day, Tom, 272-73, 274
Odd Fellows, 290
Ogalalla, 265
Ogden, Colonel Josiah, 149
Oglethorpe, 107-08, 118, 377, 387
O.G.P.U., 121, 138

Ohio
  Region, 186
  River, 32, 47, 61, 68, 184, 185, 199, 200,
    201, 208, 209, 213, 214, 316
  State of, 32, 46, 152, 153, 183, 185, 193,
    202, 214, 221, 248, 321, 401
  Valley of, 184, 216
Ohio Company, 221
Ohio Steam Navigation Company, 208
Oil, 227, 234, 287, 288, 328, 359, 446
Okie, J. B., 275, 277
Okie, Mrs. J. B., 276
Oklahoma, 84, 152, 153, 195, 233, 309, 381,
  396, 397, 399, 400, 401, 402, 403, 409,
  423, 453
Oklahoma City, 394
Old Baldy, 16
Omaha, 168, 243, 246, 250
Oneida, 248
Oneida Perfectionists, 153
Onondaga, 43
Ontario, Lake, 68
Opeleika, 362
Opelousa, 222
Oregon, 219, 224, 262, 279, 294
Oregon trail, 289
Orford, New Hampshire, 112, 117
Original Church of God, 153
Otis, Harrison Gray, 12
Otter Hat, Chief, 262
Ouachita River, 205
Overland Stage Company, 262
Owen, Thomas W., 53
Oyster industry, 320, 331, 426

Packard, Walter E., 396
Pacific Coast, 398, 407, 423
Pacific County, Washington, 301
Pacific Railway Bill, 192
Paducah, 316
Palatinate, 108, 109, 184
Palatine settlers, 42, 77
Palmyra, 162
Pamilco Sound, 45
Panama, 194, 345
Pan-Americanism, 229

Paragould, 313-14
Paraguay, 381
Paris, 96, 97, 206
Pasadena, 9, 10, 14, 20
Passing of the Gods, 143
Patagonia, 60, 66
Patrons of Husbandry, 244
Patroon, 101, 103, 114
Paxton boys, 86, 120
Peattie, Donald Culross, 28, 34, 183
Peerson, Cleng, 36
Peffer, Senator, 246, 248
Pellagra, 362, 411, 429
Penn, William, 87, 98, 145, 182
Penn family, 98, 99
Pennsylvania, 33, 52, 77, 86, 98, 99, 105,
  108, 111, 113, 115, 116, 119, 124, 126,
  145, 146, 150, 152, 153, 159, 179, 182,
  184, 249, 250, 267, 401, 403, 412, 413
Pentecostals, 152, 153, 401, 403
Pentecostal Assemblies, 153
Pentecostal Holiness, 153
Peru, 442
Peshtigo, 298
Philadelphia, City of, 33, 86, 87, 99, 139,
  147, 216
  County of, 99
Philip, King, 49
Philippines, 287
Phillips Estate, 220
Piedmont area, 184, 345, 379, 380, 453
Pied Riche, 41
Pietists, 140
Pigeons, 32-33, 196, 294
Pike, George W., 278
Pikes Peak, 195
Pilgrim Holiness, 153
Pilgrims, 77, 104, 141
Pillar of Fire, 152
Pilot Mountain, 35
Pinus monticola, 36
Pioneers, 42, 69, 119, 123-35, 183, 198, 322,
  359
Pirates, 101-03, 188, 191
Pitchford, Etta, 397
Pittsburgh, 141, 184, 208, 216

Plains Indians, 61, 305
Plantations, 67, 69, 91, 92, 98, 101-08, 113-20, 179, 180, 189, 217, 319, 358-60, 384, 387, 404, 415, 423, 425, 431, 436, 448, 453, 455
  owners, 338, 345, 346, 358-60, 362, 366, 367, 368, 369, 370, 375-76, 390, 405, 419, 436-37, 453, 457
  stores, 371, 382, 418, 455, 456
  system, 243, 377, 381, 413, 419, 420, 432, 460
Planters, 55, 99, 104, 105, 107, 109-15, 181, 221, 253, 387
Plaquemines Parish, 322, 329
Platt, Orson, 165
Platte River, 170, 171, 262
Plenn, Abel, 318
Plymouth, 49, 77, 99
Plymouth Company, 100
Pocahontas, 40
Poison Snake Creeks, 283
Poison Spider Basin, 288
Pokegama Bear, 298
Police Gazette, 18
Polk, Lou, 283, 285
Polygamy, 153, 163, 176
Popie Agie, Wyoming, 261, 288
Pop Goes the Weasel, 298
Population, 188, 194, 195, 239, 240, 243, 387, 404
  Indian, 61
  rural, 177, 217, 411-30, 431-70
  urban, 216
Populist, -s, -ism, 13, 216, 218, 238-55, 433
  Party, 245 f.
Porcupine, 61-62
Portage Canal, 224
Port Tobacco, 78
Post, Emily, 192
Potawatomi, 41, 54, 168
Powhatan, Chief, 40
Potomac, 31, 105
Poverty, 147, 155, 380-87, 389, 390, 392, 393-408, 420, 424, 428, 435, 436, 437, 453, 468
Powder River, 273, 282, 283

Powder River, 264
Powell, Ozie, 341
Prairie du Chien, 49
Prices, 436, 444-50, 453, 460
Preface to Peasantry, 388
Presbyterians, 50, 139, 147, 184, 186
Princeton University, 300
Pring, Martin, 46
Printz, Governor, 98
Production Credit Association, 391
Progress and Poverty, 253
Progressive Dunkards, 140
Progressive Party, 255
Prohibition, 245, 248, 250, 251, 252, 285
Proletariat, 218, 406
Prostitution, 96, 191, 255, 283, 284, 296
Protestantism, 136-60
Protestants, 335
Psalms and Hymns, 117
Public health, cf. Sanitation
Pueblo County, Colorado, 232
Puerto Rico, 345
Puritans, -ism, 16, 48, 50, 58-59, 81, 87, 139, 141, 142, 143, 145, 148, 184, 195, 212
Putnam, General Rufus, 207, 221
Putnam County, Georgia, 386
Putnam County, New York, 220
Pythians, 285, 290

Quakers, 49, 79, 82, 86-88, 99, 116, 120, 121-22, 139, 140, 144, 145, 147, 149, 154, 158, 159, 186
Quietism, 86, 144, 154

Race conflict, 37-64, 71, 89, 91, 253, 334-57, 318, 383-87, 391
Radisson, 299
Railroad, 61, 64, 83, 192, 193, 195, 196, 225-31, 234, 238, 243, 265, 288, 295, 302, 305, 388, 433
  Commission, 244
  government ownership, 246
  rates, 228, 229, 244
  regulation, 244-45
  stockyards and, 228, 243

Ramona, 60
Ranters, 140
Raper, Arthur E., 53, 380, 384, 386, 388, 390, 432
Rapides, 222
Raping, 338, 341, 380, 385
Rappahannock River, 31
Rappites, 141, 153
Rattlesnake Basin, 288
Rawlins, 228
Reader's Digest, 421
Reconstruction, 107, 345
Rector, Major Elias, 203
Red Bluff, 171
Red Cloud, 59, 263
Red Cross, 315, 331, 388
Red Hill Area, Alabama, 338, 341, 344
Red Jacket, 44, 157
Red River, 205, 231
Reformation, 136-49, 155, 157
Reformed Methodist, 153
Regulators, 119, 268-72
Rehabilitation, 365, 366-77, 412, 413, 422, 432
Religion, 37-38, 44-45, 48, 61, 70, 76-77, 79-81, 85-89, 121-23, 136-76, 245, 337, 344, 429
    Indians and, 38, 44, 45, 65-69
Remington, 59
Renaissance, 143, 144
Reni, Jules, 262
Reno, 163
Reno, Milo, 417
Republican Party, 247, 270, 272, 286-87
Resettlement, 340, 363, 364, 372, 394, 411, 420, 422, 425, 432, 436, 462, 467
    Administration, 411, 412
    Investigation Bureau, 343
Revere, Paul, 247
Revolution, American, 116-20, 149, 178, 179, 184, 222, 245, 248, 428
Rhett, 91
Rhode Island, 158, 412
Richmond, 101
Ridgfield, 116
Riley, Whitcomb, 249

Rio Grande, 71
Riverside, 10, 16, 17
River Travel, 185, 199
Roads, 196, 224, 232, 294, 327, 387, 405, 421, 454
Rockefeller, 142
Rocky Mountains, 28, 34, 35, 170, 194, 260, 262, 264, 321
Rocky Mountain Telephone Company, 289
Rodeos, 259-60
Rogers, Robert, 36
Rogers, Will, 18
Roman Empire, 94
Rome, 378, 392, 468
    Holy, 137
Rome, New York, 214
Roosevelt, F. D., 44, 246, 334, 392, 458, 467
Roosevelt, Nicholas, 208-09, 210
Roosevelt, Theodore, 335
Rotary Club, 283
Roumania, 192
Rowlandson, Mrs., 40, 41, 48
Royal Society of England, 30
Rum, 37, 54, 103, 116
Rural credit, 383, 391, 449, 457
Rush, Benjamin, 126
Russell, William Howard, 91, 384
Russia, cf. Soviet Union
Russians, 125
Rye, 190, 215
Ryding, H. C., 366

Sabbatarians, 158
Sacagawea, 59
Sacramento, 20
Sadducism, 80
Sahra Constant, 105
St. Bernard Parish, 320, 322, 329
St. Clements Manor, 104
St. Francis River, 310, 315, 316
St. Joseph, 170
St. Louis, 198, 205, 214, 262, 309, 319
St. Mary Parish, 320
St. Paul, 210, 384

St. Paul, Minneapolis and Manitoba R. R., 230
Salinas Valley, 405
Salt Creek, 282, 288
Salt Mines, 227, 359
Salton Sea, 396
San Bernardino, 16, 17-20
San Diego, 20
Sandoz, Mari, 156, 197
San Francisco, 22-23, 194, 230, 408
  Bay of, 22
  Fair, 22
Sanitation, 339, 365, 387, 388, 394, 402, 424, 456
San Joaquin Valley, 393, 396, 408, 423
San Luis Obispo, town of, 397
  County of, 394
San Pedro, 13
Santa Fe R. R., 226, 243
Santa Monica, 10
Salamanie River, 185
Salisbury, 100
Salmon Falls, 80
Salt Lake City, 170, 173
  Valley of, 169
Salvation Army, 290
Sargent, 46
Sassafras, 31, 67
Savine, 103
Saxon, Lyle, 204
Sayles, William, 106
Scalping, 46, 47, 49, 83, 84, 208, 262
Scandinavians, 195, 300
Schiller, 18
Schoolcraft, 60
Scotch, 72, 194
Scotch-Irish, 46, 87, 98, 147, 184, 186, 207
Scotland, 139
Scott, General, 55
Scottsboro trial, 335, 338, 341, 344, 361, 362
Screven County, Georgia, 387
Sears, Roebuck, 362
Seekers, 140
Seine, 168
Sellers, Charles Coleman, 191
Seminole Indians, 53

Senath, 314
Seneca Indians, 38, 157
Seneca Chief, 215
Seneca County, New York, 163
Separatists, 140
Sequoyah, 55
Serfdom, 102-12, 363, 418
Settlers, 31, 38, 40, 41, 45, 46, 47, 48, 50, 70-73, 74, 77-79, 83, 92-112, 125, 126-35, 185, 188, 193, 195, 197, 221, 231, 232, 233, 234, 242, 260, 262, 263, 265-72, 276, 288, 299, 301, 305, 400, 408, 429
Seven Pillars of Wisdom, 398
Sewall, Judge Samuel, 142
Seward, 196
Sex relationships, 152, 153, 155, 338, 341, 402
Shakespeare, 143, 250, 252
Share-croppers, 339, 340, 360, 362, 363, 364, 370, 372-77, 381-91, 399, 402, 403, 415, 418-63
  Union, 255, 343, 344, 346, 364, 370, 372, 373, 374, 375
Shakers, 401
Sheep, 177, 261, 275
  herders, 276, 278, 280
  herding, 280
  men, 260, 275-79, 280, 286-92
  shearing, 275-76
  wars, 276-78
Sheep Mountain, 27
Shell Beach, 331
Shell Creek, Wyoming, 261
Shenandoah, 105
Sheriff, 341, 369, 370, 387
Short Creek, 176
Shoshoni Indians, 259, 260
  Reservation, 259, 274
Shoshoni, Wyoming, 275
Shreve, Captain, 210
Sibley, Delegate, 300
Sierra Madre Mts., 9, 13, 36, 291
Silver, 78, 193, 196, 227
Sims, Dr. V. M., 371
Simpson, Jenny, 248, 249

Sinclair, Upton, 12
Single-tax, 245, 249
Sioux, 49, 59, 62, 69
Sioux Campaign, 282
Sitting Bull, 59
Skamani County, Washington, 301
Slade, John A., 262
Slavery, 55, 71, 91, 97, 103, 105, 107, 112-14, 138, 158, 189, 217, 222, 361, 384
Smith, Hyrum, 165
Smith, James, 39
Smith, Joseph, 161-65
Smith, John, 31, 40, 77
Smith, Mary Bayard, 35
Smith, Thomas D., 262
Smith, William, 46, 102
Snake Indians, 174
Snake River, 261, 262
Social Democrats, 157
Socialism, -ists, 141, 142, 145, 250
    Party, 255
Social Laborites, 157
Soil, 238, 378-80
    conservation of, 419, 458, 459, 465
    depletion of, 115, 178, 345, 378-83
    exhaustion of, 379-81, 409-13, 416, 418, 419, 434, 436, 437, 453, 454
Soil Conservation and Domestic Allotment Act, 445, 459
Soul Sleepers, 140
South, The, 15, 55, 71, 91, 92, 96, 112, 179, 195, 214, 216, 222, 243, 252-53, 334-92, 399, 402, 403, 411, 419-23, 437, 441, 446, 448, 449, 453, 455, 456, 461
South Africa, 175
South America, 175, 212, 288, 319
South Carolina, 106, 108, 111, 119, 139, 152, 153, 181, 252, 412
South Creek, 273
South Dakota, 59, 195, 274
South Pass, 161, 170, 171
Southern Pacific, 230
Soviet Union, 121, 138, 157, 218, 306, 365, 404, 428, 443, 449, 462
Spain, 138, 206, 234, 284, 322

Spain (Cont.)
    Queen of, 19
Spaniards, 47, 77-78, 186, 187, 188, 193, 199, 202, 206, 212, 222, 319, 322, 326
Spalding, Rev. H. H., 84, 161
Spartanburg, 184
Spencer, Herbert, 335
Spotswood, Governor Alexander, 118
Spotted Tail, Chief, 59
Squatters, 98-99, 112-13, 179, 185, 192
Stacy, Mahlon, 30
Stalinism, 158
Standard Oil, 228
Stanford, 23
Stanford University, 23-24
Staunton, 105
Steamboats, 61, 207-12
Steel, 295, 446
Steele, Franklin, 303
Steer farmers, 366-67, 372-74
Steinberg, Morris, 328
Steinberg and Company, 328
Stevens, 207
Stinking River, 261
Stockyard industry, 228, 243
Stoddard, Solomon, 49
Stone and Timber Act, 233, 301
Strikes, 347, 360, 405
Stuart, Robert, 261
Stubbs, Special Agent, 301
Studly, Thomas, 76
Stu-Mick-O-Sacks, Chief, 59
Stuyvesant, Governor Peter, 122, 158
Submarginal lands, cf. Land
Subsidies, 436, 444, 450, 451, 453
Sugar, 177, 198, 319, 384, 441, 457
    beets, 423
    cane, 30
Sugar River, 185
Suhr, 22, 406
Sulphur, 328, 359
Sumpter County, Alabama, 53, 338
Sun Creek Massacre, 47
Sundan, 383
Superior, Lake, 36, 303-04
Superstitions, 58, 67-68, 79-91, 120

Supreme Court, 64, 82, 222, 231, 235, 237, 246, 272

Swamp Act, 225

Swedes, 31, 98, 125, 156, 198, 306, 437, 469

Sweetwater River, 171, 262, 266, 267

Switzerland, 196

Symmes, John Cleves, 185

Syndicalists, 157

Syphilis, 342

Talapoosa County, Alabama, 361-62, 372, 375

Talmadge, 360, 387

Taos, 60

Tariffs, 245, 433, 442, 443, 444

Tate, Allen, 154

Taxation, 99, 100, 118, 120, 124, 227, 229, 233, 246, 329, 386, 414, 433, 451

Taylor, Dr. Paul, 400, 422

Teapot Dome, 74, 234, 288

Technology, 442, 449, 460, 462

Teller, Senator, 236

Tenant farmers, 112, 113-15, 147, 243, 252, 360, 363, 381, 382, 383, 387-91, 399, 415, 417, 418, 419, 420, 422, 423, 424, 425, 427, 429, 430, 431, 432, 433, 435, 446, 448, 454, 455, 456, 457, 460, 463

Tennessee, 75, 126, 152, 153, 158, 168, 185, 202, 308, 309, 343, 387, 403

Tennessee Coal and Iron Company, 363

Tennessee Valley Authority, cf. T.V.A.

Ten Sleep Country, 278

Terrebone Parish, 320

Teton Pass, 261

Texas, 34, 152, 153, 232, 264, 380, 381, 401, 426, 453, 454

Texas Pacific R. R., 230

Textile industry, 442, 445, 452

Thames, 31, 207

The World Is Mine, 137

They Starve That We May Eat, 394, 407, 424, 461

Three Harbors, 111

Thomas County, Georgia, 383, 386, 390

Thorstein Veblen and His America, 25

Tillman, Ben, 252-53, 260

Tobacco, 31, 78, 83, 84, 119, 151, 168, 202, 203, 419, 450, 458

Tobacco Road, 362, 388, 411

Tories, 108, 178, 179

Torrey, Colonel, 287

Townsend, 12

Trade, 90, 138, 167-68, 189, 196, 199, 201-2, 205, 207, 210, 212, 216, 440-41, 442, 443, 468

Tragedy of Lynching, 384, 388

Transition of the West, 60

Transportation, 192, 196, 197, 198

Trappers, 23, 37, 82, 261, 262, 264, 268, 269, 299, 318-36

Traskites, 140

Travels in New England and New York, 123

Trew, Captain William, 102

Tribune (Casper), 273

Tripp, John, 210

Troup County, Georgia, 380, 389

Troup, George Michael, 108

Trotsky, 145

Trotskyites, 157

Trumbull, Benjamin, 41

Tulare County, California, 395

Tunkers, 140, 146, 155

Turberville, Georgia, 113

Turner, Frederick Jackson, 70, 83, 189, 195, 216

Tuscaloosa County, 336, 371

  town of, 344

  University of, 344

Tush-ka-lusa, 69

Tuskegee, 340, 365, 366, 374, 375

Turkeys, 31, 77, 175, 202, 299, 344

T.V.A., 371, 436, 465

Twain, Mark, 191, 209, 211

Twiggs, Judge, 253

Twin Buttes, 280

Typhoid, 325, 402

Unemployed, 442, 452, 454, 460, 463

Union Laborites, 249, 250

Union Pacific Railroad, 61, 229, 230

Unitarians, 145

United Order of Brethren, 176
Uruguay, 218
Usher, John, 100
Usquebaugh, 32
Utah, 153, 174, 232, 233
Utica, 214
Uxmal, 66

Valesh, Eva McDonald, 252
Vancouver, 301
Vanderbilt, 213
Van Dine, D. L., 426
Van Horn, Colorado, 271
Van Rensselaer, Kilian, 101
Vauban, 28
Veblen, 10, 113, 142
Venezuela, 213
Vermilion River, 185
Vermont, 101, 129, 161, 300, 412
Vicks Plantation, 205
Vicksburg, 309, 429
Victoria, Queen, 211
Vigilantes, 289, 291, 405, 406, 407, 462, 468
Vincennes Road, 34
Violet, town of, 332
Virginia, 92, 104, 105, 106, 108, 111, 114,
    115, 118, 125, 145, 146, 153, 158, 184,
    192, 193, 195, 217, 221, 380, 403
  Governor of, 31
Voltaire, 99
Voodooism, 205
Voyageurs de bois, 321

Wabash, 54
Wabash River, 68, 141, 185
Wages, 124, 339, 357, 366, 383, 386, 421,
    422, 424, 426, 427, 433, 435, 442, 454
Wakan-Takka, 69
Wales, 410
Walker, General Francis A., 22, 195, 213
Wallace, Henry, 217, 364, 365, 366, 392,
    426, 437-67
Wallace, I. W., 300
War of 1812, 183, 210, 222
Washington, George, 105, 184
Washington, City of, 20, 35, 105, 331

Washington (Cont.)
  County (Alabama), 334
  Government at, 55, 331
  State of, 152, 231, 302, 303, 423
  Territory, 227
Washingtons, The, 221
Watson, Thomas E., 253, 360
Watt, 117
Watteau, 197
W.C.T.U., 290
Weaver, General James B., 236, 248, 251
Weber, Max, 141
Weedspatch, 400, 404, 405
Weisser, Conrad, 43
Welsh, 184, 194
Wentworth, Governor, 101
Wertenbaker, 79, 92, 142
Wesley, Cora V., 289
West, Benjamin, 67, 68
West Indies, 177
Western Union Beef Company, 268
West Virginia, 153
Westward movement, 119-20, 121-218, 238,
    239
We Were New England, 129
Weyerhaeuser, 302
Weyerhaeuser Lumber Company, 302
Wheat, 76, 131, 146, 178, 196, 215, 218,
    404, 410, 446, 449, 451
Wheatfield Riots, 406
Whiskey, 36, 55, 192, 202, 215, 220, 283
Whiskey Gap, 262
White, Father Andrew, 31
White River, 185, 205
Whitman, Walt, 27
Whitman, Dr. Marcus, 161, 262
Whitney, Anita, 22
Whitney, Asa, 225
Whittier, 88
Wilburites, 149
Wildcat River, 185
Wildcats, 10, 30, 34, 100, 320
Wilkinson, 206
Willard, Samuel, 141
Williams, Ezekiel, 261
Williams, Parson, 262

Williams, Roger, 148
Willamette Valley, 224
Wilshire, Gaylord, 12
Wilstach, Paul, 103
Wind River, 27, 274
Wind River Range, 261, 280
Winona and St. Peter R. R., 226
Winslow, Anna Green, 90
Winter Quarters, 168
Winthrop, John, 80
Winthrop, John, Jr., 30
Winthrop, Ted, 281
Wisconsin, 195, 220, 223, 229, 242, 295, 296, 302, 303, 316
Witchcraft, 121, 138, 144
Wolcott, Vermont, 129
Wolcott, Major Frank, 268, 271
Wolfram, 288
Wolton, 274
Wolves, 33, 34, 173, 196
Woodbury, Secretary, 35
Woodstock, 100
Wool, 15, 218, 275, 286, 287
Wooten, 380, 383
World War, 39, 218, 320, 326, 327, 403, 434
W.P.A., 293, 305, 432, 442
Wrangel Island, 35
Wright, Roy, 341

Wycliffe, 139
Wyeth, Nathaniel J., 262
Wyoming, State of, 26-27, 59, 60, 153, 161, 228, 232, 233, 259-92
  Stockmen's Association, 272
  Valley, 52, 99
  Woolgrowers' Association, 277, 278
Wyoming Derrick, 280

Yankees, 185, 186, 195, 201, 212
Yale Review, 154
Yale University, 123, 125
Yaqui Indians, 20
Yazoo River, 205
Yazoo Scandal, 222
Yellow Creek, 47
Yellow Fever, 187, 205, 214
Yellowstone, 35, 234, 261, 262
Y.M.C.A., 290, 462
York, North Carolina, 184
York County, Pennsylvania, 99
York, Duke of, 98
Yosemite Valley, 35, 234
Young, Brigham, 168, 170, 174
Youngstown, 185
Y.W.C.A., 290

Zara, Louis, 213